Calverton in his study, mid 1930s

IN THE SERIES
Critical Perspectives on the Past
edited by Susan Porter Benson,
Stephen Brier,
and Roy Rosenzweig

V. F. CALVERTON

Radical in the American Grain

LEONARD WILCOX

V. F. Calverton

Radical in the American Grain

Temple University Press
Philadelphia

Temple University Press, Philadelphia 19122
Copyright © 1992 by Temple University.
All rights reserved
Published 1992
Printed in U.S.A.

The frontispiece photo of Calverton is used by
permission of Margo Berdeshevsky. Photo courtesy
of The New York Public Library, V. F. Calverton
Papers, Rare Books and Manuscript Division, Astor,
Lenox and Tilden Division

Library of Congress Cataloging-in-Publication Data
Wilcox, Leonard, 1942–
    V. F. Calverton : radical in the American grain /
Leonard Wilcox.
        p.   cm. — (Critical perspectives on the past)
    Includes bibliographical references and index.
    ISBN 0-87722-929-5 (alk. paper)
    1. Calverton, Victor Francis (George Goetz),
1900–1940.   2. Radicals—United States—
Biography.   3. Radicalism—United States—
History—20th century.   I. Title.   II. Series.
HN90.R3W55   1992
303.48′4—dc20   91-30289
                                                            CIP

To my mother and father, Letha and Leonard Wilcox,
and to my grandfather, Gordon Earls

Contents

Acknowledgments

I am indebted to libraries holding manuscript materials by Calverton and his circle: The V. F. Calverton Papers, Rare Books and Manuscript Division, The New York Public Library, Astor, Lenox and Tilden Foundations; the Grant C. Knight Collection, University of Kentucky, Lexington; the Sherwood Anderson Collection, Newberry Library, Chicago; and the Eastman Manuscripts at the Lilly Library, Indiana University, Bloomington. I am extremely grateful to Margo Berdeshevsky, who allowed me to examine her private collection of letters, primarily correspondence between Calverton and Nina Melville, gave me permission to examine the considerable correspondence in the New York Public Library's Calverton Papers that, at the time I did much of the research, was designated "restricted," and gave me permission to quote from the Calverton collection.

The following people participated in personal interviews, most of them tape recorded: Michael Blankford, George Britt, Oliver Carlson, Una Corbett, Henry Hazlitt, Suzanne La Follette, Isaac Don Levine, Bessie Peretz, Eli Siegel, and Helen Letzer-Solidar.

The following people shared information with me through correspondence or telephone conversations: Roger Baldwin, Margo Berdeshevsky, Huntington Cairns, Malcolm Cowley, Robert Delson, C. Hartly Grattan, Louis Hacker, Henry Hazlitt, Will Herberg, Granville Hicks, Sidney Hook, Irving Howe, Matthew Josephson, Alfred Kazin, Corliss Lamont, John Howard Lawson, Ashley Montagu, Scott Nearing, James Rorty, Meyer Schapiro, Isador Schneider, Sterling Spero, and Bertram D. Wolfe.

I would like to thank Jay Martin for introducing me to the work of V. F. Calverton and his *Modern Quarterly* years ago and encouraging me to go to New York to undertake the daunting task of examining the enormous Calverton collection at the New York Public Library. Thanks also to Olaf Hansen for dinner and drinks in the Village and intriguing talk about Randolph Bourne and the prewar Socialists.

I am indebted to the following people for reading and criticizing the manuscript in an early incarnation: Jay Martin, Peter Clecak, Bruce King, and Elizabeth Crayford. I must thank in particular John P. Diggins, whose comments and encouragement helped me immensely during the early stages. Later, Cary Nederman generously devoted many hours to scrutinizing the manuscript and offered valuable suggestions for sharpening the direction and argument of the study. Casey Blake and Roy Rosenzweig read the entire manuscript, and I benefited enormously from their astute criticism. Regular electronic mail conversations with David C. Harlan were a lifeline, a personal link with American ideas as well as a consistent source of inspiration and encouragement. My especial thanks to Jane Dunbar for her discerning editorial suggestions, her interest, and for her warm encouragement. Thanks to Gwenith Standring and Judy Robertson in the American Studies Department at the University of Canterbury for their assistance with preparing the manuscript. Finally, I would like to thank my editors at Temple University Press, Janet Francendese and Mary Capouya, for their patience and for their assistance.

Early versions of Chapters Four and Eleven appeared, respectively, in the *Journal of American Studies* 23, no. 1 (April 1989), 19–26; and *History of Political Thought*.

V. F. CALVERTON

Radical in the American Grain

Introduction

In the summer of 1983 I walked up East Pratt Street in Baltimore to its intersection with Patterson Park Avenue. Close to the intersection sits an old three-story brick building whose address is 2110 East Pratt Street—one of a series of town houses joined together, some with brick facades, some with stone.

The day was hot and humid. The front door of 2110 was open and an old man had taken refuge from the heat under a tree near the entrance. I approached him and told him that for historical reasons I was interested in the apartment. Could I go inside and look around? "Do you want to buy the place?" he asked with a heavy Greek accent. No, I only wanted to look inside. "The place is for sale," he said.

I walked in. There was a large staircase at the end of the entrance hall. To the right there was a drawingroom with a fireplace. Other than a single table and chair, the room was empty. Yet voices from past days seemed to haunt the edges of the emptiness and silence, sounds of the numerous parties and literary soirees that had occurred here years before. I climbed to the second floor to find another large empty room. At one time this room was lined from floor to ceiling with books—an appropriate backdrop for the writers who gathered here during the 1920s. The room would bulge with people and resonate with conversation, heady and exuberant gatherings occurring at least once a week, usually on Saturday night. The latest editions of magazines dedicated to experimental writing and radical politics lay about, provoking general discussion before some formal presentation on literary criticism, economic theory, or dialectical materialism. There would then be a lengthy and often heated discussion; ragtime would be played on the piano or a Mexican named Tatanacho (said to be the composer of several Mexican popular songs) would play his guitar. About midnight, food and drink would be served. Debate would often continue until dawn.

In this salon celebrated authors read from their works in progress, hopeful concert performers played, prominent critics spoke on literature and art, social commentators discussed architecture and the city, Communists expounded on the class struggle, black artists elucidated the meaning of the Harlem Renaissance, and black academics addressed the issue of racial conflict. Over the years an impressive array of literary and political figures attended the soirees, such as writers F. Scott Fitzgerald, Sherwood Anderson, and Langston Hughes, anthropologists Robert Briffault and Alexander Goldenweiser, labor leaders Louis Budenz and A. J. Muste, black intellectuals Alain Locke and Charles S. Johnson, veteran radicals Scott Nearing and Max Eastman, and seasoned Socialists Norman Thomas and Haim Kantorovitch. Like other famous soirees, such as those of George Russell in Dublin, Mallarmé in Paris, or the famous Paris salon of those other Baltimoreans Leo and Gertrude Stein, the door always remained unlatched, allowing anyone to attend. Visitors were made welcome and were expected to participate in the discussions, presided over by a man named George, a left-wing writer who lived there, and who was known more formally as V. F. Calverton. 2110 East Pratt Street was a refuge, in the conservative and inhospitable climate of the early 1920s, where it was possible to hear fearless discussion of politics, economics, sex, and religion. It was one of the few places in Baltimore where blacks and whites met on an equal basis. By 1924 the soirees had become an institution for young intellectuals in the Baltimore area.

As I left the room, the voices and music faded. I went down the stairs and out into the street. Without moving from his chair, the old man called out to me, "Listen, I'll make you a good deal on the place, you can have it for $20,000 dollars." "I'm sorry," I replied, "I don't live in Baltimore, and I don't know what I'd do with a place here. I'm only interested because, well, they used to have these parties here, and . . . have you ever heard of the *Modern Quarterly*? Have you ever heard of V. F. Calverton?" "It would make a good investment," the man said, "and you won't get a price this good, let me tell you."

Now a depressed neighborhood filled with immigrant Greeks, East Pratt Street no longer remembers the literary coterie that gathered here in the twenties. And few Baltimoreans, even those who live on Pratt Street, recall the publication that was founded there, or its editor. Yet 2110 East Pratt Street was the birthplace of the *Modern Quarterly*, which housed the writings of some of the most prominent liberal and radical intellectuals of the twenties and thirties. 2110 East Pratt Street was the home of V. F. Calverton, whose role as editor of this journal would be crucial in the history of the American Left.

An independent Marxist who was one of the most influential noncommunist spokesmen for the literary Left during the 1920s and 1930s, Calverton's career was inextricably connected to the *Modern Quarterly*. He

founded the journal in 1923 at the age of twenty-three, and it became one
of the chief theoretical journals of the thirties "Old Left." Calverton's extraordinary energy and restless intellect carried him into such varied fields
as sex and politics, economics and religion, literature and social thought.
During his forty-year life he wrote and edited seventeen books on topics
as diverse as literary criticism, psychology and sociology, feminism, black
culture, and American history. He poured out editorials and articles for
the *Modern Quarterly* as well as contributing to numerous other liberal and
radical journals. During his career he was an editor, critic, advisor and
scout for several publishing houses, lecturer, prose and fiction writer, and
organizer of some of the independent Left's most vital discussion groups
and forums. Calverton's magazine, as well as his Baltimore home and later
his apartment on Morton Street in New York's Greenwich Village, became
open forums for radical dialogue and debate, attracting a large number
of independent and heretical thinkers in the radical movement. These
groups, nodal points of independent radical speculation and dissent, were
a unique phenomenon. His close friends and acquaintances, with whom
he carried on a staggeringly prodigious correspondence, represent a diverse and unlikely gallery of prominent intellectuals and artists of the
twenties and thirties: Max Eastman, Sidney Hook, Earl Browder, George
Santayana, Leon Trotsky, John Dewey, Havelock Ellis, F. Scott Fitzgerald,
Sherwood Anderson, Langston Hughes, Edmund Wilson, Michael Gold,
and Bertrand Russell.

Daniel Aaron has suggested that "Calverton's career is almost a one-
man history of the radical movement between 1920 and 1940."[1] Certainly
his ideas exhibit several basic premises of the early-twentieth-century radicalism of the Village "Lyrical" Left: the revolutionary potential of "modern" ideas and the notion that advanced thinking in a variety of fields
could be linked together to form a powerful criticism of bourgeois culture. His political and social awareness developed in the reemerging postwar political radicalism of the twenties; his loss of innocence coincided
with the Stalinization of the American Left later in the decade, which
registered the end of radical innocence generally. Calverton's intellectual maturity corresponded with the development of the Old Left in the
thirties. When he died in 1940, radicalism was in decline, and America
was soon to be involved in another war. Moreover, his intellectual odyssey
during the two decades reflected a characteristic pattern among American intellectuals: he early developed an interest in socialist ideas (and was
briefly a member of the Socialist Labor Party); later he developed an intellectual alliance with communism; and still later became estranged from
the Stalinist-dominated Communist Party. This movement from socialism

to communism to anti-Stalinism was accompanied by responses typical of many intellectuals, both in America and abroad—optimism, growing skepticism, and finally disillusionment.

Yet Calverton's odyssey was in many ways unique. He was among the very small number of American intellectuals investigating Marxism and literature during the twenties. He was not galvanized into radicalism by the depression of the thirties; his alliance with communism occurred in the mid twenties, years before the general leftward movement of American intellectuals. During the thirties, he was among the earliest and most vocal in his opposition to Stalinism and one of the most active in rallying every shade of opinion on the Left against the Moscow trials. His criticisms of Party policy in the late 1930s ran against the intellectual hegemony of the Popular Front. As Alfred Kazin has pointed out, Calverton was a premature Marxist and a premature anti-Stalinist, always ahead of the times, always "out of fashion."[2]

Yet in histories of the American Left Calverton figures only sporadically, chiefly in conjunction with other writers who published in his magazine. And from a contemporary vantage point, Calverton's ideas seem not to have worn well. Much of what he wrote has been forgotten. He is often remembered as a "vulgar" Marxist, a superficial thinker, at worst a popularizer, an organizer of groups devoted largely to socializing and talk, at best one whose contribution was primarily to spur other writers and intellectuals into activity, a "radical impresario" as Daniel Aaron would have it.[3]

But perhaps Calverton's work has not worn well because it has been judged by the wrong criteria. Christopher Lasch views the development of the Left in America as coextensive with "the emergence of the intellectual as a distinct social type."[4] Yet one role of the literary intellectual—the role of editor—has yet to be considered as an important factor in shaping, sustaining, and even changing the course of the American Left. It was chiefly as editor that Calverton played a crucial role in defining the critical issues of his time and in structuring the dialogue and debate on the Left. Although Calverton nominally shared responsibilities with an editorial board whose constituents changed over the years, he considered the *Quarterly* his own and treated it accordingly. He set the tone of discussion in the magazine; he wrote the editorials, organized the many symposia and debates on issues he felt crucial, and steered the magazine along an independent course through years of factional strife. A cursory glimpse through the publication suggests the pivotal nature of the intellectual discussion and argument it contained. During the thirties, symposia such as "The Doctrinal Crisis of Socialism," "Why I Am (Am Not) a Communist," "What Will I Do When America Goes to War," and "Was the Bolshevik

Revolution a Failure?" suggest the degree to which Calverton and the *Modern Quarterly* brought timely issues to intellectual attention and fashioned the discourse on the Left through the major part of two critical decades. Moreover, the participants in these debates included some of the most prominent intellectuals of the time; in fact the list of contributors to the *Modern Quarterly* reads like a "Who's Who" of the American Left.

The sources of Calverton's commitment to discussion and debate, to a shared culture of critical inquiry comes from the prewar intellectual Left with its optimistic, nondoctrinal socialism and its ideal of intellectual community. An important part of this legacy was pragmatism with its Jamesian freewheeling radical pluralism and Deweyan belief in social and intellectual reconstruction and underlying commitment to democracy. The heroes of Calverton's youth, Van Wyck Brooks, Randolph Bourne, and Max Eastman had, in Bourne's words, "taken Dewey's philosophy almost as our religion."[5] No systematic student of John Dewey, Calverton nevertheless absorbed the general pragmatic intellectual disposition of his prewar progenitors, holding to the values Bourne had earlier seen in pragmatism, "the actual unfolding of a freer, more individualistic and at the same time more communal life."[6] From this pragmatic strain with its notion of "democracy as a way of life" that unites self and society, Calverton developed a catholic ideal of community, one in which common commitments coexisted with a high degree of intellectual and cultural diversity. From this pragmatic strain he also inherited the notion of critical intelligence that defers to no authority and of a pluralistic discourse that is the very basis of communal participation. Calverton's belief in the importance of critical discourse and unfettered speculation as a means of social and intellectual regeneration is suggested in an open letter, published in the *Modern Quarterly*, to Leon Trotsky: "Whenever a revolutionary movement closes its doors to democratic discussion, criticism, and opposition within its ranks, it does so only at the expense of its own vigor, plasticity, and power."[7]

Consistent with this legacy of pragmatism, the *Quarterly* became a forum during the thirties for an attempted dialogue between Dewey and Marx. The lengthy and famous debates by Sidney Hook and Max Eastman on the ways such a dialogue might be accomplished took place in the pages of the *Quarterly*, and a number of writers during the thirties addressed the problem of a relationship between Pragmatism and Marxism in the journal. Not only was the pragmatic ideal of discourse and conversation important to the *Quarterly*'s consistently nondoctrinal and independent stance, but it opened the larger discussion about how Marx might be "Americanized," how a radical program based on Marxist ideas might be tailored for the American situation. The attempted dialogue between Dewey and Marx

and the speculation on how a native radicalism might be fashioned represent major contributions the magazine made to the intellectual culture of
the thirties—and to twentieth-century radicalism, in general. In a larger
sense, however, it was the *Quarterly's* speculative propensity, a legacy of
prewar socialism with its pragmatic bent, which sustained and buttressed
the magazine's most important contribution to the American Left—keeping alive a strain of independent radicalism during the years of Stalinist
hegemony.

Calverton's intellectual configurations were also affected by his family
history and the friends he made in his early years. Much more than the
"New York Intellectuals," he identified with an older America that he felt
to be his own, those prewar "Gentiles," Brooks, Bourne, and Eastman.
Yet Calverton was what Moses Rischin calls a "non-Gentile Gentile."[8] A
native-born American, he was nevertheless of an immigrant family, and
he felt the pressures to succeed as well as something of the sense of the
outsider characteristic of the immigrant. He was driven by the demonic
historical imperatives of an intellectual life; he wanted not only to achieve
literary recognition but to have his ideas matter. His early friendship with
Haim Kantorovitch introduced him not only to the socialist outlook that
pervaded the world of the Russian-Jewish immigrant, but also to the need
for a sustained, rigorous, and critical analysis of Marxist ideas. His magazine thus developed as something of an amalgam, hybrid, or conversation
between the gentile and Jewish strains of American radicalism (personified in two important figures in the history of the magazine, Eastman and
Hook). This conversation, often manifesting itself as one between prewar
socialist ideals and thirties radicalism (embodied in the older Eastman
and the younger Hook), between social idealism and radical praxis, between Dewey and Marx, between the American "usable past" and Marxist
analysis, was also a product of the magazine's cosmopolitan spirit. Cosmopolitanism, a distinctive feature of the magazine, allowed the journal to
represent a wide ethnic diversity; in addition to Jewish intellectuals, black
writers of the Harlem Renaissance were included in the *Modern Quarterly*
in the mid and late twenties.

Perhaps because of its American focus (and because of Calverton's limited view of modernist developments in the arts), the *Quarterly's* brand
of cosmopolitanism, not so "international" as that of *Partisan Review*, for
example, neglected European modernism. Nevertheless, its cosmopolitanism was manifest not only in its ideal of cultural and ethnic diversity,
but in its openness to intellectual variety and its suspicion of dogma. It was
evident in its tendency to go "against the grain" of thinking on the Left
in matters such as its proposed marriage of psychoanalysis and radicalism
in the late twenties. It was also manifest in the ideal of a world radical cul-

ture implied in specific matters such as its championing of Diego Rivera's murals, destroyed by order of the Rockefellers, and its defense of the integrity of Sergei Eisenstein's *Que Viva Mexico* against Upton Sinclair's alterations.

This cosmopolitanism was part of the larger legacy of independent radicalism Calverton inherited from the Village Left of the 1910s, a legacy his magazine preserved and a tradition it kept alive. Alan Wald has observed that the *Modern Quarterly* "in some respects was a predecessor of the post-1937 *Partisan Review*."[9] Unlike the *Partisan Review* in the early years of its second incarnation, the *Modern Quarterly* had no specific Trotskyist sympathies, and at no time did its editorial policy represent a Trotsky-ist direction. Yet Wald is correct insofar as the *Quarterly* gathered several strands of independent radicalism, drawing from the Village Left (prominent figures of the prewar intellectual Left such as Max Eastman, Waldo Frank, and Floyd Dell, all published in the *Quarterly*) as well as from the "Jewish Internationalists" of the *Menorah Journal* group (writers like Louis Fischer, Edwin Seaver, Louis Lozowick, Herbert Solow, Sidney Hook, Eliot Cohen, and James Rorty). Indeed a number of writers wrote for both the *Quarterly* and *Partisan Review* (the most prominent being Sidney Hook and Edmund Wilson), suggesting a common attitude of intellectual independence. More important, Calverton and the *Quarterly* were primarily responsible for maintaining the ideal of the autonomous intellectual and keeping intact a viable tradition of independent radicalism through a period of extraordinary ideological rigidity, fratricidal battles, and outright fanaticism. It was this ideal of intellectual autonomy that was continued by the *Partisan Review* in the concluding years of the thirties.

In *The New York Intellectuals* Alan Wald contends that Trotskyism was the single crucial factor in the formation of an independent Left in America. Indeed, as he puts it, "Without Trotskyism there would have never appeared an anti-Stalinist Left among intellectuals in the mid-1930s."[10] Without Trotsky, Wald argues, there would only have been a "Menshevik" anticommunism associated with various social-democratic organizations.[11] But the history of Calverton's *Modern Quarterly* suggests this appraisal is partial and partisan. Hardly a Menshevik publication with its distinguished contributors including Lewis Corey, Louis Budenz, Scott Nearing, Will Herberg, Bertram D. Wolfe, and Karl Korsch, the *Quarterly* was never allied with the Trotskyists. To be sure, Trotsky was an important influence on two of the publication's major contributors, Eastman and (to a lesser extent) Hook. Yet if Eastman throughout the thirties was working out his complex and thorny relation with the ideas of Leon Trotsky,[12] an enterprise that ultimately led to rejecting them, his writings for the *Quarterly* focused rather on the American reception of Marx, the way in which Marxism might be reconciled with Deweyan pragmatism and an epistemology of instrumentalism. Similarly, a significant portion of Hook's *Quarterly* articles was involved in this American project, the conjoining of Dewey and Marx, a project, it should be added, that Trotsky rejected outright as wrongheaded and retrogressive. Moreover, the attacks by the Communists on the *Quarterly* as a journal that "flirted" with the Trotskyist opposition were true only to the extent that Calverton opened his magazine to all political persuasions. During the mid thirties he published a variety of anti-Stalinist writing including Trotskyist, Lovestonites, and independents whose outlooks ranged from radical to liberal. But Calverton, who admired Trotsky during the late twenties as a revolutionary, writer, and intellectual, was wary of Trotskyism. He believed the Trotskyists exhibited a propensity toward sectarianism and doctrinal rigidity similar to that of the Stalinists and therefore eschewed any alliance between his magazine and the Trotskyist opposition. About Trotsky himself, Calverton would ultimately come to agree with Dewey: "a first rate mind frozen in the dogmas of revolutionary theology." [13]

Wald makes a compelling case that a significant number of intellectuals in the American thirties looked to Trotskyism as a way of breaking with Stalinism while remaining within the ranks of the Left. Yet this view does not account for the role in an independent and, ultimately, anti-Stalinist Left of an American thread of radicalism, which was largely sustained by Calverton's publication during the twenties and thirties. To be sure this thread was modified, altered, and cross-fertilized in the "cosmopolitan" context of the journal. Nevertheless, the *Quarterly* embodied a fundamental strain of independent radicalism firmly rooted in the American tradition, a radical tradition whose pragmatic character was deeply antithetical to doctrinal rigor, and whose experimental disposition led to its uniquely nonpartisan and speculative nature. Besides the notion of intellectual community, if any intellectual ideal animated the *Modern Quarterly*, it was that of the unfettered play of ideas—and this pragmatic American ideal was significantly responsible, this study contends, for the sustenance of an independent Marxist Left during that "middle generation" between the prewar intellectual Left and the "New York Intellectuals" that emerged from the *Partisan Review* circle.

In *The Rise of the New York Intellectuals*, Terry Cooney gives credit to only one figure in this "middle generation" as among the "roots and sources" of the *Partisan Review*'s independent stance—Edmund Wilson, who as Cooney puts it "gave meaning to the idea of independent radicalism." [14] But a substantial number of the many essays Wilson wrote during the thirties were published in Calverton's magazine. Moreover, Wilson served on the editorial board of the *Modern Quarterly* during 1934 and

1935. This link between Wilson and the *Quarterly* is suggestive, for it implies that the ideal of independent radicalism espoused by Wilson was supported and sustained in the radical journal he himself chose to be associated with during the mid thirties. Additionally, as Alexander Bloom points out, Sidney Hook was "a dominant figure in the political discussions among the individuals who eventually formed the New York intellectuals." [15] Hook's writings, with their American philosophical concerns, many of which appeared in the *Quarterly*, convinced many in the *Partisan Review* circle, according to Irving Howe, of "the possibility of an intelligent American Marxism." [16] What ultimately attracted the New York Intellectuals to Hook was his notion that Marxism was a method rather than an absolute truth; Hook's writings, speculative and provisional, permitted, Bloom suggests, "the very theoretical loosening which Rahv, Phillips, and other literary critics desired." [17] Thus, if the *Quarterly* writers collectively did not constitute the "root and sources" of *Partisan Review*'s literary and international outlook, the spirit of independence and undogmatic inquiry that characterized their writings had an important impact on the New York Intellectuals of the *Partisan* circle.

This study examines Calverton and the career of the *Modern Quarterly* in order to fill in the picture of independent radicalism during the interwar years. In proposing that Calverton's magazine formed a bridge of independent radicalism between the Village Left of the 1910s and the anti-Stalinist Left of the late thirties, it aims to help complete what seems missing in accounts of the Left between the wars: what Daniel Bell has called the "missing generation," that generation between the pre–World War I Left and the radicals who came to maturity in the mid-to-late thirties, who came to be known as the New York Intellectuals.[18] This study suggests that Calverton and the writers who banded around the *Modern Quarterly* in the bleak years of the early twenties and sustained the publication until 1940 constitute an important segment of that "missing generation."

An examination of the career of Calverton and the *Modern Quarterly* also serves to suggest how this American strain of radicalism, rooted in progressivism and pragmatism, gave rise to various paradoxes, to a potential for liberation from dogma as well as to contradictory impulses toward social control. Calverton's intellectual odyssey embodies the radical paradoxes of individual commitment and group identity; it sheds light on the dilemmas of an intellectual who was attracted to radicalism for deeply personal reasons, who wished to conjoin individual redemption and social regeneration. It sheds further light on salient problems of the Old Left generation such as the deradicalization of American intellectuals in the late thirties and forties. Moreover, an investigation of the continuity of independent radicalism between the wars suggests the larger continuity of an American radical tradition, the way in which the legacy Calverton inherited and extended points toward more contemporary developments on the American intellectual Left.

Finally, the study contends that neither the *Modern Quarterly* nor its editor has been accorded the distinctive place in the history of the American Left it and he deserve. Calverton's role as editor has been largely overlooked, and in some sense his own work has been wrongly judged. Calverton was never a systematic, rigorous, or academic intellectual. He was among an earlier generation that Russell Jacoby calls America's "last" generation of public intellectuals, and like them he was an urban, nonacademic intellectual who wrote for an educated audience of nonspecialists who were assumed to be familiar with advanced ideas in politics and the arts.[19] Like these earlier free-lance and "free-floating" intellectuals (of which Marx himself was one), Calverton supported himself, often with great difficulty in the depression years, by editing, book reviewing, and writing articles and books. Like these intellectuals, he drew from, and attempted to integrate, a variety of disciplines, which have now gone their separate and discrete ways. And like them, he attempted to combine the notion of intellectual autonomy and the ideal of a public culture. Some of Calverton's works were of interest to academics of his generation, but Calverton wrote largely for intelligent readers rather than academics, and given the subsequent "academization of culture" (as Jacoby terms it), Calverton's works have been faulted for a lack of rigor and disciplinary specificity they were never intended to have.[20]

To be sure Calverton did not achieve the recognition of some of the nonacademic intellectuals of his generation, of an Edmund Wilson or a Lewis Mumford. His books and articles are extraordinarily uneven, at times exhibiting flaws that range from a mechanical and unimaginative analysis of literary issues to an almost slap-dash effort to synthesize current ideas. At other times, however, they reveal an imaginative grasp of political and social problems and are venturesome attempts to grasp the meanings of their times. If his books and articles did not always offer carefully worked-out answers to complex problems, they nevertheless asked the right questions. Calverton was politically astute and he was often able to comprehend the implications of a political doctrine or policy more clearly and quickly than others. His writings are worthy of examination not only because they are often politically perceptive, exhibiting good hunches and prescient perspectives, but because they almost always isolate and explore the central concerns of his time.

As an editor, Calverton's role was crucial in setting the agenda for discussion and debate and in constituting intellectual dialogue on the Left over the major part of two decades. As a writer, he provided some of the most astute criticisms and commentary on the Left. He was a precursor, heretic, maverick, whose quest for a "complete" and distinctively American form of socialism provides a sustained critical perspective on the radical movement during his lifetime.

CHAPTER ONE

I WAS BORN—that is the way they say all autobiographical narrative should begin—on August 4th, 1914.
I had been born way back in 1900, but my real birth, my
intellectual coming of age, occurred on that memorable
day when war became a reality in Europe.
                    —V. F. Calverton, "Between Two Wars," 1940

George Goetz: Baltimore Beginnings

George Goetz was born in Baltimore, a city that left its indel-
ible mark on his life and thought. Growing up in a comfortable middle-class section of East Baltimore with the teeming
life of the wharves virtually at his front door, working at the Sparrows
Point steel mill as a teenager, and studying at Johns Hopkins University, he saw the city in all its savage contradictions and contrasts. By the
time he was fourteen Baltimore had taught him a political lesson about
America's potential for militant patriotism and repressive conservatism.
Living in a German community, he experienced the brunt of anti-German
hysteria, which bloomed in the provincial city. In Baltimore, a village of
nearly a million people, he became aware of the heavy hand of the "best
people": the board members of the Baltimore library, for example, who
often restricted books they considered objectionable from general circulation. The Baltimore environs also called attention to the plight of workers;
as a young adult he saw two thousand men mob the Baltimore Municipal
Employment Bureau to get jobs paying thirty cents an hour. Baltimore's
stifling puritanism gave impetus to a rebellious strain in his early years.
As much as the city's constricting conformism, its anti-intellectualism gave
focus to the rebellious imperatives of intellectual development. He came
to hate this pervasive hostility or indifference to ideas, something that was

part of the very character of the extended family in which he grew up, where there was a preference for card playing and bowling rather than reading. Yet in Baltimore he also learned, as a student at Johns Hopkins University, about the possibility of an intellectual life and an intellectual community.

V. F. Calverton was born George Goetz on June 25, 1900, to Charles and Ida Goetz. Both Charles and Ida were of German ancestry. Ida Geiger's grandfather was a "Forty-Eighter," one of the thousands of disappointed liberals and radicals who migrated to the United States after the Revolution of 1848. Charles Goetz's grandfather, a tailor, left Germany during the same period to escape military conscription. Charles and Ida Goetz met in their youth at a Baltimore crabfest and were drawn together by their similar family backgrounds.

Yet theirs was a marriage of two irreducibly opposed natures. Ida came from a sternly Lutheran background while Charles had a Catholic upbringing; Ida took her religion seriously while Charles was an outspoken atheist; Ida had no intellectual interests whatsoever, while Charles regularly spent hours in the Baltimore public library away from his custom tailor business. Charles was irreligious, contemptuous of "respectability," and unambitious. He escaped the disagreeable practicalities of life not only in books but in alcohol; drinking habitually, he characterized himself as a "philosophical drinker." Ida, on the other hand, was deeply dissatisfied with Charles's lack of commitment to his business and to religion and took refuge from her disappointment in long bouts of sleep.[1]

Because Charles's tailoring business was not thriving, he moved his family to his parents' home when George was still a child. It was in his grandfather's three-story house at 2110 East Pratt Street—at that time in a relatively comfortable, middle-class German community—that George grew up. But if the house was comfortable, the young George was torn by the intense contradictions of his family life, particularly when his mother encouraged him to attend church while his father denigrated religion and tutored him in the theory of evolution. Charles Goetz was the sole member of the Goetz–Geiger clan who read as a pastime, and George was drawn by his father's interest in books and ideas. He regularly stopped by his father's tailor shop on the way home from school to read the books his father had taken out of the library or to listen to the political discussions between his father and his patrons. Here in the tailor shop he was exposed to lengthy harangues and political arguments. He became accustomed to hearing his father's populist denunciations of political figures, his distrust of corporations, and his resentment toward the rich. Goetz embraced Theodore Roosevelt's politics of reform with its crusade against monopolistic trusts and the "arrogant rich." As a petty-bourgeois tailor he felt particularly threatened by the ready-made clothing industry, burgeoning in the prewar years, which was, as he told his son, "driving the merchant tailors to the wall."² This populist view of monopoly was brought home vividly to the young boy when his father announced he was taking out a loan in the form of a second mortgage on grandfather Goetz's house to keep the tailoring business from sliding into bankruptcy.

In spite of the clash of personalities, both Charles and Ida Goetz were in agreement about their son's career. Over his protests, they sent George to the Baltimore Polytechnic in 1914 to study engineering. The regimented atmosphere of the school and mechanical orientation of the class work were anathema to George. He made the long hours of his technical classes pass by reading classics from his father's library. He shared his literary interests with other members of a sparsely populated literary club at the Polytechnic and was elected president of the group.

George's tedious technical classes drove him to seek intellectual stimulation in the political discussion and debate that went on in his father's tailor shop, particularly when his mother's cousin, Henry Lucke, a patent lawyer from New York City, came to visit. Lucke, a Socialist, would become involved in lengthy and heated arguments with Charles Goetz. Goetz's individualistic temperament and general faith that, but for the trusts, capitalism was a viable system, drove him in the direction of progressivism and populism; these same characteristics evoked in him an open hostility to the socialist movement. Lucke, on the other hand, scoffed at Goetz's faith that Roosevelt could turn business back to small manufacturers and restore the frontier days of rugged individualism. Lucke insisted that the trusts prepared the way for a future collectivized society, and that the small businessman must ally himself with the working class to create a new society. Fascinated by Lucke's passionate defense of socialism and his discussions of class divisions, class antagonisms, and class alliances, George was nevertheless puzzled by his talk of the collective society of the future. He could only conclude that politics must be important if it could spark such intense arguments.

If he was still in doubt about the gravity of political conflict he could not remain so for long, for by the summer of 1914 the Goetz family, as part of the German American community in Baltimore, was shaken by the threat of a growing wave of anti-German sentiment that was sweeping the country. The atrocity stories, evidence of this growing hostility to "Huns," that began appearing in the *Baltimore Sun* sparked a furor of resentment in the German community. Predictably enough, in the Goetz household opinion was divided: the Geiger side of the family, including George's mother, was openly pro-German, whereas Charles was an ardent pacifist, his opposition to war of any kind coming from a deep-seated personal conviction.

He was not "pro-German" but rather "pro-human," he protested. Around home Goetz often raged against the impending war, in particular the possibility of American intervention, and engaged in long shouting matches with the pro-German members of the family. Goetz decried the preparedness movements and read with distress the editorials in the *Baltimore Sun*, which he denounced as "so pro-English they stank."[3] He deplored war in terms of his quasi-populist little-versus-big-man point of view, arguing that it was the "humble people" who had to do the fighting. Years later, on the brink of World War II, George would see the nature and causes of war in a different light from his father, but his antiwar sentiments would be as strong. Yet if he retained his father's strong antiwar convictions, the anti-German hysteria during these prewar and early war years made his father's populist faith in the "ordinary man" seem dubious. Indeed his suspicion of populism was formed during this time, and in later life he would consistently argue the political dangers associated with the populist impulse.

After the outbreak of war in Europe, George's political education consisted of lessons imparted to him by his family and social environment. He saw his father grow more and more disconsolate as the patriotic fervor grew. And as family arguments raged, he observed the polarization between the larger Baltimore milieu and the German community—the xenophobia and the mounting tensions caused by a hysterical patriotism that quickened to the distant sounds of battle. He watched a "Preparedness Parade" in May of 1916, a collective expression of fervent patriotism and anti-German sentiment. He heard Socialists like Henry Lucke argue that war and militarism were part of the capitalist system; he heard arguments that the Germans were barbarous and militaristic, and counter arguments that the Kaiser was on the side of all that was good and sacred. Thus after 1914, George discovered a world outside himself; as he later wrote in an autobiographical fragment, "All the world was personal, revolved around me, until August 1914—then I knew there was another world, outside, and I became a new person, was reborn, as it were."[4]

Indeed, George was reborn to a political world, a world of intense local and international conflict, a world in which Lucke's discussion of the systemic origins of war and militarism began to make more sense than his father's veneration of the small man. Yet as much as this world outside loomed into consciousness, he had his own inner conflicts to contend with, especially his growing frustration with vocational classes at Polytechnic. He felt vague and aimless. He had excelled at baseball in school, had even played semiprofessional baseball for a short period, and he now considered professional baseball as a career. His mother, however, consistently discouraged his athletic ambitions because they were not practical and would not lead to a steady job. Meanwhile his courses at Polytechnic did not satisfy a new urge to learn to write that accompanied his interest in literature. Confused, torn, and frustrated from every direction, George extricated himself from this deadlock in 1916. Without consulting his parents he quit Polytechnic and took a job as a clerical assistant in the office of the foreman of the steel metal shop in the Bethlehem Steel Company at Sparrows Point. The job promised to be tedious, dull, and dreary for a young man with literary propensities. Fortunately, however, George came under the supervision of a bookish foreman who recognized his keen interest in ideas, allowed him to read during slow periods at work, and ultimately encouraged him to enroll at Baltimore City College.

After several months at Bethlehem Steel, George left to study in the liberal arts program at the City College (the Baltimore academic high school). His father had been distressed when George dropped out of school for the job at Sparrows Point and was pleased to see him resuming his education. His mother, however, put little stock in education and would have been happier to see him continue his work in the shipyard. She gave him no encouragement in his educational aspirations and was largely indifferent to his academic accomplishments. Nevertheless, at City College George quickly became president of the "Washington Irving Literary Society." He graduated from Baltimore City after three years of study in 1918 with his interests in literature crystalized and with a determination to continue his studies at Johns Hopkins University.

W H E N George Goetz enrolled at Johns Hopkins in the fall of 1918 the country was in turmoil over the war. Patriotic hysteria had reached its peak in Baltimore. Tensions between the interventionists and pro-German pacifists ran extremely high. In April 1917 rioters broke up a meeting in Baltimore at which the pacifist David Starr Jordan was to speak under the auspices of the American League against Militarism. The mob was led by college professors, students, bankers, and lawyers. Police were called in, and rioters and pacifists alike were badly beaten.[5]

In the summer of 1918 the army began to conscript twenty-year-olds. George, however, was only eighteen. When he arrived on campus there was frenzied talk among students about whether to join the recently formed Student Army Training Corps, the R.O.T.C., or the Ambulance Corps (as John Dos Passos, Ernest Hemingway, and Edmund Wilson had already done). Students debated the war, quoting Randolph Bourne if they opposed U.S. involvement, or John Dewey if they favored it. Some discussed the Bolshevik revolution in Russia, while others argued the merits of Isadora Duncan's patriotic dances at the Metropolitan Opera in New York City. George found himself unable to take a position in these exchanges. He knew he was opposed to war, but he was unable to articulate an argument regarding his opposition to this particular war. And he had only the vaguest idea what bolshevism was.

In early November the war was over. After the initial jubilation, malaise set in. For many radical students, the war had discredited the university itself and proved liberal professors to be apologists for capitalist aggression.[6] But for George, a freshman, the university seemed a new adventure. He took an extraordinarily heavy load in his liberal arts course, and by his sophomore year he was covering his course work at almost twice the normal rate. In addition, George did enormous amounts of extracurricular reading and participated in a number of university clubs; he was president of the social science club as well as the literary club, vice-president of the oratorical society, and editor-in-chief of the university magazine. He represented the university in the Southern Oratorical contest in 1920. At meetings of the literary club, he presided over discussions of avant-garde literature and recent criticism and functioned as a contact man, bringing in guest speakers.[7]

Summers George worked with his mother's cousin, Henry Lucke, in his patent law office in New York City. Although his thinking had been influenced by his father's Rooseveltian progressivism and antiwar sentiments and he had long been intrigued by Lucke's socialism, at this point George still had, strictly speaking, no politics at all. His populistic view of the crushing power of monopoly was reinforced as, over the years, he had seen his father's business slide into bankruptcy and his father slip into alcoholism. But in New York City, even more than Baltimore, the contradictions that inhered in American society became apparent; a quiet walk at lunchtime would have brought him from the comfortable Rector Street office to the squalor of the Bowery. Moreover, in New York, Lucke introduced the young man to several socialist friends, one of whom was a leader in the New York Socialist Party. George found that the Socialists' concern for building a better society stirred his "profound respect and admiration." He admitted that the socialist ideals seemed to confirm his growing sense that American society was "degenerate and corrupt" and helped him to understand the plight of the worker. But he remained doubtful about the capacity of any new order established after a revolution—socialist or otherwise—to cure the maladies that existed in the present social order.[8]

In the year 1919, however, George was less concerned with political questions raised by the Socialists than he was with theological issues raised by a friend, Herman F. Miller, a young teacher at a Lutheran seminary in New York. Perhaps because of the influence of his mother's unrelenting religiosity, George had begun recently to consider religion as a calling.

Yet because of his love of intellectual activity, his emerging interest in social problems, and his progressive sentiments, he found it difficult to accept religious belief detached from independence of thought and social responsibility. His ambivalence toward the religious calling is revealed in an exchange of letters between him and Miller in the summer of 1919.

George wrote Miller that he was considering the ministry as a career, but that he had not arrived at his religious convictions through religious experience but through thought and contemplation. He contended that his religious convictions were strong and felt that each man should have the right to interpret the message of Christ as he pleased. Miller, for his part, felt that "a purely philosophical approach to religion," such as George's, was not a solid foundation for anyone contemplating a religious life. "Your religion is too individualistic and cannot be put into the hearts of the masses," he wrote.[9] Nonetheless George wrote again to Miller reaffirming his plans to study for the ministry. He admitted experiencing nagging misgivings that stemmed from his difficulty in reconciling institutional religion with his speculative impulses and progressive inclinations. He had been influenced by Walter Rauschenbusch and other Social Gospel thinkers and wrote to Miller of his hope that religion would become "more progressive."[10] Miller averred that religion would, in time, become increasingly tolerant and broad-minded, but felt George was excessively concerned with the life of the mind and overly preoccupied with secular and social issues: "personally I believe you will emerge from your pool of philosophy and find yourself on the sandy beach of faith."[11]

George's letters to Miller continued to argue for an intellectual and antidogmatic approach to religion, a religious belief based on a liberal freedom of individual interpretation, and a religion with a progressive concern for social change. Believing his ideas would find a receptive audience, George arranged a number of speaking engagements at various churches in Baltimore, including the Lutheran, United Brethren, and Methodist. But as he later wrote, "My ministerial career was drastically brief."[12] His progressive message was hardly welcomed in the churches of conservative Baltimore, and he began to reappraise his plans for the ministry.

Meanwhile, George's socialist inclinations were receiving further stimuli from a young poet and radical, Eli Siegel, to whom he was introduced in 1920 by a friend and university classmate, Adolphus D. Emmart. Siegel considered himself the most radical of radicals in the Baltimore area. To Siegel, a young man infatuated with his own radical purity, most Baltimore leftists—including members of the Socialist Labor Party—were merely sentimental liberals. George was attracted to this young, eccentric, self-styled literary leftist who argued passionately for socialism as though it

were at once a self-evident truth and a metaphysical ideal that encompassed every aspect of human life. After hearing a talk George gave to
the Johns Hopkins student body on the necessity of free speech, Siegel
criticized him for delivering pale liberal homilies and vaguely defined
statements. What George needed, Siegel claimed, was a more rigorous
social analysis that could come only from a radical perspective. Siegel
then sent George a barrage of letters in an attempt to sway him from
his progressive liberalism. He chided George for being too "fainthearted"
and urged him to be more committed to socialism. Assuming the role of
mentor, Siegel insisted that George attend political meetings and lectures.
On one occasion he invited George to hear Robert Minor speak on am-
nesty for political prisoners "as part of the very necessary effort for the
salvation of your mind." [13] Thus in almost the same evangelical tone that
characterized Miller's attempt to win George to the Christian faith, Siegel
sought to win George to radicalism. This "contest" had an earlier parallel,
when George found himself between the differing ideological positions of
his populist father and his Socialist cousin. Perhaps because of these early
experiences, he later tended to see himself, if not as a political moderate,
at least as a man in the middle, one open to dialogue, if not a synthesizer
of opposites.

In any case Siegel's inducements were more effective than Miller's.
Under Siegel's tutelage George read *Das Kapital* as well as other books
that increased his theoretical understanding of the socialist movement.
George, Siegel, and "Dol" Emmart began meeting regularly and informally to discuss radicalism. They perused the latest issues of the *Liberator*
and talked excitedly about the writings of John Reed. They discussed the
legendary earlier socialist magazines like the *Masses* and *Seven Arts* and
talked about their heroes of the prewar generation of radicals—Randolph
Bourne, John Reed, and Max Eastman.

Now totally immersed in intellectual life and preoccupied with his ex-
plorations of American radicalism, George's plans to study for the min-
istry seemed distant. In 1922, one year after his graduation from Johns
Hopkins University, he joined the Baltimore branch of the Socialist Labor
Party (SLP) and began a project of reading Marx's three volumes of
Das Kapital yet again. He also avidly read Charles Darwin, Lester Ward,
William Graham Sumner, Henry Thomas Buckle, and Thorstein Veblen.
He wrote an essay entitled "Concerning Partnership in Poverty," which
marked a shift from his progressive belief in institutional reform toward
a new sense of the need for radical social change. The unpublished article
contended that war was primarily the result of capitalism's inexorable
expansion in its constant search for markets to absorb its surplus. [14] Moreover, while at Johns Hopkins he had become part of a small coterie of

young literary radicals including Eli Siegel, A. D. Emmart, and Savington Crampton, an aspiring poet. These young men shared an enthusiasm for radicalism and they all wanted to be writers. After graduation George made a somewhat more formal arrangement for the group, inviting them to "2110" regularly to discuss literature and politics as well as to propose collective writing projects.

G EORGE GOETZ graduated from Johns Hopkins University in 1921. In 1920, as a junior, he had taken a teaching job at a local junior high school, at Asquith and Orleans streets, known as Public School No. 40. After graduation he continued teaching there. The school was in a Jewish section of the city. Many of the students were from immigrant and working-class families—primarily from Russia and Poland—with socialist backgrounds. George enjoyed teaching in the school with its working-class character, delighted in an environment in which his socialist ideas were received with interest.

Also in 1920 George's cousin, a teacher at Peabody Music School, invited George to her house to meet one of her friends, eighteen-year-old Helen Letzer. After their first meeting, George and Helen began to see each other regularly. He found her spirited, vivacious, attractive, and although having no aspirations to a university education, bright and intellectually curious. As for Helen, she found his wide-ranging intellectual interests intriguing, and although he was short at five feet, six inches, she found his dark, athletic good looks appealing. She was also stirred by his desire to become a writer. By 1921 they were passionately involved and they married in December of that year.[15]

George's father had recently died, after a long period of depression and ill health that coincided with the steady decline of his business as customers abandoned the older neighborhood shops for uptown department stores. The Pratt Street residence now housed an extended family comprising George's mother, his grandmother (who owned the house), his uncle, two brothers, and a sister. But George's sister was about to marry and leave home, and the house was large, so George and Helen moved into "2110."

Helen got a job teaching elementary school and so both she and George were subject to the demands of full-time work. In spite of this, they kept alive the soirees at the Goetz home. Soon the number of participants grew, and by 1922 they had become weekly Saturday-night affairs. George invited friends from the varied artistic and literary milieux of Baltimore, former classmates from Johns Hopkins, and on occasion the brightest students from Public School No. 40. By 1922 the Goetz home was fast becoming known as a center where advanced ideas flourished.

During this time George had been writing short stories and submitting them for publication, but they were all rejected. Although a rejection by the *Dial* stung particularly badly, it had the effect of turning his interest to essay writing. More important, it led him to consider the role of editor. He had been the editor of *Black and Blue Jay*, the student magazine at Hopkins, and he now wrote to the editor of the *Midland*, a literary magazine published in Iowa, offering his services to help build the magazine up and proposing to join the magazine as coeditor.[16] George's offer was not accepted, yet this display of chutzpah suggested the degree of his ambition to make a mark in the world of letters.

In 1922 he discovered, however, that the opportunity to be an editor lay no farther than his Pratt Street home. He proposed to the core members of the discussion groups—Siegel, Emmart, Crampton, and a new addition, John Hubner—a plan for a magazine devoted to literature and social thought. Having eagerly read magazines such as the *Dial, Seven Arts,* the *Freeman*, and the *Liberator*, the men jumped at the chance to initiate a similar publication, combining advanced ideas in art and politics. Like Russell Jacoby's "Last Intellectuals," these young men were essentially nonacademic intellectuals who grew up in the peppery environment of Baltimore, who looked to an integrated public intellectual life centered in urban areas and who drew inspiration from the Village Bohemia of New York.[17] Like the independent intellectuals of Greenwich Village, their speculations were uninhibited by disciplinary boundaries. In intellectual attitude, they resembled the earlier Village radicals who evidenced, as H. L. Mencken put it, "the natural revolt of youth against the pedagogical Prussianism of professors."[18] Some of the group either were or had been associated (as in George's case) with *Black and Blue Jay* at Johns Hopkins. All were offended by the false sophistication, vapid humor, and general lack of relevancy to life that characterized college publications including the Hopkins magazine. As they conceived it, their magazine would have nothing to do with the typical university magazine's genteel posturing, pretty metaphors, and unbearable triviality. Theirs would reject the bourgeois pretense that so infected college campuses and would combat the compartmentalization of thought that typified college learning.

On these premises the young men, under George's principal direction, brought out a publication called *Horizons* in May of 1922. They announced in the magazine's foreword their rejection of niceness, good manners, reticence, and the "humorous way"—what Malcolm Cowley was later to call the "life-is-a-circus type of cynicism," which, inspired by Mencken, had became the standard pose of the college student of the day.[19] They dedicated their magazine to serious issues and speculative thought; the sort of issues, they claimed, that might have engrossed a Spinoza or a Veblen. Yet for all its seriousness, the magazine was a conglomeration of impassioned but vague discussions of socialism, ungainly attempts to connect the philosophy of Randolph Bourne with Lenin, mediocre efforts at short fiction, and spectacularly bad attempts at poetry.

Horizons folded after the first issue. Nevertheless, the publication reflected the mood of the group who conceived it. These young men had not witnessed the disillusioning spectacle of war at firsthand, and so shared little of the malaise that characterized the postwar intellectual temperament. Rather than sharing the skeptical disposition of many slightly older members of their generation—the "lost" stance of Malcolm Cowley's "exiles" with their sense that social idealism was a form of self-deception—these young intellectuals drew inspiration from the optimistic years of prewar radicalism. If they resembled the "exiles" in their opposition to the moribund genteel tradition, they were not, like Cowley and his friends, "disillusioned and weary." [20] Rather, their disaffection from middle-class gentility was accompanied by a positive view of their own capacity as young radicals to bring about social change. Their defiant attitude was based primarily on the prewar example of Randolph Bourne, an attitude of youthful rebellion that saw the essence of the struggle as being against bourgeois gentility and complacency, a complacency they saw their slightly older contemporaries unwittingly embracing, by espousing glibness and world-weariness, the dead end of the genteel tradition.

Horizons also revealed another mood or attitude, part of the legacy of the progressive era, which characterized these youthful radicals. In their rejection of intellectual compartmentalization, they upheld the ideal that areas of thought should be interrelated and interwoven into a holistic and complete criticism of literature, society, politics, and life. This notion of a complete criticism would be taken up again in their next venture, which followed closely in the wake of the *Horizons* experiment. The most significant achievement of that experiment was its serving as a mock-up or prototype for the next publication from these young literary radicals—the *Modern Quarterly*. Furthermore, the *Horizons* venture revealed the ambition and enterprise of its chief editor, who, within a year, would be leading these young men in launching the new magazine.

 For George Goetz, at age twenty-two, socialism had supplanted the social gospel as the hope for a decent society. In 1922 an incredulous and disheartened Herman F. Miller wrote George demanding that he reevaluate his socialist convictions: "Look what your motley retinue are [*sic*] doing to poor Russia. The church may have exploited the people gradually on a retail basis; the Bolsheviks hope to do it on a wholesale basis." [21] But the two concerns of George's early life—religion and socialism—were not by any means diametrically opposed. His religious orientation had always been "progressive." Like many other progressive thinkers he found his religious interests moving naturally into a concern for social reform, and concern for progressive social reform seemed to move him naturally toward socialism. As he was later to write, "It was the study of the Christian texts that first drove me in a socialist direction." [22]

The two concerns of his early life could doubtless be traced back to the contradictions in his home environment that resulted from the enormous disparity between his mother's and father's view of the world. Influenced by his father's Rooseveltian progressivism with its adamant antimonopoly sentiment, he later rejected his father's populist inclinations for socialist convictions. Yet his father's political progressivism raised questions about social change and social justice that he later found answered in socialism. Initially influenced by his mother's religiosity, his interest in religion later dissipated, yet he retained a religious temperament, which manifested itself not only in his commitment to the ideal of socialism, but also in his subsequent interest in utopian communitarianism.

In later life George would become preoccupied with the inmost self (what he termed the "man inside"), as well as the potential of socialist community to redeem the lonely self from isolation and the fear of death. If these concerns have a general "religious" resonance, they suggest more specifically the radical personalism he inherited from the Village Left and from writers of the *Seven Arts* group, particularly Randolph Bourne, for whom politics was a "means to life" and properly extended itself into the most intimate areas of human existence. [23] Like prewar intellectuals such as Bourne and the young Lewis Mumford, George would come to see the redemptive process of self-renewal tied up with cultural renewal, and the key to this was the community—as Bourne had put it, "the good life of personality lived in the environment of the Beloved Community." [24] From the prewar intellectual Left, itself influenced by the thought of John Dewey, George inherited a pragmatic strain with its notion of the "organic" intellectual who participates deeply in the life of the mind and relates ideas to action. But beyond a future-oriented instrumentalism that deploys thought as a means to enable effective action, he inherited the pragmatic concern for a culture of radical democracy in which self-creation and communal participation are coextensive.

Indeed, the dominant theme that would run through his writing and career was that of community, a concept that for him provided an organic interrelation between private and public realms. If his thought embodied the desire to integrate self and society that lay at the heart of prewar progressivism, it was also influenced to some extent by another strain of progressive and pragmatic thought, the idea of social control, something that would preoccupy him during the mid thirties.[25] Yet increasingly he would look to intellectual community to solve the deeply personal problems of loneliness and angst; ultimately he would view the participation of the individual in the community as a possible answer to the most elusive existential problem that confronted the self—death. Moreover, concern about the problem of individual and community and a desire to discover some organic interrelationship between self and society that could transform American life, a legacy of prewar intellectuals such as Bourne and Brooks, would preoccupy George throughout his career and shape his vision of a socialist society of the future.

The influence of the prewar radicals on George Goetz's thought cannot be overestimated. He considered Van Wyck Brooks one of his intellectual progenitors, maintained a lifelong correspondence with Brooks, and always eagerly awaited Brooks's opinion of the books he wrote. Like Brooks, his criticism, at its best, fanned out to encompass cultural criticism; it assumed, as Brooks put it, that "literary criticism is always impelled sooner or later to become social criticism."[26] But more in the manner of Randolph Bourne, George looked to politics as a possible remedy for private concerns, for the deepest anxieties of the self. Like Bourne, who sought out friends to allay his "dreadful pessimism,"[27] he would seek out the group and search after radical community to assuage his personal anxieties.

The degree to which such anxieties pressed upon and preoccupied him is indicated in an unpublished autobiographical novel written toward the end of his life, "This Thing of Darkness."[28] The novel provides several clues to the inner world of its young protagonist "George." The novel, a *bildungsroman,* charts his awakening to sex: the pleasures and guilts of furtive and defiant sex in a repressive, morally censorious, and puritanical Baltimore environment. Scenes of adolescent masturbation are vividly recounted, as well as the anxiety, guilt, and conflict experienced because of them. Guilt-ridden and burdened by the views of his church toward sex, George nevertheless continues to explore his awakening sexual desire. His first sexual encounter occurs at sixteen, with a working-class girl who labors in a factory on the docks. They meet secretly; he is stunned and elated by her sexual frankness and aggressiveness. The initiation is not only into sexuality, but into a dawning awareness of the possibility of sex without guilt, and George, at sixteen, sees the experience as the first step in a break with the middle-class prudishness of Baltimore.

But if there is Eros there is also Thanatos, and death enters the novel in the form of a traumatic incident in which the young George watches with terror as his grandfather dies of a heart attack on a New York subway train. Dazed, the boy observes the family's solemn preparation for the funeral. At the funeral, filled with horror, George watches the casket being lowered into the grave: "He knew he would never forget the noise of those ropes, the cling and crawl of them, as they slid into the grave, and that thud when the casket bumped against the earth, and the uncanny stillness that followed it." [29] Witnessing his grandfather's death apparently left a lasting trauma: although George lived much of his adult life in New York, he never ventured into the subway. The awareness of death precipitated by this traumatic experience permeates the narrative of the autobiographical novel. Yet in a more general sense, the heavy pall of death in the novel is associated with his parents' leaden bourgeois existence, with his father's alcoholism and his mother's somnolence. Ida Goetz, in fact, exhibited propensities toward a deep melancholia, often manifest in her withdrawal and her love of sleep. At intervals in his own life George would be brought low by similar bouts of depression. As if forming himself in rebellion against his mother's docility and withdrawal, he would work compulsively and sleep sparingly. Yet throughout his life he was also frightened by the specter of death: not only by the horror of abrupt and complete extinction he had witnessed as a child as he watched his grandfather die, but perhaps even more by the death-in-life that the lure of Thanatos—like his mother's attraction to passivity and sleep—represented.

During the twenties, George, like the prewar radicals before him, would condemn the puritanism of American society. He would wage an open war against the Victorian and repressive attitudes toward sex he associated with the middle-class milieu in Baltimore, embracing the works of the "new psychology" and entering into unorthodox and experimental relations with several women. He would have numerous relationships with women; these relationships, however, were more than a desire to explore new and "unrepressed" sexual relations. They emerged from a deep-seated need for approval—particularly in the area of intellectual accomplishment—that he never got from a mother who was indifferent to education. In his relationships with women George searched for security, for approval, for acceptance, and for answers to his personal fears, his profound anxieties about loneliness, isolation, and death.

Indeed it was death—the "thing of darkness"—that would increasingly preoccupy him. The various crises of his early family life contributed to the insecurity and instability that he felt during his early years. His father's response to the crisis of his business, depression and drink, as well as his mother's withdrawal and sleep, generated anxieties about the integrity of the self and about the dark possibilities of the disintegration of the will and the dissolution of self. They also engendered a sense of aloneness, of the singularity of the self confronting its own extinction. This sense of separateness and awareness of mortality, a continual source of dread and at times the source of panic-terror, would make George crave friendship, would drive him to seek solace in relations with women, and would ultimately compel him to look to the group for relief. If socialism had replaced religion for George, he nevertheless would attempt to assuage the anxieties of the isolated self by seeking a merging of self and other that verged on the religious—in a passionate love affair or by submerging individuality in the group. Moreover, as an inheritor of the prewar Socialists' belief in the coextensive relation of the personal and the political, the desire to find release from the anxieties of the self provoked his quest for the ideal of socialist *gemeinschaft* in the revolutionary party or political fraternity. Nevertheless the burden of the isolated self would continue to plague him throughout his life, to plummet him periodically into black depression, and to induce him in later life to adopt his father's solution to personal problems—heavy drinking.

A *bildungsroman* frequently concludes with the protagonist's discovery of some goal or purpose around which life might be organized. Appropriately "This Thing of Darkness" concludes with the young protagonist's discovery of socialism. Stopping at this point, however, it fails to account for the way in which private preoccupations, such as loneliness and fear of death, and public, intellectual concerns, such as a commitment to socialism, would later converge and influence one another. Nor does it depict the interesting features of its protagonist's later life: the transformation of George Goetz of Baltimore into V. F. Calverton, the internationally known radical editor; the development of a career that extended through two crucial decades of American radicalism. Nor does it account for an intellectual life embodying the conflicting desires for the individual and communal, an intellectual life that, motivated by deeply personal matters, desperately sought community yet preserved a fierce independence of mind. It tells nothing of the story of V. F. Calverton, a lone rebel within the American Left. All this was to be depicted in an autobiography Calverton began in 1940 entitled "Between Two Wars." But he died suddenly that year with only two pages completed and the advances spent. He was never to write his own intriguing story.

In 1922 that story was just beginning. In Baltimore he had gained a university education, discovered an intellectual world, found socialism, and gathered an intellectual community of friends around him, all of whom were, like himself, enthusiastically committed to political and cultural radicalism. He was writing and planning to launch a new radical journal. In the mornings he would get up, go into the second floor study of "2110," with its chintz curtains, pleated parchment lamp shades, tables littered with book reviews, and its smell of stale smoke from the gathering of the night before, and begin writing. On one of those Baltimore mornings so full of the promise of beginnings he wrote: "The milk wagons break the stillness of dawn—the sky is already gleaming with light and the river beyond my window is imprisoned by its radiance. Why sleep with summer in the air?" [30]

CHAPTER TWO

We are a Socialist magazine. That is, we belong to no
brand of socialism save the kind described above and *that
is* The Complete Socialism. As a Socialist magazine, our
considerations are for all things, literature and biology, as
well as the economics of supply and demand.
                    —Editorial, *Modern Quarterly*, March 1923

The Birth of V. F. Calverton and the Genesis of the *Modern Quarterly*

T he early 1920s were bleak years in American radicalism. For
many radicals, socialism seemed a lost cause. The anti–Red
crusade of Attorney General A. Mitchell Palmer, the arrest
and deportation of anarchists Emma Goldman and Alexander Berkman,
the arrest of Nicola Sacco and Bartolomeo Vanzetti, and the breakdown
of leftist loyalties and organizations made it abundantly clear that political
radicals had no place in Woodrow Wilson's postwar world. Moreover, the
continuity between past and present seemed fractured by the war. Struggling to gain their bearings in chaotic times, many radicals became too
discouraged to hope for a change in social organization or social values.
Randolph Bourne was dead and with him the spirit of rebellion that had
permeated, in such a thoroughgoing fashion, the Village environs and the
"Lyrical Left" of the 1910s.

Moreover, Bohemia itself had broken into pieces and factions: literary
expatriates who went to Europe after the war felt little sense of political
responsibility. Those who remained were divided between the approach
of Van Wyck Brooks, who continued the search for a viable cultural heritage, and the political radicals who remained in the Village and published
first in the *Liberator* and later in the *New Masses*. Yet if Bohemia had been
fractured or decentered, it had also become, as James Gilbert has pointed

out, an international phenomenon quite independent of Greenwich Village in New York. It could be constituted in any highly evolved urban community where there was a "belief in the existence of a community of intellectuals united in function and persuaded of the need to associate with one another."[1]

Such was the case with the young intellectuals—George Goetz, Eli Siegel, A. D. Emmart, and Savington Crampton—who gathered together at 2110 East Pratt Street in Baltimore, seeking models in the *Seven Arts* and the *Masses* of the 1910s and the more contemporary *Liberator*. Like members of the Village Left—and other Bohemias—they were hostile to the middle class, whose bourgeois oppression in both sex and politics seemed to them to have reached its apotheosis in Baltimore. But they did not imagine they had to travel to New York to be part of the intelligentsia. Rather they confidently believed they could live the life of ideas in Baltimore, that their group could provide a source for the dissemination of radical values in both literature and politics. What they now needed was a journal.

Late in 1922, George Goetz outlined plans to the group for a new magazine to be called the "Radical Quarterly." He proposed a magazine that would merge revolutionary politics and modern ideas in art and literature in the best tradition of the Greenwich Village Left. The group discussed the idea and agreed that the new magazine would be directed to socialist thinkers regardless of factional persuasion or differences of outlook. They sought a "complete" perspective on politics and culture that would help to mend the strife-torn factions on the Left, and to revitalize radicals with new purpose. But the young Baltimoreans, caught up in the first flush and enthusiasm of their plans, had little sense of strategy for funding and distributing such a publication.

George Goetz had conceived of the project, and, as was the case with the *Horizons* experiment, quickly became the driving force within the group's push to launch the new publication. Unabashedly, he sent out letters to prominent radicals soliciting contributions (Upton Sinclair agreed to write for the first number) and to socialist groups (such as the socialist cooperative Charles H. Kerr & Co. of Chicago) to inquire about details of printing costs and advertising space.[2] He soon realized the difficulty he faced in launching a radical publication in the inhospitable climate of the early twenties. The League for Industrial Democracy (a broadly socialist group that worked to establish liaison with labor leaders), for example, advised him that "before the war it was possible for a small idealistic group to publish a quarterly or monthly and rush around after publication for enough money to pay for its issue, but it is no longer possible."[3] And from the editor of a Baltimore socialist periodical came another gloomy prognosis:

"You are sitting amidst the wrecks of progressive journalism of all sorts and conditions. . . . Our local venture The Voice of the People is at this time sending out an S.O.S call."[4] Nevertheless Goetz persisted, applying to the American Fund for Public Service, which administered the Garland bequest (provided by the young Harvard graduate Charles Garland who dedicated his paternal inheritance to the radical cause). When he was turned down, he managed to get modest financial assistance from several local Baltimore liberals including a wealthy dowager, Elsie Sise, who would make periodic contributions to the magazine throughout its life.

But these contributions scarcely met the costs of launching the journal. From the very beginning, George and Helen Goetz found themselves covering much of the magazine's expenses out of the income they made as teachers. The lack of funding also meant they did all the laborious organizational work themselves—seeking articles, soliciting funds, reading proofs. It became a regular occurrence for George and Helen to arrive home from work at three-thirty in the afternoon and immediately go to work reading and correcting copy until one or two o'clock in the morning. Finally Goetz recruited several students from Public School No. 40 to assist, including an immigrant from Russia named Bessie Peretz who did typing and copy-work and later translated pieces from the Russian. And he found a printer, an aging Jewish man with socialist sympathies and an occasional participant in the Saturday night gatherings, who agreed to print the magazine at cost.

Other problems became apparent as December 1922 approached and the text of the magazine was readied for the printer. Aware that George and Helen's teaching jobs might be jeopardized by serving on the editorial board of a magazine called "The Radical Quarterly," the editors unanimously agreed to change the title to something more ambiguous that would not draw undue attention to its radical contents. They settled on *The Modern Quarterly* as best evoking the spirit of youthful, challenging thought that would characterize the magazine. In giving the magazine this name they implicitly acknowledged the example of the Village Left and critics of the *Seven Arts* such as Bourne and Brooks for whom the term "modern" meant an urban, antiprovincial cosmopolitanism that sought to conjoin political and cultural currents that reflected advanced thinking.[5] Indeed the editors intended to fashion their publication around this notion of the modern.

To ensure that their teaching jobs were further protected, George and Helen Goetz (Helen was to serve as circulation and advertising editor) adopted pseudonyms. For radicals during the early twenties this was a common practice, a legacy of the Palmer raids of 1920 when many leftists adopted pen names to protect themselves from the wholesale arrests and deportations conducted by the red-baiting Attorney General Palmer. Helen took the name "Ruth Merdon" (later she settled on "Ilene Hood") while George came up with the name "T. Z. Georgas." But later in a moment of inspiration he decided on "Calverton," the name of one of the early Baltimore manors named after Lord Calvert, founder of Baltimore. He was drawn to the name because it was intimately connected with Baltimore. He also liked the playful irony of placing a name associated with the landed gentry on the editorial board of a radical publication. In such a context, the name suggested that the very spirit of Baltimore itself was being radicalized. He prefaced the name with the initials "V. F." because he thought they sounded good juxtaposed to the surname he had chosen.[6]

Finally, all difficulties surmounted—or at least held at bay—the magazine appeared in March 1923 in much the form the editors had imagined. On the masthead the following editors were listed: M. G. Shelley, Ruth Merdon (Helen Goetz), Morton Levin, Savington Crampton, and Richel North (A. D. Emmart). They were all under twenty-three years old; several were Johns Hopkins graduates. V. F. Calverton was the name at the head of the list, for George Goetz–Calverton was plainly the journal's prime force, both organizationally and financially. The name would remain at the head of the editorial board for the life of the magazine. Indeed, the publication and its editorial policies would come to be indelibly associated with the name Calverton.

AMERICAN radicalism during the early twenties tended to be eclectic and amorphous. As Richard Pells notes, to be a Communist or a Socialist during those years often meant very little; one "was simply a radical, more or less influenced by Marx."[7] The early *Modern Quarterly* was a testament to the eclectic radicalism of this period, still strongly influenced by the prewar intellectuals' preoccupation with diverse absorbing contemporary ideas. Three words dominated the declamatory manifesto and the articles of the fledgling publication—*complete, scientific,* and *modern*. These catchwords were virtually interchangeable. All implied the ideal of a comprehensive perspective able to synthesize political and aesthetic issues, as well as the ideal of a nonpartisan vigor that would unite political rebels in the struggle to create a socialist society. The truly modern sensibility, explained the editors in their manifesto "Modernism And The Modern Quarterly," would be able to grasp the interconnections between economic, political, and cultural matters by examining them *metaphysically*—which was to say, in the editors' special use of the term, in terms of their ultimate causes. The term *metaphysical* conjured up, in a vague manner, notions of the Hegelian dialectic with its preference for totality over separate parts. The word also had overtones of a Marxist dialectical materialism: to be metaphysical was not only to understand that all aspects of reality are integrally related, but to examine them by way of their "root" causes, which were essentially material, environmental, and economic. The metaphysical attitude meant understanding that "the truth is the whole and cannot be divided"; thus the editors repudiated "all false distinctions" such as those "between intellectual and worker, between pure art and propaganda." To be a "complete socialist" meant embracing a non-doctrinal radicalism that would see no contradiction between the various forms of resistance to capitalism, but rather would see these forms as part of a larger rebellion, part of socialism in the broadest sense:

> We feel that all brands of Anarchism, Syndicalism, State Socialism etc., must work toward the same end, and as such, are merely parts of socialism; if they don't do it, they are working toward incomplete ends, as do all false schemes like Dial [*sic*] awards, W.C.T.U.'s, Leagues of Nations, and liberals' ideals of internationalisms.[8]

The editors declared their independence from any particular party. The *Modern Quarterly* would transcend the boundaries of factional groups in the same way that its interests transcended the boundaries of compartmentalized fields of study:

> We are a socialist magazine. That is, we belong to no brand of socialism save the kind described above and *that is* The Complete Socialism. As a socialist magazine, our considerations are for all things, literature and biology, as well as the economics of the law of supply and demand.[9]

Each article in the first issue of the *Modern Quarterly* elaborated on the notion of a "complete socialism." To be "scientific" was also to be "complete" in one's perspective. This required bringing an analytical comprehensiveness based on socialist principles to bear on the "object" whether it be social phenomenon or literature, as Eli Siegel explained in an article on literary criticism. To be scientific, in other words, was to fashion a critical perspective grounded in socialist thought. He concluded that a scientific criticism was "too great a thing to practice under capitalism," yet he dedicated the *Quarterly* to the attempt to forge such a criticism based on Marxist principles.[10] Similarly, Goetz advocated understanding human intelligence in "complete" terms, that is, in terms of economic conditions, availability of education, leisure time, and the quality of stimulation during early life. Combining a progressive faith in social engineering with a mechanistic behaviorism (he was still very much under the influence of the behaviorist psychology courses he had taken at Johns Hopkins), he concluded that under socialism, material conditions that produced persons of talent could be discovered and engineered. Socialism would usher in a new epoch in which genius would be commonplace rather than rare.[11]

In a feature article A. D. Emmart held up the *Modern Quarterly* as a vehicle for a comprehensive radicalism. He juxtaposed what he considered to be "The limitations of American Magazines" against the comprehensiveness of the *Modern Quarterly*. Magazines such as the *Nation* and the *New Republic* suffered from the liberal's refusal to think in ideological or broadly conceptual terms. Radical publications suffered in part from the same malady. The *Liberator*, though often "sharp and penetrating," failed to integrate Michael Gold's socialist interests with Eastman's and Dell's aesthetic interests. If the *Liberator*'s socialism was "incomplete," the *Freeman* (a journal of the Westport Bohemian set edited by Albert Nock and Van Wyck Brooks) was beleaguered by old-fashioned progressivism and a watered-down Fabianism. Literary magazines such as *Harper's, Scribner's,* and *The Century* ignored politics; *Dial, Broom,* and *Little Review* were fatally marred by the aesthete's propensity to "seek after the exotic." As for the *Quarterly*'s Baltimore rival H. L. Mencken's *Smart Set,* Emmart characterized it as a publication in which a cynical "sophistication" rationalized ignoring social issues.[12]

Emmart's article provided, primarily through negative definition, a prospectus for the new magazine. The *Modern Quarterly* would not succumb to the liberal magazines' tendency to be limited and restrained in their analysis; it would not be satisfied with mere aestheticism, and it would stand opposed to cynical nihilism. It would follow the example of prewar *Masses* and *Seven Arts* in its combination of art and radical politics, but it would, Emmart emphasized, be more uncompromisingly socialist than these publications.

Indeed the first issue of the *Modern Quarterly* exhibited certain characteristics of its prewar progenitors. Like the editors of *Seven Arts,* the editors of the *Quarterly* assumed that society was fragmented and chaotic and the study of life in America was disjointed and compartmentalized. Their notion of comprehensiveness and a "complete" socialism echoed earlier calls for an "organic" social and cultural life of a Van Wyck Brooks or Waldo Frank. Their conception of science as a method and spirit rather than a body of knowledge, and hence easily transferable from physical and biological inquiry to other human activities, echoed something of Walter Lippmann's view of science in his *Drift and Mastery*.[13] Their denial of "false distinctions" between art and propaganda echoed the *Masses* call to link culture and politics. The *Quarterly*'s manifesto in fact suggested an attempt to combine the examples of the *Seven Arts* and the *Masses*: like the *Seven Arts* it projected a vision of a comprehensive socialism that would serve to criticize American culture as a whole; like the *Masses* it aspired to criticize sharply a destructive and unjust capitalist society. What formed the common denominator of these various intellectual threads in the fledgling magazine was the general progressive and pragmatic sense of instrumental reason—the notion that critical intelligence can change and shape environment, that thought can be deployed to enable effective action. Clearly the editors wished to fashion themselves as "organic" intellectuals in this progressive and pragmatic mold.

Yet the *Quarterly*'s socialist vision remained (like that of much prewar socialism) inordinately vague and unspecific. Infatuated by the idea of a complete socialist perspective, the editors described in rhapsodic terms how such socialism would heal the world's body and overcome the fragmentation of knowledge under capitalism. Carried away by youthful enthusiasm, they clearly believed they were at the cutting edge of literary and social thought. Nevertheless the first issue of the *Modern Quarterly* had a strikingly juvenile quality. It exhibited none of the wit, irony, or literary sophistication of a *Seven Arts*, nor any of the brash, impertinent cheerfulness of the *Masses*. Rather its tone was ponderous and full of self-importance. Emmart's article showed an upstart editor taking on almost every important magazine in the country and confidently assuring his readers that the *Quarterly* would exceed all other publications in depth and quality. Siegel's piece read like an undergraduate essay in introductory philosophy. Goetz's article was woefully tedious in its wooden, dogged determinism and politically dubious in its notions of social engineering. If it had not been for an article by Scott Nearing and a short piece on social art by Upton Sinclair, the first issue of the *Modern Quarterly* would have scarcely exceeded its predecessor *Horizons* in quality.

Nevertheless the first issue of the *Quarterly* indicates the direction in which the magazine would grow. The idea of a complete socialism—so replete with naive and youthful optimism, so amorphously eclectic and vague—nevertheless indicated a decided propensity toward the heterodox and nonpartisan. Indeed the general progressive and pragmatic tone of the new magazine indicated a stance that, if developed, would be naturally antithetical to doctrinal narrowness. Moreover, the first issue of the *Quarterly* precipitated an event that portended, in an utterly uncanny way, future conflicts between the magazine and doctrinal orthodoxy on the Left. Siegel was expelled from the Socialist Labor Party (SLP) shortly after the first issue appeared for the "heresies" contained in his article "The Complete Socialism," another vague essay about the all-encompassing, "wholly true and right" character of socialism.[14] In sympathy with Siegel, Goetz resigned from the SLP immediately thereafter, but the incident anticipated a long series of conflicts between the *Quarterly* and orthodox strains of the Left.

The new *Modern Quarterly* caught the attention of liberals and radicals and was favorably reviewed in both circles. John Marcey, editor of the *Nation*, congratulated V. F. Calverton on an "excellent magazine."[15] Joseph Freeman, then on the *Liberator* staff, was so impressed he wrote Calverton and Siegel to solicit contributions for another new radical journal, a publication as yet "still a fine dream, having its existence exclusively inside the heads of the Party leaders," to be called the "Daily Worker."[16] From abroad, and from an entirely different political point of view, T. S. Eliot's *Criterion* characterized the magazine as "stimulating," while the British *New Age* noted with approval the birth of a new radical publication.[17]

One thousand copies of the first issue were printed. Although all but eight were sold, financial difficulties made only two more issues possible during the first year. For the most part, these numbers featured continuations of articles from the first issue, or mediocre short stories, which had been rejected elsewhere, written by Goetz under his nom de plume, "Mark Rodson." Meanwhile he continued to write editorials, solicit articles, search for financial assistance, and pour money from his teaching salary into the publication.

Amid economic strain and overwork, rivalry began to develop among the members of the editorial board. Siegel considered himself the genius of the group whose role was that of writing on the philosophical basis of socialism rather than involving himself in editorial details. But Goetz had initiated and taken the reins of the publication whose first issue had been a modest success, and perhaps Siegel now felt threatened in his accustomed role as mentor and an undisputed expert on socialism. As in the early days of their friendship, Siegel began to rebuke Goetz for being a mere liberal, insufficiently "metaphysical" and "complete" in his socialist vision. Siegel insisted that his own work was far superior to Goetz's, and that Emmart concurred with this judgment. Siegel proclaimed that Goetz was an "intellectual careerist" with no interest in socialism.[18] In a measured response Goetz wrote that "regardless of your feeling toward me always believe me to be your friend."[19] But tensions remained in their relationship. Siegel ceased regular contributing after the third number and the tensions among members of the editorial staff were no doubt a factor in Emmart's decision to leave the *Quarterly* by the close of 1923 and take a job with the *Baltimore Sun*.

The George Goetz–Eli Siegel exchange anticipated a number of conflicts among editorial board members on the *Modern Quarterly*. It also foreshadows something that would become a central concern in Goetz's later life: the delicate and precarious nature of intellectual community. The conflict also indicates something about Goetz's role as editor: if Siegel's charges are defensive and self-righteous, it is no doubt true that Goetz now regarded the magazine as his and saw it as a vehicle for establishing a reputation as both critic and creative writer. Yet Siegel, always something of a true believer,[20] failed to comprehend that Goetz was interested both in the idea of socialism and in the enhancement of his own reputation. Certainly the history of the magazine scarcely bears out Siegel's contention that Goetz's interest in socialism was merely "opportunistic."

By the close of 1923 the *Modern Quarterly* had lost two of its original editors and contributors. However, in the spring of the following year, Haim Kantorovitch, an immigrant who left Russia after becoming disenchanted with the Bolshevik revolution, joined the editorial board. He was a veteran who had been involved in a number of factions and groups ranging from socialism to syndicalism to communism. He had the deep intellectual commitment to socialism of the immigrant Jewish intellectual. His wide reading had included Russian literary theorists like George Plekhanov and Leon Trotsky. Goetz met Kantorovitch in the Baltimore school system, where Kantorovitch was teaching Hebrew; Goetz was impressed with his knowledge and recruited him to the magazine. Kantorovitch was immediately taken with the *Quarterly* venture; he was sympathetic to the magazine's expressed ideals of a nonpartisan socialist philosophy, and like Goetz he was an admirer of socialist ideals of the prewar Left.[21] But he felt that the publication needed more ideological sophistication and focus.

Kantorovitch's presence on the board resulted in a major change of direction in the magazine. The two issues of the *Quarterly* that followed the first number had merely continued the jejune and adolescent flights about complete socialism. As an antidote to such vagueness, Kantorovitch recommended Goetz read Marx's *Theses on Feuerbach* with its injunction that materialism must comprehend human sensuous activity as practical, that "all the mysteries which urge theory into mysticism find their rational solution in human practice and in the comprehension of this practice."[22] Kantorovitch thus urged a more rigorous attention to the scientific and materialistic basis of socialism. Providing an insight that would profoundly influence Goetz and the direction of the *Modern Quarterly*, Kantorovitch argued that discrete and separate disciplines in the sciences could be unified by a synthetic approach based on a materialist methodology. This "new synthetic science" Kantorovitch called "neo-materialism." In the area of literary criticism, Kantorovitch stressed the need for a study of American literature that would provide the basis for a disciplined historical awareness and Marxist methodology in American criticism. With Kantorovitch's encouragement, Goetz began a study of literature along Marxist lines, an investigation that his new-found mentor believed would be an important contribution to Marxist criticism in America.[23]

The spring 1924 issue of the *Quarterly* testified to Kantorovitch's influence. It was an enormous improvement both in quality and scope. It demonstrated a new attention to the Russian theorists and Russian literature with its inclusion of Plekhanov's essay "Materialism and Art" (translated by Bessie Peretz), as well as a translated prose poem by V. G. Korolenko. It was the first issue that properly could be said to be radical or "Marxist" in orientation, for pointed analyses of theoretical issues on the Left now replaced the insubstantial writing that characterized the first issues of the magazine.

One of these articles probing radical concerns (and by far the most impressive piece in the issue) was Kantorovitch's own article, "The Rise and Decline of Neo-Communism." Kantorovitch's article was singularly important because it set a tone of critical independence and willingness to subject socialist premises and developments on the Left to scrutiny. Kantorovitch characterized John Reed's writings on the Bolshevik revolution as an "artist's dream," which read "more like a fairy tale than a statement of facts."[24] He accused the communist regime of using terror against both friends and enemies. He argued that the Bolshevik revolution—a revolution by a small group—was in direct contradiction to Marx's notion that social revolution would be made by the mass action of the majority of the workers rather than by a small minority heading the unconscious masses. Furthermore, said Kantorovitch, Lenin's and Bukharin's rejection of the idea that each country must inevitably pass through capitalistic development and capitalistic exploitation before a socialist revolution could be possible was "precisely the reverse of Marxism." Not only was Lenin's revolution premature, he protested, not only did the revolution occur before the majority of workers had attained consciousness, but in their zeal to avoid "reformism" the Communists drove away potential allies such as the European socialist parties and hence remained isolated from the working-class movement.[25]

Kantorovitch's article anticipates critiques of Stalinist Russia and of the legacy of Leninism itself that were to emerge on the Left more than a decade later. In the late thirties, Goetz would embrace a view similar to that expressed in Kantorovitch's article,[26] but in 1924 he disagreed strongly with its conclusions. Nevertheless he respected Kantorovitch's opinions and ran the article in the spirit of the magazine's proclaimed editorial policy: providing a variety of perspectives and ideas by intellectuals on the Left. Moreover, if Goetz disagreed with Kantorovitch on this issue, he was nonetheless profoundly influenced by Kantorovitch's critical spirit and his independence of thought. Kantorovitch had displaced Siegel as Goetz's mentor, and Kantorovitch not only encouraged him to write a work of literary criticism, but provoked him to put the magazine's stated policy of independence on the line over a crucial theoretical issue.

The inclusion of Kantorovitch's article in the spring 1924 issue, then, initiated the heterodox and often controversial character the *Modern Quarterly* would assume in the arena of radical political debate over the next two decades. For his own part, Kantorovitch felt that the spring issue had made significant headway toward becoming an important socialist publication. Moreover, he felt it had made a "splendid impression. . . . The Modern Quarterly," he wrote Goetz, "is the only scientific socialist magazine in the country—something to be proud of." [27]

Certainly the *Modern Quarterly* was now one of the most theoretically oriented independent radical magazines in the country. And during this dry period of the mid twenties the *Quarterly* was one of the few socialist periodicals that was growing and developing. The *Liberator*, for example, was alive, but after its becoming a Workers (Communist) Party organ in 1922, writers and artists began to lose interest in its purely political character.[28] It would expire in only six months, leaving the *Quarterly* virtually alone among literary radical journals until the *New Masses* appeared some two years later. Kantorovitch's prognosis for the future of the magazine would prove to be essentially correct: "I believe we have a great future before us." [29]

A**FTER** the spring 1924 issue, the *Quarterly* continued to improve. The format broadened to include symposia, book reviews, articles on the state of criticism, economics, and race relations. And the publication was now attracting contributions from prominent figures. The 1924 numbers contained essays by art critic Herbert Read, black economist Abraham Harris, and veteran Socialist Scott Nearing; they also contained a debate on American labor that included Charles E. Ruthenberg, secretary of the Workers Party, James Oneal, editor of the socialist *New Leader*, and V. L. Reynolds of the Socialist Party.

These early issues of the *Modern Quarterly* not only reveal the budding potential of the magazine but establish literary criticism as one of its dominant interests. From 1924 on, issues of the *Quarterly* clearly sought to bring a Marxist dimension to literary study in America. The translations of Plekhanov suggested an emphasis on Marxist aesthetics, as did Goetz's lengthy work presented in installments in the second and third numbers of 1924, entitled "The Sociological Criticism of Literature." At Kantorovitch's encouragement, Goetz decided to publish these essays in book form. The ensuing volume, entitled *The Newer Spirit*, appeared in the spring of 1925.

Immediately before the book was released, the publishers, Boni and Liveright, wrote Goetz insisting there was no good reason to use the pseudonym "Calverton" since the book, scholarly and academic, would not likely offend the Baltimore school board.[30] In spite of this advice, Goetz requested that the book's author remain "V. F. Calverton." For in the process of establishing a magazine and writing his first book, he had discovered a direction for his life. During those years of 1923 and 1924, George Goetz, the young Baltimorean, the Johns Hopkins graduate, had created V. F. Calverton, the radical critic, writer, and editor. In doing so George Goetz had given birth to a public version of himself. To the readers of the *Modern Quarterly*, and to his literary contacts, he was known as V. F. Calverton. To his close friends he was still George, but they acknowledged the newly developed aspect of his personality; they called him by a name that united the old and the new, the public school teacher and the Marxist critic—"George Calverton."

V. F. Calverton's *Newer Spirit* is in one sense a response to the inchoate state of criticism that existed in America. As William A. Drake (editing a volume of American criticism in 1926) summed up the case, American criticism was vigorous yet it lacked firm theoretical precepts.[31] At mid decade several critical strains dominated the American scene. The humanist movement, represented by Stuart Pratt Sherman, Irving Babbitt, and Paul Elmer More, stressed classical models and felt that literature, a medium for exhibiting humanist values, should revolve around the twin notions of ethical insight and restraint. The aesthetic critics, on the other hand, represented by Joel Spingarn (a student of Benedetto Croce's), were primarily concerned with the work itself, undistorted by psychological or political preconceptions, the moral standards of the humanist critics, or other "extrinsic" concerns. The historical and cultural critics, embodying a progressive impulse and represented by Van Wyck Brooks, Randolph Bourne, and Lewis Mumford, stressed the cultural shortcomings of America and protested against the domination of cultural and collective life by commercial values and materialistic pursuits that repressed native talent. Like Floyd Dell, a few critics attempted to apply Freudian insights to literature, while others, such as H. L. Mencken, proceeded along totally individual and idiosyncratic lines.

In this context of conflicting critical principles and a paucity of theoretical guidelines, Calverton voiced the need for a rigorous and "scientific" criticism. In an article in the *Modern Quarterly* on the state of criticism, he lamented the "critical myopia" on the American scene, while attacking the dominant critical schools of the time. The "Spingarn–Croce" aesthetes lacked any sense of social or historical reality; they were critics who "imagine we paint before we eat, that men fought originally for art expression and not for food." Professor Stuart Pratt Sherman and the Humanists he found muddled and ultraconservative. The idiosyncratic individualists like Mencken were largely negative in spirit and substance, as well as lacking a consistent philosophy (Mencken was "anti-bourgeois in morals," but a "thorough bourgeois in economics," Calverton wrote). Calverton concluded that only a sociological criticism based on materialist premises could be properly exacting in method.[32]

Thus for his own critical work he drew on the historical and social approaches of Buckle, Hippolyte Taine, and J. M. Robertson, but also the Marxist work of Plekhanov with its notion of literature as typifying and socially reflective, as a reflection of the "social mentality" or ideology of a particular historical period. Calverton was also strongly influenced by the sociological criticism practiced by Dell (such as his collection of essays "Literature and the Machine Age," published in installments in the *Liberator*) and Eastman. Such criticism emphasized the work's political, economic, and cultural background.

The Newer Spirit argues that the aesthetic precepts implicit in any body of literature are an expression of the society in which they emerge. All art springs from a dominant way of seeing the world that is related to the ideology of an age. Class concepts shape and determine aesthetic consciousness. Every revolution in aesthetic ideas is the consequence of a revolution in social structure. Not only art but critical principles are subject to the changing patterns of history: "All the theories and concepts, the dicta and shibboleths, of creative and critical effort are but the outgrowths of the social system in which they have their being, and which is in turn the product of the material conditions of the time."[33]

In support of his thesis Calverton argues that aesthetic categories such as tragedy—aristocratic and feudal in origin—were altered as a declining nobility became increasingly dependent on the rising bourgeoisie. Just as the rise of the bourgeoisie modified prevailing aesthetic categories (tragedy being transformed from a falling from illustriousness to a falling from sincerity and rectitude), the rise of the proletariat is presently transforming critical and artistic notions in a number of ways that are only recently being recognized. Increasingly the working class is becoming a force in molding social and aesthetic ideas. In America an interest in the common man was signaled early in the work of Walt Whitman. Calverton saw a trend to explore the life of the common man developing in writers as diverse as Émile Zola, Victor Hugo, Thomas Hardy, D. H. Lawrence, James Joyce, Theodore Dreiser, and Sherwood Anderson. These writers may not have identified with the proletariat—indeed they are, strictly speaking, bourgeois writers—yet a concern for the working class became a part of their work as a "social reflex," a function of the fact that social conditions shaped their consciousness.[34]

For Calverton, Sherwood Anderson is the "avatar of the proletarian movement," not only because Anderson's works often deal with laboring men, but because his works embody an aesthetic concept derived from the outlook of a modern postindividualistic age—that of "scientific determinism." The proletarian motif in fiction thus exhibits the logic of "inevitability" that is part and parcel of modern realism. In Anderson's fiction, "The sins of the characters spring from their environment, not from any ineradicable wickedness of human nature"; the system, not the individual is described as the cause of the existing evils of society.[35]

Calverton's conception of literature embodying the "proletarian concept," then, was virtually synonymous with nineteenth-century naturalism. Moreover, the guiding aesthetic principle of this proletarianism was realism: a "deeper realism" in matters of sex, breaking through the barriers of bourgeois reticence. Gustave Flaubert, for example, provided an early example of this "anti-bourgeois" impulse, revealing virtues like honesty and chastity to be deceptive and ideological in nature. Essentially, greater realism was equated with an unmasking of bourgeois pretense. This criterion, less than precise, allowed Calverton to enlist in the ranks of proto-proletarian literature just about any major writer of the nineteenth century.

As for contemporary art that embodied the "proletarian concept," Calverton argued that although it should deal with working people or with the disenfranchised, it need not be a creation of the working class. Unlike Gold, he did not see "proletarian literature" as a literature by and for the masses. Nor did he believe it should be patterned after "Proletcult" models emanating from the Soviet Union. Perhaps the most distinguishing feature of Calverton's theory was that proletarian art would ultimately seek to annihilate the class basis of culture:

> The realism toward which proletarian art is driving in its annihilation of class-distinctions possesses a comprehensiveness of content, singularly communistic in its development. Contrary to the usual belief there is no unilaterality in the attitude, considered in its fullness, no puffery of a single group at the expense of others except as an immediate situation in society might necessitate—as at the present time—but the promise of a complete synthesis of them all.[36]

Calverton's notion that the destiny of the proletariat was the eventual annihilation of class culture suggests Trotsky's influence. In a review of Trotsky's *Literature and Revolution* in the *New Leader*, Calverton praised Trotsky for opposing the "class chauvinists" who condemned all bourgeois literature and praised all literary effort of the working class. He agreed with Trotsky that the proletariat presently existed in an uncrystallized and untutored state and was therefore unable to create a culture particular to itself. Yet he was not willing to say, like Trotsky, that there could *never* be a proletarian art. Trotsky contended that since the ascendancy of the proletariat means the annihilation of class distinctions, in a classless society there can be, strictly speaking, no proletarian art. Calverton agreed with this theory, but felt that in the *transition* period between capitalism and communism—a period of indefinite length in which class conflict would continue to exist—a proletarian art might come into being.[37]

In a more general sense, however, the book with its Whitmanesque phrases (as in the above passage) like "no puffery of a single group," reveals a distinctively American vision of art and cultural radicalism. It suggests the legacy of writers like Van Wyck Brooks who called for a national culture in which society could fully participate. Calverton's formulations for proletarian art have obvious progressive echoes and are shaped by a fundamental vision of community that he inherited from the prewar Left: if "the immediate situation in society" requires an exposure of class differences, a classless and complete literature would ultimately emerge from the temporary proletarian phase, synthesizing all contradictions and projecting a vision of an organic interrelationship between self and society that would, in progressive fashion, reshape American life. More than the influence of Trotsky, the book suggests this progressive and pragmatic tradition with its democratic ideal of self-creation flourishing with communal participation, a vision shared alike by Brooks and Dewey. Moreover, the work not only indicates Calverton's indebtedness to the intellectual tradition of the Progressives, but implies an intellectual strategy he would later develop—a flexible, pragmatic amalgamation of the progressive tradition and Marxist ideas.

Calverton's work exhibited the beginnings of an effort to combine, in a pragmatic and experimental fashion, these two strains, but in general the *Newer Spirit* was conceptually sloppy and fraught with problems. His notion of the "proletarian concept" remained vague and ill-defined, while his preoccupation with naturalistic determinism as the sine qua non of advanced radical literature left him stuck, aesthetically speaking, in the nineteenth century. He was completely unable to deal with important modernist writers such as Kafka, whose works might have been seen from a more sophisticated and dialectical point of view, such as Georg Lukacs's, as constituting an indictment of bourgeois society. He remained confined by an undialectical and deterministic analysis he had gleaned (and oversimplified) from Plekhanov, and his reductive determinism, which he equated with a "scientific" view, left him with an utterly mechanical conception of the relationship between literature and society. The artist, finally, was absolutely determined by the environment, his writings a mere "social reflex." Shakespeare, pontificated Calverton, "did *nothing more* than represent the aesthetic conceptions of his period" (emphasis mine).[38] Moreover, the fact that Calverton chose Sherwood Anderson as the contemporary writer of chief importance suggests that his scheme provided no sophisticated criteria of aesthetic evaluation.

Thus although Calverton set out to clear up the critical confusion of his time by applying the Marxist method, he failed rather badly in his task. The mechanical nature of his inquiry made the study more positivist than Marxist: it did not account, as more developed Marxist perspectives might, for the complex interrelationship between the economic base and the cultural superstructure, for the fact that the relationship between art and society is neither direct nor mechanically determined. Calverton's vision of proletarian culture as a radical community represented the high point of the book, but in general Marxist analysis remained a blunt tool in his hands.

Critical responses to the *Newer Spirit* were mixed. John Dewey, sympathetic to its progressive approach, found the book "the best statement on behalf of the sociological criticism which I have read."[39] Herbert Read, then editor of T. S. Eliot's *Criterion*, praised Calverton for his "great service to the cause of criticism."[40] Less complimentary was H. L. Mencken in the *American Mercury*: "Calverton is full of the astonishing discoveries that socialists are always making—of facts known to all of us since childhood."[41] And Waldo Frank wrote an utterly scathing review in the *New Republic* entitled "No Spirit at All." Frank, who had long contended that criticism must be practiced as an art, not as a science, was hostile to any criticism that claimed to be scientific; but his primary complaint was Calverton's simplistic and mechanistic scheme, his tendency to see socioeconomics as "the one governing factor in the genesis of art." That the *Newer Spirit* was being taken seriously in radical circles indicated to Frank "the intellectual and spiritual bankruptcy of our revolutionary labor movement."[42]

Probably the most measured and perceptive criticism of Calverton's work came from Kenneth Burke in the *New York Herald-Tribune*. Burke saw merit in Calverton's sociological criticism, but objected to the problematic thesis of the impermanency of aesthetic values, as well as the fact that Calverton's procedure offered no criterion of aesthetic evaluation: "It seems quite plain that social change has produced a change in the *creative force* of the feudal aesthetic; but it is doubtful whether this change also makes us readers unable to enjoy the 'cream of feudal art.' . . . I still wait for Mr. Calverton to explain in what way his feudal-bourgeois-proletarian scheme contributes to, or detracts from, our evaluation of, say, *King Lear*."[43]

But Burke's balanced perspective was the exception among the ranks of the Left, where responses ranged from ecstatic praise to angry denunciation. James Oneal's praise in the *New Leader* was totally enthusiastic,[44] while H. M. Wicks, a Party ideologue writing in the *Daily Worker*, attacked Calverton, less over theoretical concerns than over matters of a doctrinal nature. In his belief that a transitional stage of proletarian culture might well arise before a truly classless society was possible, Calverton had contradicted Trotsky, Wicks charged. Since Trotsky at this time was still regarded as a leader in theoretical and cultural matters, Calverton had obviously committed a cardinal error: *The Newer Spirit*, according to Wicks, was to be regarded as contrary to Marxism.[45]

Michael Gold, however, who was at the time basically nonpartisan and busily assisting in the launching of what was planned to be a nonpartisan radical journal, the *New Masses*, wrote to Calverton:

> I want to tell you with what joy I have been reading your book. . . .
> It delights me that we have at last a real philosopher in our revolutionary ranks. Your book is on a plane with the best writing of the Russian critics—the first class men among them.[46]

Gold favorably contrasted Calverton to the older generation of writers associated with the old *Masses* and the *Liberator*, writers like Eastman ("a thorough bourgeois in his aesthetics") and like Dell ("the historian of the phallic hunting girls of Greenwich Village"). "I believe you are at the beginning of an interesting and perhaps great intellectual career," concluded Gold, adding however in his typical hard-boiled fashion, "that is if you don't get scared of your own thoughts and turn liberal and soft."[47]

The Newer Spirit brought Calverton to the attention of radical circles and launched his career as a spokesman for the literary Left. The book's less than deft analysis in part suggests the infancy and theoretical paucity of American radical criticism. Yet it also represents one of the first studies in the United States that consciously attempted a Marxist analysis of literature.[48] Floyd Dell's series of essays "Literature and the Machine Age," formerly published in the *Liberator* and published as *Intellectual Vagabondage* in 1926, was described by its author as "a kind of Marxian essay in literary criticism," but it dealt primarily with the intellectual alienation of his own generation in capitalist civilization. One other critic had attempted to articulate a theory of radical literature in the United States at this time: Michael Gold, whose essay "Toward a Proletarian Art," published in 1921 in the *Liberator*, was less a discursive study than a rhapsodic prose poem, which proclaimed a revolutionary culture produced by the "masses."[49]

Calverton's study lacked Gold's fervent rhetoric, but it was finally more serious and scholarly than Gold's. It was also less doctrinaire than theories of proletarian literature were to become in the late twenties and thirties.

To his credit, Calverton did not impose fixed and orthodox definitions on a body of literature yet to be written (as many "proletarian" critics of the thirties were later to do), but rather attempted to identify emerging trends in existing literature and from this speculate about future possibilities. If Calverton's initial attempt at Marxist criticism in the *Newer Spirit* was blunt and unsophisticated, it was at least not doctrinaire.

By the summer of 1925 the fates of the *Modern Quarterly* and its editor were thoroughly intertwined. George Goetz–Calverton had, with the help of his Baltimore radical coterie, successfully launched the *Quarterly*, and with Haim Kantorovitch's assistance he had shaped it from an adolescent journal into a magazine that was emerging as a serious radical publication. By the end of 1926 the magazine had an impressive list of contributions, which included, besides translations of Plekhanov's works, articles on black literature and art by W.E.B. Du Bois and Alain Locke, on the labor movement by David Saposs, on sociology in America by Harry Elmer Barnes, poems by Genevieve Taggard, Mark Van Doren, and E. Merrill Root, criticism by J. M. Robertson, and pieces by luminaries of the Left, literary and otherwise: Floyd Dell, Michael Gold, Benjamin Stolberg, Bertram Wolfe. Moreover, although financial difficulties continued, the circulation of the magazine had increased to 1,500 copies.[50]

Coextensively, the publication was bringing notoriety to its editor who was rapidly establishing his reputation as a promising young literary leftist. He now published not only in his own journal, but in a variety of left-wing and liberal journals like the *Nation*, the *New Republic*, and *Current History*. He was receiving invitations to lecture from New York's radical intelligentsia, and he gave a series of talks on "An Economic Interpretation of American Literature" at the Rand School of Social Sciences in the summer of 1925.[51] By this time he had met Mr. "Proletcult" himself, Michael Gold, who paid him the ultimate Goldian compliment: "I was glad to make your acquaintance, and to discover that you are a quite normal cigar-smoking young American, despite the tremendous themes you write on and tremendous Veblenian phrases."[52]

The Workers (Communist) Party now began considering Calverton as a potential Party member and radical theoretician. The severity of the "Third Period" of the International Communist movement—a period of Party militancy based on the idea that revolutionary activity would ensure the collapse of an already destabilized capitalist economy—was still some years away, and there was a greater latitude of opinion among Party officials. Hence, Earl Browder, William F. Dunne, and William Z. Foster received the *Newer Spirit* enthusiastically in spite of the attack by H. M. Wicks. At Browder's recommendation, the *Newer Spirit* was translated into

Russian in 1926. "We have a great need of a revolutionary intellectual who can analyze the broad developing social situation and help us map out policies," Foster wrote Calverton.[53] Dunne, editor of the *Daily Worker*, went even further: "I think you should consider, if you are not a member of our party, making application and getting in touch with the Central Executive Committee. If you carry your Marxian knowledge into other fields of activity, then you belong in the Communist Party."[54]

While Foster, then Party leader, saw promise in Calverton, his general attitude toward the young man was ambivalent. Foster was uneasy in the presence of Calverton's restless energy and wary of his tendency to write on a plethora of subjects with little regard for orthodox opinions or factional positions. When Calverton announced his intention to undertake an analysis of Plekhanov and Trotsky, Foster explained to him the Party's position on the two men. Everybody knew about Plekhanov's Menshevik weakness, but the Trotsky question was more difficult. Trotsky had performed a real service to the Russian revolutionary movement in the early years, but now the political situation between Trotsky and the Stalinist faction had become problematic and volatile. Foster warned that given the present political climate one could easily "break one's neck on the Trotsky issue," and cited Max Eastman as an example. Eastman, of course, had returned from Russia in 1924 with Lenin's last "Testament" calling for Stalin's removal from the post of general secretary. The following year Eastman wrote *Since Lenin Died*, which purported to expose the Stalinist faction's cynical power plays and their malicious campaign against Trotsky. Foster's cautionary tale was that Eastman not only had broken his political neck, but had "killed himself in the movement by his treatment of the Trotsky question."[55]

But Calverton, youthful and enthusiastic, wanted to make his mark on the literary and political world and to write on large topics without regard to fussy ideological distinctions. Indeed George Goetz had created Calverton as a public persona, a public intellectual who would write on a variety of topics for politically informed readers on the American Left and who would shape his magazine to include debate and dialogue on the Left. Calverton now presided over a journal of independent radical opinion whose central premise was that various radical factions were merely part of a greater unity of purpose, part of the complete socialism. This notion was to become a constant source of friction between Calverton and the Communists, but for the moment he was a respected fellow traveler, and in the many letters to Calverton from Party members during the mid twenties, he is addressed as "comrade."

CHAPTER THREE

There is more to be solved by the criss-cross of argument
than by the isolation of dogma.
            —Editorial, *Modern Quarterly*, November–February
                1927–28

Red Love and Lost Innocence,
1926–1928

Nineteen twenty-six was a good year for George Calverton.
He was thriving both intellectually and socially. His soirees
attracted a prestigious group of intellectuals for whom Baltimore had previously been a mere stopover between Washington and New
York. He held the first of many fund-raising dinners for the *Quarterly*.
Scott Nearing, declining the rich food and drink and eating his raw vege-
tables from a brown bag, was the principal speaker at this first *Quarterly*
function.

Calverton's house swelled with people every weekend, making his gatherings worthy of the party spirit of the twenties. Exhibiting a cosmopolitanism characteristic more properly of larger centers like New York, these
Baltimore assemblages epitomized the ideal of diversity and plurality, both
intellectually and ethnically. The black educator Charles S. Johnson and
black economist Abraham Harris often attended; on one occasion Langston Hughes gave a lecture on the structure of the blues. Often the soirees
were highly structured with Calverton reading from his works in progress
and soliciting comments from his audience. At other times the sessions
were raucous and freewheeling. On one occasion the psychologist J. B.
Eggen, standing formally at the head of the room, leaning on the mantelpiece, began a discourse on behaviorism. But something he said triggered
a discussion of the Sino-Japanese situation. Eggen was left with his elbow

on the mantelpiece, while an argument raged. After some time, he turned to Helen Calverton and asked, "Helen, do you think I'm *that* boring?"[1]

Because the Calverton residence had become by this time a hub and refuge for liberal and radical intellectuals (and hence a "black spot" on the conservative neighborhood), and because of the bootleg liquor available there, people now referred to 2110 East Pratt Street as "Cal's Black House" in joking contrast to Calvin Coolidge's White House—a symbol of Waspish complacency and prohibition.[2] Calverton's notoriety among Party members was also growing. Foster's recognition of his talents and Dunne's invitation to join the Party greatly enhanced his standing on the Left and bolstered the confidence of this ambitious young man, who was so eager to be recognized and accepted and so desirous of having his ideas matter. Yet in spite of Dunne's invitation, Calverton did not join the Party. He wished to maintain his role as the organic intellectual and "complete socialist," contributing to critical discourse on the Left rather than belonging to a party or camp.

Calverton had dedicated the *Modern Quarterly* to independent criticism and analysis on the Left, and his publication of Kantorovitch's controversial critique of Leninism initiated this policy. But during the mid twenties Calverton's thinking began to move increasingly in the direction of Leninism, and he wished to work with and further the cause of the Communist Party. If his friend Kantorovitch had criticized the fundamental tenets of Leninism, he had also recommended that he reread and reconsider Marx's *Theses on Feuerbach*, of which the eleventh thesis read: "The Philosophers have only *interpreted* the world differently, the point is, to *change* it." Believing in the necessity of transforming the world, Calverton advocated the Party's political position and continued to do so well into the thirties. Yet in spite of his close associations with the Party, he held to his stance of critical autonomy. For if the eleventh thesis' call to act on the external world appealed to the pragmatic strain in his thinking, that same strain made him wary of allegiances to Party and doctrine. Initially, moreover, his position of independence was a "naive" one, an optimistic and heady response to the enthusiasm with which he and his publication had been received in radical circles. His assumption that an independent position on the Left was unproblematic was largely a combination of his youthful hopefulness about the possibilities of a complete socialism and a relatively flexible political climate on the Left. But as time went on and the political atmosphere grew more troubled, Calverton began to realize the stakes involved in maintaining his independence. This was especially true after his trip to Russia in 1927, a journey in which he saw at firsthand the increasing Stalinization of the Soviet state. For Calverton the journey not only pointed up what was at stake but reconfirmed his commitment to intellectual autonomy and to an independent journal.

Early in 1926 the flexible practice of a complete socialism that transcended sectarian boundaries did not seem an impossible dream. Indeed, both the Socialists and Communists were eager to be associated with Calverton. In the spring of that year James Oneal readily accepted Calverton's offer to write a regular column for the socialist *New Leader*. Oneal introduced him to the magazine's readers as "the keenest, most informed writer we have today."[3] Shortly after his column began appearing in the *New Leader*, William F. Dunne, editor of the *Daily Worker*, invited him to become a regular contributor to the magazine's *Sunday Supplement*, which dealt with literary and cultural affairs. By the summer of 1926 Calverton was contributing to both the *Supplement* and the *Daily Worker* on a wide range of political, literary, and cultural topics ranging from labor disputes to a subject heretofore virtually unknown in the pages of the *Worker*—black literature.

Increasingly, the twenty-six-year-old Calverton was coming to be regarded as a sort of *Wunderkind* of the radical movement. Word had spread about the Russian translation of the *Newer Spirit* that was being prepared for publication in Moscow. Now he was in demand more than ever as a lecturer. He was soon traveling between Baltimore and Boston to speak on subjects as diverse as sex and economics. Still holding on to his junior high school teaching job, he taught courses in the evenings at the Baltimore Labor College and during summers traveled frequently both to New York City to teach at the Rand School of Social Science and to Katonah, New York, to lecture at Brookwood Labor College, run by A. J. Muste, a minister who had become a labor organizer. Harry Freeman, secretary of the Proletarian Artists and Writers League (a Moscow-organized group dedicated to workers' education and the fostering of "proletarian" culture), invited Calverton to serve on the organization's National Executive Committee.

Calverton's multifarious connections and his associations with both the Socialist Party and the Workers (Communist) Party could have only existed in the mid-decade climate, when factional disputes were ill-defined and had yet to be set along rigid "party lines." Consequently, the cooperative efforts of various radical groups could be united in such struggles as the Passaic Strike of 1926. But from mid to late 1926, there was an emerging tenseness and uncertainty in the political atmosphere. This tenseness was related to the disputed issue among the Left of "dual unionism" versus "boring from within."

The industrial union policy continued to be one of the most contentious issues on the Left and showed no signs of resolution. As early as 1912, William Z. Foster had formed the Syndicalist League of North America, devoted to "boring from within" the American Federation of Labor (AFL) to capture it for the revolution, rather than building a rival, separate, Red or "dual" union, the approach the Industrial Workers of the World (IWW) was then taking.[4] Yet there was an essential contradiction inherent in the communist policy of attempting to wrest control of existing unions while simultaneously pressing for a full-fledged Marxist program that could only lead to isolation from the rank and file. Furthermore, the bitter hostility of the AFL leaders as well as the abysmal failure of "boring from within" in conflicts such as the Passaic Strike eventually pushed the Party toward the rival-union policy. By 1928 a reversal of the trade union policy would be announced in Moscow commensurate with Third Period strategy, Foster would fall into line, and dual unionism would be the inflexible order of the day.[5] In 1926, however, the Party was experiencing an interregnum, and the political atmosphere, particularly in relation to this issue, was extremely unstable. It was at this point that Calverton, at the peak of his naive confidence in his role as complete socialist, suddenly found himself embroiled with Party officials over this controversial issue.

The conflict was sparked by a review Calverton wrote and published in the *Modern Quarterly* of labor economist David Saposs's book *Left Wing Unionism*. In his review, Calverton praised Saposs's study for its freedom from "partisan-rationalization" and agreed with the author's thesis: circumstances determine whether establishing separate, rival, "dual" unions, or "boring from within" established unions such as the AFL, is the better strategy for radicalizing the working class. Calverton took the opportunity to castigate the rigidity of both socialist and communist approaches to the issue: "The Socialist Labor Party of today, with its firm faith in dual unions as the only solution, is as absurd as the Workers Party when it declares itself inflexibly opposed to dual unionism."[6]

Calverton's reasoned call for greater flexibility failed to gauge the conflicts and uncertainties that seethed beneath the surface of the Party's policy of "boring from within." Foster's quick and edgy response suggested Party touchiness about the industrial union question. Foster wrote expressing irritation that Calverton's review "took a dig" at the Workers Party. Because the review had caused "something of a flurry" in communist headquarters, Foster felt obliged to correct Calverton on the union question. The Party's position was not inflexible: it was militantly opposed to splitting mass organizations but was not opposed to forming separate unions where no unions existed or where existing unions were decrepit.

The Workers Party position was "scientific," declared Foster: "while not overlooking the fact that in some cases independent unions are necessary, it nevertheless puts tremendous emphasis on a united labor movement."[7]

This was the first rap on the knuckles by the Party, and Calverton was stung. Nevertheless, he quickly sought conciliation and admitted he was at fault for oversimplifying the Party position.[8] Foster let the matter rest, and it might have ended in a private exchange of letters. But Dunne took the opportunity to castigate Calverton publicly in the *Daily Worker*. In a tense piece entitled "The Confused Mr. Calverton," Dunne charged that Calverton was "trying to make a case against the communists in his review of Saposs's book."[9] Although Dunne relented somewhat when Calverton submitted his correspondence with Foster for publication, Dunne nevertheless rebuked Calverton for "the detached manner in which you spoke of the Party and its program," which was "just the sort of thing I personally and as a Party member resent very much."[10]

This minor skirmish over the "dual union" question revealed something of the nervousness and confusion at the heart of the Party. Certainly Calverton had touched a sensitive issue on which there was as yet no united policy. But Calverton's otherwise inconsequential five-hundred word review may also have provided a welcome distraction from the factional disputes now beginning to plague the Party. These disputes, gaining momentum from the middle to late twenties, culminated in Stalin's expulsion of the Lovestonites at the Comintern's American Commission in Moscow on May 12, 1929, which effectively transferred leadership from Lovestone to Foster. Operating in a political vacuum because of their inability to establish any real rapport with the masses of American workers, the American Communist Party was already beginning to take on a defensiveness verging on paranoia, which would typify the ideological atmosphere of the Third Period strategy initiated in 1928. At any rate Foster's and Dunne's reactions were ominous. The incident foreshadowed future stormy conflicts with the Communists, which would arise because of Calverton's critical spirit (his "detached manner," as Dunne put it), his speculative flexibility, and his unwillingness to think along factional lines.

For the present, however, Calverton faced further immediate problems. No sooner had tensions with the Communists simmered down than difficulties with the Socialists emerged. Because he was contributing articles to the *Daily Worker*, his status as an independent free-lancer fell under scrutiny by the Socialists. "The *New Leader* is not in sympathy with the communists," Oneal reminded Calverton when he rejected a review in which Calverton had praised a book by a Communist Party member.[11] Oneal became even more irate when he read the *Daily Worker*'s account of a lecture

Calverton had given at the Workers' School, in which he stated (according to the *Worker*) that the Communists should join with the Socialists to fight for some major issues in spite of the "bankruptcy" of the latter.[12]

Calverton defended himself in a letter to the associate editor of the *New Leader*, Edward Levinson:

> While I did not say that the Workers Socialist Party was bankrupt, I most likely did say, and do believe, that it is at present inactive, unalert, uninviting to youth and unexciting to the intellectual . . . . If comparisons are to be made, despite their small size, the Workers' (Communist) Party has been far more active. That does not mean that I approve of all the tactics of the Workers' Party. I do not. Nor does it mean that I have made application to join the Workers' Party. I have not. I do not intend joining either party and intend saying exactly what I think if I am convinced that I am correct . . . if my independent position, with its criticism of the S.P. is a handicap to the *New Leader* and you fear misunderstanding, then I'll cease "Critical Cruisings" at once. If not, I'll continue as usual—independent, unallied.[13]

Despite Calverton's resolute insistence on his right to a nonpartisan and independent position, Oneal ousted him from the *New Leader*: "the *Daily Worker* is the filthiest thing that ever appeared in the United States," Oneal wrote Calverton in his letter of dismissal. Stressing the need for free expression in the radical press, Calverton protested, but Oneal was adamant. "Your trouble began," Oneal admonished him, "the moment you departed from consideration of books and historical opinions and ventured into an open opinion regarding two movements that are deadly enemies. . . . I believe you sincerely tried to do the impossible—write for two movements without giving offence to both."[14] In the spring of 1927, after writing for the *New Leader* for almost a year, Calverton's relationship with the Socialist Party was severed and his friendship with its editor terminated.

Although Calverton continued publishing articles and book reviews in liberal magazines as well as in radical magazines that were not party affiliated, and thus technically maintained his independent position, his expulsion from the *New Leader* led him to look to the *Daily Worker* as an outlet for much of his writing. Haim Kantorovitch had previously objected to Calverton's writing for the *Daily Worker* and voiced alarm as his friend's political opinions moved progressively to the left of the socialist point of view. But in spite of their strong intellectual ties and close friendship of nearly four years, Calverton's viewpoint had diverged radically from Kantorovitch's. Calverton's recent reading of Lenin only strengthened his growing conviction of the necessity for communizing the world. By contrast, Kantorovitch, the staunch Social Democrat, the disenchanted Russian immigrant who had lived through the revolution, remained skeptical of the Leninist approach to achieving socialism: "I don't believe Lenin has found the right way for the realization of our common ideals. . . . As far as I know what communism is, and especially what communists are, I am convinced that communism is just the opposite of Calvertonism."[15]

In view of the conflicts between Calverton and the Communists that lay ahead, Kantorovitch's remarks were prophetic. Nevertheless, in spite of the fracas with Dunne and Foster, mutual esteem between Calverton and the Workers Party continued to grow. Fully recognized in Party circles for his expertise in literary and social criticism, he was now also considered—because of his essays on black literature—something of an expert on the race question. When the Party asked George Schuyler—a black leftist—to prepare a series of lectures on the race question, he was given Calverton's name by the Workers' School as a source of "scientific data" on the subject.[16] And as Calverton's sphere of expertise expanded, he was drawn into political action under Party auspices. His appointment in April 1927 as chairman of the "Hands Off China" committee, organized to protest British intervention into Chinese affairs, marked a high point in his relationship with the Workers Party.[17] Another incident, a letter from Earl Browder, written from Moscow, urging Calverton to come to the Soviet Union to study, further deepened his ties to the Party.

Like many other radicals, Calverton looked to the Soviet Union as a model of cultural renewal and human liberation. As Browder (later to become leader of the Communist Party) wrote him from Russia, "for a keen student of cultural problems such as yourself Moscow would be the most fruitful field I can think of. You really owe it to your work to learn the language and spend a year here. Ready to hand, you will find the most gigantic laboratory in full operation."[18] Browder's letter was filled with anecdotal examples of the new social forms and new human relationships that were being developed in this "gigantic laboratory." As early as the spring of 1926, Foster (who had himself journeyed to Moscow in 1921 and had undergone a kind of conversion to communism while there) advised Calverton that a trip to Moscow was "indispensable" to the personal development of any serious young radical intellectual.[19]

Although a greater number of American radicals were to visit the Soviet Union in the following decade, serious radicals in the twenties viewed the journey as an obligatory pilgrimage. Max Eastman, Scott Nearing, Robert Minor, Mike Gold, Joseph Freeman, and Theodore Dreiser were among those who journeyed to Moscow. Accordingly, Calverton was eager to study new developments in Soviet culture. But since he remained an independent he could not expect the Party to assist him financially with the trip, and he was forced to borrow from several friends and to draw heavily on his teaching salary. Nearing, who had previously traveled in Russia, advised him to go alone, travel light, and stay in dormitories wherever he stopped.[20]

Now reconciled with the Workers Party leaders in the wake of the skirmish over dual unions, Calverton sailed for Russia on July 2, 1927, a trusted fellow traveler in good standing, an acknowledged "expert on cultural problems," and with a letter of introduction from Foster himself. He set out believing that his research would increase not only his knowledge of cultural issues, but the demand for his writings, particularly in Workers Party publications. In short, he hoped that his journey to Russia would make his place in radical intellectual circles more solid than ever.

LIKE many young intellectuals of advanced opinion in the twenties, Calverton was interested in the customs of love in the new society. Caught up in the larger discussion of sex and psychology, the criticism of marriage, and the search for alternate arrangements between the sexes that was rife during the decade, he had read Engels on marriage and was coming to view these issues from a radical point of view. A trip to the Soviet Union, he felt, would be a splendid opportunity to investigate a timely and crucial topic: "Nearing has studied education in Russia . . . a dozen men have studied economic conditions, but no one has studied sex life in the new Soviet Republic," he argued in a note to his publisher.[21] Only weeks before leaving, he clinched a contract with Macauley Book Company for a study of sexual mores, marriage, and the family in the Soviet Union.[22] Furthermore, he fully intended to send back his observations for publication in the *Quarterly* regarding this "modern" topic.

Even before the journey to Russia, Calverton had written a work in which he attempted to link his interest in sex with a radical viewpoint. In *Sex Expression in Literature* (1926), he attempted to analyze the reasons for the steady decline of sexual candor between the Renaissance and the Victorian period when sexual expression was virtually "castrated" in literature. This phenomenon he attributed to the rise of the upward-struggling, pleasure-denying bourgeoisie, but he speculated that the postwar attitudes critical of bourgeois values had resulted in a new generation of writers who exhibited sexual honesty. More to the point, he conjectured that the most important single factor in the new questioning of middle-class sexual attitudes was the revolution in Russia. In the concluding chapters of the work, he held up the Soviet Union as a society where a new sexual morality was evolving, quoting with approval psychologist Paul Blanchard's observation that the young in Russia "discuss sex relations, abortions, and love with the candor of obstetricians."[23]

Calverton's second book suggests the degree to which the Soviet Union represented not only a daring new social experiment but a sexual one as well. It reflected a pervasive feeling that a revolutionary society, free of middle-class values and the puritanical repression that characterized bourgeois society, held out possibilities of sexual liberation. Love in Russia was the love of the future. Thus Floyd Dell, long considered the Left's sexologist, wrote to Joseph Freeman, who journeyed to Russia one year before Calverton, "I hope you will write to me about their new sexual conventions in some detail."[24]

Calverton's interest in the subject of sexual behavior and the search for alternative relations between the sexes—both within and without the bounds of marriage—was not purely theoretical or academic. Shortly after he founded the *Modern Quarterly*, Bessie Peretz, the young immigrant from Russia, joined the staff of the magazine. She had been his student in junior high school and lived with her parents several blocks from "2110." She assisted in typing, editorial work, and translating Soviet literature. Of Russian-Jewish origin, she was only sixteen years old and fresh from Russia with all the romance of the revolution. She worked closely with George and Helen and devotedly typed Calverton's manuscripts. She came each afternoon when Calverton arrived home from teaching, and after work concluded in the late evening he would walk her home. She faithfully attended the soirees at "2110," and Calverton would excuse himself from the lingering discussion of late night to see her home. Together nearly every afternoon and evening, and deeply attracted to each other, it was not long before Bessie and Calverton were emotionally and sexually involved. And since they worked together at "2110" their affair could scarcely be concealed from Helen. When Helen surmised their intimacy she was initially angry, but she considered herself as much a sexual progressive as Calverton and Bessie, and the three decided to form a ménage-à-trois as an experiment in rebellion. The influence of André Maurois's book *Ariel*, describing the life of Shelley, provided the inspiration for this arrangement. But problems inevitably ensued: besides resentments and jealousy, Calverton refused to restrict his sexual activity to Helen and Bessie. He wanted no restrictions whatsoever on his sexual adventures, but he denied the women with whom he was involved the same freedom. Helen found it unendurable that he would become frightened and angry at the mere mention of her involvement with another man and that he categorically forbade her the sexual freedom he expected for himself. Thus the triangular relationship disintegrated shortly after it was initiated.[25]

In fact the experimental relationship, however justified by ideology and the desire to overthrow bourgeois marriage, was largely a product of Calverton's compulsion to have relationships with women. His urge to have affairs was an aspect of his deep-seated insecurity—perhaps a desire for approval and acceptance from women that he had never received from his withdrawn and passive mother. In any case Calverton had numerous affairs with the women who came to the parties at "2110." During the mid twenties a schoolteacher named Una Corbett joined the Saturday-night gatherings. She had met Helen in a bookstore, and when she mentioned to Helen that she subscribed to the *Modern Quarterly*, Helen announced that she was the wife of the editor and invited Corbett to the Saturday-night discussions.

A schoolteacher who embraced advanced ideas and radical politics, Una Corbett was isolated and lonely, finding no one of like mind at work or in the larger, respectable Baltimore environs. Thus she was delighted to meet people who shared her interests at the Calverton home. Moreover, one of her few friends was black, and there was no place in Baltimore they could meet socially. Since there was no place in Baltimore a black person could eat, they could not even go out to dinner together. But at "2110" she and her black friend were welcomed.

Una Corbett was taken with George Calverton, with his energy and enthusiasm for ideas, with his deep resonant voice displayed to good advantage when he read from his works in progress. She was, unlike Helen, college educated, having graduated from Goucher, the Baltimore women's college, and she shared with Calverton a passion for literature and literary culture. When he asked her to write book reviews for the magazine she was thrilled. Shortly after beginning her work for the magazine she and Calverton began a passionate affair. She adopted the pseudonym "Vera Fulton" for her *Quarterly* book reviews; the initials of the name, identical to Calverton's first and second initials, announced, albeit in a private code, her attachment to him. She shared with him an enthusiasm for advanced ideas in sexual matters. She had read Engels on marriage and the family and was caught up in the ideas on the "new woman" coming into vogue by the mid twenties. When she became pregnant with Calverton's child, she decided to have it in spite of the fact that an abortion could have been arranged by a physician friend and in spite of the fact that a child out of wedlock might well have endangered her job with the Baltimore school system. Nor did she have any illusions about eventual marriage. She and Calverton talked the matter over and, subscribing to the experimental life, viewed having the child as an adventure, a willful act that flew in the face of bourgeois morality. They named the child, born in 1926, Joy.

For Una Corbett, the task of giving birth and bringing up a child without a partner was an ordeal. She took leave from her teaching position (supported by a letter from a doctor friend of Calverton's that said Corbett had "hypertension") and was taken in by a nursing home in Philadelphia. She went back to work only months after having the baby, and a woman doctor friend in Philadelphia found a trained nurse who took Joy into her home. For two years Joy lived with the nurse and Corbett visited her on weekends. She then brought Joy home, identifying her as her "niece." But teaching and taking care of the child proved to be extraordinarily difficult, and when Corbett went to a lecture given by Bertrand Russell she decided to send her daughter to the Beacon Hill School run by Dora Russell in England. Through all of this Calverton and Una Corbett remained close. She found Calverton consistently concerned about her and the child. He contributed money where he could, although the major support for Joy came from Corbett's teaching salary. Nevertheless, she believed she never could have survived the ordeal of raising Joy without Calverton's loyalty. She well understood that his loyalty was by no means exclusive—he was also "loyal" to Bessie Peretz and a number of other women—and it sprang, in part, from his inability to break off a relationship with any woman. She understood such loyalty was to some extent an aspect of deep insecurities and anxieties, yet she also felt that it was, viewed in a certain light, one of his more appealing qualities.[26]

In 1927, then, as he readied for his trip to Russia, Calverton was reeling from the intricate and knotty series of relationships that included Helen, Bessie, and Una. For her part Helen was fed up with "experimental relationships," which she believed simply fed Calverton's compulsive desire to have affairs. She was angry about his prolonged relationship with Una and bitter about their child. And if this were not enough, if she was taken ill at work or decided to come home when she was not expected, she was obliged to call first to find out if Calverton had a woman there. She would have put up with this had Calverton agreed to let her have the same freedom. She was devoted to him, but she was spirited and independent and wanted to share whatever marital arrangements were made— however unconventional—on an equal footing. But Calverton denied her that freedom, and Helen's self-esteem deteriorated. She wanted to leave the marriage.[27]

Calverton seemed blind to the contradictions in his behavior and unaware of the reasons behind his desperate need for one affair after another. He seemed oblivious to the contradiction between his espousal of sexual freedom for both sexes and his own fear of granting that freedom to either his wife or the other women in his life. He left for Russia convinced that the enforced monogamy of institutional marriage was stifling and inadequate, yet painfully aware of the difficulties created by alternatives such as he had attempted. Sex and marriage seemed a dilemma, a series of perplexing questions to which Calverton hoped the Soviet Union might provide some answers.

He thus began his journey in a state of emotional instability and found his stay in Russia difficult. He was not a good traveler, hated to be alone, and missed his Baltimore home intensely. The language barrier also presented a problem. Like Dreiser, who visited the same year, Calverton was upset by the physical aspects of life there; the food and accommodations were poor, and he particularly deplored the absence of creature comforts.[28] Nevertheless, like Dreiser, he found the cultural transformation, especially regarding marriage, encouraging. He was particularly impressed with the advanced attitude of the people toward birth control, especially since in Baltimore the sale of birth control devices or even the dissemination of information about them was illegal. Amazed at the enlightened attitude and sexual candor of the Soviet people, he noted that:

> At a railroad station I picked up a pamphlet on birth control (entitled *Prevention of Childbirth*, by Dr. M. Z. Shpak), which sold for a pittance and had already gone through numerous editions. In the pamphlet were described a number of methods to prevent conception, with admonitions as to certain methods that experience had proven precarious.[29]

Calverton was impressed with the implementation of sex education as an integral part of the curriculum in Soviet schools and the Soviets' active struggle against prostitution and venereal disease. His observations led him to conclude that by abolishing the concept of private property the Soviet Union was eradicating the subordination of women to men. He noted with approval that women were rapidly gaining political, economic, and sexual equality with men. Consequently, the double standard in sexual relations was disappearing, as was the disapproval of women who bore children out of wedlock. All women were equal before the law and were not obliged to follow their husbands from one place to another. The divorce laws were humane and uncomplicated, divorce being merely a declaration to separate, which could be obtained either by mutual consent or at the instigation of one party. Perhaps the most encouraging aspect regarding sexual attitudes was the total lack of the prying puritanism found in the United States. In an article entitled "Red Love in Soviet Russia," published in the *Modern Quarterly* shortly after his return to the States, Calverton wrote enthusiastically that in the USSR, the "ecstasy of sex contact, the joy of erotic communion, are regarded as private to the participants, and not subject to social intervention or restriction. It is only when children are involved that sex-relations really become a matter of social interest or consideration."[30]

For Calverton the importance of the new cultural revolution in Soviet Russia lay in its utopian possibilities. The new society offered a glimpse of the erotic potential of human relationships, a glimmer of ultimate human freedom. He wrote in the same article that "while it would be sheer folly to picture these new changes in the moral life of Russia as the background of a new paradise, it is the direction toward which they point that holds for us such great hope for the ultimate liberation of man." [31]

Although there were objective reasons for Calverton to be impressed with the Soviet Union, such comments suggest that his conclusions were those of a sexual idealist rather than a critical observer. While Max Eastman, writing in 1924, could observe that "the Moscow I lived in was, in its sexual code, a sort of generalized Greenwich Village," [32] Joseph Freeman noted about his own visit to Russia in 1926 that those radicals who had been in the Soviet Union for any length of time understood that the sexual revolution, and particularly the equality between the sexes, was largely illusory. [33] Calverton's visit to the Soviet Union nevertheless came at a dynamic period. The vitality of Russian culture under communism supported the American tourist's belief that altering the economic base of society could alter the relations between the sexes.

Calverton may have been uncritical in his conclusions about sex in the Soviet Union, but such was not the case about politics. The Soviet Union seemed to hold out hope in the cultural realm, but it posed nothing but questions in the political sphere. Like a number of radicals who visited the Soviet Union during this period, Calverton soon detected the tenseness in the political atmosphere as Stalin amassed his power. When he left for Russia, a friend wrote him that, "If, as the papers say, Trotsky and Zinoviev are expelled, you'll have to watch your p's and q's." [34] After arriving and talking to intellectuals such as Serge Dinamov, a professor of American literature at the University of Moscow (who would disappear during the Moscow Purge Trials), he gained some sense of the growing paranoia, terror, and treacherousness of the Central Committee's tactics. An admirer of Trotsky as a Red Army chief and revolutionary, Dinamov despaired at the Stalinist political intrigue and the growing repression designed to crush the Trotskyist opposition.

Lonely, weary, and strapped for money, Calverton prepared to push off for home a mere six weeks after he had arrived. He had heard nothing from home and was concerned about his relationship with Helen. It was paradoxical that he was unable to realize or even permit the equality of sexual relations in his personal life that he so admired in Soviet society. In fact, he had spent a large portion of his time in this land of unfettered "red love" fretting about his marriage. Still, his journey had been by no means wholly negative: he was genuinely impressed with Soviet culture and he had been treated warmly by writers like Serge Dinamov, who had offered to coedit a volume of American criticism with him. Yet long talks with Dinamov and others about Stalinist political grotesqueries left him dispirited and depressed. Roger Baldwin, also in the Soviet Union in the late summer of 1927, met near Red Square a disappointed Calverton, who asked, "Is it for this we had so much faith?"[35]

CALVERTON arrived home in October 1927, and his worst marital fears were realized. Helen told him she had been seeing another man and was considering leaving. He was devastated to think she might leave him and implored her to reconsider. But Helen had decided to take the sexual freedom he had forbidden her and she was not disposed to patch up a relationship in which the balance of power and the prerogative of freedom were so onesided. George and Helen would continue to live at "2110" until well into 1928 and only finalize their divorce in 1930, but their marriage was virtually over in the fall of 1927.

Beyond this severe emotional upheaval, Calverton arrived home that autumn haunted by the taut and nervous political atmosphere he had experienced in Russia. Yet his hopes for the People's Republic outweighed his doubts and overshadowed his severe misgivings about political developments in the Soviet Union. Like many other radicals who wished to remain loyal to the Soviet Union and the revolution in spite of the power struggles now occurring, Calverton suppressed his reservations. He set to work writing *The Bankruptcy of Marriage*—a treatise, in spite of the personal resonances of its title, about the transformation of sexual mores in the Soviet Union. He assured H. M. Wicks, the Party's ideological watchdog, that he was getting down in book form his impression of the Soviets "with the great inspiration of their work vivid in my mind, and the cordial greetings I got there still a splendid memory."[36]

Nevertheless, an editorial he wrote for the *Modern Quarterly* reflected a change in attitude from his pretrip fellow traveling. He now expressed a new antagonism to sectarianism and factional warfare of the sort he saw emanating from Russia and infusing the ranks of the Left at home. In the atmosphere of increasing political intolerance, the independence of the *Quarterly* became an urgent issue. Writing early in 1928, and obviously sensing the growing rigidity and dogmatism in American radicalism that was the product of Stalin's victory over the opposition, Calverton reaffirmed and underscored the independence of his magazine:

> We plan no compromise with the truth as we see it. While we accept the logic of the class struggle, the preponderating importance of the Bolshevik revolution and the logic it has taught . . . we refuse to accept a boxed-in and codified interpretation that is not resilient to the ever-changing conditions and crises of our contemporary world.[37]

Furthermore, after his return a strain emerged in his thinking that was to be a consistent preoccupation: the need to build a distinctively American radical movement based on American realities rather than doctrinaire policies originating in the Soviet Union. In the same editorial, he condemned the bitter internal disputes of the left wing, and blamed the increasing isolation from organized labor on its tendency to cling to dogmatic programs unsuited to the specific needs and psychology of the American worker. Thus far, Calverton concluded, the history of the Left in the American labor movement had been "a record of failure."[38]

Calverton's comments were astute, even prophetic. Yet given the political climate of 1928, now moving into Third Period militancy, criticisms of Party programs and critical evaluations of the Party's history were not taken lightly. Response from the Party came swiftly. Calverton's old adversary, H. M. Wicks, published an attack on his reputation as a critic and writer in the *Daily Worker*, February 4, 1928. If Wicks had earlier attacked the *Newer Spirit* because it deviated from Trotsky, he now attacked it because much of it had been plagiarized. Calverton's modus operandi, he claimed, was to copy without qualm from anything at his disposal.[39]

Calverton was an easy mark for such charges; a synthesizer, he drew on numerous sources in writing his books and was notoriously careless about citing sources. Furthermore, as Max Eastman noted, he was "a man of prodigious memory who would sometimes, when referring to another scholar's thoughts, reproduce the man's words almost verbatim without knowing it."[40] Even while he was away in the Soviet Union, Joseph Freeman had written a satiric attack on Calverton's criticism in the *New Masses* of August 1927. In "Bulgarian Literature or the Perfect Critical Method," Freeman accused "Vincent Chatterton" of writing equipped only with the chutzpah to plagiarize from any source at his disposal including "whole passages" from Upton Sinclair and Floyd Dell as well as the *Encyclopaedia Britannica*.[41]

Freeman's article struck one of the few lighter satirical notes in a series of attacks that were to become increasingly bitter as the Communist Party became more militant. At precisely the same time that Wicks attacked Calverton in the *Daily Worker*, Bertram D. Wolfe attacked the *Modern Quarterly* in the *Communist* (the theoretical organ of the Communist Party). The Stalin–Trotsky "question" having now been "settled" in Stalin's favor, any hint of the taint of Trotskyism was a matter of extreme seriousness. Wolfe accused all those associated with the *Quarterly* of supporting the Trotskyist opposition and of championing Eastman, Trotsky's staunchest defender on the American scene.[42] As evidence, Wolfe pointed to an article by Samuel D. Schmalhausen that appeared in the *Quarterly* next to Calverton's editorial on radical "failure."

Schmalhausen had initiated a correspondence with Calverton in 1924, and by 1927 the two men had a close intellectual collaboration. Ten years older than Calverton, Schmalhausen had been an instructor of English at De Witt Clinton High School in New York City who was fired, during the war years, for encouraging his students to write "unpatriotic essays."[43] He then took up free-lance writing and the study of psychoanalysis. After running across an issue of the *Modern Quarterly* in New York in 1924, he wrote Calverton expressing his enthusiasm for the magazine; he continued to correspond with Calverton and later submitted articles for publication. Schmalhausen joined the editorial board in August 1928, and became one of the chief forces in the *Quarterly*'s move toward the topics of sex and psychology in the later years of the decade. But in the summer of 1927 he was already involved in editorial meetings and functioned informally as a temporary editor while Calverton was in Russia.[44] Schmalhausen's interest in psychology notwithstanding, he was a sort of court jester of radicalism. His articles, displaying a comic sensibility absorbed from vaudeville, made his Marxism less the brand of Karl's than that of Groucho's.

His article, "These Tragic Comedians," to which Wolfe objected so strongly, was actually a literary burlesque of the Left that bristled with puns, alliteration, and wisecracks. Schmalhausen's theme was the demise of revolutionary socialism in the United States. "The Socialistic shambles all about us are like fevered ghosts returned to plague our false serenity," he wrote.[45] Schmalhausen lampooned the entire spectrum of the Left, from liberals like Lippmann and Dewey who had supported the war to Socialists like Morris Hillquit and Victor Berger, "the distinguished undertakers of the Socialist Party." He dismissed as inconsequential Floyd Dell ("a mere playboy of the socialist revolution") as well as Scott Nearing, William Z. Foster, and head of International Publishers (the Party's press) Alexander Trachtenberg ("good scout Trachtenberg who is helping build a museum for the housing of Bolshevik specimens of higher learning"). Schmalhausen concluded his article by calling for a "new type of radical" to lead the younger generation of American leftists. He drove home his ironic point by holding up one possibility, hardly a "new type of radical," and moreover a pariah to the Communists in 1928—Max Eastman.[46] Plainly, the article was to be read as a comic piece, but Wolfe objected to Schmalhausen's "smart-alecky article . . . in sophomoric style."[47] Wolfe construed the article as an endorsement of Eastman, and by extension, of the Trotskyist opposition.

"These Tragic Comedians" appeared in the November–February issue of the *Modern Quarterly*, and as Calverton claimed in his editorial in the following issue, "few articles have stirred such wide and excited comment."[48] He then proceeded to publish a full page of correspondence arising from

Schmalhausen's burlesque, ranging from Egmont Arens, editor of the *New Masses*, who called it "a knockout," to Sam Ornitz, himself a comic writer, who asserted that Schmalhausen was "what we need in America: a Voltaire." [49] Calverton also published excerpts from Wolfe's *Communist* attack, and a further attack on Schmalhausen in the *Daily Worker* by H. M. Wicks. But the most curious response came from Max Beer of the Marx–Engels Institute in Moscow, who enjoyed the "vigorous onslaught on the Liberals and pseudo-Socialists"; Beer had apparently been deputized by the Institute to enquire into Schmalhausen's pedigree: "Sophie Marx, the elder sister of Karl Marx, was married in 1842 to a gentleman by the name of Schmalhausen. . . . We are interested in getting information as to whether you are connected to the Marx family." [50]

Calverton printed the letter in full, and, always the entrepreneur, used this prestigious response from the Moscow Institute to enquire of his readers whether "a critical revolutionary writer in America must seek revolutionary appreciation of his endeavors in Soviet Russia instead of in the United States where his work actually appears?" [51] Nevertheless, despite the furor the article caused, its satiric style was a deviation from the *Quarterly*'s usual seriousness. Whatever cogent criticisms of the Left it made were lost in the dazzle of Schmalhausen's virtuoso performance. Calverton had anticipated that the article might create an uproar and refrained from publishing it until his return from the Soviet Union. [52] He had decided to publish the article in the interests of free expression, doubtless hoping to inject some humor into the factional warfare among radicals that was now growing in intensity. But if he felt a little lampooning on the Left was not a bad thing, he was in a tenuous position to defend the article to a Party official who viewed the matter in deadly earnest. Calverton pointed out to Wolfe that no united attitude toward Trotsky existed on the *Quarterly* staff. Hence the magazine could in no way be construed as an "organ of the opposition." Personally, he assured Wolfe, he was no Trotskyite and found Stalin's position "correct." [53]

Ironically, this first major crisis in Calverton's relations with the Communists was precipitated by a spoof, a comic travesty that sent a paroxysm of laughter through the less humorless ranks of the Left. But the Communists were never known for their sense of humor, and despite his avowals to Wolfe, by the spring of 1928 the *Daily Worker* refused to print Calverton's work, and Jack Wasserman, secretary of the Proletarian Artists and Writers League informed him that among Workers Party members antagonism toward him was now "more or less the official attitude. . . . The majority of the Party officials," Wasserman wrote Calverton, "are against your reaction toward the party, some are against you personally, and those that are interested to an extent were not convinced of your personal contribution to the labor movement and are not enthusiastic enough to put up a fight for you."[54] Calverton's close ties with Party officials such as Foster, Browder, and Dunne were now for all intents and purposes severed. He suddenly found himself shunned by the Party with which only a year earlier he had hoped to establish good relations.

The nature of Calverton's rejection by the Communists was precisely what Wasserman indicated—"more or less" official. There was as yet no Party "position" on dissenting radicals; this would come later when the Third Period (which assumed the United States was on the verge of a revolution) had gained full momentum. Thus Calverton was not completely cut off from the more orthodox radicals of the left wing. He continued to publish in a number of radical publications and he remained on good terms with individual literary radicals both in and out of the Party. In the spring of 1928, Joseph Freeman invited Calverton to lecture on modern American literature at the Workers' School along with such distinguished speakers as John Dos Passos, Floyd Dell, and Michael Gold.[55] Gold and Calverton remained friends. As editor of the *New Masses* (not yet officially Party affiliated), Gold continued to accept Calverton's articles for publication. Even the *Communist,* which contained Wolfe's attack on the *Modern Quarterly*, continued to publish installments of Calverton's series of articles on "Literature and Economics." And Wolfe himself remained favorably disposed toward Calverton after it became clear that Calverton was not personally involved in the opposition movement.

If Calverton's reputation in the United States had suffered among Workers Party ranks, his reputation in the Soviet Union was growing steadily. In Moscow, Serge Dinamov called him "the best Marxian critic in the U.S.A." Dinamov assisted in preparations for the translation and publication of Calverton's *The Bankruptcy of Marriage,* while D. Riasanov, director of the Marx–Engels Institute in Moscow, praised Calverton's writings enthusiastically.[56] By the end of 1928 his three books—*The Newer Spirit,* *Sex Expression in Literature*, and *Bankruptcy*—were published in Russian under the official imprint with an enthusiastic foreword by Marxist aesthetician and theorist Anatol Lunacharsky. Yet even while his articles and books were appearing in the Soviet press, the *Daily Worker,* early in 1929, swooped in for another attack on the "Trotskyist" impurities in the *Modern Quarterly*. When the *Worker* refused to print Calverton's rebuttal he appealed to Party functionary Jay Lovestone to help him, insisting he had made his own pro-Stalinist position clear to Wolfe and had even taken the Stalinist side in a debate with Isaac Don Levine.[57] He further pointed to an anti-Trotsky article in a current issue of the *Quarterly* by Louis Fischer. Depressed, exasperated, and now realizing the futility of attempting to extricate himself from the Trotsky controversy and clear himself with the

Communists, Calverton wrote to Michael Gold that "certainly I am more pained than you think at their error. After all, my attitude is a fundamentally revolutiony one. It is one, in fact, that would work hand in hand with them if they knew how to utilize it without such foolish attacks."[58]

For Calverton the year 1927 marked a turning point. He had left for Moscow in the summer of 1927 at the peak of his relationship with the Communist Party, confident about his place in the radical movement and full of optimism regarding the potential of the Left to transform American society. When he returned he quickly found himself at odds with the Party and disillusioned with radical strategy and tactics. The autonomy of the intellectual, the notion of unfettered critical intelligence and critical discourse—ideals of the prewar intellectual Left that had inspired him enormously—were increasingly under attack. Moreover, the journey to Moscow was a harsh initiation into political knowledge; it represented an odyssey from the utopian speculation of "red love" to the grim political realities of internecine warfare and power politics. Stunned by Stalin's brutal seizure of power, Calverton returned home with a sense of unease he could not shake off. His youthful naïveté had been stripped away.

Meanwhile events in America conspired to further his political education. Everywhere factional controversy and political defeat seemed to abound. The Sacco–Vanzetti case, which reached its denouement in August 1927, represented to Calverton, as to other left-wing intellectuals, a crisis in the radical politics of the decade. Failure to save the two men seemed a product of radical divisiveness and an example of radical impotence. The Communist Party policy toward the Negro emerging from the Sixth Comintern Congress of 1928—the self-determination of the "Black Belt"—Calverton saw as another example of divisiveness, a substitution of race consciousness for class consciousness. He now wrote biting editorials in the *Modern Quarterly* on factional warfare and on ideologues who assaulted one another rather than a common enemy:

> While the radicals in America annihilate each other in . . . warfare, at once unremitting and unintelligent, our trade unions become bankrupt, corruption spreads, and knavery becomes the profession of the labor bureaucrat. . . . The radical movement is so split, so small, so uninfluential that it can do little more than talk to itself through its own press and platforms.[59]

As the 1930s approached, Calverton summed up a decade in which political activity seemed to have been dissipated by factional strife, and his editorials expressed a note of deep pessimism, the sense of gloom experienced by the left-wing intellectual isolated from American political life:

> With the dominant parties there are no significant issues at stake, and with the minor parties what issues there are have either been weakened by compromise or obscured by an unfortunate, although courageous, denial and defiance of reality. Nowhere is there light or hope. The radical movements of Europe have little meaning or application in the American soil. American radicals are isolated from the American scene.[60]

This "isolation from the American scene" was not only political but cultural. After his return from Russia, Calverton despairingly expressed the plight of the left-wing intellectual of the 1920s, the predicament of being doubly estranged—estranged from a coherent radical political movement and from the mainstream of American society as well. "What is most disheartening in contemporary America," he wrote in an editorial examining the blatant prosperity and social irresponsibility of the later part of the decade, "is the absence of social sympathy. Activities like pugilism, baseball, football, lynching, are enormously popular and may be considered the psychological equivalent of social sympathy."[61] Disheartened too by the American people's indifference to the imperialistic policies of the Coolidge administration in Central America and Hawaii, Haiti, and Nicaragua, he concluded that the concept of independence "is part of a tradition that has long ago withered into a dry and desiccated formula that has little meaning for the present age."[62] And in a troubled letter to a friend he wrote:

> I find myself an alien in these states despite the fact that I was born here. . . . I understand the environment in which I live and it is for that reason that I feel so alien. There is here so much to accelerate but so little to inspire. The puritanism which you condemn, I loathe. The radical movement which you are aloof from, I yearn to be a part of, but in my zeal for that clarity of thought which is born of courage—and challenge . . . I find myself more and more removed by attack and exclusion, from its organization. The money-madness that has obsessed us as a people, undermined our art, and seduced our artists—sickens me to despair. Intellectually, of course, I do not despair, emotionally, however, I often do.[63]

If, as Joseph Wood Krutch wrote in his 1929 work, *The Modern Temper*, an existential acceptance of despair is the first sign of maturity, then perhaps Calverton's mood is a reflection of the wrenching process of education. Calverton's loss of innocence coincided with that of the American

Left, for the Stalinization of the American Left was the end of radical innocence. His effort to maintain an independent position within the revolutionary Left of the late twenties foreshadowed the even harsher fratricidal battles of the thirties in which he was to become embroiled. Nevertheless, while Calverton shared in the collective sense of futility of the late twenties, he did not succumb to it. Rather he continued to urge political action and worker education. In spite of their internal struggles and gross errors, the Communist Party seemed the only viable alternative to the dominant parties and their nonissues. During the 1928 election campaign Calverton urged his readers to support Foster as the presidential candidate.

Yet, after his trip to Russia, he began to realize the stakes involved in editing the *Modern Quarterly*, for they comprised nothing less than defending a lineage of independent radicalism now under siege in America. Accordingly, he reaffirmed the need to foster dialogue and debate on the Left. Writing in November 1927, he announced the magazine's policy of printing articles not only by radicals but by left-leaning liberals "even though we may often disagree with their analysis and conclusions."[64] Advocating a discursive pluralism, he argued that it was in the "flash and conflict of ideas" that the Left in America could grow and develop.[65] Articles during this period ranged broadly over a number of topics—calculatingly intended to challenge and to provoke fresh perspectives—from literary criticism to the plight of black Americans. The *Quarterly* provided alternatives to the Communist Party position of "dual unionism" with the viewpoint of A. J. Muste, minister and patron saint of the Labor Temple, who argued for an American labor party and for militant trade unionism.[66] It included one of Eastman's early critiques of dialectical materialism as "state philosophy" in Russia, an article that was to spark a lengthy and famous debate with Sidney Hook over the nature of the Marxist dialectic.[67] And by late 1927, a number of articles on sex and psychoanalysis was beginning to appear. Not only was the *Quarterly* fulfilling its stated policy of independence, but it was beginning to set the agenda for discussion on the Left. Indeed, within a short time it would be the center of controversy among radicals over the question of the relationship between psychoanalysis and radical politics and the possibility of uniting Marx and Freud.

Thus the period immediately after Calverton's trip to Russia represented a confirmation of the *Quarterly*'s independence. The magazine's independent stance was now more firmly established, based on a more clearly articulated set of principles that would, implicitly, provide guidelines for its future course. These principles embodied, at a fundamental level, the philosophical tenets of American pragmatism—that critical intelligence is crucial in transforming the world and that truth is various and flexible. These assumptions were buttressed by Calverton's sense, particularly after his trip to Russia, of the importance of the role of the autonomous intellectual who functioned as an independent critic of developments on the Left. For, after his trip to Russia, Calverton was utterly convinced that the fratricidal disputes and the loss of intellectual independence, more than any threat from without, had the power to paralyze and destroy the Left.

CHAPTER FOUR

> There is no doubt that one of the attractions of a radical
> movement is the greater sexual freedom it counters or
> encourages.
> —Floyd Dell to Joseph Freeman, 1952

Karl Marx of the
Sexual Revolution

After his return from Russia, Calverton set to work on *The Bankruptcy of Marriage*, a book investigating the new sexual morality gestating in the Soviet Union. During the late twenties he became increasingly interested in the interrelations between sex, psychology, and radical politics. His magazine reflected this interest, featuring a large number of articles that dealt with psychology and relevant issues: the family, marriage and relations between the sexes, and the "sexual revolution." The *Modern Quarterly* thus functioned to raise further provocative questions and to fashion a new area of discussion on the American Left. It quickly became the center of a contentious debate on the efficacy of uniting the insights provided by the "new psychology" and radical politics. Perhaps more than any radical of his generation Calverton argued for a cultural radicalism—which is to say, a radicalism having to do with transforming consciousness and changing values—that encompassed psychology, psychoanalysis, and the study of sex, and which assumed that the marriage of Freud and Marx was crucial to a revolutionary understanding.

Calverton's interest in sex and psychoanalysis at once indicates his cosmopolitan interest in contemporary ideas and his indebtedness to the prewar intellectual Left. For the cultural radicalism of the 1910s Village "Lyrical Left" contained a strong element of Eros, as Randolph Bourne's writings with their celebration of life, exaltation of youth, and devotion to individual "release" suggest. And from the early twenties both Max East-man and Floyd Dell insisted that the radical movement should come to terms with sex and psychology, and the theories of Freud, Havelock Ellis, Jung, and Adler.[1] During the late twenties Calverton was a principal figure in carrying on this legacy, one of the strongest voices in the American tra-dition of the "libidinal Left." Interestingly, his efforts to unite Marx and Freud suggest that the association between sex and left-wing politics that characterized the American sixties did not arise de novo from figures like Paul Goodman and Norman O. Brown.

Yet although Calverton's proposed coupling of sex and radicalism stirred interest in the late twenties, such interest on the Left was short-lived, gaining little of the momentum that it later did in the sixties. His proposed sexual revolution was ultimately unsuccessful for several rea-sons. The first was the decline of tolerance toward sexual radicalism on the Left as the Communist Party moved into its militant Third Period after 1929. The second was the economic depression itself, which made sexual radicalism seem either peripheral to crucial economic issues or part of the profligacy of the twenties, the "gaudiest spree in history." The third had to do with a brand of sexual radicalism embraced by young leftists of the twenties—an Americanized Freudianism that stressed sexual liberation laced with the more soft-minded aspects of Havelock Ellis's mythology of sexual release. This admixture finally failed to provide an intellectual context rich or complex enough to synthesize the conceptions of Freud and Marx or the tenets of sexual and political radicalism productively.

Yet regardless of the opposition it met from orthodox radicals, and whatever its theoretical or intellectual flaws and ultimate failure, Calver-ton's American attempt to marry psychology and Marxism is significant. Although the members of the Frankfurt School are considered to be the great realizers of the Freudo–Marxist idea, his example indicates that there was an American attempt to couple these two thinkers independent of and running parallel (and even slightly prior) to European develop-ments.[2] His writings and the direction of his magazine from the mid to late twenties provide a new chapter in the history of a distinctive American brand of sexual radicalism in the twentieth century. And in terms of the history of the American Left in the late twenties and early thirties, his pro-posed sexual revolution provides a unique example of a clash between a distinctive American radicalism—permeated with assumptions about per-sonal growth and cultural revolution inherited from the "Lyrical Left" of the 1910s—and the increasingly militant and doctrinaire communism of the Third Period, only beginning to get underway.

CALVERTON's interest in psychoanalysis is evident as early as 1925 when he started corresponding with Dr. Samuel Tannenbaum, the "Village" analyst. Calverton doubtless became aware of Tannenbaum by way of Floyd Dell who was analyzed by Tannenbaum and wrote extensively about it.[3] Tannenbaum was favored by the young Village residents like Dell during the 1910s because his interpretation of Freud stressed the dangers of sexual repression.[4] Tannenbaum's American approach to psychoanalysis—his tendency to dispense with Freud's tragic vision of civilization's inevitable discontents in favor of a sexual metaphysics of primitivism—made perfect ammunition for the attacks on puritanism and gentility that were gaining momentum during the twenties.[5] His liberative psychology and his vision of health as release from forms of bourgeois repression were extremely influential not only among Village radicals of the 1910s but also among young radicals like Calverton coming to maturity in the twenties. And in 1926 Calverton initiated a correspondence with Havelock Ellis, "granddaddy of the new sex hygiene." Calverton had recently finished writing his first book, *The Newer Spirit*, which was among the earliest examples of Marxist literary criticism written in the United States. He then began to consider the relationship between sex and economics and how such a relationship might be taken into account by a Marxist criticism of literature. He solicited Ellis's comments on sex and literature and brought out a book on the topic late in 1926 dedicated to Ellis. In his preface to *Sex Expression in Literature* he credits Ellis for bringing him to understand that "sex enlightenment" is furthered by examining sexual expression in social and anthropological terms. It is in this same spirit of examining the historical tendency of human sexuality that Calverton conducts his investigations, while nonetheless stressing the class factors consonant with his own Marxist approach to literature.[6]

If Calverton's study of sexuality in terms of broad social and historical patterns was inspired by Ellis, the general intellectual ambience of the twenties was another important influence. Like other young intellectuals of the decade, Calverton saw an absolute correlation between the rise of the bourgeoisie and sexual repression. He was influenced by the anthropological studies of Bronislaw Malinowski, which at once fostered a cultural relativism in regard to sex and seemed to throw into bold relief—by contrast to the sexual permissiveness in primitive societies—bourgeois sexual repression. Accordingly, Calverton's narrative in *Sex Expression in Literature* describes an increasing suppression of sexual subject matter in the literary text, from the relative freedom of sexual expression in courtly literature to the sharp taboos on sexual expression in Victorian literature—the height of bourgeois hegemony. His historicizing impulse led him to eschew the more fashionable varieties of popular Freudianism prevalent at the time. When Horace Liveright, the book's publisher, objected that the book was too dry and scholarly and concerned more with history and economics than sex, Calverton responded:

If I took a Freudian attitude and discovered every wistful Madonna pining after phallic scenery and architecture I certainly would have written a different kind of book. But it is not the method of Freud that will elucidate the origins and development of moral trends in literature. . . . My task was to show the social background that made this Victorian taboo so sharp and emphatic.[7]

In spite of Calverton's belief that Freudianism slighted the social and historical dimension of individual behavior, his interest in the new psychology continued to grow. One reason for this was his friendship with Schmalhausen. From the early stages of their correspondence, which was initiated in 1924, Schmalhausen put the case to Calverton that if the *Quarterly* were to uphold its claim of being modern, it should publish material on the new psychology. He proposed that the magazine run a series of articles entitled "Studies of Sex" and offered to contribute a piece entitled "The Psychopathology of Capitalism."[8] Calverton was eventually persuaded and invited Schmalhausen to work on the magazine in 1927 and formally to join the editorial staff of the *Quarterly* as associate editor in 1928.

Schmalhausen's articles, which began to appear at this point, gave the *Quarterly* a new direction. Yet his radical psychology consisted largely of the cavalier use of psychoanalytic terminology coupled with a vulgar Marxism. For Schmalhausen, capitalism had produced a "sick civilization in which the "fetish of individualism and intense competition" created "inferiority complexes" and other forms of "psychoneurotic malaise and misery." Revolution was the social equivalent of analysis, the cure for the maladies and cultural decay of capitalism. A revolutionary socialist society would eliminate the "dominance of the ego" and replace it with "cooperation and integration."[9]

Nevertheless, Schmalhausen was a strong influence on the *Modern Quarterly*; after 1927, articles appeared on such topics as the sexual revolution, marriage and the family, birth control, and prostitution. The January–April issue of that year included a debate between Calverton and Upton Sinclair entitled "Is Monogamy Desirable?" Sinclair argued that monogamous marriage ensured that sex would not interfere with the serious business of revolution; Calverton claimed that monogamy, an expression of the property relations of the bourgeois order, was nonetheless being undermined by the technology of capitalism: "Contraceptives, part of the technological advance of capitalism . . . have done more to undermine monogamy than any socialist tract or radical preachment."[10] In the November–February 1928 issue, Harry Elmer Barnes argued in favor of the greater sexual freedom of the jazz age, while Gilbert K. Shaw buoyantly asserted that after the "pathological fear and distorted shame" regarding sex had been overcome, prostitution would be swept away forever as people came to realize that "sex love" was the "sweetest reality in the living universe."[11] The issue also reviewed glowingly A. S. Neill's *The Problem Child* as a work that drew on Freud and Adler to plead persuasively for the "rights of natural impulse" and for the fact that "children are not bad . . . only adult morals are."[12]

During the late twenties, then, the *Modern Quarterly* championed the cause of sexual freedom that was of concern to young intellectuals of the postwar generation, many of whom sought answers to America's repressive puritanism by embracing Freud and the new psychology. Many of the articles that appeared in the magazine intimately associated psychoanalysis with the desire for sexual liberation. Yet if the *Quarterly*, reflecting to a large extent Schmalhausen's influence, espoused an admixture of Ellis's sexual enthusiasm and a romantic Freudianism that identified sexual health with instinctual liberation, Calverton's editorials remained, as usual, running commentaries on radical politics. For as much as Calverton was eager to be a sexual modernist, he was uneasy with Schmalhausen's sexual reductionism. He had been persuaded by Schmalhausen's earliest letters of 1924, which argued that his Hopkins-inspired behaviorism (expressed in several early articles in the *Modern Quarterly*) was mechanistic and narrow; "your conception of determinism is too deterministic and your conception of objectivity is too naive," Schmalhuasen wrote, recommending Calverton study Freud.[13] Yet it was also during this period that Calverton came under Kantorovitch's influence and began studying Marxist theoreticians such as Plekhanov under his tutelage.

Thus if Schmalhausen stimulated his interest in psychoanalysis, Calverton remained fundamentally Marxist in his perspective. Now he argued repeatedly that Marxism needed a psychology and that psychology needed to be grounded in a radical analysis of society. In an article for the *New Masses* he insisted that "the nature of psychology has been neglected by the radical" and, conversely, that "there is no original psychologist who, in his examination of mental reaction and his attitude toward social evolution, is a profound radical."[14] And in a review of Floyd Dell's *Love in Greenwich Village* (Dell's nostalgic fictional recollections of his bohemian days in the Village), he charged Dell with radical "failure." If Dell had indicated a desire to explore the social background of art in his earlier book *Intellectual Vagabondage*, he was now devoting himself "to the trifling pastime of writing sexy novels for the adolescent Menckensians and the jaded Bourgeoisie." That Dell was so easily diverted from social and economic considerations and caught up in literary "sex playboying" displayed the inadequacy of American literary radicals, revealing their inability to achieve an integrated perspective that included both psychology and radical politics.[15]

Calverton brought the emerging debate about psychoanalysis and politics into his magazine and framed the terms of the discussion by publishing Dell's rejoinder entitled "A Literary Self-Analysis." One of the earliest debates about sex and Freudianism on the American Left was now under way. Dell conceded that Freudianism was a major factor in his retreat from literary radicalism, but he viewed this development positively: Freud had given him "a keen insight into the neurotic origins of much political radicalism." Moreover, Freud had helped him work out his own conflict between the "narcissistic impulse" and the "sexual impulse" and the result was a new appreciation for marriage and family. Far from being a "sex playboy," Dell had settled down and was happy being a family man writing about family themes.[16]

But for Calverton, both Dell's sexual reminiscences and his later retreat into the privatized world of the family amounted to the same thing—a retreat from radicalism, a Freudian backlash. Thus when Dell extended the debate over the sex question to the entire radical community via the *New Masses* ("What is the correct revolutionary attitude toward sex?" he asked in a questionnaire appearing in March 1927),[17] Calverton responded that Freudian psychology was profoundly conservative if not wedded to a radical analysis of society. Radicals were "timid in sex" because of their inability to see "the relationship between forms of family life and modes of production." Sex and family life would inevitably change as the economic structure itself changed, and for radicals to fight for the family and against the economics that perpetuated it was a "farcical contradiction." Addressing Dell's question, Calverton contended that

> a proletarian revolutionary attitude toward sex . . . must oppose the bourgeois family with its system of monogamy, must repudiate the ethics of private property which makes of possession a virtue and freedom a crime, and must construct its relationships in harmony with its social vision.[18]

Calverton's most forceful and extended argument for linking sex and radical politics, however, was his critique of the bourgeois family in his 1928 book, *The Bankruptcy of Marriage*, his study of sex under the revolutionary regime in Russia. In what is perhaps the strongest statement of sexual radicalism to emerge from the American Left during the twenties, he argues that monogamous marriage and the bourgeois family are responsible for the subservience of women to men and for a repressive morality that generates guilt about and fear of sex. Bourgeois marriage is "bankrupt," however, not because of the unhappiness it creates, but because historically it emerged in the context of private property—a system in decay. Moreover, the war produced a radical break in conventional morality. The flapper is a "vivid symbol" of this change: "Cigarette in hand, shimmeying to the music of the masses, the New Woman and the New Morality have made their theatric debut on the modern scene."[19] Indeed, an entire younger generation in the West now embraced a new code of sexual ethics:

> All over the western world it is the same. This new girl, this modern flapper, with her lack of respect for the ideals of her predecessors; and this new masculine youth, with his disregard for the old responsibilities, his disdain for marriage, and contempt for virtue—both were born in the fury of their revolt, in the days of the World War and those that have immediately followed.[20]

All this led Calverton to pronounce the death of middle-class family life. "The old family has decayed. The old home has been replaced by the movie, the club, the dance hall. Home has become a place to dine and die."[21]

As a counter to the bourgeois family, Calverton proffers the working-class family for the sublimated utopian aspirations and sexual possibilities it reveals. Because of its oppressed state, working-class family structure remains to some extent outside bourgeois norms and values; hence it might be seen as a potential site for imagining and nurturing nonrepressive sexual values. "The proletariat, by the very nature of its labor and the disintegration of its family by the demands of industrial production, could never have observed, in any strict sense, the demands of bourgeois morality . . . it is only when proletarians become bourgeoisified that they crusade in favor of virtue."[22] The proletariat contains within itself the seeds of a new morality that challenges bourgeois sexual codes. In the Soviet Union abortion and contraception, companionate marriage, easy divorce, laws establishing the equality of women, and the abolition of the concept of the illegitimate child all provide early signs of just such an "anti-bourgeois" morality, gestating in the working class, and now able to emerge by virtue of a new economic order.

Calverton's attack on the family as an expression of the bourgeois commitment to private property to a large extent follows the classic Marxist analysis of Engels's *The Family, Private Property, and the State*. Like Engels, he sees the patriarchal authority and the sexual double standard being undermined in the working-class context. Like Engels, he opposes rigidity of laws governing sexual behavior and marriage. Yet Calverton does not reach the conservative conclusion Engels does in arguing that communism will bring about the fruition of monogamy—for men as well as women. Rather, his speculations more closely resemble those of Wilhelm Reich who was conducting his explorations between psychosexual behavior and politics in Germany at approximately the same time Calverton was doing so in the United States.

Although Reich's theories were not to reach America until the post–World War II period, the two men arrived independently at a position that saw nonrepressive sexual values latent in proletarian culture and felt that the development of proletarian culture would undermine repressive bourgeois institutions including monogamous marriage itself. Calverton had no developed notion of the family structure as a transmitter of society's repressive values as Reich did, yet both men privileged instinctual liberation and felt that the Soviet Union might prove to be a place where sexual repression would ultimately be vanquished. Both felt that Marxism needed a psychology and that psychology needed to be politicized. Reich's vociferous advocacy of a marriage between Marx and Freud, of course, was ill rewarded by the Communist Party. In 1934 Reich was expelled from the Party for Freudian deviations and accused of being a counter-revolutionary.[23] Nothing quite so dramatic would happen to Calverton, yet trouble lay ahead with the Communists over the sex question.

WIDELY reviewed, the *Bankruptcy of Marriage* enhanced Calverton's reputation as a champion of sexual radicalism. In England the book received high praise from Havelock Ellis, Robert Briffault, and H. G. Wells. Also from England, Huntley Carter wrote, "your book has positively paralyzed the reviewers in England. . . . Reverend St. John Ervine has asked the police to stop you and your immoral book from coming into the country." And in the United States, praise came from Judge Ben Lindsey, a proponent of the revolution in morals in America.[24]

But the critical reception on the Left of the *Bankruptcy of Marriage* was cool at best. A reviewer in the *New Masses* approved of Calverton's publishing "his analysis of the attitude toward sex in Soviet Russia along with his exposition of the cross-currents of contemporary sexual revolt in America," but concluded on a peevish note: "For the thousands who are fussing and fuming about companionate marriage, who know more about immaculate conception than immaculate contraception, the book will be stimulating and richly provocative."[25] Michael Gold, then editor of the *New Masses*, took exception to the reviewer's opinion but only privately, writing Calverton a note explaining he believed *Bankruptcy* was a valuable study.[26] Upton Sinclair, predictably puritanical, lashed out at Calverton's destructive criticism of marriage: "When human beings have all the license they want, then they will discover they are in desperate need of self-control—that is assuming they are ever to think of anything but sex."[27]

Yet even before the *Bankruptcy of Marriage* appeared, orthodox radicals were beginning to take a dim view of Calverton's sexual radicalism. Calverton's earlier reply to Dell's *New Masses* "sex questionnaire," in which he charged radicals with sexual timidity, caused a minor controversy and prompted the *Daily Worker* to characterize him as "a writer who has the correct method of analysis but lacks the horse sense to apply it in specific situations."[28] The *Worker*'s statement riled John Darmstadt, a *Quarterly* writer sympathetic to Calverton's views on sex and radicalism. Darmstadt wrote a rebuttal in the *Quarterly* in which he described the *Daily Worker* as a publication written by "puritanical radicals" and "middle-class moralizers who set themselves up as infallible guides to the workers."[29]

This volley from the *Quarterly* considerably increased tensions over the sex question. Darmstadt had knowingly kicked a hornets' nest, and the *Worker* struck back furiously in an article by H. M. Wicks. In his "An Apology for Sex Anarchism Disguised as Marxism," a ranting attack on the *Quarterly*, Wicks asserted that

> such people are perverts of the revolution, and their doctrine, if accepted by the working class, would lead to the swamps of anarchism, where every person would consider their own self-expression the most important thing in the world, and his sex life just as important as the control of industry by the working class.[30]

Like an Increase Mather of the Left, Wicks complained that "it is precisely sexual excesses and not repression which most seriously affects the workers."[31]

This ideological skirmish between the *Modern Quarterly* and the orthodox Communists—a kind of "sex war"—takes on the character of a rehearsal for the later literary wars of the early thirties between those of liberal and orthodox persuasion: the conflicts over sex reflect an ideological tightening on the part of the Party, and an offensive posture toward heterodox radicals that would come to fruition several years later in the battles over literature and politics. The sex dispute also portends the degree to which sexual radicalism would fall into disfavor among Stalinists by the early thirties. In any case, the battle lines were now clearly drawn between the *Quarterly*'s sexual radicalism and the Communists' sexual conservatism. For the moment there were no further volleys exchanged between the two groups.

But the Communists could not have been happy about the *Quarterly*'s increasing prominence and growing reputation among young intellectuals and sexual modernists. Nor could they have been particularly pleased with Calverton's growing popular reputation as a champion of new ideas. Traveling between lectures in Baltimore and debates in Boston, he was a frequent featured speaker at gatherings considering the sex question. He shocked members of the liberal Twentieth Century Club in Boston with a lecture attacking monogamy.[32] He gave frequent lectures on college campuses; after a lecture at Dartmouth, the president of the discussion group told Calverton that the coeds were circulating a copy of the *Bankruptcy of Marriage* and "arguing and considering the possibility of your sexual revolution."[33] His stature as a deadly opponent of old values and antiquated morality was enhanced when fundamentalist John Roach Stratton died shortly after a debate with him. According to the *New York Telegram*:

> In the death of John Roach Stratton, American fundamentalism loses its most colorful vocal leader. . . . He literally gave his life to their support. As Bryan broke down in his clash with Darrow, so Dr. Stratton's health gave way last Spring after a debate in Boston with the brilliant young freethinker V. F. Calverton.[34]

Riding the wave of interest in sex and psychology, Calverton and Schmalhausen raised money for the *Quarterly* by sponsoring debates and symposia in Baltimore and New York. In March 1927 Calverton and Dell squared off for the first of a series of debates on the question "Is Monogamy Desirable?" These debates were enormously attractive because they presented a radical freethinker of the new generation challenging a sexual-anarchist-gone-conservative of the older generation. Calverton and Schmalhausen also organized and participated in a series of symposia; one symposium in December 1929 at the John Hayes Holmes Community Church in New York City struck out at puritanical repression with the title "Sex Is Necessary! Or, Why You Don't Feel the Way You Should." Another, held at the same venue, provided arguments for more permissive attitudes by examining anthropological data and the sexual practices in other cultures made popular by Malinowski and Margaret Mead. Entitled "The Great Meeting on Sex and Civilization," it included Phyllis Blanchard, Ira S. Wile, Judge Ben Lindsey, and Calverton. In covering the event the *New York Times* reported that "Blanchard and others draw optimistic conclusions from the Trobriand Islanders."[35]

As undisputed champions of sexual modernism, Calverton and Schmalhausen were now more readily able not only to raise money for the *Quarterly* but to extend its readership. Furthermore, organizing the sex debates and symposia situated the two men strategically at the center of a network of intellectuals, and this facilitated their next project, a series of anthologies that would collect the best essays on sex, the new morality, and cultural radicalism. The first of these, entitled *Sex in Civilization*, appeared in 1929.

An outgrowth of "The Great Meeting on Sex and Civilization," the anthology included essays by the decade's foremost exponents of the new knowledge—Havelock Ellis, Joseph Jastrow, Alexander Goldenweiser, Phyllis Blanchard, and Judge Ben Lindsey. The collection took as its fundamental premise the need to link psychoanalysis with a social perspective and to further a "psycho-sociology" that "promises to open up a brilliant new chapter in intellectual history."[36] Articles ranged from the Viennese psychoanalyst Fritz Wittels's discussion of narcissism to Robert Briffault's "Sex and Religion" and Margaret Sanger's piece on birth control. In his own article included in the volume, Calverton attempted to spell out the ground rules for a psychosociology. He criticized Freudian psychologists for a "failure in social vision" and asserted that individuals could never be isolated from their social situation. Radical social movements, however, were in need of psychological insights, and the real task was to enrich the Marxist framework with psychoanalysis. A radical psychosociology, then, would not only reveal that sex was an integral part of the social struggle, but would provide the missing link between individual and society, and between a cultural and political radicalism. Calverton viewed a volume such as *Sex in Civilization*—bringing together the foremost thinkers in psychology and social thought—as the first step toward a radically new interdisciplinary way of thinking.[37]

When *Sex in Civilization* appeared, the *Los Angeles Times* called it "a milestone in sex enlightenment."[38] Within the next two years Calverton and Schmalhausen had produced two new anthologies, again with prominent contributors in psychology, anthropology, and social thought. The first, entitled *The New Generation*, embodied another strand of social thought embraced by the young intellectuals of the twenties, a legacy of the progressive preoccupation with children as the hope for the rejuvenation of American life. Buttressed by Ellis's notion of the essential innocence of infantile sexuality, and Bourne's view of the child as a vessel of spontaneous creativity and cultural renewal, the essays examined the patriarchal nuclear family as well as the "tyranny" of middle-class life that was assumed to be inimical to the child's creative self-development.[39] The second collection, *Women's Coming of Age*, assumed that feminism and socialism were integrally connected; only under a socialist order could one expect to see "the subtle sublimation of raw sexuality into communal comradeship," a comradeship, the editors asserted in their introduction, that would exclude the domination of women by men.[40]

To a certain extent, this vision of socialist comradeship between the sexes expressed the emerging ideal of "companionate" marriage and the notion of the wife as "pal" and sexual partner rather than a subordinate, retiring, and merely maternal figure. Yet *Women's Coming of Age* was by no means an unproblematic view of the "new woman," nor an uncritical celebration of the ideology of sexual emancipation. The volume represented a wide spectrum of opinion ranging from sexual liberalism to sexual conservatism, from Ellis's contention (based on questionnaires and data relating to "auto-erotic practices") that women's sexual drives are as strong as men's, that inherently "there is no special sexual psychology of women,"[41] to Charlotte Perkins Gilman's cautionary approach to notions that would justify sexual "indulgence. . . . The women of to-day, emerging from long repression, finding themselves overcharged with sex-energy and warmly urged to use it, in the justification of [a] highly masculine psychology, seem quite largely to have adopted the theory that the purpose of sex is recreation," Gilman warned.[42] The volume contained two conflicting strains of twenties feminism.[43] The first was embodied in Dora Russell's enthusiastic paean to woman's uniqueness and her maternal destiny ("vigorous women have even been known to find creative ecstasy in the pangs of birth," Russell wrote).[44] The second was Lorine Pruette's empirical and tough-minded discussion—which radically undercut poetic notions of a "special destiny" or feminist mystique—of the socioeconomic forces that shaped women's lives in contemporary America. In discussing "Why Women Fail," Pruette surveyed the obstacles—both economic and psychological—to fulfilling work and a career for women and concluded that "they fail because they lead contingent lives and depend for their satisfaction upon pleasing someone else; they fail because their men do not want them to succeed; they fail because they seldom have wives."[45]

Many of the articles in fact countered sentimental ideas of feminine uniqueness and discussed specific social and psychological impediments to the liberation of women. In an article in which he attacked the myth that women were inherently more monogamous than men, Calverton concluded with the observation that "it can only be with the final dissolution of all economic differentiations between the sexes . . . that women can be as free and creative as men."[46] George Britt found antifeminist attitudes persisting amid seemingly progressive change. His study of professional women in the South revealed changes in personal habits such as smoking, involvement in women's clubs, and women's social reform, yet he concluded that the new woman of the South "may like to earn a little money and have her fling, but the ideal in the back of her head is a nice house in the home town and a decorative position in society."[47] And Judge Ben Lindsey contended that the flamboyant freedom of the twenties did not necessarily mean the victory of a feminist consciousness. Based on his experience in working with youth in Denver, Colorado, during the twenties he predicted that the flapper would become "a happy, loyal wife with several children."[48]

Calverton himself was primarily interested in feminism as a manifestation of the decay of the nuclear family and the emergence of the new morality. Yet *Women's Coming of Age* was perhaps the most balanced, thorough, and challenging of the Calverton–Schmalhausen anthologies. It raised the central problems faced by the feminist movement and attempted to grapple with them from a number of points of view. In fact each of the Calverton–Schmalhausen anthologies represented some of the best examples of the changing morality of the postwar twenties, if not some of the best writing on advanced ideas to emerge from the decade. The astute and critical writing exemplified particularly by *Women's Coming of Age* notwithstanding, however, the anthologies suggest, taken as a group, the extent to which the young sexual modernists of the twenties were sexual enthusiasts whose lyrical talk about the naturalness and beauty of sex reflects the far greater influence of Ellis's optimistic vision of sexual release than Freud's austerity. Examples of the "Americanization of Freud," these collections displayed an interest in psychoanalysis insofar as it could be appropriated to the cause of liberation and cultural renewal. Certainly too, their lyrical vision of cultural radicalism emphasizing social cooperation, creative self-fulfillment, and youth as a rejuvinative cultural force suggests the Village connection, the degree to which young intellectuals of the twenties such as Calverton were heirs of radicals of the teens like Randolph Bourne.

What was unique in these anthologies was their interdisciplinary spirit and their advocacy of a new science of psychosociology, both motivated by Calverton's insistence that psychoanalysis was confined by its individualism and that Marxism was limited by its failure to account for the inner world of the psyche discovered by Freud. Calverton's ground rules for reconciling Marx and Freud were, to be sure, extraordinarily sketchy. Yet his primary contention, expressed most forcefully in the *Bankruptcy of Marriage*—that Marxism needed a psychology and that psychoanalysis needed to be politicized—was received initially with a mixture of coolness and derision on the Left and found no intellectual context in which to develop. An idea well before its time, it found expression not in dialogue or debate on the American Left—for the skirmishes in the "sex war" between the *Modern Quarterly* and the *Daily Worker* had produced a virtual standoff—but rather in the more popular context of anthologized essays on the revolution in morality. If the call for a psychosociology contained in these works was ignored or scorned by most orthodox radicals, the anthologies nonetheless indelibly associated Calverton and Schmalhausen in the public mind with the sexual revolution. As one reviewer in the *New York Times* put it, "If the two men are not authors of the lyrical ballads, they are at least jointly the Karl Marx of the Sexual Revolution."[49]

As EARLY as 1927 signs appeared indicating orthodox radicals' growing impatience with the individualism of the twenties. During that year Michael Gold and his colleagues at the *New Masses* polled their readers with a questionnaire entitled "Are Artists People?" that asked:

> If you prick an artist does he not bleed? If you starve him does he faint? Is heaven his home or can he properly take part in our mundane struggle for the fact of bread and the concepts of liberty, justice etc.? As a social critic and evaluator, can he not merely see what's wrong, but also by more than negative implication declare what's right?[50]

Many responded that the artist, indeed prone to faint when he starves, should produce works that transcend individual concerns and demonstrate social commitment. This now famous questionnaire, as Daniel Aaron has pointed out, registers a shift of sentiment on the Left, a sense that "politics and economics were supplanting sex in the literary consciousness."[51]

No doubt a change in the wind was clearly signaled the same year by the *Daily Worker*'s attack on the *Quarterly* writers as "sex anarchists." Yet even before that there were hints of a sexually conservative backlash. When Calverton wrote his review of Dell's *Love in Greenwich Village* in late 1926 for the *New Masses* (charging Dell with radical "failure"), he was amazed to find the piece, already very critical of what he considered Dell's exclusive preoccupation with sex, embellished upon publication with a damning and distasteful indictment of Dell—one he had not written. The review had been altered with the result that Dell was now sneeringly depicted as a radical who had achieved "ineffectuality, sterility, and a place in *Who's Who*."[52]

Calverton had suspected Gold of tampering with the review and had written to Dell apologizing profusely ("the last paragraph with its conclusion as to Who's Who is an absolute atrocity. . . . If the New Masses continues this tactic, it will have nothing more of my work").[53] He had then given Dell a chance to reply in the pages of the *Modern Quarterly*. The result was the famous "A Literary Self-Analysis," in which Dell embraced Freud and acknowledged his own increasing distance from political matters. But by 1929 Dell's involvement with radical politics was all but finished when he resigned from the *New Masses* because of his disinclination to follow the publication into an ever more rigorous orthodoxy. Upon Dell's resignation Gold assaulted him as an unregenerate "Village playboy" whose "main interests were in the female anatomy."[54] Thus Dell was cast out of the fold; better to say he departed with shouts of "playboy" at his back.

Ironically, little more than six months after Dell's leavetaking, Calverton—who earlier criticized Dell for "sex playboying"—found himself branded a "sex boy" in the *New Republic* by Malcolm Cowley. Cowley's review, with its novel title "Sex Boys in a Balloon," lambasted the writings of Fritz Wittels, Joseph Tannenbaum, Schmalhausen, and Calverton and characterized these men as sexual renegades whose commitment was not to serious revolutionary aims but rather to "the importance of sex and the high value of the books they write about it." Cowley added,

> Now when physical love is treated in a metaphysical manner, it becomes something more than a subject for scientific or sentimental speculation: it becomes a new religion, an erotic pantheism, of which Schmalhausen, Tannenbaum, and Calverton are the high priests. . . . The sex boys, in their balloon of rhetoric, go sailing far above the physical reality of their subject.[55]

Cowley's attack on Calverton and Schmalhausen was tantamount to a condemnation of the *Modern Quarterly*'s sexual radicalism. And his inclusion of Tannenbaum in the review was an implicit indictment of the tradition of Village cultural radicalism that persisted into the twenties and was preserved in publications such as the *Quarterly*. Certainly Cowley's "Sex Boys" piece, featured so prominently in the *New Republic*, announced a further "shift of sentiment" on the Left. Now, it would seem, many radicals were out of patience with speculations about the links between revolution and sexual freedom, and the sex question was to be considered a subject for satire rather than for serious consideration. In case this was not understood, Cowley came back for a second attack (again in the *New Republic*) several months later in "Oedipus: The Future of Love," a speculation on sexual utopia that satirically projected a future

> in the bright sexological by-and-by when the world will have been made safe for the universal libido. Divorce, frigidity in men, Bolshevism, crime, the drug habit, unemployment, hippophagy, athlete's foot and manic depressive insanity—all will have been cured by the new sexology.[56]

Committed as he was at the time to communist orthodoxy, Cowley's onslaughts reflect the Party's Third Period ideological rigidity and its increasing hostility toward the sex issue. Beyond this, however, it is significant that the "Sex Boys" piece coincided with the onset of the depression. For it suggested a more general feeling on the Left that beside the exigencies of the "economic earthquake" a preoccupation with sex now seemed trivial, part of the larger extravagant irresponsibility that characterized the decade of the twenties. Cowley's reviews implied that the literary Left should purge itself of peripheral and frivolous matters and turn its attention to a sustained political and economic analysis of America's maladies.

Cowley further expressed a general feeling of guilt and a related intellectual backlash on the Left, for his lambasting disparagement of the "sex boys" contained more than a hint of the "reformed playboy." As such it prefigured sentiments he later expressed in *Exile's Return*, which renounced the "easy, quick, adventurous age" of the twenties (personified in the "religion of art," emotional profligacy, and the decadence of Harry Crosby) and welcomed its eclipse by the grim and ugly yet "reassuring" realities of the thirties.[57]

Certainly Cowley's campaign against the "sex boys" marked a turning point. After 1929 one could not be both a political and cultural radical, an exponent of both Marx and Freud. As Daniel Aaron has observed, "The dual life was no longer possible."[58] The title of an article written by Hook in the late twenties summed up the matter succinctly: "Marx and Freud, Oil and Water."[59] As the thirties progressed antagonism toward any remaining discussion of sexual radicalism intensified on both the Left and the Right. In 1934 (the same year that Wilhelm Reich was expelled from the Communist Party), Calverton's *Bankruptcy of Marriage* was banned in Germany by the Nazis.[60] Earlier, from Russia, where plans were afoot to publish Calverton's works, came a disheartening letter from Serge Dinamov, the Soviet writer with whom he had established a friendship while visiting Russia in 1927. Apart from an alleged "shortage of paper," Dinamov's 1930 missive informed Calverton that a "more particular reason for reluctance to publish your works is the lack of interest in sex problems in our country (the cause of which you no doubt understand)."[61] Dinamov's only slightly veiled reference to the loss of tolerance and growing prudishness under Third Period communism notwithstanding, Calverton was bitterly disappointed to see his books dropped by Soviet publishers and dismayed to see speculations about sexual radicalism disappearing as a Third Period Marxist hegemony defined the new psychology and studies of sex "individualistic," "bourgeois," and "reactionary."

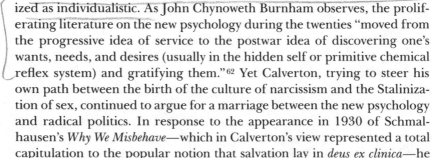

To be sure the new psychology might have been legitimately characterized as individualistic. As John Chynoweth Burnham observes, the proliferating literature on the new psychology during the twenties "moved from the progressive idea of service to the postwar idea of discovering one's wants, needs, and desires (usually in the hidden self or primitive chemical reflex system) and gratifying them."[62] Yet Calverton, trying to steer his own path between the birth of the culture of narcissism and the Stalinization of sex, continued to argue for a marriage between the new psychology and radical politics. In response to the appearance in 1930 of Schmalhausen's *Why We Misbehave*—which in Calverton's view represented a total capitulation to the popular notion that salvation lay in *deus ex clinica*—he wrote to Schmalhausen: "If it were my study it would never come to grips with contemporary psychologists be they Freudians, Jungians, Adlerians, or whatever without . . . pointing out the inadequacy of any psychology without social basis." Calverton further argued that being a "revolutionary psycho-sociologist"—that is, bringing together psychological and social perspectives on the terrain of radical politics and revolutionary praxis— was "one of the most significant tasks, however a thankless one for the time being, of our age."[63]

Calverton's partnership with Schmalhausen would later break over their diverging views and differences. But if he continued to argue the need to combine psychology and Marxism, *Women's Coming of Age*, published in the depths of the depression in 1931, stands as his last effort toward a synthesizing cultural radicalism. Like the concerns with sexual liberation generally, feminism underwent an eclipse after 1930, not only as a distinctive force in national life, but also as a force within the Left. Now the pervasive hostility to Calverton's ideas on the Left and the pressing problems of the depression would turn his attention—and the attention of his magazine—away from sexual radicalism and toward the economic crisis, the threat of fascism, and the critical examination of Stalinism.

THE FAILURE of Calverton's sexual revolution suggests the deficiencies of the intellectual context in which American radicalism prevailed in the late twenties and early thirties. American radicals like Calverton did not have the benefit of the Frankfurt School theorists' efforts to combine psychoanalysis and politics. The Frankfurt School's writings on the possibility of synthesizing Freud and Marx did not begin to appear until 1932, and even after that date there is no indication that Calverton was familiar with them.[64] He was of course aware of French surrealism, which did combine left-wing radicalism with a species of Freudianism, but he remained suspicious of these European-influenced avant-garde experiments, which, he felt, undermined the communicative function of language.[65] During this time, however, Calverton was unaware of Reich's efforts to bring about a marriage of Marx and Freud. The similarity between the ideas of Calverton and Reich might be explained by the fact that the core of Reich's thought—his notion that without sexual liberation a healthy and just society was an impossibility and that neurosis and hence human unhappiness can be traced back to sexual repression— was very much the way that Freud was "read" in America during the years of Village radicalism and well into the twenties.[66] And although Calverton was critical of what he saw as Freudianism's inherent individualism, he nevertheless was influenced profoundly by this Americanized and liberative version of Freud.

But neither this Americanized Freudianism nor the enthusiasm for other varieties of the "new psychology" was able to sustain the development of sexual radicalism during the next several decades in the United States. Like the members of the Frankfurt School, American radicals such as Calverton turned to psychoanalysis because they felt that Marxism failed to deal with the subjective in human life and because they wanted to go beyond the instrumental utilitarianism that permeated vulgar Marxism. But the Frankfurt School had the rich tragic vision of Freud to work with while Americans embraced a diluted Freudianism with its optimistic teleology of sexual liberation or the less complex and more lyrical psychology of Havelock Ellis. Calverton's theoretically thin efforts to wed sexual and political radicalism suggest that in the American context there was no fertile ground for psychoanalytic concepts to develop, no intellectual matrix dense enough to unite productively Freudian and Marxist perspectives. This failure of intellectual context, as well as the increasing hostility of orthodox leftists to the issue of sexual radicalism, the shock of the economic earthquake, and consequent reaction against the profligacy of the twenties combined to make Calverton's sexual revolution an abortive one.

Yet, if it was abortive, it was nonetheless significant. An expression of an American tradition of cultural radicalism, Calverton's sexual revolution drew on the optimistic belief in the cultural revolution of the Village 1910s and looked ahead presciently to the 1960s when men like Paul Goodman, whose ideas were buttressed with Reichian theories, would carry on this essentially American sexual radicalism, which saw a coercive society dependent on instinctual repression and viewed sexual liberation not only as healthy but as revolutionary and creative. To this would be added the "darker" Freudianism of the Frankfurt School and the Frankfurt School's richer and more complex analysis of the relationship between Marx and Freud, largely through the writings of Herbert Marcuse. In any case it would be during the 1960s that cultural radicals like Goodman and Marcuse would turn again to what Calverton had already identified in the 1920s as a crucial project, a "significant intellectual task"—that of combining sex and politics, psychology and a radical analysis of society.

CHAPTER FIVE

I seek in you a woman who will lead me beyond life itself.
—V. F. Calverton to Nina Melville, 1928

New York: Metropolitanism and Love

As Calverton's reputation as a radical freethinker grew in the late twenties, he received many invitations to lecture outside the Baltimore area. By early 1928 his lecture schedule included Brookwood Labor College in Katonah, New York, the Workers Forum in Philadelphia, Howard University in Washington, D.C., the Cosmopolitan Club at Syracuse University, the Community Church in New York, the Manhattan Lyceum, and the Rand School of Social Science, also in Manhattan. Calverton now traveled frequently between Baltimore and New York, hub of American radicalism, for regular lectures at the Rand School and to make contacts for his magazine.

In 1928 he also quit his teaching job in Baltimore and moved to Greenwich Village to devote himself entirely to literary activities. Besides the attractions of New York's metropolitanism, he felt the need for change. His relationship with Helen had continued to deteriorate after his trip to Russia; she was planning a divorce and was preparing to move out of "2110." Teaching brought in much-needed money, but increasingly it seemed an impediment to the job of publishing the magazine. He found a small but attractive studio apartment at 52 Morton Street in the Village and felt a sense of relief when he moved to New York City. Yet Baltimore still made claims on him. Aside from the fact that it would always feel like home, the base of operations for the *Quarterly*—the staff and printer—remained in Baltimore, and Calverton took the train back to "2110" every weekend to conduct the magazine's business as well as preside over his established Saturday-night gatherings. During weekends in Baltimore he also visited

Una Corbett, to whom he remained very attached, his daughter Joy, and Bessie Peretz, with whom he continued to be emotionally and sexually involved.

New York was a breath of fresh air for him, a blast of cosmopolitan stimulation. During the late twenties there was a remarkable collection of magazines in the Village area centering on Thirteenth Street between Sixth and Seventh avenues. The *Dial*, the *Freeman*, the *New Masses*, and the *Menorah Journal* all huddled in close proximity on Thirteenth Street; a block away on Fifth Avenue W.E.B Du Bois was editing *Crisis*, and not far north in the Chelsea area the *New Republic* had its home.[1] Calverton's coeditor, Schmalhausen, lived in New York and they were now able to meet on a daily basis. As a result their partnership bloomed, and it was during this period that they collaborated on the various sex symposia, began to put together their anthology *Sex in Civilization*, and planned for anthologies on feminism and the "new generation." Calverton found the atmosphere intensely stimulating, and he resolved to stay in New York and partake of the city's intellectual life and the radical thought that flourished there.

Now without a teaching salary, he took a job as a book review editor for the Book League of America just launched by Isaac Don Levine, and soon landed two more literary jobs: literary editor of the MacCaulay Company and literary advisor for the Macmillan Company. With astonishing energy, he continued nevertheless to manage and edit the *Quarterly*, write his own books, and contribute articles to a dozen periodicals. In 1929 *Sex in Civilization* appeared, as well as the *Anthology of American Negro Literature*, edited solely by Calverton, and his short-story trilogy *Three Strange Lovers*. During this period Joshua Kunitz wrote Calverton:

> Say George, to me you are an amazing psychological phenomenon: Publisher, Editor, Critic, Sociologist, Psychologist, Anthropologist, Rebel Fighter, Lover, and now—creative artist. Hell and damnation—I'm envious of you! Your tireless energy and versatility are enough to drive any normal, plodding, phlegmatic guy like myself to despair.[2]

Of the three works, the *Anthology of American Negro Literature* stands as his most important. Of Calverton's edited anthologies it is no doubt among the best and the most significant and it reflects a cosmopolitan spirit in his work, which bloomed in New York.

In his early years Calverton had been influenced by the cosmopolitan ideal articulated by prewar radicals like Randolph Bourne, which embraced the notion that metropolitan life would give rise to a vital proliferation of subcultures, and that such subcultures would exhibit tolerance and engage in conversation with each other. Such an ideal held that cultural differences were valuable for what they could bring to the larger socialist perspective.[3] From the outset Calverton organized his soirees at "2110" with this cosmopolitan ideal of diversity and difference, rejecting parochialism whether regional or ethnic.

Outraged by the conservatism and underlying racism in the Baltimore environs (the black Baptist church, St. Paul's, for example, was stoned in 1924),[4] Calverton developed an interest in black culture and by the mid twenties he was corresponding with economist Abraham L. Harris, a professor of economics at West Virginia Collegiate Institute, and speaking on radicalism and its implications for race relations at the institute under Harris's auspices. Through Harris he began to see the limitation of the Communists' view of the race question, the notion that revolutionary interracial trade union organizations alone were sufficient to deal with the economic disabilities of blacks under capitalism. Harris pointed out to Calverton that the crucial issue for blacks in America was the development of a cultural identity, that what blacks were looking for was cultural recognition and renewal. Harris wrote Calverton, "You spoke last time of not letting the race problem absent so much of our energy that we may not be able to do bigger things. But Goetz, someone has to tell you and others equally ignorant [about] the Negro's cultural and artistic efforts."[5] Harris also made Calverton reevaluate his uncritical belief that blacks could be easily "proletarianized." "I still believe," Harris wrote him, "that the Negro masses are as receptive to communism and socialistic doctrines as the hide of a rhinoceros is impressionable to the stimulus from the sting of the most infinitesimal species of mosquito."[6] Calverton began, at Harris's advice, to study the emerging black artists of the Harlem Renaissance, and his correspondence with black intellectuals grew to include George Schuyler (the black columnist of the Pittsburgh *Courier*), Charles S. Johnson (editor of the black journal *Opportunity*), Walter White (an official of the NAACP), Alain Locke (professor of philosophy at Howard University), poet Langston Hughes, and fiction writer, historian, and civil rights champion, W.E.B. Du Bois.

By the mid twenties the *Modern Quarterly* featured writing on black culture. In the October–December 1925 issue W.E.B. Du Bois initiated a discussion of the Harlem Renaissance, and its significance for black culture. "Already this art expression," Du Bois wrote, "is showing its peculiarities, its unique content." In later issues Charles S. Johnson wrote on "The New Negro," assessing the emerging black art and literature of the Harlem Renaissance, Alain Locke on "The American Literary Tradition and the Negro," and Clarence Cameron White, a black composer, on "The Labor Motif in Negro Music." The black sociologist E. Franklin Frazier's sharply perceptive article, "La Bourgeoisie Noire," undercut what was to become party dogma about the black working class.[7] Frazier analyzed the reasons that black intellectuals were not "class conscious," pointing to the fact that the primary struggle on the part of blacks in America had been to acquire a culture; the cultural concerns of the Harlem Renaissance were largely divorced from political and class issues, while black political radicals were not interested in cultural problems.[8] And in the Winter 1930–31 issue, Carl E. Gehring made a claim for jazz (which was generally seen at the time as distinct from "serious music") as a unique expression of black culture as well as "this country's individual contribution to musical composition."[9] After its numerous articles on psychology and sex in the mid to late twenties, the *Modern Quarterly* was clearly setting another agenda for discussion by publishing some of the most intelligent and trenchant writing on black culture to appear in any radical journal of the period.

Calverton's *Anthology of American Negro Literature*, published in 1929 and dedicated to black activist Walter White, was an outgrowth of the increasing association of black intellectuals with the *Quarterly*. The volume included an extraordinary range of offerings (fiction, drama, poetry, literary, historical, and sociological essays, as well as examples of blues, work songs, and spirituals) and contributions by the most prominent voices in the black cultural world: Jean Toomer, Claude McKay, W.E.B. Du Bois, Langston Hughes, Alain Locke, Walter White, Charles Johnson, and Abraham Harris. It provided historical perspective with offerings by Paul Lawrence Dunbar, Frederick Douglass, and Booker T. Washington. This astutely constructed volume was introduced with an essay by Calverton asserting the uniqueness of black culture and its importance in the growth of American culture as a whole. In one sense, he argued, the black arts are more important to a uniquely American culture than the white arts, since the latter carried on a European tradition whereas the development of black culture in the United States was an original phenomenon.[10]

Calverton's *Anthology of American Negro Literature* was hailed by Bernard Smith in the *New Masses* as one of the very best works on Negro literature and culture.[11] Yet in spite of isolated praise from within the orthodox Left, many of the ideas on black culture expressed in the *Modern Quarterly* (and by extension in Calverton's anthology) were, as Harold Cruse put it "trenchant criticisms of the whole Communist Party approach to literary and cultural affairs."[12] In a sense the perceptive analysis of black culture that came about through Calverton's close and congenial association with black intellectuals succumbed to the same forces that aborted Calverton's "sexual revolution": the tightening ideological rigidity of the Party. As Cruse argues forcefully, the articles in the *Quarterly* during this period had a direct bearing on the Negro struggle in politics, economics, and culture. But because of increasing tension between Calverton and the Communists, none of the ideas raised in the *Quarterly* was discussed in Party circles. Meanwhile all literary and cultural questions relating to the Negro were left to Gold's sectarian care in the *New Masses*—which blindly followed Party policy. As a result, Cruse asserts, "the Negro radical intellectuals and the Harlem Negro Communist theoreticians either learned nothing at all from the wealth of critical material printed in the *Modern Quarterly*, or else were so subordinate to the ideas and influence of the Communist whites that they dared not express a single idea themselves that was independently critical." [13]

One might add that the *Modern Quarterly* explored the implications of the "New Negro" and the Harlem Renaissance more fully than any radical journal of the period. It took seriously Alain Locke's contention that the black artist aspired to become a "collaborator and a participant in American Civilization." [14] Such a contention, itself expressing a cosmopolitan ideal, however, ran against the grain of a parochial, backward, and segregationist policy adopted by the Party in the late twenties—the idea of considering southern blacks a subjugated nation with the right of self-determination. Thus on the issue of race along with the more general issue of the metropolitan disposition of the modern intellectual, the intellectual's responsibility to cultural diversity, Calverton's *Modern Quarterly* found itself once again at loggerheads with the Party.

Calverton's cosmopolitanism was also expressed in his interest in psychology and psychoanalysis, an interest associated with a metropolitan sensibility and urban environment. By 1928 this interest had brought him into conflict with orthodox opinion on the Left. Nevertheless after his arrival in New York he undertook a work of fiction that explored the neurotic convolutions of obsessive relationships and the interrelationship of love and death. *Three Strange Lovers*, his most successful work of fiction, was published by Boni and Liveright in 1929. These three stories, depicting a world of compulsion, anxiety, and suicidal impulse, focused on the ennui that settles upon a relationship and the inevitable decay and death of romance. Exhibiting an hyperbolic romanticism and sense of anxiety about the death of love, one of the "strange lovers" complains that the romantic ardor and beauty of a new love inevitably fades and is transformed into a "living corpse." Obsessed with preserving the height of romantic passion, he insists on suicide for himself and his lover: "We must end life before life ends love." [15] As the passage suggests, the stories are melodramatic and self-conscious, the characters are wooden, and the plots contrived and exorbitantly Gothic. Nevertheless, the trilogy drew interested comments from psychologists Wilhelm Steckel and Fritz Wittels regarding their insightful probing of the world of inner compulsion and psychosis.[16] Interesting though they were from a psychological standpoint, the stories fail as good fiction in part because they too closely mirrored Calverton's own private preoccupations. These concerns, especially about death, now haunted him increasingly and were to become a dominant motif in his next relationship.

Shortly after his arrival in New York, he met Hortense Goodsitt, who was born in New York City in 1908. Her father, like Calverton's, was a tailor who was interested in ideas and culture; a Russian immigrant, he loved the opera and the violin and would leave the family Saturday afternoons to go to the Metropolitan Opera. Her mother, like Calverton's, had prosaic interests and was primarily concerned with the material well-being of the family. Unlike Calverton's family, hers was Jewish. Hortense went to Hunter College in New York City, majoring in sociology and literature, and when she heard Calverton discussing the relationship between the two topics at a public lecture, she was taken with him and introduced herself at an informal gathering after the talk. She was a fledgling actress, seeking parts on stage and teaching acting in summer camps. She was twenty years old, intelligent, and had a dark, exotic beauty.[17] George Calverton fell in love again.

From the outset her parents opposed her involvement with Calverton. Theirs was not a particularly religious family, but Calverton's gentile background became an issue of contention. Calverton had yet to be divorced, a fact Hortense kept from her parents. When "Horty" ran off with Calverton, she told them that she and Calverton had married in Baltimore. Her parents contacted the Marriage License Bureau there and found no record of the marriage. They wrote Hortense a number of angry letters condemning her behavior and threatened to sabotage the relationship. Away for a weekend in Baltimore, Calverton wrote her that "your parents . . . have enough people on our trail now . . . watching for me to take you out of New York in order to get me on the Mann Act."[18]

After a short retreat at Croton, New York, to escape family conflicts, the couple began living together in the Morton Street apartment, and Calverton gave Hortense Goodsitt a name with literary echoes—Nina Melville—when she became theater critic for the *Modern Quarterly*. She loved her involvement in a literary milieu. She relished living in the Village in the daring and unconventional role of Calverton's bohemian lover and enjoyed participating in a world of letters and political thought. She was enormously devoted to Calverton, planning his schedule, assisting him with research, acting as his secretary, helping with the magazine, making dinner dates, and arranging his soirees. Her youth, poise, and sociability made her the perfect hostess for the literary parties Calverton now began to organize at the New York apartment. Calverton told her about Una Corbett and Joy, even Bessie Peretz, and she accepted the fact that his weekend visits to Baltimore included seeing them.

From the outset of the relationship Calverton told Nina Melville about his ideal of the sexually liberated life. Immediately after they met, he wrote her about his notions of sexual freedom, which, he contended, contrasted sharply with her own traditional upbringing: "Your own theories of life, your own notions of action, your own conceptions of behavior, your own ideas of right and wrong, conflict, if they do not clash, with mine. . . . I believe in a certain spontaneity of living, a desire to live without restraint and repression that are [sic] alien to one of your nature." [19] His calculated "warning" ("I should be the first to warn you against myself," he admonished her) had the desired effect. Precisely because of her traditional upbringing, Nina Melville was attracted to this young man with his unconventional notions of the sexually free, nonpossessive relationship. But later, when she became aware that Calverton often had flings when he went on lecture tours, she felt hurt and betrayed. She soon became aware, like the women before her, that his affairs had less to do with advanced ideals than with his own profound insecurities and that his ideals of sexual freedom rationalized his infidelities.

Calverton's attitude toward love and relationships was profoundly dualistic and ambivalent. He was a dialectical materialist in his writings on bourgeois marriage, yet he was an incurable romantic. He understood that romance was a myth, an ideological device used to perpetuate bourgeois marriage and family, yet he was constantly preoccupied with romance and completely dismayed when it disappeared from a relationship. He disliked the dependency of one person on another that often occurred in marriage, yet he remained attached to and emotionally dependent on nearly all the women with whom he became intimate. In a sense Calverton suffered from what Joseph Wood Krutch called an "unstable equilibrium of forces" surrounding love that plagued the "modern temper" of the twenties generation: the tendency to see love as a legitimate subject for rationalistic consideration, yet the sense that the disappearing transcendental value attached to love as a result of such rational inquiry "leaves a mighty blank in existence." [20] Calverton's inflated romanticism and his preoccupation with love and its relation to death seem an effort to retain a sense of the "transcendent" qualities of love that were being undermined by rationalistic, "scientific" scrutiny. Indeed his letters to Melville combine an overwrought celebration of romantic love with the sense that love, rather than having transcendent value, is intensely perishable, even illusory: "Our love does go beyond our wildest dreams, as you so exquisitely said. It is a miracle, a marvelous illusion. Our miracle and our illusion—

and if we always breathe softly upon it, it will be an ever sweeter and sweeter illusion."[21]

All this was complicated by Calverton's psychological make-up. During her time with Calverton, Una Corbett had noted that he sought relationships with women as an answer to his deeply rooted insecurities and fears. When she found that Calverton and Nina Melville were involved, she wrote him a letter that wished him well yet expressed her belief that his anxieties ultimately could never be assuaged in a relationship. "I know you will be momentarily happy," she wrote, "and I'm glad for you. I wish I could spare you the suffering you endure. . . . I hope you two will love each other as madly and happily as we did."[22] Corbett believed that Calverton was searching for his mother in women, for the security, unconditional acceptance, and approval of the maternal feminine.[23] Nina Melville soon became aware of his fears and craving for approval, too; indeed Calverton asked for her adoration, saying that he needed it to function, to motivate his work, that without it he would be lost.[24] Calverton thus sought love and approval to fill a profound sense of emptiness. Yet his insecurities disallowed a sense that he might be wholly accepted by a woman, and he obsessively sought alternative relationships and affairs. And because he sought what was impossible in an adult relationship, the totally approving mother, he could not believe that a relationship could be stable or permanent. The initial ecstasy of love was doomed to exhaust itself, burn itself out, and become a form of living death. Love, as he wrote in *Three Strange Lovers*,

> cannot survive constant familiarity, and the inquisitorial intimacies of a possessive life. It exhausts itself in its very ecstasy. And love without passion is a lame, limping thing indeed. . . . It is a love grown senile and crippled of charm . . . another living corpse.[25]

On one level this represents another criticism of marriage's "bankruptcy," a protest against what a character in one of Floyd Dell's earlier novels called the "matrimonial illusion"—the idea that possessive and exclusive relations become tedious and static. But its inflated rhetoric and romantic lament on the death of love again suggest a fundamental conflict between the desire to scrutinize love scientifically and a profound sense of the loss of love's transcendental value.

This is precisely the conflict between Calverton's Marxist writing and his fiction. What is most striking about *Three Strange Lovers* is its utter contrast with the Marxist "scientific" approach of the *Bankruptcy of Marriage*. Taken together they suggest not only this conflict but also a conflict between an optimistic social vision of sexual amelioration and a dark subjective world where love and death cohabited and where death ultimately took the fore. His friend Kantorovitch had commented on the obvious split between the themes of his fiction and his Marxist criticism some years earlier when he wrote Calverton, "I do not want to be a prophet of evil, but as far as I know science and poetry are bad bedfellows, and God help the one whose heart becomes a battle ground of the two."[26] Indeed, Calverton felt a continual conflict between his desire to write fiction and criticism, to explore the world of unconscious desire and to be a radical critic. Such conflicting impulses were not unknown among American radicals; both Eastman and Dell felt the conflict between dreaming and acting, between being a self-centered artist and a servant of society. Yet each had come to terms with this conflict, and both had managed to explore the two realms with relative success.[27] Calverton's fiction writing was sporadic and relatively unsuccessful, and he continued to feel the pull of the subjective realm, the split in himself between the discursive and the artistic, between his social and individual impulses. As he wrote Melville: "What do I want in life? What do I seek? In a social sense I know deeply and well. In an individual sense I am lost in cruel chaos."[28]

Ultimately, this personal chaos had to do with the failure to find an expressive form for his preoccupation with death. Calverton retained something of the Victorian religion of love, looking to the relationship to obliterate the fears of the lonely self and solve existential riddles. At the same time, like a Victorian brooding about the death of God, he brooded over the remnants of love's "living corpse" in the modern world. The fear of death drove him to seek relief in relations with women; conversely his search for total acceptance, for the ultimate haven of the maternal principle, was a manifestation of the dual impulse, the fascination with and fear of death. For Calverton, the maternal was associated with his mother's impulse toward stasis and inertness, finally with both the lure of the death instinct as well as the terror of death's presence.

Melville soon became aware that his Gothic notion of love as an enervated and precarious state hovering constantly on the verge of its own extinction reflected his own anxieties about love's capacity to redeem him from loneliness, anxiety, and death. His letters made her aware of his overwhelming sense of loneliness: "I am frightened of myself these days, frightened of the despair which overtakes me, the terror of being alone."[29] He complained of the deep depressions that often struck him and the sense of isolation that could not be assuaged by his weekly soirees, social activities, and numerous friendships: "I am unspeakably lonely at times, and depressed. My acquaintances and friendships are exceedingly numerous and yet, in their own way, profoundly superficial."[30] The fear of death obsessed him, he confessed, and for this reason his life would "always . . . be one of extreme suffering and anguish."[31] She would write back, reassuring him: "Don't let sadness, depression, wariness of soul or the like ever touch you or me."[32] But her reassurances helped little, and as they continued to live together she found that Calverton's anxieties often cast a pall over her happiness and over their relationship.

Yet the life they made together was in many ways satisfying. Nina Melville gave Calverton consistent affection, support, and encouragement; he was often passionate, wrote her daily love letters when he was away (as he did with all his women), and brought her into a milieu that provided intellectual inspiration and a sense of purpose. Their life together made some envious. Several years into their relationship, a young Alfred Kazin visited Calverton's apartment to assist with the magazine. Dropping by one winter day to read proof on the *Quarterly*, he found Melville, suffering from a cold, draped on a couch at the center of the room, and to the young man's eyes she became the center of a particular ambience and style of life he viewed with a mixture of awe and envy:

> The sight of her in that room at the back looking out on the frozen little New York garden outside, of the winter light from the back yard turning everything steely and grey . . . of the proud girl lying there in perfect serenity, was the most rewarding experience I ever had reading proof in Calverton's house. There was an odor of herbs from the kitchen preparatory to some "French" dish, there was Calverton writing another book at his desk, there was I doing editorial chores, and there was the girl. Calverton's life was all before me, and I was grateful for sharing so much of it. Everything about the girl immediately suggested a delicate offering, a subtle power to give pleasure, that contrasted sharply with the steady dates that were the rule in our neighborhood.[33]

Calverton and Melville's relationship would endure until his death twelve years later. Neither initially desired marriage, but they eventually declared themselves married by common law (Calverton would later give October 5, 1931, as the date they entered into a common law marriage).

The period after Calverton moved to New York in 1928 was a particularly creative one, filled with the intellectual energy of New York City and all the possibilities of a new love. He often celebrated his new life and the renewing capacity of his love for Melville: "You are not living any longer with the George you first met," he wrote her some time after they began living together. "You are living with a new George, made by you, transformed by your love."[34] Yet Calverton's compulsive infidelity was a continual strain on the relationship. He expected complete sexual freedom, yet expected Melville to be loyal to him.[35] Several times she threatened to leave. He would promise to stop seeing other women, promises, she realized, he would not keep. And Calverton's depression and fear of death continued to plague their intimacy, as one of Melville's letters to him indicates:

> Last night some sort of shadow hung over you. . . . I felt it edge closer and closer to you all through the evening even when you tried to be playful, even when you were beautifully dear. . . . God I was frightened, it was almost as if your concept of the living corpse was haunting the background—almost as if that cold grip of dark emptiness which I dreaded so infused my being.[36]

The fact that Melville adopts his portentous terms suggests the overwhelming quality of his obsessions, the degree to which they impinged on her life and were a continual source of anxiety. Yet in these early years of their relationship, Calverton managed to sublimate his neurotic fears in inflated gregariousness, parties, group projects, and frenetic work punctuated by bouts of heavy drinking. But as the years went by, his anxieties increased, and Melville found his obsessions, more than his infidelities, increasingly difficult to contend with. She found it difficult not to be pulled down into the vortex of depression with him, not to think of their relationship in terms other than those he articulated—terms centered around an uncertain world where a relationship could implode and intimacy collapse into stagnation, centered around the death of love, and around the specter of death itself. Yet she continued to help him with his projects, encouraged him when he was depressed, and continued to be the vivacious hostess at his parties, which were becoming an institution in New York as they had in Baltimore. But she was coming to realize that nothing could eradicate the anxieties and deep melancholia that plagued him and darkened their relationship.

CHAPTER SIX

Politics and literature are no longer viewed as conflicting
categories. If the American writer has not become class
conscious yet, at least he has become social-conscious.
—V. F. Calverton, 1932

The New Agenda: Literary
Radicalism and the American
Revolution

The economic catastrophe of autumn 1929 brought an abrupt
end to the decade of the twenties. What F. Scott Fitzgerald
called the "orgiastic future," beckoning Americans onward
with ever increasing frenzy, had been snuffed out with a suddenness that
left the country reeling and directionless. Yet in spite of the catastrophe and slide into the Great Depression many intellectuals felt something
akin to relief. Malcolm Cowley, for example, concludes his account of the
twenties in *Exile's Return* by describing his exit from a mad, nightlong,
surrealistic party to confront dawn and a street "bathed in harsh winter
light, ugly and clear and somehow reassuring." The episode has a metaphoric dimension, signifying the end of a decade of frivolity: "It was an
easy quick adventurous age, good to be young in; and yet on coming out
of it one felt a sense of relief, as on coming out of a room full of talk and
people into the sunlight of the winter streets."[1] Cowley's suggestion of a
"fortunate fall" from the illusions of the glamorous twenties into the harsh
realities of the thirties was echoed by Matthew Josephson after the stock
market crash: "One feels infinitely closer to reality than one did in 1929."[2]

Indeed, a heady sense of confronting reality was a dominant mood
among writers during the thirties. As Josephson commented, American
writers felt as if an "arrears of social consciousness had accumulated be-

cause for a long period we had acted in the belief that artists could ignore the conditions of society." Now, according to Josephson, "We had to ask ourselves continually 'What is to be done? How can we be useful in these times?'"[3] The desire to renounce the individualism of the twenties and to be socially useful was indicated by the famous 1932 pamphlet "Culture and Crisis," which Josephson helped draft. Signed by fifty-two writers and artists who proposed that the two major political parties were "hopelessly corrupt," the pamphlet supported Communist Party candidates Foster and Ford.[4]

In an article published in August of 1930 Calverton astutely and presciently designated the thirties the "decade of convictions." The leftward turn of American intellectuals was now a "mainstream affair," he announced.[5] And in a *Quarterly* editorial he argued forcefully that the Communist Party remained the only viable alternative to the two major parties.[6] In spite of personal misgivings and his growing history of conflicts with the Party, Calverton, like many other intellectuals, endorsed Foster and Ford.

If the *Quarterly* had kept alive something of the libidinal and celebratory paganism of the Village Left during the twenties, it now emerged into the "harsh winter light" of the thirties with a more prosaic tone. Even during the sexual heyday of the late twenties, Calverton had never let the *Quarterly*'s radical perspective lapse, but now he felt the economic earthquake required a single-minded analysis of political and cultural issues. The publication entered the new decade with a weighty symposium on "Marxism and Social Change," which included essays by John Dewey, Max Eastman, Sidney Hook, Louis Boudin, and Waldo Frank.[7] From this point on, the magazine assumed the character it would maintain through much of the thirties as the chief theoretical journal of the independent Left.

Convinced that the overthrow of capitalism was necessary, Calverton approached the reality of the depression largely through a reestimation of the American cultural and literary vision, through a reexamination of the American tradition. In part this search for tradition was evoked, in Calverton and other writers on the Left, by a desire to find a sense of value through social commitment. Yet Calverton explored the past in order to demonstrate its failures and retrieve what was relevant for socialist values; he used the past in order to set the agenda for the present. In a dialectical fashion, he used the American literary tradition to demonstrate that it contained the seeds of its own transformation into revolutionary (proletarian-conscious) literature. From the outset of the thirties, he insisted that the revolution be rooted in the distinctive features of the American scene including its cultural life; thus his literary criticism undertook its initial explorations of a larger project of Americanizing Marxism. During this time the *Quarterly* marked out the discursive terrain and set the agenda for dialogue and argument about some of the decade's most pressing concerns: the role of the American intellectual in the economic crisis, the American artist's responsibility to the revolution, and the nature and function of radical literature and art.

THE winter 1930–31 issue of the *Modern Quarterly* contained not only the debate on "Marxism and Social Change" but another timely symposium, "A Challenge to American Intellectuals: A Controversy." The two symposia signaled the decided change in the magazine's emphasis. The former suggested the new importance attributed to Marxist theory and the desire to make Marxism relevant to American conditions. The latter indicated the degree to which intellectuals were now concerned about their own role in the economic crisis.

The centerpiece of "Marxism and Social Change" was a lengthy debate between Eastman and Hook on several key issues of Marxist philosophy. This debate had been initiated in the pages of the *Quarterly* in 1928 when Hook reviewed Eastman's *Marx and Lenin: The Science of Revolution* and announced that Eastman had "bungled a great theme."[8] Eastman argued that the Marxist dialectic was tainted with the residues of Hegelian "animism," which projected human purposes onto historical processes and developments. The dialectic with its trappings of Hegelian metaphysics was a "disguised religion," a form of "wish fulfillment" that saw class struggle not as a dynamic that made revolutionary ends possible, but as a sweeping historical process by which these ends (a successful proletarian revolution) were inevitably produced. Eastman believed that Marx's discovery of the class struggle was as important as Darwin's breakthroughs. But he also felt that the scientific elements in Marx's thinking had to be separated from the religious. Eastman claimed that Lenin had in fact done precisely this, "rescuing" Marxism from metaphysics and transforming it into a modern engineering science. Yet, Leninism notwithstanding, most Marxists continued to labor under the antiquated Hegelian elements in Marxist philosophy.[9]

Eastman's view of historical materialism as the "animistic personification of history" was vigorously opposed by Hook. In his review, Hook countered with his own notion of Marx's philosophy of praxis and transformation. He stressed that dialectical materialism was a scientific method and that Marx viewed the mind as the instrument of social action. Marx was not a fatalist who believed in the inevitability of socialism independent of human activity. Rather, he was a voluntarist who underscored human purposes, however much they might be contained or delimited by objective conditions. The dialectic involved neither animism nor mysticism, but was a necessary element of all thinking where class conflict, human action, and history were involved.[10]

Hence, for Hook, Marxism could very nearly be made compatible with modern instrumental pragmatism. But Eastman also subscribed to the philosophy of pragmatism (like Hook he was a student of Dewey), and he was convinced that traditional Marxist philosophy could not ultimately be squared with modern science. Thus the two exponents of American pragmatism created a storm of debate regarding the instrumental efficacy of Marxism, and the winter 1928 issue of the *Modern Quarterly* featured a "controversy" between Hook and Eastman. The titles of the pieces indicate the splenetic tone the debate had already taken on: "As to Sidney Hook's Morals" and "As to Max Eastman's Mentality." From this tone of rancor the debates unfortunately intensified into virulence, venom, and out-and-out character assassination as the two men raged at each other in the pages of the *Quarterly* over the course of the next five years.[11] At any rate, the symposium on "Marxism and Social Change" revolved around the Hook–Eastman debate and implicitly addressed the question: is Marxism a viable philosophy in the new age of science, and can it be reconciled to the spirit of American pragmatism?

Recognizing the importance of John Dewey in any discussion of an American reception of Marx, Calverton led off the symposium with Dewey himself. Conceding that his knowledge of Marxist philosophy was limited, Dewey nonetheless criticized those who "correctly or incorrectly" interpreted Marxism as an automatic working of historical forces. Such an interpretation saw the past, rather than human volition, as the agency in shaping the present. It reduced history from an active mode of understanding and acting upon the present to a passive accomplice of the policy of drift. Nevertheless Dewey implied that Marxism might be seen in a more "instrumental" light, which stressed consequences and ends, that indeed there was much in the theory of Marx, "which is of immense significance in the analysis and understanding of the present, of the conditions that make it what it is, and that suggest the direction that human desire, purpose, and sustained effort should take."[12]

Dewey obviously rejected interpretations of Marxism that stressed its Hegelian-inspired teleology, thus implicitly supporting Eastman's position. Yet he also implied that Marxism might be seen as an instrumental mode of thought that could enable effective action and bring about positive social change, a position resembling Hook's. Dewey's response to Marxism was a complex one, true to the American pragmatic vein in which any essential "truth" or "falsity" of a set of ideas is less important than the way they were "read" and acted upon. Given this complexity, it is not surprising his students could take differing positions regarding the dialectic.

Eastman and Hook followed, each reiterating his respective position. "In Marx," Eastman contended, "the Hegelian metaphysician was domi-

nant over the scientist; in Lenin, the scientific thinker gained the victory."
Nevertheless Marxism as a philosophy lacked the skeptical disposition of
contemporary science; dialectical materialism was "the last cold shred of
religious consolation."[13] For Hook, on the other hand, Marx's contention
that "men make their own histories" was pivotal in understanding the
dialectic. Certainly men made their histories within certain conditioning
limits of society and culture, yet Marxism was not a scheme of historical
fatalism or a Hegelian metaphysical system. Marxism was a method, and a
scientific one at that, an instrumental means toward a revolutionary end.[14]

A general discussion ensued and there was unanimous agreement with
Hook's position. The sociologist Arthur W. Calhoun defended Marxism's
claim to scientific validity, while Louis Boudin characterized Eastman's
talk of modern science and engineering as "Hooverized jargon." Waldo
Frank further claimed (in characteristically organic terms) that, contrary
to Eastman, the "dynamism of Lenin as an Engineer lies precisely in
his being nurtured by the *Weltanschauung* of Marx, his intuition of life
as organism *with an internal direction*."[15] That the participants sided with
Hook suggests less about the relative merits of the theoretical positions
in the Hook–Eastman debate than it does about the urgent sense of the
relevance of Marx's philosophy and the pressing nature of the debate
over Marxist dialectic. For two years after its inception, the question raged
in the general intellectual community indicating a belief in the scientific
status of Marxism and its relevance to contemporary social ills.

The *Quarterly*'s other symposium, "A Challenge to American Intellectuals" (Winter 1930–31), also indicates a shift of emphasis. A provocative
debate between Lewis Mumford and Calverton, the symposium was crucial, for it concerned the role the intellectual should play in radical social
change. It represented the tensions between Mumford's "evolutionary"
radicalism that stressed communitarianism (a legacy of prewar socialism)
and Calverton's secular political radicalism, now emerging as a dominant
stance of literary radicals.

Mumford contended that revolution in the United States was unlikely
and probably undesirable. Unlike Russia in 1917, America was a highly
complex industrial society, and the revolutionary disruption of its industrial base could amount to irreparable disaster. Mumford therefore contended (along the lines he developed in *The Golden Day*) that the intellectual should preserve general cultural values that included an opposition
to bourgeois society with its conspicuous waste and materialistic values.
Meanwhile society would be fundamentally changed, in a gradualistic
fashion, by "the control of an industry, the socialization of a municipal
utility, the nationalization of a resource, the planning of great public
works." Individual and social regeneration are integrally related, Mum-

ford averred, and looked to Thoreau as a figure who embodied individual values that would serve to renew culture. To keep alive Thoreau's ideal of the "whole human life," which opposes the extravagance and waste of capitalism, would provide guidelines for a more humane society of the future and would stress the need for "the good life," for a reorientation of American values rather than for sweeping political solutions.[16]

Calverton countered that Mumford's liberal values and his concern for the individual's quest for the "good life" were deeply ideological. "It is futile to talk about the 'good life'—unless it be for philosophers, literati, professors, and the upper class in general—until we have revolutionized the control of society so that the good life is attainable by all." Wresting power from the bourgeoisie would necessarily be accomplished by force, and the intellectual would inevitably be drawn into the struggle. The intellectual's task therefore was to analyze the class nature of society rigorously and to align with the working class in upholding pressing revolutionary ideals rather than liberalism's vague notions of "ultimate" cultural values. The domain of the intellectual was to be the realities of contemporary America—"class struggle, class exploitation, class suppression."[17]

Although Mumford argued for social cohesion through a humane regard for tradition and environment, Calverton's depiction of him as merely liberal was clearly reductive. Mumford's notion of "organicism," which sought a reconciliation of the individual and the domains of civic life and culture was more complex than Calverton acknowledged.[18] Nevertheless Calverton was correct in pointing out that Mumford's "evolutionary" approach to social change lacked any analysis of power relations and class struggle and that Mumford's position was politically uncommitted. And herein lay the crux for Calverton, broadly humanistic values could no longer be class neutral. Literary arguments were now to be seen as ideological manifestations of class conflict, and the intellectual could not remain uncommitted.

Calverton's position in the debate announced the *Quarterly*'s change of direction with a new focus on ideological and class realities. Indeed, this issue of the *Quarterly* registered a sharp change in mood among radicals not only in the Calverton–Mumford exchange but in Hook's attack on Frank and "The Non-Sense of the Whole," a review of Frank's *Rediscovery of America*.[19] Frank's book, a response to modernism's sundering of the medieval synthesis, advocates a return to organic culture by embracing the concept of the "whole" and by a new appreciation of group life. Hook correctly pointed out that Frank's notions were vague and mystical and that their political implications were dubious, even reactionary. But Hook's criticism of Frank also represented a criticism, by a younger generation of intellectuals, of the idealistic and optimistic "lyric" socialism of the prewar radicals. Clearly, the *Quarterly* was delineating the role of a new generation of American radical intellectuals in the new decade: as radical analysts of social conflict, as intellectuals of the revolution.

Beyond this redefinition of the intellectual's role however, the salient symposia and debates in the *Modern Quarterly* were now setting the agenda for discussion about the role of the intellectual in the economic crisis and for debate between radicals of various persuasions. From the very beginning of the decade, the *Quarterly* was raising the questions, defining the dialogue, and shaping the discourse that would persist on the American Left throughout most of the thirties.

THE *Quarterly* also set the discursive agenda and the terms of the debate concerning radical aesthetics and revolutionary art. In late 1929 the *Quarterly* became the locus of conflict between radicals and modernists over the famous "Revolution of the Word Proclamation" that appeared in the Paris-based publication *transition*. Probably the most important of the American expatriate "little" magazines of the late twenties, *transition* (edited by Eugene Jolas) came to represent for Americans at home and for a smaller number of English intellectuals all that was new in contemporary writing. Two years after its inception in 1927, the magazine numbered among its regular contributors Franz Kafka, Samuel Beckett, Hart Crane, and Gertrude Stein. But its shining light was undoubtedly James Joyce. As French critic Marcel Brion stated, *transition* was "la maison de Joyce," and indeed issue after issue was devoted to Joyce's "work in progress"—*Finnegan's Wake*—as well as explanations and defenses of the work.[20]

The provocative proclamation of *transition* was thus a defense of Joyce and by extension of literary modernism. It struck out against the conventions of realism, the "banal word" and its hegemony and denounced the artistically stifling influence of "monotonous syntax," "static psychology," and "descriptive naturalism." It defended the "autonomous and unconfined" imagination in search of the "fabulous word" and asserted that the literary creator had every right to "disintegrate the primal matter of words imposed on him by text-books and dictionaries." It renounced any interest in sociology, "except to emancipate the creative elements from the present ideology." Summing up, the statement repudiated the communicative function of literature and affirmed imaginative expression: "The writer expresses, he does not communicate."[21]

The proclamation in *transition* appeared in June 1929, and its antisociological and anticommunicative aesthetic was clearly a battle cry against Marxists. Calverton, ever the astute editor, moved with remarkable speed, for he contrived not only to devote nearly the entire issue of the fall 1929 *Modern Quarterly* to a rebuttal of the *transition* stance, but to include contributions from Eugene Jolas, Stuart Gilbert, and Robert Sage (Jolas's two advisory editors) in further defense of their position. Thus arose the *Quarterly's* "Revolution of the Word" symposium, no doubt the most vigorous and intriguing clash between literary modernists and Marxist critics to emerge during this period.

The principal standoff was between Jolas and Calverton over the contentious issue of expression versus communication. Jolas charged that photography made the tradition of realism in fiction obsolete. Furthermore, depth psychology had thrown into question what had previously been construed as "psychological realism" and demanded wholly innovative uses of the word to chart new "psychic frontiers." The writer was therefore obligated to disregard traditional syntax and grammar in the quest for expression and verbal innovation, for a language of "the instinctive or demonic nocturnal":

> We want to hammer to pieces a world conception which, philosophically and psychologically, has ceased to answer our deepest needs. . . .
> We must discover ways and means of expression in which the word reproduces the chthonian and is charged with explosive energies. . . .
> We hope to destroy the world with an apocalyptic vision.[22]

Calverton responded that if the contemporary literary artist insisted that his task was to "disintegrate the primary matter of words," then the artist unwittingly moved himself and his audience "further and further away from the synthesis of self and society that is necessary for the perpetuation of social reality." For language was essentially social; the primal matter of words was "imposed" on the writer not simply by "text-books and dictionaries," as the *transition* spokesmen insisted, but rather by the communicative nature of the artist's culture. The crux of the problem for Calverton was that the avant-garde aesthetic threatened the social function of art, its ability to unite individual and social concerns, and ultimately provided the justification for an antisocial retreat into solipsism.[23]

Calverton was by no means the only critic on the Left who was suspicious of modernist experimentation. Malcolm Cowley and Edmund Wilson, for example, also saw the literary avant-garde retreating into a world of private sensibility. Yet if Wilson in *Axel's Castle* (1931) charged that the symbolists neglected the social arena, he credited them for enlarging human perception by charting the irrational world of fantasy and dream. And Wilson, a largely sympathetic observer of European avant-gardism, was intrigued rather than disturbed by the innovations of Eliot, Joyce, and Stein. Calverton, on the other hand, drew his critical premises primarily from the social-realist aesthetic of Plekhanov (he had published several of Plekhanov's translated pieces in the early issues of the *Quarterly*), which

asserted that literature should disdain elaborate aesthetic theories and become an instrument of social development. Calverton insisted that to be
revolutionary "one must experiment with better means of communication
rather than with more muddled methods of expression, for the aim of our
age with its new logic is to clarify rather than confuse."[24]

The *Quarterly–transition* debate raged on, reaching its climax when
Harold Salemson, a defector from the *transition* camp, wrote in the *Quarterly* that Joyce and the modernist experimenters were "up against the
wall."[25] Stuart Gilbert rebutted from the *transition* camp that the "social
reality" the Marxist so fondly defended was the domain not of artists but
politicians, propagandists, and "other such practical people."[26] Finally,
when *transition* published one of Calverton's short stories, "After Dark,"
the editors placed within the story a sketch by German artist George
Grosz (who would later join the art department of the *Modern Quarterly*).
Entitled "The Little Agitator" it depicts an explosive little man wielding
a rattle, truncheon, sheathed sword, and bullhorn heckling an audience
equally grotesque.[27] The strategic implications of placing such a sketch in
the middle of Calverton's story were obvious: the editors of *transition* considered the writer of "After Dark" to be an ideologue and a propagandist.

Although the *Quarterly–transition* debate ended less than productively,
it sheds light on the arguments between Marxists and modernists in the
thirties. First, it suggests that both Marxists and modernists, lacking a
language-based model of the literary text, were similarly limited in their
formulations of the nature and function of literature. For both groups
language was mere "medium": for the modernists a medium of vision, for
the Marxists a medium of social information. Neither group addressed
the way ideology and the "demonic nocturnal" of unconscious impulse
converged on the terrain of language; neither group grasped the potential of the literary text to disrupt, reproduce, or recode ideology. These
issues, however, would not be widely addressed in critical discourse for
some decades. Yet the debate might have gone beyond the extraordinarily
limited poles of expression and communication had the two groups been
familiar with the Russian formalists. The modernists might have then
understood (as Bertolt Brecht did) that their own linguistic project of
"making strange" had political implications that went beyond the artist's
need for expression. And for American Marxists like Calverton, Russian
formalism would have revealed the simplistic nature of the notion of art
as mere communication, as reflection of social experience. Calverton was
correct in pointing out that *transition*'s modernist impulse was to transcend
the social world completely, to create a disembodied vision that owed little
to existing reality. Yet had he read the Russian formalists he might have
been less a dogged antimodernist in his criticism, might have understood

that a revolution in poetic language had a role to play in social revolution as well.

Besides being less than informed, Calverton's antimodernism was, in terms of his own fiction, contradictory. Ironically, even as he battled with the *transition* group over aesthetic principles, his story published in *transition*, "After Dark"—morbid in its preoccupation with private sensibility and its obsession with death—ran counter to the socially oriented critical premises he defended. An earlier story he published in the *Modern Quarterly* entitled "The Undertaker," a study of necrophilia, resulted in the suppression of the November–February 1926–27 issue of the magazine by the U.S. Post Office.[28] And the 1928 trilogy, *Three Strange Lovers*, explored modernist devices such as the distorting lens of the obsessional narrator and shared with the modernists a concern with unconscious impulse.

The contradiction between his role as fiction writer and scientific Marxist was, as already indicated, an unresolvable tension in Calverton's life. His concern with the irrational, springing from his own private obsessions, ran counter to his impulses toward a radical analysis of society, and the concerns of his novels and his social criticism remained separate and compartmentalized. Later in the decade he would write a novel exploring the fear of death and its implications for socialism, yet his attempt to bring together the two worlds of private obsession and social concern would result in a novel whose form was utterly conventional and whose social ideas were dubious. At this point Calverton must have felt the inconsistency between his fiction and criticism, as well as the inadequacy of his own critical position. In fact, shortly after the "Revolution of the Word" symposium, he wrote Scott Nearing with a proposal to set up "a self supporting monthly emphasizing revolution in the arts," based on the French publication *Monde* and using half of *Monde*'s articles in every issue.[29] Perhaps Calverton, the free-lance intellectual, always desiring to be in the thick of things, wanted to lay claim to yet another strain in the current discussion. Yet his interest in the new publication suggests that he felt a need to explore modernist ideas further. Particularly revealing is that he wanted to keep the two matters, revolution in politics and in the arts, bifurcated and compartmentalized in two separate journals.

Calverton's predicament, underscored by the debate with *transition*, also indicated the larger dilemma of the American left-wing critic during the thirties. The ideal of a rich interweaving of radical politics and advanced or modern art, heritage of the Village Left, faded as the twenties wore on. Psychoanalysis, a major expression of modernism among radicals in the twenties, had succumbed, by the end of the decade, to ideological onslaughts. There existed no theoretical terrain on which to reconcile the revolution in language with a revolution in society. There were radicals on the American scene like William Phillips and Philip Rahv who, deeply steeped in European cosmopolitanism, later came to realize that modernists were often crippled by their failure to understand Marxism, while radical critics were equally limited by their failure to understand modernism. But at this point in the early thirties Rahv's and Phillip's efforts to link modernism and Marxism had yet to begin; in these early years of Marxist enthusiasm, even Rahv denounced bourgeois writers and proclaimed himself "an intellectual assistant of the proletariat." [30] The *Modern Quarterly*'s debate with the *transition* group in the late twenties, then, was important not only for setting the terms of the debate between Marxists and modernists, but for revealing the respective limitations of the two positions. The debate suggests why a Marxist like Calverton, encountering the limits of his critical premises, was driven back toward traditional artistic forms. This accounts at least in part for the fact that like other radical critics of the thirties, he found himself exploring the past, driven toward a quest for a "usable" American literary tradition.

THERE were other reasons for the search for tradition on the American Left, such as radicals' desire to find a sense of order and identity through shared values. The discovery and perpetuation of a "usable past" based on collective values was a pressing issue in the larger concern of forging a new American literary tradition, indeed of Americanizing Marx. "It seems to me," John Dos Passos wrote in the *Modern Quarterly* in 1932, "that Marxians who attempt to junk the American tradition, that I admit is full of dry rot as well as sap like any tradition, are just cutting themselves off from the continent. Somebody's got to have the size to Marxianize the American tradition or else Americanize Marx." [31] Calverton agreed: "There should be a concerted effort on the part of the left wing group to find itself in terms of the American scene." He added that "we do need a tradition, but it must be a new tradition in consonance with a new age. The task that confronts us is to establish that tradition." [32]

Contemplating the task of discovering a collective radical identity and establishing a radical tradition, Calverton assessed the major critical movements of the new decade and concluded that all were searching for direction. The New Humanism, the new regionalism, and the emerging proletarianism all rejected the individualism, the cultivation of cynicism (evident in Mencken), and the contempt for tradition that reached its peak in the twenties. As disparate as these movements were in their assumptions and social values, all three demonstrated what Calverton called "the desire for tradition."

Yet he held that the new regionalism of the Southern Agrarians (gathered around the *Fugitive*) displayed a rural utopianism and reactionary economics. He dismissed as anachronistic *I'll Take My Stand* (1930), a symposium by twelve southern intellectuals (including Allen Tate, John Crowe Ransom, Robert Penn Warren, and Donald Davidson), which denounced the mechanistic fragmentation of contemporary capitalism and proposed as an alternative a southern agrarian life of harmony and community. If the Southern Agrarians' program was obsolete, the New Humanists were simply "reactionary to the core": their standards of good taste, gentlemanliness, reticence, and the "inner check" reflected leisure-class ideals. The proletarian movement, however, embraced both the agrarian and humanist critique of America's social and cultural fragmentation, while linking this issue to a historically progressive ideology. Humanism's polar opposite, the proletarian movement, was collectivistic rather than individualistic; it was materialistic rather than religious, and it looked to a revolutionary transformation of American society. Within the proletarian movement the best possibilities existed for rediscovering an American tradition relevant to the new decade of convictions and for formulating a Marxist literary criticism for America.[33]

The nature of radical literature and criticism was hotly debated in the early thirties. The "Literary Class War," as Edmund Wilson called it, was sparked by Mike Gold's famous 1930 attack on the novelist and playwright Thornton Wilder. Wilder's Victorianism outraged Gold and provoked an audacious article in the *New Republic* entitled "Thornton Wilder, Prophet of the Genteel Christ." For Gold, Wilder's works willfully ignored the realities of American life: "Where are the child slaves of the beet field? Where are the stockbrokers' suicides, the labor racketeers or the passion and death of the coal miners?" Wilder's works, declared the hardboiled proletarian critic, functioned as an escape into "that newly fashioned literary religion that centers around Jesus Christ, the First British Gentleman."[34] Gold's attack on Wilder polarized opinion and evoked an outpouring of critical response; as Edmund Wilson noted, "The people who applauded Gold seemed to be moved by a strange animus; those who defended Wilder pleaded or protested in tones of persons who had seen a dearly beloved thing desecrated."[35]

Wilson, then literary editor of the *New Republic*, agreed that Wilder's books served as a sedative for sick Americans but he criticized Gold's appraisal of Wilder for neglecting the issue of craftsmanship. Issues of craftsmanship and literary form should be of the utmost importance to the Communist critic, Wilson asserted, since ignoring them was, in effect, "denying the dignity of human work for the purpose of political propaganda."[36] No such measured criticism came from the *Nation*; its literary editor, the cultural conservative Henry Hazlitt, characterized Gold's critical standards as "ridiculously narrow" and denounced his "communist criticism," which "hoots or hails a work of art in proportion as its seems to oppose, ignore, or support the opinion of a German economist who died in 1883." [37]

Calverton entered the controversy in one of the chapbooks published in 1931 by the University of Washington. In his extended essay entitled *American Literature at the Crossroads*, he asserted that Gold's position, correct in principle, reflected the general immaturity of Marxist criticism in America. Gold's criticism unfortunately shared some of the same limitations as humanist criticism: it was essentially moral albeit with a social emphasis. Yet Gold's failures, particularly his neglect of issues relating to form and craftsmanship, were not sufficient to constitute an indictment of Marxist criticism. Plekhanov, Franz Mehring, and Trotsky had used the Marxist method with precision, paying close attention to both formal excellence and social significance. Calverton similarly advised American Marxist critics to evaluate works of art both in terms of craftsmanship or formal organization and in terms of the social purpose they serve: "Revolutionary criticism departs from reactionary criticism not in its disregard for form, *but in its stress upon* the end that form should serve." [38]

Calverton was correct in arguing that the great theoreticians of Marxism had not ignored the issue of form in a dogged pursuit of political content. Yet his simplistic notion of form as an artifice that is imposed upon content and serves a particular political end overlooked Trotsky's contention that form and content existed in a dialectical relation, that changes of form result from significant changes in ideology. Nevertheless Calverton's theoretical limitations were no greater than his adversaries', and the debate that emerged—particularly the ensuing exchange between Calverton and Henry Hazlitt—remained limited by this static notion of the relation between form and content.

Seizing the opportunity to bring another controversy into his magazine, Calverton featured two essays in the winter 1931–32 *Quarterly*: "Art and Social Change: The Eclectic Approach" by Hazlitt and his own "Art and Social Change: The Radical Approach." In an earlier editorial in the *Nation* on the Gold–Wilder dispute, Hazlitt had written that "no one of sense withholds his estimate of Joyce as a novelist until he learns his ideas on socially necessary labor time or the five-year plan." [39] Hazlitt now reiterated that the work of art, an end in itself, needs no social justification and that critical evaluations based solely on alleged class differences result in "absurdities of judgment." [40] Calverton, on the other hand, contended that art is always bound up with society and that literary values are inevitably the product of groups, not individuals. The prevailing cultural values at any given time are determined largely by the period's dominant social classes: "To understand the morality of art of a community . . .

necessitates a study of the classes that constitute it, especially the ruling class."[41] Hence moral values could not be dissociated from certain ideological values, and certain types of humanist criticism had used literature to further a moral position that implied a particular (conservative) form of politics. In any case, Calverton argued, criticism itself could never be objective, could never be wholly detached from moral and political issues as Hazlitt insisted it could.

This led Calverton to a startling new turn in the discussion. Developing a point he had only touched upon in the *Newer Spirit*, he asserted that criticism is not an innocent discipline and never has been. Criticism is subject to the same ideological structures as art in a given society. The critic is never a free agent, and critical objectivity always conceals class allegiances: "Consciously or unconsciously the critical position one adopts inevitably reflects the cultural attitude and conception of a social class."[42] The aesthetic philosophy of literary liberalism is based on an Olympian disinterestedness, yet such "disinterestedness" is itself ideological in nature and expresses the interests of the status quo—the leisure-class philosophy of the upper middle class. Calverton charged that Hazlitt, subscribing to the aesthetic philosophy of literary liberalism, could not see that critical debate and criticism itself are ideological manifestations of class conflict: Hazlitt's "above the battle" aesthetic was "blind to its own class allegiances."[43]

Calverton further asserted that the literary liberal's cherished notion of critical objectivity is accompanied by another myth—that of art as a purely personal form of expression transcending class ideology. But both criticism and art reveal, however unconsciously, the ideological values or "cultural compulsives" of a particular class and thus are in a certain sense propagandistic. The very term "propaganda" implies a distinction between political and nonpolitical forms of criticism and art, and clearly such a distinction is false. Thus the proletarian critic, unlike the liberal critic, readily admits his own political interests and is attentive to the social function and class assumptions of a work of art. Yet while the proletarianist understands that all art is ultimately propagandistic in the broadest ideological sense, such a critic does not neglect to consider the formal elements without which art becomes "propaganda" in the narrowest and worst sense. Calverton unfortunately expressed this notion rather crudely: "What we want to fight today is not propaganda in art, but bad propagandists who ruin art."[44]

Calverton's suggestion that all art is in a certain sense propagandistic and that all criticism is ultimately political brought an enthusiastic endorsement from Granville Hicks and Newton Arvin who leapt into the argument in the summer of 1932. Hicks claimed that social philosophy in criticism was a strength rather than a weakness (thus exonerating Gold's brand of proletarian criticism). Arvin agreed that Hazlitt's art and propaganda dichotomy was a false one, and if the individualist critics called the expression of Marxist insights in literature "propagandistic," then "the sooner our letters turn propagandistic the better."[45] As this uncritical equation between art and propaganda suggests, these responses demonstrated more radical enthusiasm than intellectual rigor, and the debate itself was not without its crudities and oversimplifications. Hazlitt's notion of the relation between literature and society was glib and unthoughtful, and Calverton was unable to overcome the bifurcation between idea and execution in the text. Their discussions reveal an absence of any notion of literature as a particular organization of language with its own laws, structures, and devices. If their debates about the nature of literature and art indicate an inadequate understanding of the relation between ideology and propaganda, and between society and the text's own relatively autonomous life, they also indicate an undeveloped theoretical awareness of the complex relationship between economic base and cultural superstructure and of the text as mediating between these two realms.

Nevertheless, the debate is important, first and most obviously, because it suggests that by the summer of 1932 (when Arvin and Hicks joined the argument) Calverton's *Modern Quarterly* had become a major forum for debate on revolutionary art and radical criticism. The debate is also significant because it went beyond the crudities of Gold's attack on Wilder and raised important questions about literary theory and the radical intellectual. Calverton was astute and innovative—particularly during these early years of the thirties when critical pronouncements (like Gold's) were theoretically unformed and doctrinaire—in suggesting that the critical act itself takes place within a set of ideological formulations, that criticism does not arise spontaneously and is not "transparent." Moreover, the debate was significant because it gave criticism a new and vital importance, positing it as a way of formulating a countermorality for an American tradition in which capitalist and liberal values had achieved hegemony. Criticism was now viewed as the chief means by which the radical could not only oppose capitalist culture but revitalize and radicalize the American literary tradition.

Calverton elaborated on the nature of a radical criticism and its place in the American tradition in several essays during the early thirties including the chapbook, *The New Ground of Criticism* (1930). During the late twenties he had concluded that a new science of psychosociology was needed to bridge the gap between psychology and radical politics. Now, pointing to the synthesizing studies of Briffault and Malinowski, he urged that interdisciplinary methods be applied to critical analysis. The "new ground of criticism" would be broken by the critic who constructed an analysis on a thorough understanding of a work's social and economic background and the ideological factors that shaped the author's point of view.[46] Yet formal and structural elements were also important in any consideration of a literary work. Here Calverton made the distinction between Marxist *criticism* of literature and Marxist *interpretation* of literature. The former analyzes the work in terms of its style, structure, and design in relation to its social vision, while the latter merely stresses the social outlook and implied class convictions of a work. He concluded that most radical criticism in the United States unfortunately fell into the latter category: a narrow interpretation of the work in terms of social background and class rather than a broader synthesizing criticism of the work's formal elements in relation to its social determinants.[47]

Calverton's call for a synthesizing Marxist criticism of literature as opposed to a mechanical and limited interpretation is significant. It stressed the need to recognize that the logic of content is ultimately social and historical in character, that there is a dialectical relation between art and history that overcomes the dichotomy between the work and its background. Moreover, his call constitutes a criticism of Marxist literary theory as then practiced in the United States. In spite of his own critical shortcomings, he recognized the need for American radical critics to go beyond the simplistic categories they were accustomed to using.

Calverton further argued that American radical criticism often overlooked its relation to an indigenous radical literary tradition and attempted to impose an alien tradition on the American writer. But proletarian literature, strictly speaking, was as yet a theoretical impossibility in the United States. He criticized Trotsky's wholesale rejection of the notion of proletarian literature (Trotsky insisted a revolutionary literature, strictly speaking, must be "classless") and sided with Lunacharsky's idea of an emerging proletarian culture.[48] Nevertheless, he insisted that as yet no proletarian ideology had taken root in America and American writers were unaccustomed to thinking in terms of class and ideology. Thus Marxist critics who demanded that the American writer conform to rigid formulae and preconceived models were profoundly unMarxist in their approach. In fact, given a culture that had been until recently "overwhelmingly bourgeois," it was "nothing short of absurdity to expect a proletarian literature to spontaneously crop up and multiply."[49]

Because proletarian literature in the strict sense of the definition—a literature emerging from a rigorous working-class ideology, or a literature written by workers about workers—was not presently possible in the United States, Calverton made a distinction between proletarian and "revolutionary" literature. Revolutionary literature, which sympathized with the viewpoint of the working class and espoused anticapitalist values, was not only a distinct possibility in the United States, but was already beginning to emerge in the socially conscious new decade. A proletarian literature would develop later when the working class itself arrived at a mature level of consciousness. In the meantime, a revolutionary literature that identified and depicted the dilemmas and aspirations of the working class would function to prepare the way for a fully developed proletarian literature of the future.[50]

Calverton therefore disagreed fundamentally with literary radicals who expected American writers to immediately produce a proletarian literature. Rather than holding such unrealistic expectations, the radical critic should foster literature that exhibited a general socialist value system. Meanwhile, radical criticism should not only shed light on the ideological nature of literature and art but reveal the ideological and class bias of criticism itself. Criticism would then become an instrument for class and social analysis and finally for creating the values of a revolutionary culture.

Calverton's conception of the revolutionary literature of the future was squarely in line with a social-realist aesthetic; he favored older, naturalistic, realistic, and even "epic" genres over contemporary modernist and experimental forms. Again, this suggests his limited antimodern bias. Nevertheless his notion of the development of revolutionary, as opposed to a formulaic proletarian literature, set him apart from those who saw the critic as a soldier, or perhaps more accurately, as a strategist, allied with the artist in a class war. His notion of the critic's crucial role in building a revolutionary culture stressed the need not merely to embrace tradition but to reshape and transform it. As he argued in his 1931 chapbook *American Literature at the Crossroads*, radical criticism embraced revolutionary values while exhibiting a "desire for tradition."[51] Yet tradition would not be considered immutable, but would be constituted in a dialectical process leading to liberation in the social and cultural realm. For Calverton, finding and isolating strands in the American tradition that might be appropriated by radicals was coextensive with Marxianizing that tradition, of forging the tradition of the future in a radical direction.

Calverton's search for and redefinition of American tradition was his primary project during the early thirties. His 1931 study, *American Literature at the Crossroads*, was followed one year later by his most ambitious book, *The Liberation of American Literature*, a work Walter Rideout has characterized as "the first of the very few whole books in the thirties attempting a Marxist analysis of literature."[52]

AFTER looking at the preliminary chapters of the *Liberation of American Literature*, Maxwell Perkins of Charles Scribner's Sons observed, "The great opportunity for the book is that it formulates ideas and feelings which are generally, but vaguely felt—that it sets the course for Americans which many of them are stumbling to find."[53] The book was in fact based on the premise that the literary radicals of the present belonged to the main tradition of American letters. "They are not outsiders clamoring for entrance into the literary field, but are already intrinsic parts of it," Calverton insisted, pointing to writers such as Theodore Dreiser, Edmund Wilson, Newton Arvin, Granville Hicks, Malcolm Cowley, Waldo Frank, and Lionel Trilling.[54]

The *Liberation of American Literature* thus takes up John Dos Passos's suggestion regarding the need to Marxianize the American tradition. Yet the work is nonetheless modest in its claims for critical analysis. Clearly the work falls short of the properly Marxist criticism for which Calverton had earlier called—a criticism that explores the relation between aesthetic and ideological factors. Rather, the study might more accurately be described (according to Calverton's categories) as "Marxist interpretation" with its concern for social and historical issues as distinct from aesthetic considerations. By his own admission, his work "does not fall as closely into the category of literary criticism as social history." Calverton frankly acknowledges the infantile state of Marxist criticism in America[55] and calls his book "spade work," which attempts to put criticism on a "secure social basis," recognizing that aesthetic criticism is "fundamentally social in character." He explicitly sets out "to interpret American literature in terms of American culture. . . . It is only by an appreciation of the class psychologies dominant at the time, as Marx has shown, that we can understand the nature of a culture or the direction and trend of a literature."[56]

Calverton theorizes that historically the American writer has labored under a double bondage: that of a sense of cultural inferiority, a "colonial complex," and a continuing petty-bourgeois insensitivity to artistic values reinforced by a legacy of puritan hostility toward art. The first was manifest especially in the nineteenth century: writers as diverse as Bryant, Cooper, and Hawthorne labored under the weight of the colonial complex, which prevented them from discovering their national identity. Like Hawthorne, they may have treated American themes, but their forms and styles were derived from Europe. At the same time the ideals of a petty-bourgeois individualism were at work countering this European influence. Calverton draws on Frederick Jackson Turner's frontier thesis and argues that the American frontier enabled petty-bourgeois individualism to gain a foothold in the United States that it never held in any other country. This individualism began to express itself in Thoreau, Whitman, and Emerson (whom Calverton refers to as the "prophet of the petty bourgeoisie"). These writers established a "spirit of revolt" against the increasing mechanization and industrial alienation that came with the rise of the wealthy upper bourgeoisie. They thus provided, Calverton suggests, an incipient tradition upon which radicals might draw. Furthermore, this individualistic spirit that manifested itself particularly in writers like Artemus Ward, Whitman, and Twain—writers who consciously broke from the European tradition—helped America escape from the colonial complex and find its own new and distinctive idiom.[57]

America eventually freed itself completely from the colonial complex when it became an economic equal of the parent country at about the time of the Spanish–American War, a period that marked America's achievement of imperial power and a new phase of capitalist growth. Yet with the emergence of a corporate economy, the individualistic ethos of the petty bourgeoisie began to crumble. As a result gloom and despair became the dominant note in writers like Edwin Arlington Robinson, Dreiser, O'Neill, and Hemingway. Calverton sees the American writer facing a radical crisis in culture occasioned by the collapse of the very individualistic values that enabled national identity to emerge. Now liberated from the colonial complex, American writers have no viable chart to interpret the world unless they ally themselves with an incipient proletarian tradition just becoming visible in the United States. This emerging proletarian tradition might be nurtured and reinforced by the spirit of revolt and faith in the common man that emerged in nineteenth-century American letters and is now a part of the American literary heritage. Thus the classic American writers could be appropriated to further a proletarian revolution. What was needed was a sense of a new historical moment in which once progressive individualistic values would now be transformed into socialist and collectivist values:

> The faith in the common man which Emerson and Whitman entertained was faith in him as an individual and not as a mass. . . . In that sense, their faith was founded on a false premise; fitting and persuasive enough in their generation it led only to disaster in the next. . . . Their belief in the common man was a belief in him as a petty bourgeois individualist; our belief must be in him as proletarian collectivist. In that belief lies the ultimate liberation of American literature—and American life.[58]

Calverton identified writers who presently allied themselves with this new proletarian collectivism—heir of the American tradition of individualistic revolt and harbinger of "ultimate liberation"—as John Dos Passos, Michael Gold, and Charles Yale Harrison.

Certainly Calverton's terms, his emphasis on "faith" and "belief" mark his study as a product of the "decade of convictions." Yet unlike the mechanistic determinism of his first critical work, *The Newer Spirit*, *Liberation* contains a dialectical thrust, a sense that ideology is a product of a particular historical moment, that ideas once progressive can now be seen to be historically limited, but can also serve as a starting point for new speculation on a higher level. Another dialectical aspect of the book is the conjunction of the disparate political perspectives of Marxism and progressivism, its attempt to formulate a Marxist methodology while drawing on an American "usable past," particularly an American liberal tradition. Indeed, Calverton's book was profoundly influenced by Vernon L. Parrington's three-volume work, *Main Currents in American Thought* (1927–1930), as well as by Van Wyck Brooks's earlier study, *America's Coming-of-Age*. All three looked for a new and vital literary tradition; all searched for a usable past by which to praise certain writers and reject others. All three propounded the general themes that the American environment had crippled its writers in various ways and that in order to revitalize a stagnant culture art should function as a social force drawing on the present state of revolt. Calverton's book especially resembled Parrington's in its encyclopedic sweep, in its tendency to dismiss certain writers and ignore others, and in its propensity to deal with social history at the expense of aesthetic considerations or considered analyses of individual works.

Calverton shares with Parrington a deep intellectual affinity with progressive historiography with its commitment to progress, its tendency to trace a lineage of historical figures who struggled against reactionary forces for a future of greater democracy, and its impulse to unmask the material roots of cultural conflict in politics, economics, and class struggle. Calverton's effort to formulate a Marxist literary heritage for America stands as a hybrid affair, a conjoining of progressive historiography with the eschatology of a Marxist revolutionary. The relationship between progressivism and the eschatological vision of Marxism in the study is an uneasy one, yet clearly Calverton was searching for a way in which to ground a revolutionary impetus in the American tradition, and by extension, a way to achieve revolutionary consciousness in America.

In a review of the *Liberation of American Literature*, John Chamberlain criticized the influence of progressivism on the book, arguing that Calverton's Marxist terminology could be equated with the Jeffersonian icons of Parrington's works. "Alter the phraseology of *The Liberation of American Literature*," Chamberlain wrote, "discount the final chapter as an elaboration of a wish fulfillment—and you have a book that is as American as *Main Currents in American Thought*." [59]

Chamberlain's charge that the conclusion of Calverton's study falls into the category of wish fulfillment seems just, especially with regard to Calverton's claims that the writings of John Dos Passos, Michael Gold, and Charles Yale Harrison evidenced an emerging proletarian tradition. [60]

Yet his implication that Calverton is a liberal clothed in Marxist rhetoric is overly simplistic. For Calverton's study differs from Parrington's in one essential respect: Parrington put his faith in the liberal motivation of the individual, while Calverton saw the future of American letters in class terms, in the liberation from class domination that only a revolution could bring about.[61] Calverton's study also constitutes a diagnosis of the past and a program for the future that is linked indissolubly with a revolutionary impetus and the developing consciousness of the proletariat itself.[62]

In this sense then, Calverton's was a pioneering Marxist treatment of the history of American literature. And it was, in general, enthusiastically received. The historian Charles Beard disagreed with its "communist thesis," yet praised its astute historical analysis; Newton Arvin disagreed with Calverton's theory of the colonial complex, yet he was struck with the skill with which Calverton handled his materials. Even the pundit of communist criticism, Granville Hicks, was impressed. Although the study was "crude and incomplete," no other book in American criticism had given such intensive consideration to the development of American culture from a Marxist point of view.[63]

If Calverton's work was "crude" in Hicks's estimation, Hicks nevertheless benefited enormously from Calverton's "spade work." Within a year after Calverton's work appeared, he published *The Great Tradition*, which Richard Ruland calls a "sensitive rewriting of Calverton's work."[64] Yet Hicks's "sensitivity" in handling the themes Calverton had explored earlier seems dubious: Calverton's work is free of Hicks's glib and self-righteous tone, his "art as a class weapon" mentality, and his naive belief that the writer should not merely shoulder the cause but try to become a member of the proletariat. *The Great Tradition* outlined the doctrinaire critical principles of the *New Masses* with its formulaic conception of the proletarian novel and its celebration of industrial realism in writing. Calverton's work, on the other hand, eschewed formulas and remained open to new possibilities in charting a radical tradition in American letters. Rather than imposing critical precepts for a "perfect proletarian novel," Calverton believed the American writer could find impetus in his own tradition for creating a revolutionary literature. In this sense, at least, his *Liberation of American Literature* stands as a speculative and thoughtful attempt of the early thirties to "Marxianize the American tradition."

CALVERTON's impulse to Marxianize the American tradition and embrace the "main currents of American thought" also reflects as early as 1932 the decade's quest for commitment within the American experience. In his 1930 article, "The Decade of Convictions," Calverton had noted that the major American literary movements, whether conservative

Agrarians or radical proletarians, exhibited a new sense that literature should be tied to a time and place and centered in a tradition. He saw this as part of the larger search for social value, part of the quest for convictions in the new decade.[65]

Calverton's article captured the dominant note of the decade itself. Surveying the thirties retrospectively Granville Hicks comments that the young writers of the depression years were searching for some way to realize their sense of social responsibility, for a mode of action, for something "basic and real."[66] Warren Susman characterizes this impulse as a quest for "belonging and belief" in the face of social, cultural, and metaphysical uncertainty that was given impetus by the essential precariousness and instability of life during the depression.[67] Calverton's desire to embrace an American tradition suggests to some degree this need to belong and to find a center of gravity. Certainly his call in *Liberation* for a "new faith in the masses" expresses the search for belief and community in the face of isolation and uncertainty.[68]

Yet his book does not merely reflect an impulse on the Left to reenter American life and seek reconciliation through an American tradition. If, as Richard Pells has contended, radical intellectuals like Calverton sought a "philosophical rapprochement with the liberal values of their countrymen,"[69] this was done in an effort to salvage what was best in both the liberal and Marxist tradition. What seems most significant in Calverton's *Liberation of American Literature* is the narrative of liberation itself: liberation from the colonial complex, liberation from petty-bourgeois ideology. It at once suggests the heritage of the prewar intellectual Left, with its concern for how American writers might free themselves from an oppressive culture in order to change the course of history, and a newer impulse to transform tradition, to find in the shell of the past the liberating seeds of a revolutionary literature.

Calverton's notion of literary criticism as a source of cultural renewal links him not only to figures like Brooks, Mumford, and Parrington but to a Deweyan pragmatic tradition, which sees criticism as a branch of moral philosophy, or at least part of the moral life of humankind.[70] If Calverton began the decade by renouncing Mumford's alleged liberalism, his works of the period, particularly the *Liberation of American Literature*, suggest he had more in common with Mumford than he would have cared to admit. His works were influenced by a critical strain to which Mumford, Brooks, and the earlier *Seven Arts* critics belonged, a strain that insisted it was the responsibility of each generation of intellectuals to recover and reshape American history to its own purposes, to rewrite it on behalf of a better future.[71]

Yet Calverton's critical works during the early thirties exhibit an emerging radical analysis that distinguishes it from the prewar Left. His notion that cultural values are relative and ideological, an insight of anthropologists and sociologists of the time, took on a contemporary ring when he applied it to literature and criticism. His view that not only art but criticism itself is inextricably involved in ideology was novel, a surprising insight to have emerged from the thirties Left. Its inherent critical self-reflexivity looked ahead to Calverton's later theory of "cultural compulsives," which demanded that Marxism acquire a self-critical understanding of its own ideological make-up. And it looks ahead to the increasing awareness of the role of ideology that would emerge in contemporary analysis of "discourse" and culture.

Calverton's criticism in the early thirties suggests his effort to synthesize prewar ideals and current realities. It drew deeply on ideas whose roots lay in the progressive era, yet it extended them in an effort to forge more precise tools for an ideological analysis in service of revolutionary ideals. *Liberation of American Literature* represents an initial probing in the project of combining a progressive and pragmatic Americanism with Marxist analysis. Meanwhile, his *Modern Quarterly* set the agenda for debating the role of the literary artist in the economic crisis and posed questions regarding the possibility of forging a native radicalism. Ultimately such an agenda would lead to a defense of the very idea of independent radicalism. The *Quarterly* provided space for a dialogue essential not only for the sustenance of radical independence but for any effort to Americanize Marx. Yet Americanizing Marxism would pose practical difficulties and theoretical dilemmas as Calverton was later to discover. The Americanization of Marx—not to mention the idea of an independent radicalism—ran against the grain of orthodox radical opinion, particularly in 1932 as the Third Period of the Communist International reached its full momentum.

CHAPTER SEVEN

Still, who does not feel the continued poignancy in the yearning for community, which seems so widespread in our time?

—Irving Howe, *Socialism and America*, 1985

The "Literary Rotary"

By 1932 the depression had reached its nadir. Depression conditions convinced many American intellectuals that individuals would have to join together in the group if they wished to transform society. Radical intellectuals frequently denounced the individualism attributed to the American liberal tradition in general and the legacy of the twenties in particular. One aspect of this rejection of individualism was that writers of the early thirties embraced the Marxist concept of the collective and the socialist ideal of *gemeinschaft*. Drawing on the collectivist tendency of progressive thought—with the central axiom that mass society was already moving toward a collective entity in the form of industrial organization—they speculated that community would arise out of the organic relations of the industrial state, provided such a state was truly socialized. Individualism would give way to contours of industrialization in a socialist society; and out of a "collectivist economy" true community would emerge.[1] Thus many writers concluded that the individualistic ethos was obsolete. In 1932 Newton Arvin could write that "individualism, both as a social force and as a general philosophy is in an advanced state of collapse; socialism, in both senses, is even for us in America, on the horizon."[2] Similarly, for Calverton, individualism was necessarily giving way before the ideals of social commitment and the values of collectivism: the economic crisis, he concluded, had "reduced . . . individualism into a remote recollection."[3]

Calverton, profoundly influenced in his early intellectual development by the ideal of community of prewar socialist intellectuals like Bourne, now insisted that the American writer should engage in group action, not only to bring about radical social change but to provide the basis for true community. Perhaps more than any radical of his generation he endeavored to bring writers together, to establish a sense of community on the Left. In keeping with his pragmatic, open-ended, complete socialism, he believed that the Left would be strengthened by creative interchange, dialogue, and criticism within a community of writers and intellectuals. He believed it crucial to establish an intellectual and cultural collective in the midst of an indifferent and fragmented bourgeois society, to form a true community of thinkers who would conduct an ongoing critique of capitalism through symposia, books, and various group projects. Thus during his first years in New York he extended the tradition of weekly discussion groups he had already established in Baltimore and quickly became a pivotal figure in a variety of left-wing discussion and work groups.

Beyond Calverton's commitment to the idea of collectivism on the Left, he loved the sense of intellectual excitement and comradeship that the discussion and work group generated. His enthusiasm for the group, for the open-house gathering, arose in large part from very private needs. For Calverton there could never be enough friends. The gathering, the group, the literary–political soiree as an emblem of *gemeinschaft* was in part a defense against the fears of the solitary self, not the least of which was the fear of death.

Perhaps Calverton's private obsession sheds light on the appeal of the idea of community for writers on the Left in general. Many writers during this period saw community as a way of surmounting the preoccupations of the individual self. Arvin no doubt caught the prevailing mood when he asserted that men must learn to merge themselves with the group not only to bring about social change but to become more integrated personalities.[4] Yet a major strain of American radicalism stressed individual autonomy. Thus the archetypal dilemma that confronted the American radical was precisely to find some balance between individual and communal identity, between intellectual independence, on the one hand, and the claims of the group on the other.

Calverton embodied this dilemma. The primary tension he experienced during the thirties was between his ideal of fraternal community and his own deep commitment to intellectual independence. In a sense Calverton was profoundly American, seeking to reconcile his own fierce individualism with community. But this project became increasingly difficult. Christopher Lasch has pointed out that "in the absence of a mass movement, literary radicals could hope for social change only by postulating the intellectuals themselves as a kind of revolutionary 'International.'"

But, Lasch continues, this position "merely reinforced their isolation" from larger society.[5] Certainly Calverton, who saw intellectuals banded together in a community as a kind of "revolutionary international," ironically fell prey to the primary syndrome of the Left's isolation from larger society—internal conflict, sectarianism, and dogmatism. By 1932 the ideal of collectivism had become infused with a spirit of militancy and conformism that gripped the American Left during the Third Period. Thus, if collective activity held out the possibility of redemption from the fears of the lonely self, it also demanded the renunciation of individuality and intellectual autonomy.

As the dispiriting thirties wore on, with continuing financial and emotional difficulties and his growing isolation from the orthodox Left, Calverton struggled to keep alive a sense of community on the Left by forming his own group of independent radical spirits. But his groups and open-house gatherings were increasingly marginalized and shunned by orthodox radicals after Third Period hegemony enveloped the literary Left, and their status as isolated islands of fraternal spirit reflected the degree to which the ideal of community on the Left generally had succumbed to divisiveness and sectarianism. Calverton continued to be preoccupied with how the claims of the self and the group or larger movement might be reconciled, how the self might find refuge from its loneliness and its fears, how it might be supported in group activity without surrendering its uniqueness and separate identity.

AFTER his move to New York, Calverton sought to extend his reputation as an orchestrator of literary activity and to recreate an intellectual community such as the one he had engineered in Baltimore. Early in 1930 he attended the "Meeting Place," a dinner and cocktail club in Greenwich Village, founded by Max Eastman as a haunt for the New York intelligentsia and patterned after the Liberal Club, or "Polly's" (the Greenwich Village Inn operated by Paula Holladay) where prewar radicals had met. Here he became friends with Eastman, whom he had admired for many years (early in their acquaintance Calverton told Eastman of his desire to write Eastman's biography).[6] Club members included Sinclair Lewis, Theodore Dreiser, Malcolm Cowley, Gorham Munson, Art Young, John Chamberlain, Louis Adamic, and James Rorty.[7]

Calverton began inviting people from the "Meeting Place," as well as other acquaintances, to his Village apartment at 52 Morton Street. He quickly gained the reputation of being a "genius" for rounding up a miscellaneous group and for "setting the whole gang to extravagant argument."[8] In 1931 when Benjamin Stolberg and Henry Hazlitt conceived of starting a small discussion group consisting of writers and editors, they told Calverton about the plan and he took the initiative and soon organized a group that became a kind of institution.[9]

Finding more recruits among his left-leaning associates in the publishing business, Calverton would send out reminders to the group's "regulars" every month, confirming time and place. The band would usually meet at Teutonia Hall on Third Avenue at 17th Street under the Third Avenue Elevated or in a downtown restaurant such as Scheffel Hall. Friends recall that, after a good meal during which there was loud talk, joking, and gossip, the members would make their noisy exit and meet at the apartment of one of the regulars. Often the group would wind up at Calverton's studio apartment, which was lined from floor to ceiling with books. Calverton overflowed with gregariousness and warmth; he would welcome visitors into his home with a "How are you, you old horse thief!" and a devastating slap on the back. With his high forehead sloping back to unkempt black hair and his nose set prominently on his face over a well-trimmed mustache, George (as everyone called him) talked in a booming voice, while drawing on a large briar pipe, and urged the group on to conversation and argument. The talk would become more heated as the evening wore on and alcohol took effect. The guests would continue their debates, shouting at each other outside the apartment as they took their leave at about three o'clock in the morning, winding their way through the narrow Village streets to the subway.[10]

Over the months people drifted in and out of the circle. But regular group members consisted of Carleton Beals, well known for his writings on politics in Latin America; Harry Hansen, book critic for the *New York World*; Lewis Gannett, a literary columnist for the *New York Herald-Tribune*; Louis Hacker, a history professor at Columbia University; Benjamin Stolberg, a free-lance writer and student of the American labor movement; Maxim Lieber, a literary agent; Walter White, secretary of the NAACP and Calverton's close friend; Jacob Baker of Vanguard Press; Claude Cockburn, a young Englishman and New York correspondent for the London *Times*; and Louis Adamic, an immigrant from Yugoslavia who later provided an account of these gatherings in his book *My America*.[11] Robert Briffault, author of the influential anthropological study, *The Mothers*, was often at Calverton's, as was Sidney Hook, the historian Harry Elmer Barnes, the young writer Michael Blankfort, and Kyle Crichton (who later wrote a column in the *New Masses* under the name "Robert Forsythe").

The interchange among group members was lubricated with alcohol even before prohibition came to an end. Bertram Wolfe recalls Calverton's gatherings prior to Roosevelt's election as "a monthly law-breaking session to violate the Eighteenth Amendment and the Volstead Act."[12]

The group's regulars often brought guests, including Sinclair Lewis, Mike Gold, Stuart Chase, Matthew Josephson, Waldo Frank, and Granville Hicks. The group was catholic in its viewpoints, which ranged from the conservative Henry Hazlitt, financial editor of the New York *Evening Post* ("the only out-and-out capitalist in the group," Hazlitt recalls[13]), to the doctrinaire Marxism of Party member Granville Hicks, who was converted to communism at one of Calverton's gatherings.[14]

The success of these groups of such diverse constituency was in large part accountable to the complex phenomenon of V. F. Calverton. George Britt recalls that his multifaceted personality bridged the gap between men of a variety of outlooks; his sheer energy sent out rays of attraction, and his eagerness to be in the company of literary luminaries was disarming. Britt of the *New York Telegram*, himself captivated by Calverton's warmth and friendliness, was enlisted early on and recalls that "George was bound to meet and appraise and add to his list any new arrival on the horizon."[15] According to Michael Blankfort, this included young and promising writers as well as established and celebrated ones. Blankfort, a Princeton graduate who was trying to get his footing in the New York literary world, was invited by Calverton to the group and was then recruited to the *Quarterly* staff in the capacity of literary editor.[16] Similarly, Calverton invited Alfred Kazin to the gatherings, introduced him to prominent radicals, and set him to work writing book reviews for the *Quarterly*.[17]

Yet there was an overwrought, almost desperate quality in Calverton's eagerness to impress and enlist, and his ingratiating attempts to meet prominent writers and bring them into his circle were sometimes embarrassing. Britt reconstructs an incident in Lee Chumley's restaurant in the Village where a big party was given in honor of Sherwood Anderson. There was a terrific mob, more than the restaurant could hold. Someone whom Britt thought looked familiar came in, worked his way through the crowd and said, "I'm Bill Faulkner, where's Sherwood Anderson?" Britt led Faulkner through the crowd, and as they worked their way past Calverton, Calverton spotted them and yelled, "That's William Faulkner." Calverton eagerly put his hand out: "Mr. Faulkner, I'm George Calverton." But Faulkner ignored Calverton and again asked Britt, "Where's Sherwood Anderson?" Britt led Faulkner to Anderson, leaving Calverton with his hand extended.[18]

On another occasion early in 1931, Louis Adamic brought Sinclair Lewis to Calverton's Scheffel Hall gathering. Calverton sat at the same table with Lewis and was eager to talk to him. Lewis, however, mumbled to Adamic that he didn't like this bunch; he noted contemptuously that they were "highbrows," not proletarians. Finally Lewis's gaze fixed itself on Calverton who had recently written an article entitled "Sinclair Lewis—

Babbitt" for the *Literary Review*. Lewis looked straight at Calverton. "So I am a Babbitt, am I?" he asked. Calverton attempted to laugh it off, unsuccessfully, according to Adamic's recollection of the incident, while "Red" Lewis's "eyes burned holes into him."[19]

A fascinating assemblage of contraries, Calverton was clearly driven by complex, deep-seated needs to meet and fraternize with others. He was both a communitarian idealist who sought on one level to form groups of writers, and on another an archindividualist and pragmatist, opportunistically practising his art of celebrity hunting and literary "contactmanship." He was absolutely shameless in his pursuit of "contacts," single-minded in aggrandizing his own reputation and that of his magazine. Such characteristics made some conclude that he was an "ideological racketeer." Yet his opportunism was unassuming, above-board, and open, and his warmth and extraordinary capacity for friendship overshadowed his politics of contactmanship. Hazlitt observed that Calverton never broke off any friendship over political differences. On the contrary, he attempted to bring those who were of different ideological persuasions into his group, and he was friendly to a fault to those who had attacked him in print.[20]

Certainly the fact that Calverton pursued, wooed, and maintained an enormous correspondence with his generation of writers accounts largely for the fertile diversity of contributors to the *Quarterly*, as well as its non-dogmatic character and the intellectual excitement it conveyed. In short, his sense of contactmanship was largely what made him such an extraordinary editor. His groups were also organized with editing in mind; Calverton seldom acted without considering the "spin-off" effects and advantages for the *Modern Quarterly*. On the other hand, the ideological catholicity Calverton demonstrated in his social activities sometimes spilled over into his writing and editing with adverse effects, spreading him thin in his writings and diffusing his energies. Certainly also, this catholicity, springing from his desire to bridge the gaps among factional disputes, made it difficult to stay out of the lines of fire. As much as Calverton wished to belong to the group, as much as he felt the need for intellectual community, his efforts in the praxis of a nonpartisan and independent collective of radical intellectual workers ran into trouble in an atmosphere of increasing collective uniformity and ideological regimentation on the Left.

THE Scheffel Hall group and the various open-house gatherings at Calverton's were all organized on the same general premise that collectivity should supplant individualism, that intellectuals should strive to form a community of thinkers that would forge new values for Americans. This same premise animated a new group, initiated in the spring of 1930 (thus running concurrently with the less formal Scheffel Hall gathering) and devoted to examining American culture from a radical point of view. In the midst of organizing the group, Calverton wrote to Mike Gold, inviting him to participate and making explicit his ideal of a radical collective:

> I wonder if you, Joe Freeman, Jack Kunitz and a few other of us "left wingers" couldn't get together more often. We have got something to say, and the only way we could say it effectively is to act less like individuals and more like communists. I would like to start the idea of our getting together by having us meet next week.[21]

Calverton, Nearing, and Hook formed an executive committee that would direct the collective efforts of the group which was to meet every Thursday night, in writing a book that Calverton believed would "dynamite a vast array of prejudices" dear to bourgeois society and culture.[22] Among the active participants, mostly communist intellectuals, were Joseph Freeman, Mike Gold, Joshua Kunitz, Bernard Smith (critic and Marxist editor at Knopf), artist and critic Louis Lozowick, film critic Harry Potamkin, Samuel Schmalhausen, and Joseph Tauber. After the first meeting Calverton was optimistic and exuberant. The next day he wrote to Gold, "By God, Mike, I think we have started something in this idea and I am depending on you to lend your support and enthusiasm to it. . . . It was great to have all the activity we did last night."[23] Calverton contacted Dos Passos and urged him to join, but Dos Passos felt the group was too heavily pro–Soviet Union. Calverton assured him that the aim of the project was not to prove that the Soviet Union was a "Garden of Eden," but rather to examine American culture from a radical perspective.[24] Even so, Dos Passos remained skeptical and refused to join.

The project made headway, and the Thursday-night meetings at Calverton's were filled with planning, discussion, and argument. At a meeting in early April Hook and Gold got into a fracas over cultural radicalism that ran on until three-thirty in the morning—at which time Gold took on Joshua Kunitz and the arguments raged until dawn. The project was still underway in October when Michael Gold read a paper at Calverton's apartment that was to be included in the group's book, tentatively titled "America at the Crossroads."[25] Despite the sectarianism that had been growing on the Left since the mid twenties, the project shows an effort at cooperation between radicals of various persuasions. Yet beneath the spirit of group camaraderie, planning, and spirited debate, tension suffused the group, due in large part to Calverton's ambiguous relationship with the Party. By 1930, Bertram Wolfe's 1928 attack on the Quarterly as a journal that flirted with Eastman and the Trotskyist opposition was still reverberating. There remained an uneasiness among communist intellectuals about working with Calverton. In spite of the fact that Calverton and Freeman had paired off to work on a chapter on the "radical Marxist position" vis-á-vis American culture for the group's book and that Gold himself was working actively in the same group with Calverton, Gold balked when it came to making any public statement about Calverton and his works. When Calverton asked Gold to make a critical comment on a piece he had published, Gold refused. "I am damned sorry that you feel too embarrassed to write about me in the New Masses," replied a disappointed Calverton, "because I would appreciate something [sic] you could say, however enthusiastic or critical." Calverton urged Gold to recognize the crucial need, as part of intellectual comradeship, for "sincere honest evaluation" among those on the Left.[26]

But the atmosphere on the Left in 1931 seemed less characterized by "sincere and honest" evaluation than by political sniping. Early that year William Z. Foster, secretary of the CPUSA, had written an "Open Letter" to Calverton in the Party's official organ, the Communist, denouncing him as a "social fascist"—the excoriating term coming into vogue as the Third Period gained momentum. Foster had taken exception to an article Calverton had written in the Quarterly arguing that the democratic tradition in the Western world was disintegrating. Either a fascist or a communist dictatorship would "solve" the economic crisis, Calverton contended, but for those who believed in the masses there was one choice—to work for the dictatorship of the proletariat.[27] Foster found in Calverton's argument the "familiar fascist thesis that the weakness of modern society is not to be found in the contradictions of capitalism, but rather in bourgeois democracy," and that the "solution to the capitalist crisis is to be found in the establishment of the fascist dictatorship. . . . According to your article," Foster wrote, "what is wrong is not capitalism as such, but democracy. Your arguments echo the views of Mussolini and Hitler; they are poles apart from those of Marx and Lenin."[28]

Calverton was shocked and stunned by Foster's attack and the absurdity (whatever the theoretical problems of his own piece) of likening his ideas to those of Mussolini and Hitler. Calverton defended himself in a lengthy rejoinder printed in the Modern Quarterly. The Foster–Calverton interchange, as well as the implications of Foster's attack, are examined in the next chapter. But Foster's charge of "fascism" reflected a desire to discredit Calverton, who was coming to occupy a pivotal position in left-wing study groups and whose nonpartisan magazine, which fostered independent radical viewpoints, was becoming increasingly influential and prestigious.

Foster's condemnation of Calverton sent shock waves through the

American Left, and in its aftermath many in the left-wing intellectual community began to shun Calverton. When his publishers contacted Gold for a comment on his 1932 manifesto "For Revolution," Gold again emphatically refused to make any public statement:

> I read your pamphlet and it reads O.K. Publishers wanted some quotation, but I'd rather not until you get yourself cleared up with the Party. You ought to do it, somehow; it ought not to be difficult. This is my opinion of course, which is why I don't want to come out and say anything until I see how far you will go toward a better relationship.[29]

In February 1932, Granville Hicks, Newton Arvin, Bernard Smith, and Clifton Fadiman picked up the idea of a Marxist symposium. Hicks wished to pursue the plan only if it did not touch too closely on the "America at the Crossroads" project. But since the latter had by now languished and died, Calverton gave Hicks his approval. The new symposium was to include primarily middle-class critics and writers recently converted to Marxism. Calverton was eager to participate in this symposium and offered his services. In February of 1932 Hicks responded curtly that "after talking with various persons, we feel there are a good many reasons against including you as a contributor, for otherwise we should certainly count on your cooperation."[30] Among these "good many reasons," of course, was Foster's denunciation. It was no longer safe for Party regulars to be associated with Calverton.

The projected book that would emerge from this new left-wing study group, another "Marxist Study of American Culture," was to be published by Harcourt, Brace and Co. But this project also languished. Some of those who were to participate and to represent the "definite leftward turn of American intellectuals" like Edmund Wilson ultimately refused to join, while other non-Communists like Arvin and Fadiman became increasingly uncomfortable with the Communists and backed out after agreeing to participate.[31] The failed project was a monument to the growing sense of isolation and ineffectuality that plagued heterodox radicals. Calverton himself felt great frustration at being excluded from the group. He was further dismayed at seeing one project after another fall apart and at having his hopes for achieving collective action and a sense of community among radical intellectuals demolished by Party-provoked intraradical rivalry.

POLITICAL problems were only part of the story. To a certain extent, Calverton's disappointments during the first years in New York, as well as his frustration at what seemed the failure of community, were related to the enormous problem of economic survival in a severe depression. Calverton tried all sorts of schemes to make ends meet and to raise money for the *Modern Quarterly*, but many of these died in a hostile economic environment.

In late 1929, just before the stock market crashed, he attempted to start a new publishing house devoted exclusively to social science textbooks, which would have an editorial board (recruited from his many friends and contacts) of professional distinction. At the same time Calverton was at work with Nearing to raise money for a magazine Calverton had recently conceived of, patterned after the French publication *Monde* (edited by Henri Barbusse), which would emphasize revolution in the arts. But with the crash both projects collapsed.[32]

In early 1930 Calverton contacted editor Suzanne La Follette (journalist, feminist writer, and art critic for the *Nation*) regarding the possibility of working with her on the recently established *New Freeman*, funded by Peter Fireman. Impressed by Calverton's reputation as a writer and his experience as an editor, La Follette invited him to run the literary department of the new magazine, but after meeting with him several times, she began to change her mind. She found Calverton's personality overbearing and was fearful that he would be aggressive in his editorial role and simply take over. La Follette also knew that Calverton and Nearing were working closely on a variety of literary projects, and she became fearful that the two men would attempt to turn the *New Freeman* into a communist publication.[33] She therefore withdrew her offer to employ Calverton.

Calverton was bitterly disappointed at losing this opportunity for an influential and high-salaried position. He wrote La Follette complaining that he had turned down a job with a commercial magazine to work for the *New Freeman* and demanded some sort of recompense for the financial loss he had sustained. Fireman acted as an arbitrator between Calverton and La Follette, who now found it impossible to behave amicably toward one another. It was agreed that Calverton would write for the magazine in whatever capacity he was needed.[34]

But before the *New Freeman* got off the ground, Calverton received a timely offer for the position of literary editor from Richard M. Smith. The position came none too soon, as the Macmillan Company, bothered by Calverton's freewheeling approach, had already decided against renewing his contract for the position of literary advisor. Calverton joined Long and Smith in the summer of 1930 and was put to work on a project to develop a series of books dealing with changes in the sciences to be marketed as college texts. He also worked on a project of his own, an anthology of American literature, which the company agreed to publish. Again the depression killed both of these efforts: Long and Smith were bankrupt within a year, and the series and the anthology were never completed.

Calverton was out of work only a short time before Alex Hillman offered him a job as literary editor of William Godwin. For a steady salary of one hundred dollars a week, a considerable amount of money for the time, Calverton was to devote full-time service to the Godwin corporation. Meanwhile the *Modern Quarterly* was to appear under the imprimatur of William Godwin and Co., but Calverton and Schmalhausen were to remain the magazine's editors, and the policy of the company would in no way be identified with the policy of the magazine. Certificates of shares of William Godwin were to be delivered to Calverton in negotiable form, "fully paid and non-assessable." [35] The arrangement seemed beneficial to both Calverton and Godwin: Calverton would have available capital with which to fund the *Quarterly*, and since he owned shares in the business, he would, presumably, have an interest in increasing the corporation's profits.

Such a capitalistic scheme looked promising for ensuring the survival of the socialist magazine. But there was one major flaw in the plan: Calverton was no businessman. For all his ambitiousness in literary matters, he showed a profound lack of interest when it came to financial issues. Moreover, after his move to New York, his energy was scattered in a dozen different directions, and he devoted little time to the *Quarterly*. Between the fall of 1929 and the winter of 1930–31 the magazine lapsed; not a single issue appeared. The *Quarterly* had in effect become, for the time being, a yearly.

The magazine's editorial offices remained in Baltimore until May 1931, but even when they were moved to New York in the interests of efficiency, the magazine failed to come out regularly or on time. The fall 1930 issue did not make its appearance until two days before Christmas, rendering most of the advertisements it contained obsolete and drastically reducing its sales potential. Hillman was furious. "From the way this whole damn thing has gone and the way you managed it, letting it come out two days before Christmas, I have a good mind to burn the whole god damned issue," he raged at Calverton. Hillman further complained that Calverton had misrepresented the *Quarterly* when he joined William Godwin, making it appear that the magazine was well distributed when it had in fact "absolutely no distribution." Hillman had therefore decided to "turn the entire mess over to the American News Company and let them sell what they can." [36] Calverton's position with William Godwin was, then, short-lived. He lost his position as literary editor of the company as well as the advantages of having Godwin as an "umbrella corporation" for the magazine.

Now Calverton found himself financially up against it. Lee Furman of MacCaulay was hounding him for five hundred dollars, the amount of an advance Calverton had received from MacCaulay for a book he had proposed and failed to write. At the same time the British Communist Party's leading ideologue, R. Palme Dutt, was threatening to take Calverton to small claims court for fifty dollars, the amount he owed on an article Dutt had written for the *Quarterly*.[37] "Dutt is practically the leader of the Communist Party," Calverton fretted to Schmalhausen, worrying that if the matter were not cleared up, it would invite even more trouble with the Communists.[38] Meanwhile Calverton was being sued by his Baltimore printer ("a totally bourgeois" printer, Calverton snorted) who reneged on his agreement to extend him time on payments due.[39] As of May of 1930 he was eighteen months in arrears on the payment of ground rent on the "2110" property in Baltimore, which he had bought from his grandmother after the death of his parents and which was pledged to the Broadway Savings Bank in Baltimore.[40] The depression had caused the near-total collapse of lecturing as a steady secondary income, and as Calverton wrote to Albert H. Gross of Liveright, appealing for a loan to pay Dutt's fee, "I am not even able to pay the rent over here, not to speak of paying for anything else."[41]

Financial difficulties were also accompanied by problems on the editorial board of the *Modern Quarterly*. In October 1931 Oakley Johnson resigned from his position as assistant editor complaining of Calverton's propensity to regard the *Quarterly* as *his* magazine and thus to dominate the editorial meetings as well as the policy of the magazine.[42] To complicate matters, relations between Schmalhausen and Calverton had become increasingly strained. With the direction of the magazine redefined after 1930, the emphasis was now on literary radicalism and radical politics rather than sex and psychology. Consequently, Schmalhausen's articles with their cavalier approach to psychoanalysis and mocking sense of humor seemed peripheral, if not counterproductive. Tension developed until things snapped in late 1932 when Schmalhausen ran across an advertisement in another publication for the *Quarterly* in which his name did not appear among the editorial staff but was relegated to a footnote among miscellaneous book reviewers. Schmalhausen was furious and wrote a letter to Calverton resigning from his post as associate editor of the *Quarterly*.

> The major reason why, contrary to many impulses, I knew I had to quit after so much humiliation and double dealing, was precisely this apparent uncontrollable tendency of your brain to use everyone who crosses your path for purposes of ego aggrandizement. I suppose the key is simply that infinite egocentric narcissism hitched to an infinite energy of personal ambition that makes it literally impossible for you to realize some other person exists except to serve your private ends.[43]

Calverton retorted that Schmalhausen's resignation was unnecessary; the advertisement was correct, and his sacking was a fait accompli.[44] Schmalhausen shot another letter back to Calverton complaining bitterly of the humiliating years of collaboration with Calverton that were riven with "underground rivalry." Finally Schmalhausen called a halt to the exchange, reiterating his resignation, a "sabbatical leave for clarity's sake and new composure of mind."[45] But the "sabbatical leave" marked the end of Calverton's and Schmalhausen's seven-year collaboration. Calverton replaced Schmalhausen with Michael Blankfort, who had recently joined the *Quarterly* staff as book review editor.

Calverton's treatment of Schmalhausen no doubt reveals some highhandedness, and Schmalhausen's feelings about Calverton's imperious editorial practice were shared by Oakley Johnson who resigned earlier. In the last analysis, Calverton saw the *Quarterly* as his own publication (which technically and legally it was), and he maintained a nearly autocratic control over its direction and editorial policy. Yet the split between the two men seemed inevitable. Calverton had always felt Schmalhausen's treatment of psychological topics insufficiently grounded in radical analysis and on several occasions had found himself apologizing for his partner's caustic, if occasionally entertaining, assaults on other intellectuals. Now that the two men had come into direct conflict, Kantorovitch, whose health prevented him from participating in editorial matters, wrote Calverton supporting his decision to jettison Schmalhausen. Kantorovitch insisted that Schmalhausen had "no idea" of how to conduct any sort of Marxist analysis and that he was a "total nihilist."[46] Kantorovitch's opinion notwithstanding, the *Modern Quarterly* had outgrown Schmalhausen: his contributions now seemed extraordinarily lightweight beside the articles the magazine was attracting by Dewey, Mumford, Beard, Hook, and Eastman.

Yet Schmalhausen's charge of Calverton's personal ambition was doubtless correct. Calverton, as editor, was an archindividualist who wanted to figure in American intellectual life. And as editor he tended to see his own career and that of his magazine as indistinguishable: self-aggrandizement and the success of the magazine went hand in hand. But such ambition and individualism had its costs and ran head on against his commitment to intellectual community. If the frenetic, scattered, and divided work involved in a variety of proposals, projects, anthologies—all meant to keep him afloat in New York in hard times—increased his feeling of isolation, so his impulse to run his magazine unilaterally undermined the community he sought. By the end of 1932 Calverton had established himself in New York, but one of his most important intellectual associations and friendships of the twenties had dissolved, and he now faced financial uncertainty and the difficulties of running the magazine if not alone, then without his partner of seven years.

CALVERTON'S was, then, a deep and continual conflict between his archindividualism and a need for intellectual stimulation and intellectual community. His fear of death continued to permeate his private life and to adversely affect his relationship with Nina Melville. Certainly the two had difficulties enough with continual emotion-fraying financial problems. Anticipating problems at Long and Smith, Calverton told Melville that if the company foundered they might be forced to leave their Village apartment and to move into "2110" in Baltimore, where, with no rent, they could live on twenty to twenty-five dollars a week.[47] He admonished Melville regarding her inability to "hold in restraint" her dislike of his associates in the literary world: "If Smith goes under, and such things these days are all too possible, it is such contacts alone that will make it possible for us to survive economically in New York."[48] The two struggled together, laboring on the *Modern Quarterly*, Calverton taking editorial work where he could get it (after the collapse of Long and Smith he picked up some work with Book League Monthly) as well as lecturing whenever and wherever he could, Melville taking up sporadic work typing for publishing houses or for the office of social welfare. Pitted against this extraordinarily precarious and uncertain world Calverton wrote her that "if there is anything religious in me, it is the worship of what we have created in our own lives amidst a world that is so loveless."[49]

Yet the haven of their relationship ultimately could not protect him from his loneliness and anxiety. As he told her, "I dread this loneliness more than anything, but it always returns no matter whom I'm with or how much I'm in love."[50] His letters to her returned compulsively to the issue of death: "I'm sick of heart, spirit, and body . . . only the thought of death seems to haunt and obsess me."[51] He continued to seek out affairs as a measure of relief. Love letters would inevitably follow him home from lecture tours. When Melville protested and threatened to leave because of the other women, he would tell her, "I am going to do all you ask and get rid of them all, absolutely and completely. . . . I'm never going to hurt you again, ever, I promise."[52]

Calverton felt himself caught in the constricting snares of a series of double binds. The "constant familiarity," of the relationship, the continual association and intimacy with one individual (as he had noted in his fiction), gave rise to feelings of loneliness and an inertial and entropic stasis that threatened the love relation itself. The relationship, sought out to alleviate fear, magnified it; the fear of death for which the relationship promised some amelioration was replaced by a dreadful sense of closure that threatened to destroy the relationship; the protective harbor and sanctuary of the relationship settled into a stasis resembling death. Moreover, no number of affairs could alleviate his feeling of aloneness. Calverton therefore looked to the group as an antidote to the anxieties that the love relation could not solve. Overwhelmed with work from every direction, he became ever more obsessive about his soirees and fearful of what he would do without the gatherings. He would ask Melville, who did most of the work organizing these soirees, to "get people in, darling, I want them around. . . . I can put on a face with people and forget myself. . . . I can't put on a face with you; you are myself."[53] She would dutifully help organize his groups, "get people in," so that his personal problems would find a collective outlet. But Calverton's obsessions frayed her nerves and left her emotionally exhausted. After his death in 1940 Nina Melville retreated to a rest home. She wrote in her diary that "death lived in George [like] a cancer that was with him every waking moment" and admitted to herself that Calverton's preoccupation with death had nearly driven her insane.[54]

NOTWITHSTANDING that deeply neurotic and obsessive needs motivated Calverton to form his groups, they were, like his magazine, extraordinary experiments in nonpartisan radical politics and intellectual community. In spite of financial and personal problems during the early years of the thirties, Calverton's open-house gatherings continued. The Scheffel Hall group died out after its inception in 1931, but by then the gatherings that followed at Calverton's apartment had become a kind of tradition among New York radical intellectuals. Louis Adamic, in *My America*, called Calverton's meetings "The Literary Rotary," implying an innocuousness similar to a group of Rotarians who engaged in small talk, gossip, and indulged their own sense of self-importance. Writing in the late thirties, with an end-of-the-decade mood of pessimism, Adamic satirized the group's participants for believing that they were in the vanguard of revolutionary thinkers. Adamic saw a collective self-deception in the group's belief that its ideas would have some bearing on the revolution seen to be just around the corner.[55]

But most others who attended Calverton's gatherings viewed them in a different light. Two men at opposing ideological poles—Henry Hazlitt and Bertrand D. Wolfe—saw Calverton and his groups as crucial for stimulating diverse opinion and debate on the intellectual Left. Wolfe saw Calverton as an important "catalyst," while Hazlitt noted that "one reason George attracted so many intellectuals to his home was that they felt they could come there, speak their minds freely and even bluntly, and leave in the same atmosphere of cordial good will. . . . He created an atmosphere in which ideas of all sorts were expressed and encouraged."[56] Michael Blankfort evaluated the significance of these parties from the perspective of a young writer coming to New York in 1932, fresh out of Princeton: "In

Calverton's house were Trotskyites and Lovestonites and Gitlowites and Socialists, leftwing Socialists and Norman Thomasites, and they talked— it was my education, my university."[57]

In fact the importance and uniqueness of Calverton's meetings and open-house gatherings can scarcely be overestimated. The Calvertonian group or soiree, as Sidney Hook observed, was "the only thing of its kind in America,"[58] bringing together independent spirits, and, like his magazine, keeping alive the spirit of critical debate and discussion, utterly unfettered by Party doctrine, through the years of Stalinist orthodoxy. For Hook, the greatest tribute to these open-house sessions, many of which he attended, was their open and speculative character. Hook notes that some of the group's regulars were not even Socialists, but rather "individuals who enjoyed the argument and the free play of ideas that whirled around him [Calverton] and his guests."[59]

Calverton's parties were still going on in 1936 when Alfred Kazin attended, and, although the constituency had by then changed to some degree, they continued to be islands of independent thinking and community in an ocean of ideological entrenchment and divisive sectarianism. Kazin best depicts the vitality and rich eclecticism of the Calvertonian soiree:

> Suddenly you saw Thomas Wolfe looming like a boy mountain in Calverton's inadequate doorway, crusading journalists like Walter Liggett of Minnesota who would soon be murdered for his exposés of the local political machine, sensitive and skeptical anthropologists like Alexander Goldenweiser who were contemptuous of Marxism, ex-radicals like Eugene Lyons who had gone completely sour on socialism and all its works, a man named Schmalhausen who was a wild imitator of Mencken's assaults on all radical intellectuals, pretentious and otherwise; labor experts, news commentators, student leaders, Harlem poets. Calverton gathered them all in and tried to give equal welcome to them all.[60]

In spite of the worsening relationship with the Communists, Calverton's parties and soirees went on. As Kazin further comments, the "more isolated Calverton felt as the Communists calumniated him, the more parties he gave and the more he sought contact with every independent spirit in the literary and radical world."[61] The more he felt the possibilities for intellectual community undermined by sectarianism, the more he strove to preserve a spirit of community and independent thinking.

Although Calverton's desire for radical community was primarily emotional in source, it was also distinctively American in two senses. James Gilbert has written that the thirties radicals "placed the values of the community above those of individuals, if only to save individualism."[62] Certainly Calverton's groups, devoted to collective thought and action, were nevertheless based on the individualistic values of free speculation and independent thinking, of pluralism and dialogue. Secondly, as Richard Pells has pointed out, an individualistic premise was at the very core of the American notion of the collective: writers embraced the ideal of the collective not simply for economic and political reasons but for reasons having to do with the self. Moreover, in espousing collectivity, Calverton was embracing what Pells calls the decade's "dominant assumption," namely "that one could overcome inner turmoil by becoming part of a stable community, that private problems could be solved by collective outlets."[63] Haunted and obsessed with private fears, Calverton sought collective activity as a form of temporary redemption.

Yet in spite of the relative success of his own New York soirees, Calverton never ceased to be preoccupied with the failure of community on the Left in general and continued to be dismayed by his own isolation from the radical movement. He failed to find in his groups more than a temporary respite from private anxieties and he was coming to believe that the fear of death was a condition of bourgeois civilization where an ideology of individualism prompted in the self an obsession with its own extinction. The problem of death, then, was part of the problem of individualism and community, a problem Marxist philosophy had yet to address.

The conflict Calverton felt between individualism and community is not only an archetypal American problem, but his failure to find a balance or integration of the two demands underscores the dilemma of the thirties radical. Calverton could have entered the community of orthodox Communists only on terms unacceptable to him. Given the extreme collectivism and ideological rigidity now gripping the American Left, Calverton could have entered into the community only by the submersion of his own individuality, intellectual independence, and sense of self.

If his fear of death sprang from deeply private sources, it may nevertheless have been in part an expression of the profound and more public conflict of self and the group: the self with its need to find solace from loneliness, existential anxiety, and mortality in the group, the group demanding as antidote to existential angst the renunciation of self and identity—a form of death itself. The preoccupation with death—the death of self, the submersion of individuality—may have been intensified by having to walk a fine line between the concerns of the individual and the group and, finally, a dangerously thin line between social commitment that affirmed the self on the one hand and commitment that resulted in the loss of self in the mass on the other.[64] Nowhere was the latter indicated more strikingly than in the Marxist poet and philosopher Rebecca Pitts's

1934 essay in the *New Masses*, "Something to Believe In," which asserted a rediscovery and transformation of the self after the individual assumed a position "functionally subordinate" to the group.[65] As the decade continued, Calverton would become increasingly caught up in the dilemma of individualism and community and would search in the Marxian ideal of community for some solution to the problem of death. Concomitantly, he would continue to confront the dilemma that collectivism could become authoritarian, that the spiritual quest to merge with the group—however much it seemed desirable—could easily become a mystical renunciation of identity: the subordination of the self to the group's conservative or even totalitarian logic.

CHAPTER EIGHT

New Masses should once and for all dispense with the tradition of "rotten liberalism" which allows it to throw open the hospitality of its columns to sundry exponents of social fascism. At the same time the journal should begin a ruthless exposure of the social fascist spokesmen, not contenting itself with merely keeping silent about them as in the case of Calverton and Max Eastman.

  —A. Elistratova, *International Literature*, Moscow, 1932

Excommunication and Exorcism: Calverton and the Party

As the peak of the militant Third Period of the international Communist movement advanced, Calverton's dilemma—that of the intellectual committed to the idea of communism yet determined to maintain his intellectual independence—became an acute personal conflict. Tension between Calverton and the Communists had been intensifying since 1928, but as 1933 approached the aggressive and doctrinaire policies of the Third Period and Calverton's independent stance moved toward an inevitable collision. In 1933 Calverton became the target of a series of ferocious attacks by the Stalinists. The enormity and fantastic character of these charges shook him personally, forced him to reevaluate his ideological position, and resulted in a dramatic alteration of the direction of the *Modern Quarterly*.

The history of conflict between Calverton and the Party notwithstanding, the question remains: why was he singled out for such an ideological blitz? The answer largely lies in the politics of Third Period communism and the psychology of its central theory of social fascism. Max Schachtman describes the various periods in the history of the communist movement, as they were defined by the Communist Party after 1928:

According to the new communist doctrine, events since the First World War ended were divided into three periods. The first was the period of unprepared and unsuccessful storm assault on European capitalism, which proved stout enough to defeat it. The second period was the relative stabilization of capitalism. And the "Third Period," which was now ushered in, was the period of the final collapse of capitalism throughout the world and its burial under the revolutionary offensive of the proletariat led by the Communist parties.[1]

Thus the Third Period (lasting roughly from 1927 to 1934) was a period of new militancy. The precarious stability of the capitalist economy was assumed to be ending—indeed the depression seemed to prove capitalism was near death. The Comintern therefore considered it an appropriate time for a revolutionary offensive. The Stalinist drive during the Third Period for social, economic, and political unity in the effort to consolidate the revolution resulted in an intolerance of political programs considered to be less than totally revolutionary.

In this contentious atmosphere, the notion of social fascism emerged, based on the theory that liberalism—particularly its political expression in social democracy—and fascism were both expressions of the same repressive bourgeois state. As Joseph Stalin had put it in 1924, "Social democracy is objectively the moderate wing of fascism."[2] It followed that Socialists and liberals were thus "class enemies" of the communist movement rather than allies; such groups stood between Communists and the working class and therefore served the interests of the enemy. But during the peak of Third Period militancy, this dubious notion had all but lost any theoretical dimensions and had become a means of rationalizing the simplistic idea that all those who are not Communists are Fascists. The Social Fascist provided a threat from within against which the group might consolidate itself. As Irving Howe and Lewis Coser observe, "It was essential to the politics of the Third Period that the Party feel itself both profoundly threatened and on the verge of triumph; beleaguered by enemies and, if only it could purify and steel itself, within the reach of power."[3] The psychology of the Third Period, then, demanded scapegoats. Calverton, committed to tolerance of viewpoint and free inquiry, was a likely candidate. Certainly the attacks on him were consistent with a major impetus of Third Period strategy—the denunciation of writers who maintained an independent position. Calverton was at this time probably the most influential independent radical spokesman on the American intellectual Left who also presided over the most important journal of independent radical opinion. Moreover, some of his writings during this period—particularly a piece on his theory of "Cultural Compulsives"—offended and riled the Party cadre. Given these factors, Calverton and the *Modern Quarterly* were inevitable targets for Third Period belligerence.

SURVEYING the history of conflict with the Party until 1933, it is significant that as early as 1928 when Wolfe attacked the *Modern Quarterly* for its "flirtation" with Eastman and the Trotskyist Opposition, the campaign bore directly on the *Quarterly*'s ideological flexibility and Calverton's failure to take a hard line against Trotsky. And as tensions between the Stalinist and Trotskyist factions increased, there was a growing intolerance of "free spirits" (as Wolfe characterized the *Quarterly* group).[4] A general antagonism toward Calverton had now become, as we saw earlier, "more or less the official attitude" among Party members.[5]

Nor were Communists about to let the Trotsky issue drop. Further evidence to discredit Calverton appeared in January 1929, when the *Daily Worker* came out with a front-page headline:

REVOLUTIONARY RENEGADES AID CANNON'S GROUP:
Modern Quarterly and Lettish [*sic*] Splinter with Eastman
and Cannon PART OF WORLD PLOT[6]

When it appeared, Calverton thought the accusation a desperate joke. As proof of the *Modern Quarterly*'s complicity in a "world plot" the *Daily Worker* displayed a letter from Armstead Collier, business manager of the *Quarterly*, offering James P. Cannon, leader of the Communist League of America (the Trotskyist opposition), space in the *Quarterly* to publish suppressed Trotskyist material.

Collier's letter indicated something far simpler than the *Quarterly*'s involvement in any "world plot," and that was the pluralism of the magazine, its policy of publishing a variety of factional viewpoints. Nonetheless the *Daily Worker* berated Calverton as a "busy propagandist of anti-communist, anti-Marxist, and anti-Leninist philosophy" who hid behind "the long-winded, super 'intellectual' attacks of Eastman on the dialectical materialist basis of Marxism."[7] Calverton wrote an angry letter to the *Worker* denying that Collier had any influence on the overall editorial policy of the magazine and reaffirming his own sympathies with the Communist Party.[8] He also appealed to Jay Lovestone (whose tenure as Party leader was about to come to an untimely end by Stalin's order), pointing to an anti-Trotsky article in the current issue of the *Quarterly* by Louis Fischer as evidence that his magazine had no pro-Trotsky direction or policy.[9] But all this was to no avail. The whole uneasy situation was rendered more complex because at this time Calverton was running afoul of orthodox opinion due to his sexual radicalism. At any rate, correspondence from Moscow suddenly dwindled, and it was at this point that a project Calverton was working on with the Soviet literary critic Serge Dinamov was suddenly canceled because of the alleged "shortage of paper."[10]

Party ideologues now moved in, mining Calverton's writings for impurities and theoretical errors. In the May 1929 issue of the *Communist*, A. B. Magil accused him of being "petty bourgeois" in outlook since he had failed to distinguish between bourgeois and proletarian intellectuals in an article on European and American intellectuals. Behind Magil's quibbling was an obvious resentment that Calverton had gained "a sort of official status as *the* revolutionary critic in America" while presiding over a magazine that included the writings of splinter groups:

> Were it not for the fact that Calverton exercises considerable influence among many uncritical workers, I shouldn't spend so much time and space discussing his last effusion. His magazine, the *Modern Quarterly*, has become a rallying point for all sorts of enemies of the Communist Party—Trotskyites and other breeds—who volubly profess their "revolutionary" fervor, at the same time graciously pointing out the "errors" and "stupidities" of the American communists.[11]

The sense of increased militancy behind this attack was heightened in 1930 with the Second World Plenum of the International Bureau of Revolutionary Literature, which convened in Kharkov from November 6 to November 15. The conference resulted in the affiliation of the John Reed Club with the International Union of Revolutionary Writers (IURW). The theory of "social fascism," declared essential doctrine by the Comintern in 1929, was also impressed on the American delegates. It was no longer sufficient for the revolutionary writer to oppose imperialism and fascism in a general sense. The writer must also fight against that "concealed fascism which parades under the mask of socialism—that more insidious type that has come to be known as social fascism."[12]

Only months later, a manifestation of this new "hard line" against social fascism emerged in the American communist press. In February 1931— the same month the *New Masses* carried glowing accounts of the Kharkov conference—William Z. Foster published his derisory and influential article in the *Communist* entitled "Calverton's Fascism" attacking Calverton's editorial, "Democracy *vs.* Dictatorship."[13] Foster's disagreement with Calverton's thesis that both communism and fascism were expressions of monopoly capitalism's erosion of an individualistic ideology (although Calverton hastened to add that the proletarian dictatorship was the only logical "answer" to capitalism's crisis), prompted Foster to liken Calverton's views to those of Mussolini and Hitler. Furthermore, the *Modern Quarterly*'s refusal to line up with the orthodox Communists was a particularly sore point for Foster:

> The social fascist and liberal elements whom you gather together to debate Marxism in the columns of the *Modern Quarterly* in no sense represent the revolutionary foment now going on among intellectuals. They are defenders of revision, not capitalism. They are enemies of the revolution.[14]

Calverton should have understood that an attack by a functionary as formidable as "Big Bill" Foster signaled the end of his relations with the Stalinists, but he was slow to sense the ironfisted logic of the Third Period. Still retaining his naive faith in rational discourse and reasoned debate, he wrote Foster a modest and explanatory letter, asking Foster to stop the attacks on sympathizers and calling for reconciliation. In spite of a pledge from Foster to print the letter in the *Communist*, it never appeared.[15]

Meanwhile, Foster's condemnation of Calverton as a Fascist was having its repercussions. His long-standing relationship with the Friends of the Soviet Union was severed when members simply stopped inviting him to lecture.[16] Earl Browder, general secretary of the Communist Party, suddenly demanded that his name be removed from the masthead of the *Modern Quarterly*.[17] Michael Gold, as we saw earlier, refused to write reviews of Calverton's works. The *Daily Worker* admonished its readers to beware of his social-fascist ideas.[18] And the *New Masses* closed its columns to him. Kantorovitch, long critical of the Party (and of Calverton's close relationship with it), spoke for many non-Party leftists when he provided Calverton with his own succinct definition of "social fascism": "It simply means you do not belong to Foster's party."[19]

AMONG Party loyalists, Foster's attack transformed the general antagonism toward Calverton into open hostility. The earlier charges of collusion with the Left opposition were now overshadowed by the accusation of social fascism and a steady stream of articles pummeling Calverton for his deviations poured from the communist press. Party ideologue A. Landy's "Cultural Compulsives, or Calverton's Latest Caricature of Marxism," appeared in the *Communist* shortly after Foster's attack.[20] Landy's assault began with Calverton's theory and underscored a fundamental and profound disagreement between Calverton and the orthodox Communists over the possibility of scientific objectivity in social thought and, ultimately, over the Party's scientistic rendering of dialectical materialism.

Calverton had articulated his theory of cultural compulsives in the 1931 edition of the *American Journal of Sociology*.[21] A study in psychosocial inquiry, his article explored how the supposedly objective social sciences are inevitably colored by class interests. He examined the reception by scholars of the works of two anthropologists—Lewis Morgan and Edward Westermark—to illustrate how anthropology had served as a prop for class ethics and a class outlook. Morgan's theory hypothesized that the family had passed through evolutionary stages in human history on its way from primitive communism to private property and monogamous marriage. Morgan's ideas had appealed to many radicals, including Engels, Kautsky, and Plekhanov, precisely because they fit well with the Marxist notion of social evolution through thesis, antithesis, and synthesis. Moreover Morgan's ideas implied that the institution of monogamous marriage was not fixed or permanent but rather developed out of economic conditions. This buttressed the radical view of the family and the Marxist interpretation of culture as an economic unit. Morgan's ideas therefore were eagerly and uncritically adopted by radicals. But in the same manner, bourgeois academics uncritically seized upon Westermark's theories because they implied the essential and timeless nature of marriage and family and thus justified the perpetuity of monogamy and patriarchy. Westermark's notion that monogamy was basic to the human species (being seen even in other mammals) had in fact arisen, Calverton argued, as an ideological defense against the influence of Morgan's ideas.

Calverton contended that class factors had acted as a determinant in the reception of both anthropologists. Neither the bourgeois scholars nor the radicals could be entirely aloof from their own vested class interests, their own mind set, their intellectual rationalizations. Calverton termed these factors "cultural compulsives"; they colored all social thought and made objectivity in the social sciences impossible. Since all human thought arises in a definite social milieu, not in a vacuum, sociology was necessarily a *relative* rather than an *absolute* system of thought. Sociological inquiry could not escape the influence of class and history; the social sciences were inevitably based on a class viewpoint, consciously or otherwise.

As a system of thought or constellation of ideas that rationalizes the material interests of a particular class, Calverton's notion of cultural compulsives resembled the Marxist concept of "ideology." There was, however, a crucial difference. According to the Marxists—at least of the contemporary Stalinist variety—the distorting lens of ideology was exclusive to the bourgeois outlook, while the proletarian view, being free of bourgeois interests and at one with the movement of history, was objective. Calverton disagreed with this formulation and claimed that "all social thought is colored by such [cultural] compulsives, reactionary as well as radical; and those who think they can escape them are merely pursuing a path that is socially fallacious."[22] Furthermore, the class coloration of cultural compulsives was not only inevitable but to some extent essential to give social thought unity and coherence. Rather than emerging from an objective point of view, "knowledge" in the social sciences, then, could only be produced by rival views of reality and "the very processes of social conflict." But Calverton warned that if cultural compulsives were to a certain extent organizing structures through which the classes viewed reality, they could also be a source of excessive distortion—of "false consciousness" pure and simple. Social theorists therefore should not simply acquiesce to the pervasive force of cultural compulsives, but should be on guard against their more extreme forms, their manifestations in the form of ideology as false consciousness. Radical thinkers should take the lead in understanding the compulsives that shape social thought, so that their own thinking might be at once more self-critical and more flexible.

Will Herberg criticized Calverton's thesis, arguing that "the class bias of the bourgeoisie is a *truth distorting* bias, while the class bias of the proletariat is a *truth inducing* bias."[23] Given this pervasive assumption, even on the part of a Lovestonite opposition spokesman like Herberg, it is hardly surprising that Calverton's theory appeared scandalous, for it implied that radicals, not unlike bourgeois thinkers, were entangled in "ideology." If all systems of thought—Marxism included—were subject to process, change, and class bias, then the dialectical method could not provide absolute knowledge that transcended history, and communist ideology would have to acknowledge its kinship with other ideologies of the superstructure. Calverton did not go so far as Eastman, who maintained that the residues of the Hegelian dialectic in Marxism brought with them a "mystical" element in Marxian philosophy. Yet his theory bore some resemblance to Eastman's contention, expressed in his *Marx and Lenin: The Science of Revolution* (1927), that Marx's mind was influenced by cultural factors that prevented him from seeing the genesis of his own ideas.[24]

If Eastman's influence was evident in Calverton's theory, so was the larger influence of pragmatism. The relativistic and ungrounded characteristic of Calverton's theory of cultural compulsives suggests the influence of Dewey and his instrumental view of knowledge—particularly Calverton's contention that the interpretation of social phenomena presupposes a purpose, end, or mind set. Certainly Calverton's theory was threatening to the orthodox Communists, because he relativized all class perspectives, suggesting that a totally objective and transparent view of history and society was impossible. If such were the case, how was it possible to measure various social theories and find them wanting as "false consciousness"? How was it possible to impute to the proletariat a position somehow outside ideology?

Calverton's contemporaries in Europe were wrestling with precisely this issue. In *History and Class Consciousness*, Georg Lukacs had asserted that only the proletariat, by virtue of its members' pivotal position in the labor process that made them both subject and object of history, could aspire to the *total* vantage point from which true moral–cultural–practical knowledge emerges.[25] The Party ideologues in the United States, unfamiliar with Lukacs's complex epistemological arguments, put their position very crudely and undialectically: the proletariat's objectivity arose because, having no vested interests in the established bourgeois order, it provided the Archimedean point in which "true" consciousness was grounded. Calverton's position, however, resembles the theory of the European social theorist who is often placed against Lukacs—the Hungarian sociologist Karl Mannheim. Calverton may or may not have read Mannheim; nevertheless Mannheim's *Ideology and Utopia*, published in New York in 1929, noted that the analysis of thought and ideas in terms of ideologies was becoming a weapon that could be used from a variety of political positions.[26] Certainly, Calverton's theory bears some resemblance to Mannheim's sociology of knowledge thesis—that mental structures are inevitably differently formed in different social and historical settings.[27] Mannheim attempted to salvage totalistic knowledge by hypothesizing a collectivity of "free floating" intellectuals whose integrated viewpoint approached truth as an appropriate reflection of the social reality of a given period.[28] Calverton on the other hand (reflecting a bent toward pragmatism) simply relativized and historicized social knowledge, making it a function of the class alignments and sympathies of the individual intellectual or of groups of intellectuals. Yet both saw Marxism as merely one ideology among others, not a standard of truth by which false consciousness could be evaluated.

Calverton's cultural compulsives thesis was unique in America for problematizing social knowledge as well as the crucial issue of "true" versus "false" consciousness. Certainly his position demonstrated that he was developing a keen awareness of the limitations of a scientistic Marxism. Yet his speculations won him a ferocious thirty-three-page attack in the *Communist*. Landy denounced him as "an enemy within the ranks of the proletariat" who was trying to disarm the revolutionary working class of a weapon with which to transcend the ideological distortions of bourgeois thought. Even such renegade social theorists as Georges Sorel, Max Beer, and Sidney Hook, who denied the objectivity of Marxism as a science, did not go so far as Calverton and his notion that *all* social sciences lacked objectivity.[29]

The theoretical disagreement was fundamental, but the strenuousness of Landy's attack suggested a ritualistic dimension, a rite of purification. The tone of ceremonial purgation characterized his entire article:

> When one who claims to be a communist introduces among the masses the uncertainty, the impotence, the doubts and contradictions that characterize the bourgeoisie in its last stages—he is in every respect an enemy within the ranks of the proletariat. It becomes the immediate duty of Marxism to expose and combat this counter-revolutionary poison.[30]

Calverton, not only a notoriously unorthodox radical but a prominent one, provided a convenient symbol of the threat of "poison" from within. Concurring with Foster, Landy concluded that Calverton was indeed "a social fascist ideologist."

Calverton had remained silent up until now. But after yet another charge of "social fascism" by Foster in his book *Toward Soviet America*,[31] his forbearance finally gave way. Meeting the charge of social fascism head on, he published "An Open Letter to William Z. Foster" in the *Modern Quarterly*. Calverton attacked "the general stupidity of the tactic of making various outsiders, especially those close to the Party, scapegoats for inner factional fights." The theory of social fascism was "tragically mistaken"; it was an ideological bludgeon used by the Communists to beat all criticism and dissent into retreat.

> Calling everyone and everything fascist that does not meet with the approval of the moment, instead of preparing the way for the success of communism . . . make[s] it all the more easy for Fascism to rise to power. Fascism is the great menace in America tomorrow. To fight the menace, we must combine rather than divide our strength, and learn to cooperate.[32]

Calverton's admonitions to Foster were prophetic: in Germany, Hitler had been in power for two years, Nazi terrorism was growing, and the strength of the Nazis continued to rise. Nevertheless, the Communists insisted that the collapse of Hitler's regime was imminent and continued to wage war on the Social Democrats in the belief that fascism and social democracy were both aspects of the same evil. In 1932, Calverton foresaw that the costs of pursuing such a mistaken policy would be high, but his reasoned plea for a unified front against fascism was contemptuously dismissed by the Party.

Calverton's "Open Letter," however, won him support from opposition groups. The Lovestonites, now a renegade group calling themselves—with a certain amount of self-delusion—the "majority" group (Stalin himself had condemned them as "right wing," and their ranks were considerably depleted), cheered Calverton on, finding evidence of "sectarian sterility" in the official communist treatment of him.[33] Will Herberg, in spite of his reservations about Calverton's cultural compulsives thesis, praised his article as "a striking piece of social-historical analysis."[34] In the meantime, however, literary radicals who sympathized with the official Communists (led by Foster) busily severed their public connections with Calverton.

Joshua Kunitz, for example, who once praised Calverton's work highly, now wrote a review for the *New Masses* criticizing Kenneth Burke's *Counter Statement* on the basis that Burke had been influenced by Calverton. Echoing the official opinion that Calverton's work was steeped in bourgeois ideology, Kunitz claimed that Burke had been "taken in" by Calverton's "much trumpeted" Marxism, which, he claimed, many bourgeois writers "mistakenly identified with real historical materialism."[35]

Calverton immediately sent Kunitz a note stating that he was "a bit nonplused" by the review, and Kunitz replied:

> It may surprise you to know that I cherish a warm feeling for you and that it pains me to have to fight you on the ideological front. . . . The article in the [New] Masses was a talk I delivered at the John Reed Club in the presence of Burke. When I assaulted his conception of Marxism, Burke exclaimed: "I got it from Calverton." Everybody laughed. Under such circumstances it was my revolutionary duty to assail the source itself.[36]

Kunitz made light of the incident, but Calverton was hurt by the attacks of old cohorts. Newton Arvin, who once considered Calverton his mentor in Marxist criticism, attempted to reassure Calverton:

> I have talked with Freeman, Hook, Gold, and other people who you know; and I can assure you that such people never speak of you as a person except pleasantly and even cordially. My very strong impression, as an outsider, is that there is no personal resentment of any kind in the attacks on you that have been made.[37]

Yet Calverton was scarcely reassured by the lack of "personal resentment" in these attacks. He was, indeed, deeply disturbed by the tendency to bifurcate so neatly the public and private realms—to attack viciously publicly and to speak pleasantly privately—and the tendency on the other hand to fail to distinguish the person from the cause, the individual from the political category. He was appalled that, under the sectarian logic of the Third Period, individuals were subsumed under the monolith of ideology according to which they became abstract political categories, mere symbols, scapegoats to atone for the sin of deviation.

Nevertheless, Calverton's name had indeed become a symbol of deviation, not only among Party members but among many literary radicals associated with the John Reed Clubs. Attacks on Calverton and the *Modern Quarterly* were becoming commonplace at meetings of the John Reed Clubs. In May 1932, a conference of twelve John Reed Clubs of the United States was called at the suggestion of the International Union of Revolutionary Writers (IURW), an international organization guided and directed from Moscow. When the clubs met at the Lincoln Center Auditorium in Chicago, Calverton and the *Modern Quarterly* came under open attack. Sidney Hook was invited to the convention to speak from the point of view of the "fellow traveler" (a Party term for those of like mind who were not Party members). Hook was immediately perplexed by the fact that Joseph Freeman informed him of new plans to draw "a great many fellow travellers" into the John Reed Clubs, while club members were busily attacking fellow travelers associated in any way with the *Modern Quarterly*. He wrote back to New York that one of the topics discussed at the convention was the "deviational" material that had been appearing in the *Modern Quarterly*. Hook was a lone dissenter. "I made a plea for printing stuff that was deviational in the minds of the editor [*sic*]," Hook wrote Calverton, "and said that the trouble with the *Modern Quarterly* was not that it did print the deviations, but that it did not correct them." Hook reported that his defense had prompted one of the members of the convention to refer to him as an "arch enemy of the working class." Hook concluded his report to Calverton in a tone of exasperation: "In the fall if they still stay sane I'm going to propose for discussion an open meeting [on] 'V. F. Calverton' and straighten things out once and for all. If they reject that I'm going to suggest a meeting be held on fellow travelers. If they turn that down, I'm through."[38]

The hostility toward Calverton and the *Quarterly* that charged the atmosphere of the Chicago John Reed Clubs was hardly surprising: the IURW had only recently censured the *New Masses* for its past association with Calverton. A. Elistratova (a twenty-year-old woman and putatively an eminent Russian authority on American literature) charged the *New Masses* with "petty-bourgeois passiveness," "insufficient politicization," "rotten liberalism," and with failing to fight social fascism adequately. Writing in *International Literature*, the central organ of the IURW, Elistratova attacked the *New Masses* specifically for its past mistake of entrusting Calverton, "who was without a doubt connected with social fascism," with leadership in the fight against Humanism. Elistratova here referred to Calverton's article, "Humanism, Literary Fascism," which had appeared in the *New Masses* back in 1930. Ironically, Calverton had taken precisely the same stand on Humanism as had orthodox radicals like Freeman and Gold—that Humanism as a literary movement was backward looking, anachronistic, and reactionary. Nevertheless because of the grave error of giving Calverton a prominent voice in the humanist controversy, the magazine would now be watched with "closest attention" by the IURW to see that the editors overcame the "most serious shortcoming" of failing to speak out against the social fascists. Elistratova informed the editors of the *New Masses* that the IURW expected them to launch "a ruthless exposure" of such "social fascist spokesmen" as Calverton and Eastman.[39]

The demand for a "ruthless exposure" of the social fascists was not long in being met. In January 1933 the *New Masses* devoted an entire issue to an onslaught on Calverton. Entitled "The Marxism of V. F. Calverton," it was written jointly by David Ramsey and Alan Calmer. The two men were not only upholding Third Period ideology but were engaging in an Oedipal confrontation that emerged from their own "anxiety of influence": both had been Calverton's students in the Baltimore public schools and had participated in the "2110" evenings of the early twenties. Calmer had also served on the editorial board of the *Quarterly* in 1927 and 1928. They justified the length of their attack on the basis of Calverton's great influence among leftist intellectuals, particularly the impressionable (as they had once been), the "least experienced of them."[40]

In the longest article in the magazine's history—some sixteen pages, virtually the entire issue—Ramsey and Calmer accused Calverton of being everything from a "sex racketeer" to a plagiarist. They seized upon quotations from editorials he had written as far back as 1928—editorials critical of the Communist Party's divisive tactics and chronic inability to speak to the American masses—as evidence of his sins against the Party. They rehashed H. M. Wicks's attack of years before, dragging up the old issue of plagiarism. Calverton's theory of cultural compulsives was cited as evidence of his "ideological attack on the revolutionary movement," and his pamphlet *For Revolution* with its notion of American exceptionalism (the idea that the United States must develop its own revolutionary strategy and tactics based on its particular conditions) was offered as further proof of his heresy. Calverton was in sympathy with the petty bourgeoisie, and therefore a Fascist. He was a "maturing fascist," a "radical fascist," an unscrupulous "real racketeer," and an "open collaborator of the ruling class."[41]

By this point Calverton was becoming accustomed to being the target of the steady stream of onslaughts and denunciations issuing from the communist press. But he was still amazed by the virulence of the *New Masses* attack. He now realized that further appeals for cooperation on the Left, like his "Open Letter" to Foster, were fruitless and that a counteroffensive was necessary. He published a vigorous defense of himself, an "Open Letter to the *New Masses*" in the March 1933 issue: "While I knew you would go to great lengths to satisfy Moscow . . . I did not think you would bend so far backwards to gain absolution."[42] Well aware of the directives issued by *International Literature*, Calverton asserted that the *New Masses* attack reflected the Communist Party's tendency to consider "everyone a social fascist who does not accept the absolute infallibility of the Party's approach and tactics." He felt compelled to answer the attack publicly, because "it is characteristic of a tendency to attack all writers who deviate from your superimposed, regimented, pseudo-Marxian norm."[43] Calverton argued that the marked change in the Party's attitude toward him was quite obviously a manifestation of increasing ideological regimentation during the Third Period:

In 1928 and 1929, my articles were being used in the Soviet Press, and I was constantly getting letters to send more; in 1930 and 1931 when the power-fight became more intense and official parties were being ripped to pieces in the process, and it became known that I did not think a healthy communist movement could be built upon such a basis, the favor with which my work was looked upon in Moscow suddenly turned to disfavor.[44]

To the charge that he had attacked the scientific basis of Marxism, Calverton retorted:

The great danger which Marxism faces today is exemplified by your approach. Marxism is dynamic and not static; it is significant as a scientific method but dangerous as sterile dogma. When used to praise those who are politically in favor at one time and then to denounce them when they are not in political favor at another, the scientific aspect of Marxism is lost. It has then become the dogma of a ruling sect instead of the scientific yardstick of revolutionary analysis. The significant truth of Marxism must be tested in the scientific world of fact and not in the closed chambers of authoritarianism.[45]

Calverton's astute critical assessment of the Third Period mentality again attests to his good political sense, and he was supported by others critical of Stalinism. Max Eastman, who received a copy of the Ramsey and Calmer article in the mail (sent to him by several fellow travelers as a challenge), defended Calverton on the issue of cultural compulsives. He asserted that "Calverton . . . was attacked under orders from Moscow . . . because he would not swallow the deluge of stereotyped lies and vulgarizations of Marxian thinking with which revolutionary intelligence has been swamped for the last ten years all over the world."[46] Still, the complete reversal of the official Communists' attitude to Calverton between 1928 and 1933 baffled many on the literary Left. As Harry Hansen wrote in the *Virginia Pilot* of Norfolk, Virginia,

> Zowie, Biff, Swat! as they used to say in the comic strips. The *New Masses* for January 16 prints 16 pages to say that V. F. Calverton is not a true revolutionist or communist; he is just a bourgeois worker in disguise, masking the coming of fascism. And we thought he was a red.[47]

But Calverton's new status as a social fascist and the fact that the *New Masses* attack was becoming widely known as the "Calverton issue" of the magazine raised him in the estimation of some. A member of the editorial board of *Labor Unity* wrote Calverton that

> I am afraid I owe you an apology. Until I read the Calverton issue of the *New Masses* I rather underestimated you; Ramsey's article has duly impressed me of your importance. I doubt if *New Masses* would run a longer article if someone should discover that Stalin is a traitor to the revolutionary cause—which may happen any day, I guess.[48]

Ultimately Calverton would find himself in good company; in 1937 the *New Masses* would devote eleven pages to attacking the *Partisan Review*, its editors, and the arguments of their camp.[49] The viciousness of the *New Masses* attacks make William Phillips's statement that New York writers during the thirties "often acted as though they were in a primitive struggle for survival" a moderate one.[50] Terry Cooney explains the *New Masses* strategy of "overkill" as a result of the fact that political allegiances were not a distant abstraction but an inescapable part of daily life and that factional enemies literally rubbed elbows in New York.[51] For Calverton, who preferred not simply to rub elbows but to maintain friendships, the result of the attack was particularly devastating. Besides intense isolation, he felt a crushing moral anguish as he witnessed the movement he had wished to remain allied with now abandon reason and embrace authoritarianism. He felt an urgent need to reassess his own ideological commitments. For if Calverton had long-held private misgivings about Stalinism, he had kept them in check, publicly supporting the Party and calling for unity on the Left even in the face of attacks on his views and his magazine by Party officials. Now he realized, as he wrote a friend late in 1933, "Stalin's tactics . . . must be fought tooth and nail," and he set about this battle with all the energy and resources he could muster.[52]

I F FOSTER's first attack in 1932 had marked a devastating blow to relations between Calverton and the Communists, the *New Masses* attack signaled the final and irrevocable break. After 1933 the *Modern*

Monthly (the magazine's new monthly format initiated that year) took on an adamant anti-Stalinist character. Calverton introduced the magazine's new policy by publishing a letter he had recently written to Leon Trotsky: although he disagreed with the Left Opposition on many points, Calverton endorsed the absolute necessity to speak out against "the indescribable harm done to the communist movement by the Stalinist triumph."[53] Accordingly, he began inviting opposition spokesmen from both the Left (Trotskyists) and the Right (Lovestonites) into the pages of his magazine. In the June 1933 issue of the magazine, Calverton ran a symposium entitled "The Crisis in Communism" with J. B. Field articulating the Trotskyist position and Will Herberg representing the Lovestonite faction. By the end of 1933, both Will Herberg and Bertram D. Wolfe (who by this time had gone over to the Lovestonite faction) contributed regularly to the *Monthly*.

The same year, Eastman's "Artists in Uniform," a harsh criticism of the suppression of cultural freedom in Russia under Stalin (later published as a book), appeared in the *Monthly* as part of Calverton's new campaign. Hook's "The Fallacy of the Theory of Social Fascism" lent further weight to his cause. Hook struck a forceful blow against the theory of social fascism by arguing that if social democracy had functioned historically to suppress revolutionary movements around the world, it nevertheless held as its premise of survival the perpetuation of mass labor movements. By contrast, fascism was devoted to the suppression of mass labor organizations. Contrary to the doctrine of social fascism, social democracy and fascism were in irreconcilable conflict.[54]

Calverton also used the *Monthly* to express his own critical indictments of Stalinism and Third Period tactics. Writing of the "crisis in communism"—signaled by the collapse of the Communist Party in Germany— he asserted that while the Nazis had been steadily gaining power, the German Communists had pursued a course of "tragic error," blindly following the theory of social fascism, directing their fire against social democrats rather than Nazi terrorists.[55] Like Trotsky, Calverton believed that a Left united front was imperative to stop fascism. In editorial after editorial, he persistently pointed out that fascism represented the most immediate and potentially devastating threat to the civilized world. Several years later, when it became obvious that fascism was no passing phenomenon, the Communists would drop the notion of social fascism, and in a volte-face, would adopt the Popular Front policy of a united front against fascism— a united front not only with other factions of the Left, but with liberal bourgeois parties as well. By 1935 most radicals would share Calverton's feelings regarding the tragic error of Third Period tactics.

But in 1933 orthodox radicals found Calverton's idea of a "crisis in communism" utterly reprehensible. Early in 1934, in the wake of the *New Masses* controversy, *International Literature* printed an even longer attack on him. The twenty-eight-page article echoed the *New Masses* attack and added a few new offenses to Calverton's lengthy list—among others, the transgression of printing Eastman's "Artists in Uniform" in the *Monthly*.[56]

Many of the literary radicals of an orthodox bent who had been associated with the *Quarterly* now began to abandon the magazine. Granville Hicks, whose book reviews had been appearing quite regularly, was the first to leave: "Insofar as I am compelled to take sides, I side with the Party," Hicks wrote. "Now it seems increasingly clear you and your magazine are allied with the Opposition."[57] Newton Arvin left shortly thereafter. Kyle Crichton, who had been writing a commentary column for the magazine resigned, as did Stanley Burnshaw, a young poet and critic who had been promoting the magazine on college campuses; both went over to the *New Masses*. Edwin Seaver, who had written proletarian stories for the magazine, stopped contributing after the *New Masses* attack, and Eli Siegmeister, a Marxist musicologist, resigned angrily after the publication of Eastman's controversial "Artists in Uniform." From Paris, Robert Briffault wrote Calverton expressing his disapproval of the magazine's new direction and voicing the philosophy of the Third Period: "I don't see any use of using any intermediate terms in the political vocabulary now. If you're not a communist you're a fascist. Nothing else matters."[58]

Calverton took all these leave-takings hard. Briffault had been one of his close friends; a short time earlier when Briffault had run out of funds in New York and found himself facing starvation, Calverton had lent him money. Michael Blankfort's resignation from the magazine, however, probably hurt Calverton the most. Blankfort had become Calverton's close friend while serving as associate editor. Blankfort had resisted his impulse to resign after the magazine took its anti-Stalinist turn, because, as he wrote Calverton, "my loyalty was greater than my conviction."[59] Calverton protested Blankfort's resignation, warning him that he was aligning himself "with the most vicious elements, at least as I see them, in the official communist ranks which are tending to destroy the world rather than build up the possibilities of a future communist world."[60] Yet characteristically Calverton appealed to Blankfort to "keep circumstances from hurting a friendship so precious as ours," and in spite of their ideological differences they remained close friends.

But his friendship with Mike Gold did not fare so well. In November 1933 Gold published an article in the *Daily Worker* entitled "Against V. F. Calverton." "I must confess to a political error," Gold began his mea culpa. Gold explained that Calverton had exhibited the usual "complexes" of literary men, but for a time it seemed he would "adjust," and it seemed he was influencing many American intellectuals toward a general sympathy for communism. Gold had opposed the *New Masses* attack, primarily because he felt it a "tactical error" to give so much space to one man's mistakes. But a recent reappraisal of Calverton and his magazine had forced him to change his mind, especially when he read Eastman's "Artists in Uniform":

> Looking back over the files of the *Modern Monthly*, and reading carefully Max Eastman's article, I am forced to the conclusion that this magazine now exists to poison the minds of intellectuals, and to excite in them hatred and prejudice against the Soviet Union, and the communist movement. As such, of course, it must be fought and condemned.[61]

After this public confession, Gold totally severed his relationship with Calverton.

The breakdown of relations with people Calverton had considered friends for years was certainly the most painful outcome of the *New Masses* attack and Calverton's subsequent decision to steer his magazine away from the Communist Party. Now when old friends—like Freeman, Gold, and Kunitz—were conspicuously absent from his parties, Calverton was very nearly devastated. He fell into periods of black depression and frequently brooded about the *New Masses* attack, the leave-taking of friends, and the departure of associates who had worked with him on the magazine. George Britt remembers consoling him: "George, why give a damn about that, it's good riddance; you'll find in the long run that the *New Masses* attack is one of the principal claims to your credit." But Britt observed in retrospect, "I don't think he ever got over it."[62]

The attacks by the Communists, no doubt precipitated because of the enormous influence Calverton and his independent publication had gained in radical and liberal intellectual circles, were ultimately the result of circumstance (the Party's hostility to those who refused its discipline and dogma) and intellect (Calverton's unorthodox views and theories) intersecting with profound consequences. At the conclusion of 1933, Calverton's situation was both ironic and tragic: he had been victimized by the same "self-devouring internecine warfare" that he had spoken out against for years. An outspoken critic of doctrine and dogma, he was made to fit the Procrustean measure of the social fascist. Theoretically astute in his refusal to accept a narrow and scientistic version of Marxism, and prophetic in his commentaries on the dangers of fascism, Calverton had become an outcast, one of the foremost "enemies of the revolution."

Sidney Hook has argued that Calverton would not have turned away from the Stalinists had he not been attacked by them.[63] But by 1933 a history of continuing disagreements between Calverton and the Party made it clear that Calverton's free-ranging speculations and Party doctrine were on a collision course, and that he would have broken with the Party sooner or later. Certainly as his theory of cultural compulsives suggests, he was moving in an intellectual direction that made peaceful coexistence with Party orthodoxy impossible. Beyond his private misgivings about Stalinism, which went all the way back to his Russian journey in 1927, what seems clear is that Calverton's calls for unity on the Left, his criticisms of Party policy, and his insistence on the independence of his magazine in the face of Party orthodoxy all indicate that he was moving irrevocably away from the Party even before the attack.

Moreover, Calverton's critical indictment of Stalinism in the post–1933 period sprang from sources far deeper than literary politics. Rather than being simply reactions to the attacks against him, his work represented a sustained and systematic criticism of Stalinist policy that arose from deeply held convictions. These criticisms were extensions and developments of criticisms he leveled against the Party before his break, and they arose from a continuing independence of mind. But no doubt the communist attacks forced Calverton to confront publicly the dangers of Stalinism and to alter his alliances. Now he urged prominent intellectuals to join him in the task of fighting Stalinism and to face the task that he now believed crucial for American intellectuals: the creation of an independent socialism that took into account American conditions and the American intellectual tradition. Calverton thus redirected his magazine, as well as his own energies, to the objective not only of battling Stalinism but of Americanizing Marx.

Chapter Nine

If the American workers can be taught to be proud of the revolutionary development of their tradition, they can be inspired with renewed faith in the revolutionary possibilities of the future.

—V. F. Calverton, *For Revolution*, 1932

The Americanization of Marx

After his trip to Russia in 1927, Calverton became increasingly convinced of the wisdom of Lenin's advice that "the development of the revolution in different countries proceeds along varying paths in varying rapidities."[1] One of the first radicals to call for the Left to adjust its policies to the particular conditions and opportunities of the American situation, his editorials after 1928 began to insist on the uniqueness of the American cultural pattern and to reproach the Communists for failing to adapt their programs and language to the psychology of the American worker. Now, having witnessed the Stalinization of the American Communist Party and the devastating effects of the doctrine of social fascism, Calverton was adamant about the need for American Communists to break with the Comintern and reformulate their program to fit American conditions.

Calverton's interest in the Americanization of Marx originally stemmed from his contact with Brookwood Labor College, where he lectured intermittently during the mid and late twenties, and with A. J. Muste, labor leader, pacifist minister, and director of the college. Ideas of an American approach to Marxism had been gestating at Brookwood during this period; the labor organizer Louis Budenz had given a series of lectures on the topic at Brookwood in 1928,[2] and ideas relating to America's special conditions and problems were expressed in the Musteite *Labor Age*, which Calverton read avidly. So taken was he with the project of Americanizing Marxism that when Muste formed a party committed to this end in 1933—the American Workers Party—Calverton joined and became an active participant.

But if his notions of an American approach to Marx were provoked initially by Brookwood and the Musteite movement, Calverton adopted these ideas with a singular devotion, and the formation of a uniquely American radicalism became a highly personal quest. Early 1933 represented a distinct turning point for his journal as he dedicated it to a careful analysis of "the American scene in American terms." Calverton's interest in Americanizing Marx led him further in search of a usable past, an indigenous radicalism rooted in the American tradition. For it was during the period between 1933 and 1935 that Calverton, suffering from the *New Masses* attack and profoundly disillusioned with the Communist Party, turned away in large part from literary criticism in an effort to redefine his own political outlook. He sought to reappraise the American past in an attempt to grasp a coherent tradition of native radicalism that would provide some meaning in the face of the destructive policies of the Stalinist regime. His work during this period is simultaneously an explanation and a critique of the failure of the Communist Party to have a broad impact in the United States, for he believed that the Party's categories and its very terminology were simply alien and inapplicable and hence its praxis barren. Thus the project of Americanizing Marxism was not simply providing a better theoretical appraisal of American conditions but fashioning a praxis that would transform radical action from something foreign into terms of the American experience.

For Revolution (1932) was Calverton's first and most polemical statement for Americanizing Marxism. Written at the nadir of the depression, the pamphlet argued that revolution in America was a necessity. Lenin had maintained that there were two fundamental prerequisites for a successful revolution—a high development of the productive forces and the preparedness of the proletariat. In the United States, Calverton contended, only the first of these conditions was realized:

> Our technology is advanced but our ideology is backward; we have built up an industrial structure which can easily be converted from a competitive into a co-operative one, but we have not built up a working class which has learned as yet the advantage of cooperation or the wisdom of communism. . . . America is faced today with an objective situation which is potentially revolutionary, but with a working class which is ideologically unequipped to take revolutionary action.[3]

Calverton claimed that this contradiction—between a potentially revolutionary situation and a backward proletariat—was a result of a unique quality of the frontier experience in America. In line with the turn-of-the-century study by Werner Sombert who attributed the absence of socialism in America to the open frontiers and the many opportunities for social ascent through individual effort,[4] Calverton contended that the unsettled regions of the West once provided a means of escape for the oppressed bourgeoisie from the East and held forth a promise of escape for the worker. The myth of rugged individualism that this situation fostered captured the imaginations of both the working class and the middle class and persisted into modern times. The presence of the frontier, with its agrarian orientation and individualistic promise, made the American workers and especially America's farmers amenable to a retrogressive agrarian populist philosophy with all of its fundamental contradictions: the opposition to corporate capitalism and Wall Street but at the same time the desire to preserve private property and the profit system.

The tenacity of bourgeois values and middle-class outlook made the task of transforming the American people into a "creatively class conscious" nation particularly difficult, Calverton wrote. Change would be brought about only by appealing to them in American terms as well as utilizing the American past. Here the influence of the Musteites (who advocated building on an American revolutionary tradition) is apparent: "The American revolutionary tradition is a tradition which the American masses will quickest understand, and which to neglect, as has been done in the past, is to hinder rather than to help the second American revolution."[5] In preparation for this "second American revolution," America's revolutionary tradition was to be revitalized and reconstituted: Jeffersonian individualism was not to be salvaged but rather the "progressive spirit of revolt" in the Jeffersonian philosophy should be upheld. Revolutionary figures of the American past were to be resurrected as "symbols of challenge and advance." If radical theoreticians could stir within Americans a "national pride" in their own revolutionary tradition (while rejecting the narrow chauvinism associated with an emphasis on nationalism), they would inspire the American people to overthrow the present ruling class of financiers and industrialists.

Calverton wished to tap the roots of the progressive strain in the American past while at the same time rejecting the objectives of traditional liberal reform. Yet there are obvious theoretical problems in the kind of selective rewriting and remythologizing of the past that he advocated. His interest in the persuasive popular appeal of myth and symbol demonstrated here was to have some rather dubious implications for his later thinking.[6] Moreover, his pamphlet concerned itself with the ideological rather than the social aspects of the coming revolution and was very unclear about political parties, class alliances, and the specifics of a revolutionary program. Nevertheless, the work was one of the earliest to address the specific conditions in America—the lack of class consciousness among the workers and the persistence of bourgeois values among all segments of the population.[7] And although the *New Masses* would later furiously castigate Calverton's "American exceptionalism" and his "bourgeois nationalism," his pamphlet, when it appeared, was admired by a number of radical intellectuals. Writers as diverse as Waldo Frank, Benjamin Gitlow, and Mike Gold praised Calverton's analysis (although Gold did so only privately).[8] Members of the Lovestonite faction welcomed the pamphlet's emphasis on national peculiarities.

But the most notable response to *For Revolution* came from Leon Trotsky in a lengthy letter in the *Militant*, organ of the Left opposition. Trotsky harshly criticized Calverton's failure to specify the role of political parties and factional struggles in the coming revolution and implied that this omission revealed Calverton's faint-heartedness and explained his failure to join the Trotskyist movement. Trotsky warned against submitting the foundations and methods of Marxism to revision in the effort to Americanize it and pointed to Max Eastman's rejection of the materialist dialectic, "an obviously hopeless and, in its possible consequences, retrograde adventure."[9] But Trotsky was in agreement on the general issue of translating Marxism into American terms:

> You are totally right; the vanguard of the American proletariat must come to base itself on the revolutionary traditions of its own country. . . . To Americanize Marxism signifies to root it in American soil, to verify it against the events of American history, to explore by its methods the problems of American economy and politics, to assimilate the world revolutionary experience under the viewpoint of the tasks of the American revolution. A great Work! It is time to approach it with the shirtsleeves rolled up.[10]

Calverton was pleased to have Trotsky's qualified endorsement and later reprinted Trotsky's letter in his magazine as support for the project of Americanizing Marx. He also responded by publishing an open letter to Trotsky, which summed up his case against the Stalinists and underscored the points of agreement with the Trotskyists: "We agree then that whenever a revolutionary movement closes its doors to democratic discussion, criticism and opposition in its ranks, it does so only at the expense of its own vigor, plasticity and power."[11] Yet he expressed his suspicion that the Trotskyist opposition itself might go the way of the Stalinists, suppressing opposition once it attained power: "There is no final guarantee that the Left opposition or any other opposition might not degenerate into a power-perpetuating machine, modifying its policies to preserve its own dominance, once it was able to outlaw all the criticisms and condemnations of its opponents."[12] Obviously, this was Calverton's answer to Trotsky's charge of faint-heartedness and a reiteration of his independent position. Calverton admired Trotsky as a great revolutionary figure and a courageous opponent of Stalin, but he was suspicious of the monolithic and antidemocratic character that the Trotskyist opposition shared with the Stalinists. Thus he avoided any alliance between his magazine and the Trotskyists.

It was nevertheless with this attitude of approaching a "great work" with "shirt-sleeves rolled up" that Calverton prepared, in late 1932, to introduce the new format of his journal, the *Modern Monthly*. The growing radical consciousness in America, intensified by the economic crisis, now made it feasible to convert the magazine from a quarterly to a monthly, he reported in an editorial for the fall 1932 issue. Foreign subscriptions, which had provided about 30 percent of the magazine's support before the crash of 1929, had doubled, while American subscribers had quadrupled and newsstand sales had increased tenfold.[13] The *Quarterly* was still beleaguered with financial problems, but the heightened interest in the magazine occasioned by the depression and the leftward turn of American intellectuals made Calverton optimistic about the future of its new monthly incarnation.

The *Modern Monthly* made its debut in February 1933, only a month after the *New Masses* attack. Calverton's editorial announced the magazine's new direction, explicitly dedicating the *Monthly* to the project of Americanizing Marx. Calverton argued that Americans were being driven toward the brink of revolt by the economic situation. But it was not just workers and farmers who were suffering. America was seeing the radicalization of a new class:

> That group, commonly known as the intellectuals, which constitutes in occupational terms the professional workers, teachers, writers, artists, doctors, dentists, lawyers, architects, engineers, has already begun to reveal signs of revolt in advance of the workers and farmers.[14]

This professional and intellectual class, like the workers, was experiencing the brunt of the depression; the supply of professional workers had outstripped demand, and with fewer and fewer jobs available, "distress and despair of the American intellectual is but part of an inevitable process." The new *Monthly* proposed to address itself specifically to this newly radicalized class of intellectuals and white-collar workers:

While we realize that the professional workers constitute . . . a much smaller section, for example, than the industrial workers, we believe it better that we should limit our appeal for the time being at least to the former group. . . . There are a number of papers and periodicals which make their appeal to the industrial workers, while there is none dedicated to the interests of the professional workers—none, at least, with any radical vision or conception of a new society. In filling that cultural gap, we believe, we are performing a significant social function. We shall be specifically concerned with the problems of the American school teacher today, the American doctor, the American engineer, the American writer, the American artist— in a word, the problems which face the American intellectuals in general.[15]

The introduction of the concept of the "professional worker" now sharply differentiated the *Monthly* from a publication like the *New Masses*, for which "workers" perforce meant industrial workers, and for which— given its proletcult bent—an alliance between worker (or artist) and the white-collar class would be unthinkable. Certainly this was a substantial shift for Calverton who had earlier supposed, like the orthodox Communists, that the working class would be primarily instrumental in revolutionary change. Now, however, Calverton was in agreement with such writers as John Dewey, who believed that the Left would have to court the middle class,[16] as well as writers like Alfred Bingham (editor of *Common Sense*) and Lewis Corey who stressed the necessity of cooperation between the workers and the middle class.[17]

Moreover, what distinguished this new tack of the *Monthly* was the assumption that the professionals and intellectuals were becoming class conscious and therefore potential agents of social change. This placed the *Monthly* in a tradition of discussion that extended back to Veblen, who argued in his *Engineers and the Price System* (written after World War I) that the war had quickened the infiltration of experts into America's industrial apparatus and that a class consciousness among American engineers was emerging.[18] Technocratic progressives, like Stuart Chase, following Veblen, affirmed the power of industrial engineers to effect social change in a collectivist direction,[19] while moderates like George Soule, although reluctant to attribute a revolutionary impetus to the new professional class, nevertheless remarked on the shift in class power toward the intelligentsia.[20] Somewhat more left-leaning writers like Alfred Bingham claimed that an urban, technical, managerial, and professional force constituted a category "between and more important than capital and labor."[21]

The major influence on the *Monthly* in terms of this discussion was

Marxist economist Lewis Corey, who had been known as Louis C. Fraina years earlier when he helped organize the American Communist Party. Corey began writing for the magazine during the early thirties. At this point he was developing the ideas that would appear in his 1935 work, *The Crisis of the Middle Class*. Corey contended that capitalism was undergoing a profound structural change, producing a drastic shrinkage of an "old" middle class of independent enterprisers and the simultaneous creation of a "new" middle class of salaried employees who had nothing in common with the small enterprisers. On the contrary, the new middle class was "overwhelmingly a class of dependent salaried employees," whose "collective forms of economic activity are the objective basis of a new social order." [22] In short, the new middle class had more in common with workers than with small enterprisers, and it was becoming further proletarianized due to the rigors of the depression. The solution to the problems of the professional class was to recognize its shared interest with the working class and commit itself with the workers to a socialist society.[23]

Indeed, following Corey's tenets, a central assumption of the *Monthly*'s "statement of purpose" was the need of an alliance between an increasingly radical middle class and the working class in the fight for socialism. Broadly speaking, America was now to be considered a unique and exceptional situation. Thus the key words in the vocabulary of the *Monthly* were "America" and "American." They dominated the titles of articles in the early issues of the publication: "Marx and America," "For a New America," "What Next for American Labor," "A Labor Party *for* America," "The NRA and American Labor."

If the *Quarterly* had turned its attention to pressing social issues after 1930, it nevertheless continued to emphasize literary and cultural matters. But the *Monthly* now focused on specific social problems, reflecting the prevailing sense that the crisis in American society overshadowed cultural concerns. Gone were the great debates about literary modernism and the raging battles over radical aesthetics. In their place were articles dealing with immediate economic and political issues. Essays on the American labor movement, the plight of the American farmer, trade unionism, Roosevelt and the NRA, the role of intellectuals in the Roosevelt administration, economic planning, the growth of fascism in America, unemployment insurance, American medical care and the AMA, and similar topics now appeared regularly. Nearly all of these essays emphasized the American context and conveyed a sense of the urgent need to analyze, from a radical perspective, the distinctive features of the American situation.

In a sense, the *Modern Quarterly* had always had a distinctively American approach to Marxism, if only in its insistence on democratic criticism within the radical movement as a whole. Beyond that, however, the battle that had raged since 1927 in the pages of the magazine between Max Eastman and Sidney Hook was in fact being fought over two differing approaches to the Americanization of Marx. Both students of Dewey, Eastman and Hook were attempting to reconcile Marxism with American pragmatism, albeit from differing approaches. Eastman felt Marxism should be approached via Lenin, who had purged it of its Hegelian "animism" and brought it into line with contemporary science, engineering, and "instrumental reason." Hook, on the other hand, argued that Marxism was inherently a pragmatic science: he denied vigorously that Marxism was "saddled" with Hegelian metaphysics and claimed that the Marxist idea of praxis had its analogue in the "epistemological activism" of Dewey and James. These differences, however, did not alter the fact that both men looked at Marxism through the lens of American pragmatism and instrumentalism. In their lengthy exchange both appealed to the authority of Dewey and the tradition of pragmatism in America. Hook's many erudite articles on Marxism that appeared in the *Modern Quarterly* and the *Modern Monthly* were attempts to restate Marxist theory in pragmatic terms.[24] Unfortunately by 1933 the six-year-long Hook–Eastman debate had descended into name calling, vilification, and accusations of plagiarism and character assassination, punctuated by several mismanaged attempts by Calverton to get the two men to make up. Exasperated, Calverton finally stepped in, denounced the debaters' "cheap shots" and called a halt to the battle between the two men so they could no longer "vent their spleen to the obscene enjoyment of the bourgeois world."[25]

But if the Hook–Eastman debate thus came to a rather unseemly conclusion, articles still appeared in the magazine exploring the connection between pragmatism and Marxism. Dewey himself was featured in a symposium on "Why I Am Not a Communist," arguing that communism was not only doctrinaire and inflexible, but that it "rests upon an almost entire neglect of the specific historical backgrounds and traditions that have operated to shape the patterns of thought and action in America."[26] Thus his criticism of communism underscored the need for the Left to address itself to American conditions, a point with which the *Modern Monthly* concurred. Dewey admitted the necessity for "some kind of socialism," an assertion that Ernest Sutherland Bates roundly applauded and held up as proof of the "ease with which Dewey and Marx can be harmonized." Bates contended that pragmatism revived the "Emersonian desire for the whole man instead of the fractional man"; Dewey's ideal was that of a radical democracy, "a harmonious society of inevitably limited individuals all of whose varying capacities are developed to the fullest possible extent." Thus pragmatic ideals and Marxist goals were compatible, and "if there were a chance for the establishment of communism tomorrow,"

Bates added, Dewey would doubtless "do all in his power to assist it."[27] Louis Budenz added to this, asserting that Americanizing Marxism meant bringing it into line with pragmatism and thus taking a flexible and non-dogmatic approach to revolution.[28]

Other articles appeared urging a reconciliation between Marxism and a Deweyian pragmatism that would be appropriate for the American context. Theodore B. Brameld (a philosophy professor at Long Island University) recommended rejecting the "absolutist side of communist theory" that had been responsible for the paralysis of the Party not only in Germany but in other countries where fascism had swept into power. Brameld, like Eastman, wished to discard the metaphysical trappings of dialectical materialism and affirm other facets of Marxism: its "methodology of dynamic social interaction," its experimental impetus, and its resemblance to instrumentalism.[29] Similarly another philosopher, Jerome Rosenthal, argued against the "monistic and necessitarian" aspect of dialectical materialism. The Hegelian impulse to conceive of truth as organic, overarching, and all-embracing had led the Left to a "block universe" conception of reality that rejected any knowledge that fell short of what was considered the "whole" as "abstract and partial." The result was a system that was inflexible and discouraged heterogeneity. In this sense dialectical materialism ran counter to a revolutionary philosophy that should properly "express the practices of the sciences."[30]

Brameld and Rosenthal's articles, with their critiques of the totalizing tendency of dialectical materialism, suggested the degree to which Dewey's pragmatism was crucial in the *Monthly*'s effort to speculate about and fashion an American approach to Marxism. To what extent the various strains of Marxist thought were "scientific" remained a matter of debate, but an Americanized Marxism, as projected by these *Monthly* writers, would stress an experimental method, a reliance on empiricism rather than preconceived ideas, an openness to process and change, and a notion of truth that, in pragmatic fashion, was not an "essence" but something that emerged through human action.

The new direction of the *Monthly* made it an appropriate forum for writers who Americanized Marx in a variety of other ways. Articles appeared, for example, by Louis Hacker, whose special interest was the reinterpretation of American history in terms of the class struggle, Louis Budenz, a well-known union organizer, and of course Lewis Corey, who was concerned with the factors that made the United States unique in terms of Marxist analysis. Calverton saw eye to eye with Budenz and Corey on the issue of adapting Marxist theory to the peculiarities of the American situation. Corey, particularly, Calverton opined, "stands out today in the field of economic theory as one of the most brilliant hopes in American radicalism."[31] Corey's theory concerning the proletarianization of the professional classes sounded a dominant note in the *Monthly* toward the middle of the decade.

The *Monthly*'s emphasis on the American scene also made it an ideal forum for the Lovestonites, often called the CP of the Right (Majority) Opposition, whose members were the chief exponents of the theory of American exceptionalism. The Lovestonites criticized the Communists for applying Marxist–Leninist ideas mechanically to American conditions rather than creatively adapting them. The early issues of the *Monthly* contain numerous articles by the leaders of the Lovestonite faction—Jay Lovestone, Bertram D. Wolfe, and Will Herberg—as well as by prominent members of the faction such as Benjamin Gitlow.

Calverton never joined the Lovestonites, perhaps believing membership would compromise his magazine's independence, perhaps feeling that the Lovestonite group was not yet precisely geared for American conditions. Yet because he embraced the notion of Americanizing Marxism, Calverton was very close to the tenets of the Lovestonites in his personal outlook, and he welcomed their writings to the magazine. The introductory editorial statement of the *Monthly*, proclaimed it to be, like the *Quarterly*, "an independent radical magazine, affiliated with no party."[32] Indeed, Calverton printed articles by any faction that wished to contribute, so that the magazine contained material by both the Right and Left opposition as well as by assorted independent spirits. Yet while he continued his official editorial policy of inviting contributions by all radical groups including the CPUSA, the Stalinists were not about to be associated with a "social fascist" nor with a magazine critical of Party policy.

Of all the oppositional voices who contributed to his magazine Calverton was most impressed with Lovestonite Will Herberg and his arguments on the need for national self-determination, if not complete autonomy, within the communist movement. Calverton immediately saw in Herberg a man who could add valuable perspectives to the issue of Americanizing Marx. Calverton asked Herberg for copies of lectures on national autonomy he had delivered at the New Workers' School and asked him to contribute an article to the *Modern Monthly*'s symposium on "The Crisis in Communism" from the viewpoint of the International Communist Opposition.[33]

In his article Herberg expressed the fundamental principle of the opposition, that the United States must develop its own revolutionary strategy and tactics. This was not merely a resurrection of the idea of American exceptionalism that had been earlier espoused by Lovestone and Wolfe, for the economic crash had made the older debate about the stability and durability of American capitalism obsolete.[34] Rather the emphasis was now on autonomy from the rigid monopoly of leadership of the Communist International. Nor was Trotsky an alternative. If Stalin was "Pope," then Trotsky was "anti-Pope": "We are against the Papal system as such." Herberg condemned the "mechanical transference" to other countries of methods suitable in Russia, as well as the "forced uniformity" of ideas and tactics that ignored the unique characteristics specific to place and culture. The collapse of the German Communist Party made it crucial for American Communists to reformulate their own strategy and tactics on the basis of democratic centrism ("the right of the free expression of opinion within the party and the free discussion of all vital issues, side by side with the disciplined execution of decisions regularly arrived at"). Finally Herberg advocated a greater respect for "objective differences" in the economic and political conditions confronting communist parties throughout the world.[35]

Buttressed with Herberg's notions of democratic centrism and American uniqueness, Calverton wrote an editorial in the *Modern Monthly* denouncing Stalinist's policies and Party strategy. The doctrine of social fascism assumed that social democracy was the real enemy of the proletarian movement, and this mistaken notion had resulted in the tragic collapse of the German Communist Party. When it became patently obvious that the Communists had misspent their energies fighting the Social Democrats, they resorted to another equally futile strategy, the "united front from below." Supposedly an appeal for unity made directly to the masses by going "over the heads" of the Socialist Party and other labor organizations, the "united front" tactic excluded from the movement all non-Party Left elements and removed the possibility of Communists entering electoral alliances with the Socialists. That the Comintern had belatedly come out in favor of a united front with the Social Democrats (a complete reversal of its previous position) only revealed that the Party was inveterately opportunistic and not interested in a genuine alliance of the leftist organizations in the United States.[36]

Calverton stressed that Hitler's victory in Germany underscored the urgent need for just such an alliance. The defeat and suppression of the German Communist Party and the Nazis' rise to power cast a pall over the American political scene where organizations such as William Dudley Pelley's Silver Shirts, the Ku Klux Klan, and the abortive organization of the "Khaki Shirts" were an ominous reminder of the threat posed by the belligerent lower middle class. Certainly the tradition of agrarian populism in the United States made this threat all the more concrete. As Calverton wrote to Mauritz Hallgren, "The Roosevelts don't worry me so much as the potential Huey Longs who, like American Hitlers, will stomp up and down the country in the near future."[37] If the fascist menace in America was to be countered, the public would have to be educated toward a proper understanding of the nature of fascism and its potential threat.[38]

Such was Calverton's intention in an article he wrote for the *Monthly* of July 1933 entitled "What Is Fascism?" He asserted, as against the Communists, that it was simplistic to see Adolf Hitler merely as a creation or agent of big business struggling to maintain economic power in a dying capitalist state. Both Mussolini and Hitler relied on the financial support of big business, but the issue of "who pays?" could be deceptive. Fascism predicated certain developments not in harmony with big business. Like the feudal kings, whose political function was to discipline the barons and subordinate their power to a central authority, the fascist dictator arose in response to a need to shape the recalcitrant forces in industrial society and subordinate them to the ends of the entire corporate fascist state. Hence the first task of the fascist dictatorship was to wrest power from the hands of the private bankers, industrialists, and landlords who comprised these "recalcitrant" forces and to exterminate the Social Democrats and Communists who threatened to seize power. Conceivably, Hitler would further the interests of big business, but he would not protect the individual interests of its owners. Nevertheless, the Nazis performed an important function for big business: they provided a buffer against the spread and success of communism.

Fascism, Calverton argued, found its mass base in the lower middle class, which had been "driven relentlessly to the wall" by big business. Eager to believe the Fascists' promise to give power back to the small businessman and shopkeeper, the lower middle class rallied around the fascist dictator. But fascism could never keep its promises because of a fundamental economic reality: it was impossible to rebuild a society based on mass production around small producers. Moreover, fascism could never give the middle class the decentralization of industry it wanted, since capitalism as a state-controlled affair would inevitably increase the further concentration of capital. Despite its promises, fascism would foster the growth of large capital at the expense of small business.[39]

Calverton's theory that fascism arose out of the economic dynamism of emerging mass production and the corporatization of the state, and ironically recruited the lower middle classes in its cause, distinguished it from the usual communist theories of the time. According to the communist line, the bourgeoisie used the Nazis as tools or agents, or alternatively the bourgeoisie handed over the political power to them in order to maintain economic control of society.[40] Calverton did share with many radicals the belief that fascism would ultimately be destroyed by its own inherent contradictions. Yet, unlike a good many radicals in 1933, he insisted that it was facile to subscribe to the popular Third Period thesis that fascism represented capitalism's "final crisis" and thus fascism's emergence indicated the inevitable and impending victory of communism. The Communists underestimated the power of the adversary (on this point Calverton was in agreement with Trotsky). The naive notion that history was on the side of the Communists rather than the Fascists was probably the most pernicious idea to emerge from the Third Period conception of fascism. The fate of the Communist Party in Germany had disproved this line of wish fulfillment. "History, on the contrary, was with the fascists this time," Calverton contended. "It is our job to make history be with us—but not let it turn against us because we theologically convince ourselves that it must be with us."[41]

The lesson for America from the debacle in Germany was obvious: the Left had to make its appeal to all disaffected and alienated groups in American society. Particularly important were those elements most likely to be swayed by the Fascists—the "petty bourgeois amalgam" of small farmers, small manufacturers and tradesman, doctors, lawyers, teachers, the *déclassé* intellectuals and students (the last two having been actively instrumental in providing leadership for fascism in Germany and Italy). In his "Pulse of Modernity" editorial for September 1933, Calverton issued a dire warning:

> In a nation such as America, which is the most middle class country in the world, with a lower middle class ideology penetrating through the very interstices of our culture, influencing proletarian as well as plutocrat, any revolutionary movement which stupidly neglects appealing to that lower middle class kills off from the very beginning all possibility of success. The Workers alone stand little chance of capturing the capitalist state. If the workers fail to effect an alliance with certain sections of the lower middle class their opportunities for success are crippled at the start.[42]

Cooperation between the proletariat and certain sections of the middle class was necessary, but Calverton insisted the proletariat would have to lead the way—if the reverse occurred and the middle class took the lead, the result would inevitably be a swing to the Right. Similarly, should the "agrarian individualistic" ideology of the farmers come to dominate a farmer–labor coalition, there would be a danger of fascism. Thus it was imperative that the left-wing elements of the working class lead the farmer and worker to an understanding of revolutionary struggle as the best way of solving the agrarian as well as the industrial crisis.[43]

Finally, Calverton believed that the disastrous Communist Party doctrine of social fascism, as well as the Communists' utter miscalculations regarding the fate of the German radicals, underscored the importance of analyzing American conditions rigorously and precisely. When the Communists attacked the Roosevelt administration and the New Deal, asserting that the Democrats as well as the Republicans were agents of fascism, they made it more difficult to deal effectively with the threat from the Right. Although the National Recovery Administration (NRA) program could be interpreted as a definite step toward state capitalism through the consolidation of industry, Roosevelt's administration lacked the essential characteristics of a "fascist" government: it was not supported by a movement of the militant middle class that advocated antidemocratic principles and used extralegal forces. Nevertheless, Calverton speculated that the NRA would hasten the centralization of industry, further paralyzing small businesses. This would increase the threat of the belligerent middle class, making it all the more critical that radicals gain allies among the middle class.[44]

Calverton continued to disseminate his urgent message that Americanizing Marx was the best way to prevent the rise of an American Hitler and the only road to revolution in the United States. He stressed the egalitarian ideals at the heart of Marxist thought—the concept of democracy as economic equality and equal freedom from economic adversity. Properly understood, Marxism should have a "direct appeal to the American people," because it gave meaning and challenge to the concept of democracy that Americans had long held dear. Indeed the factor of economic equality was precisely what was missing in America and what prevented American democracy from developing beyond an "infantile" stage. The Marxists, he asserted, were the true custodians of the democratic tradition in America, and it was their responsibility to preserve the indigenous radicalism of the American past.[45] If the revolutionary figures of the American past, such as Thomas Paine and Philip Freneau, were bourgeois revolutionaries, the democracy that informed their thinking might still inspire contemporary radicals.[46]

To a certain extent, Calverton's emphasis on the preservation of the American democratic tradition and his concern with revitalizing radical aspects of the American past sounded like the rhetoric of the Popular Front that was to emerge after 1935. Nevertheless, by 1935 Calverton opposed the Party's Popular Front as a reduction of these ideas to expedient slogans. Calverton did not favor minimizing class differences in the quest for unity on the Left—the impulse behind the Popular Front's call for cooperation between Marxists and democrats, revolutionaries and reformers. Indeed, he felt a precise analysis of class was singularly important in maintaining a revolutionary perspective and preventing the spread of fascism in America.

By early 1933, Calverton, among other American intellectuals, was looking for a political party that would "speak the American language."

Such a party must purge its vocabulary of liberal rhetoric, on the one hand, and reactionary populist rhetoric on the other, and base its program on American conditions while remaining sensitive to the worldwide revolutionary situation. Above all, Calverton was looking for a party that shared his viewpoint regarding the extreme urgency of creating a truly united front against fascism. By the fall of 1933 he believed that he had found just such a party.

LOVESTONE, Wolfe, and Herberg—all leaders of the Communist Majority Opposition (Lovestonite) Party—became familiar contributors to the *Modern Monthly* in 1933 and 1934, and during this period Calverton's articles frequently appeared in *Workers Age*, the official organ of the Lovestonite group. Similarly Trotskyists like Charles Yale Harrison and Max Schachtman contributed articles to the *Monthly* while Calverton wrote occasional reviews for the *Militant*, the Trotskyist organ. James P. Cannon invited Calverton to lecture before Trotskyist audiences on several occasions, and Max Schachtman attended some of the gatherings at Calverton's home. But in spite of his general agreement with the Lovestonites' notion of respecting the "objective differences" of various countries and in spite of his sympathy with the anti-Stalinism of the Trotskyists, Calverton found both groups wanting in their ability to bring together the diverse American groups necessary to form a strong united front on the Left. Calverton was a friend of both groups, but he remained staunchly independent while he looked for a political organization that would provide a common denominator for anti-Stalinist sentiment and would at the same time be more precisely attuned to the American context.

In the fall of 1933 Calverton's old friend A. J. Muste invited him to participate in the organization of a new political party oriented toward American conditions. Muste, who had been the leader of the famous Lawrence, Massachusetts, textile strike of 1919, and who had devoted himself to the labor movement after 1929 as dean of Brookwood Labor College at Katonah, New York, was now heading a movement to transform the Conference for Progressive Labor Action (CPLA) into a political party. The CPLA had been formed early in 1929 in order to stimulate labor thinking and to participate in trade union activities. It was led by Muste and several brilliant labor intellectuals he had gathered around him such as David Saposs, the economist, and J.B.S. Hardman, the former leader of the Jewish Socialists. With the depression, the emphasis in the CPLA turned to action. The organization led the formation of unemployment leagues in the Ohio Valley area and participated in several strikes in the same region.[47] By 1933 Muste and several other leaders of the CPLA felt that the time was ripe to form an American revolutionary party.

Muste brought Calverton into his confidence in the fall of 1933, asking his opinions on strategy and inviting his participation in the formation of the new party. Calverton was enthusiastic; he wrote Muste following their meeting expressing his confidence in Muste's leadership as well as the aims of the Party: "The more I think of our talk today the more I am convinced that we are on the right track and that it is you, with a healthy American organization such as the CPLA behind you, who should take the initiative in the creation of a genuine American radical party." Calverton also pledged to further the cause of the Party among intellectuals and students and to use the *Modern Monthly* to "give the movement the kind of support and publicity it will desperately need in the beginning." [48]

Such "support and publicity" was implied in Calverton's editorial for the October 1933 issue of the magazine. The editorial declared that the imminent threat of fascism made the formation of a new revolutionary party imperative. Whether Americans became the followers of a home-grown American Fascist like Huey Long or whether they followed the lead of the radical party depended entirely on whether such a radical party could win their allegiance. Calverton therefore called for a "new communist party" that would make its appeal in terms of the American revolutionary tradition and eschew any International (including the Fourth) that would not allow it to enter upon terms of autonomy and international equality. Although at the time Calverton described it as a purely hypothetical organization, it is clear that he was describing the general aims of the new party he had been discussing with Muste:

> What we need is a new radical party, a new revolutionary party, a new communist party which will orient itself to American conditions, speak the American language, and address itself to the American workers and farmers. Such a party should set out to do what the Socialist Party, because of its evolutionary, parliamentary emphasis and reactionary leadership, and the Communist Party, because of its Russian orientation and its bureaucratic distortions, have failed to do. It should stand to the left and not to the right, and it should attempt to rally to its support all the left-wing elements in America today that are craving the creation of such a party in which they can effectively function. [49]

A decisive step toward the proposed new revolutionary American party was taken at the Conference for Progressive Labor Action held at Pittsburgh December 2 to December 4, 1933. Muste traveled to Pittsburgh to preside over the meeting, carrying with him a report that he and Calverton had worked on, outlining the aims of a new party "frankly revolutionary in purpose," which would devote itself to a "careful, scientific analysis of the American scene and the methods for dealing effectively with it." [50]

In essence, the report stated that the new party would stand for one revolutionary labor international consisting of revolutionary parties from various countries. But it would recognize that the primary contribution that the workers of any single country could make to such an international would be building an effective revolutionary movement in their own native land. State power was national, not international; therefore the new party would be concerned with the colossal job on its own doorstep—building a revolutionary party in the United States, rooted in American soil.

The report was well received, and a Provisional Organizing Committee was then elected to organize branches and work out details of the party program. The committee decided to launch the new party "no later" than July 4, 1934. On December 5, the day after the convention ended, Calverton received the following telegram from Muste:

> DEFINITE DECISION TAKE IMMEDIATE STEPS ORGANIZE PARTY
> ALONG LINES TO BE NAMED AMERICAN WORKERS PARTY WILL
> ADD ADDITIONAL MEMBERS ORGANIZING COMMITTEE NEXT
> MEETING STOP. MEANTIME YOU ARE AUTHORIZED AND URGED
> PROPAGANDIZE OFFICIALLY FOR THE PARTY.[51]

Appointed an official spokesman for the new American Workers Party (AWP), Calverton was also elected to serve on the Provisional Organizing Committee.[52]

Calverton threw himself into party work. He organized student groups at nearby universities; he spoke frequently to radical clubs on behalf of the party. He undertook tasks such as the selection of a party organizer for the Baltimore area, advising the literary section of the AWP organ *Labor Action*, and working on a committee whose job it was to examine ways to emphasize the American revolutionary tradition in party literature. Moreover, he officially joined the party when it was launched in January 1934, along with radicals such as Sidney Hook, Ludwig Lore, James Burnham, James Rorty, Louis Budenz (Executive Secretary), J.B.S. Hardman (Vice Chairman), and A. J. Muste (Chairman).

Calverton considered the task of Americanizing Marxism so important to the success of the radical movement in America and so critical in the battle against fascism that he did something he had never done before— he put aside his status as an independent radical and joined a political party. But in doing so he put himself in a sensitive and difficult position as editor of an independent radical journal. Indeed, Calverton had already editorialized for a hypothetical new American revolutionary party. During the next year he offered space in the *Monthly* for AWP members to express the party point of view, thus fulfilling his promise to Muste to give the new party "support and publicity" in the pages of the magazine. Nonetheless he now felt that expressing the AWP point of view in the magazine was entirely compatible with, indeed an integral part of Americanizing Marxism—the single most important task to which he had devoted his journal.

ＡFTER 1932, then, Calverton was a major spokesman for Americanizing Marxism, a concept that involved the resurgence of interest in America's own revolutionary past, the appeal to the American democratic tradition and its role in revolutionary ideology, and the idea that an alliance between the working class and the middle class was crucial not only for the success of revolution in America but to prevent fascism from emerging there. Such a program could be criticized on several counts: that the American revolutionary tradition is essentially the assertion of the right of revolutionary resistance to governments that overstep their proper limits and invade the "inalienable" natural rights of the citizen and therefore has little to do with the historical dialectic.[53] Moreover, while a program to build an Americanized radicalism might provide ideological and linguistic unity to a working class that was deeply divided over matters of politics and culture, it runs the risk of shaping a working-class identity built around traditional values.[54] Nevertheless, Calverton's impulse to Americanize Marx arose out of a perceived need not only to fend off fascism, but to unite revolutionary theory and praxis, a belief that without considering the ideological and social uniqueness of America any revolutionary practice was sure to fail. His efforts to wed a Marxist vision with the American democratic tradition arose from a sense that democracy is a fragile historical potential that must repeatedly be defended, that it is the only alternative to dictatorship and the fundamental constituent of any socialist society.

Calverton, of course, was not the only literary radical during this period to urge the Americanization of Marx. Besides the efforts of Hook and Eastman to align Marxism and the American philosophy of pragmatism, radicals like Edmund Wilson wanted to "take communism away from the communists" by adapting Marx to American conditions,[55] while Kenneth Burke argued for speaking the American idiom and appealing to the middle class.[56] Yet Eastman's and Hook's speculations remained highly abstract and philosophical while Wilson's and Burke's interest in Marxism sprang largely from aesthetic considerations.

Calverton's approach to Americanizing Marx, on the other hand, stressed a praxis that took into account the distinctive characteristics of class and culture in America. What seems most unique and prescient about Calverton's Americanization of Marx was his decision to direct his magazine toward the "professional workers," intellectuals and those salaried members of the middle class who held no property, could never hope to own the means of production, and were largely unprotected by unions. This was a crucial decision. It placed the *Monthly* in an ideological position far different from Communist Party publications, opening the magazine to discussion about how a radical perspective might be preserved in the face of the coalition between radicals and New Dealers, how a leftist viewpoint might throw light on the policies of the NRA, and how short-term reforms could be effected without sacrificing a longer-ranged radical vision. It was a decision that correctly recognized the imminent danger of fascism—both abroad and in the United States—at a time when orthodox Communists failed to recognize this danger. And it was a decision that greatly broadened radical discourse, which had been contained by the Communist Party's ideological straightjacket, the taboo on American exceptionalism.

Calverton's recognition of the common interests of workers and members of the white-collar class anticipated New Left critiques like those of C. Wright Mills by twenty years. To be sure Mills took a more problematic view of the middle class and its role in radical change than did Calverton, yet for both Calverton and Mills the new middle classes were up for grabs. Standing at a point in late industrial society, Calverton saw with great perceptiveness that the boundaries between manual workers and intellectuals were breaking down, that knowledge was an increasingly important force of production in the modern world and intellectuals an important agent of social change. In so doing he isolated a crucial theoretical point that the New Left theoreticians would come back to in their analysis of postindustrial society.

Perhaps because of a Deweyesque emphasis on pragmatic action that infused his thinking, Calverton's project of Americanizing Marx moved in the direction of a political or voluntaristic Marxism. This brand of Marxism holds that the terms of the class struggle are profoundly political and hence depend for their success or failure on the regional or national organization of the various contending classes.[57] Calverton's efforts at political praxis suggest his distance from the Leninism he once embraced, for he did not think in terms of vanguardism or a disciplined party. The point of the American Workers Party was to engage in education and organization of the working class—not to take an independent role in leading (or provoking) revolutionary activity. In this sense Calverton seems closer to Antonio Gramsci than Lenin in rejecting vanguardism and in recognizing that theory must be grounded in precise historical circumstances and cultural reality and that the intellectual must be linked to ordinary people.[58] As a "public intellectual," Calverton had always held to this notion, and as a political activist, Calverton felt this link was crucial for radical change.

If Gramsci, the philosopher of praxis and power, exhibited a pragmatic spirit,[59] Calverton too was essentially a pragmatist. The openness to speculation, experimentation, and flexible praxis that characterized Calverton's effort to Americanize Marx undoubtedly indicated the larger influence of the pragmatic tradition.

During the next phase of his editorship of the *Modern Monthly* he would turn to Max Eastman and Edmund Wilson to assist in the project of Americanizing Marx. Yet his efforts to turn the *Modern Monthly* into a vehicle for Americanizing Marx—as well as his own membership in the AWP— would create a number of difficulties for him as the magazine moved into the mid thirties. He believed that in spite of his membership in the AWP he could maintain an unbiased, nonpartisan forum if he continued the magazine's policy of presenting a variety of factional opinions and independent viewpoints. He insisted that the magazine remained steadfast in its independent and nonpartisan stance. There were some who questioned this, however. The contradiction between his allegiance to the AWP and the supposed independence of the *Monthly* was to create one of the major problems to beset Calverton after he joined the American Workers Party.

CHAPTER TEN

While we are proud of our achievements during the first year of our existence as a Monthly, we feel certain that, with the new members who have been added to our editorial staff and art boards, we can promise our readers an even better magazine than we have provided them with in the past.

     —From full-page ad, *Modern Monthly*, February 1934

"Hellishly Hard Sledding"

After the *New Masses* attack on Calverton, tension and hostility remained high between the Stalinists and the opposition groups that contributed to the *Monthly*. Calverton often took the brunt of this ill will. One evening in the autumn of 1934 he and Nina Melville accepted a dinner invitation from Michael Blankfort. Calverton and Blankfort had remained friends in spite of Blankfort's resignation from the *Monthly* editorial board, and the two men were accustomed to socializing together. But Blankfort also had Stalinist associates and friends. Quite by accident Mike Gold, Joshua Kunitz, Joseph Freeman, and several other Party members dropped in during dinner. The room immediately became icy and silent. When the silence broke only Gold and Calverton spoke. Finally Freeman came over to Calverton, extended his hand, and began talking with him. But tension in the room gradually built. It was not long before Kunitz and Gold had launched into an attack on Max Eastman. Calverton and Melville, feeling themselves cornered, argued on Eastman's behalf, defending his anti-Stalinism and characterizing him as "the only one who told the truth about the Russian situation." Freeman retorted that "all Eastman is trying to do is get back in the radical movement, but he's beaten already. . . . We've beaten him at it." The whole apartment quickly became violent with argument. Before the uninvited guests left, the dinner engagement had been reduced to shouting and turmoil.[1]

Calverton, by nature gregarious, friendly, and vulnerable, was profoundly shaken and disturbed by these displays of hostility. Such episodes made him acutely aware of the widespread and intense Stalinist opposition to the *Modern Monthly*. And in 1934 when the newly born *Partisan Review*, as an organ of the John Reed Clubs, was under Party aegis, and journals like the *New Republic* had a Stalinist slant, he felt the pressure and enormous responsibility of managing virtually the only independent radical journal in the country. As early as the fall of 1933, Calverton had initiated a plan to strengthen the publication in the face of Stalinist hostility and to bring in several prominent and experienced writers who were sympathetic to the idea of Americanizing Marx. Calverton singled out three men as potential coeditors: Max Eastman, Edmund Wilson, and Mauritz Hallgren. Hallgren had amassed a prodigious amount of editorial experience in his capacity as an editor on the *Baltimore Sun*, something Calverton saw as invaluable. Calverton favored Eastman because he was a veteran of American radicalism and because of his anti-Stalinism; he wanted Wilson because of his critical breadth and erudition and his understanding of the need to translate Marxism into American terms. Calverton sought all three men, in fact, because they were (as he put it) radicals who spoke "in the American lingo."[2]

Hallgren declined Calverton's invitation to become a coeditor. Eastman expressed reluctance because he feared his work on his own books would be disrupted by an editorial commitment.[3] But Eastman had been personally denounced by Joseph Stalin for his criticisms of Stalin's regime. As a consequence, nearly all the radical publications in the United States—as well as many of the liberal ones—had closed their pages to his writing. Eastman found the *Modern Monthly* an anomaly during this period, since (as Eastman later wrote in his autobiography) it "stood for free debate on even so touchy a subject as Trotskyism."[4] Thus, the *Monthly* was one of the few outlets for his articles. Furthermore, Eastman had been close to Calverton for some time and was familiar with the magazine from the inside out, so he had a certain emotional investment in its career. After a period in which he mulled over his own conflict, Eastman agreed to join.

Edmund Wilson had also followed the growth of the magazine with interest, but he had no difficulty finding outlets for his writing and was not particularly committed to the success of the *Modern Monthly* per se. What Wilson wanted was "a really good magazine," which he felt would best be created by merging the *Modern Monthly*, *Common Sense* (an eclectic liberal-to-radical journal that appeared in 1932, edited by Alfred Bingham and Selden Rodman), and the left wing of the *New Republic*.[5] Calverton was scarcely receptive to this idea. But since the undogmatic and independent stance of the *Monthly* appealed to Wilson, he too decided to join its editorial board.

Calverton's master plan for literary and political praxis would encounter a number of stumbling blocks during the course of 1934. It may be true, as Sidney Hook has suggested, that in a larger sense any plan to Americanize Marx was doomed from the outset precisely because the American people were not prepared to accept a serious alternative to the system that had produced their distress.[6] But what impeded Calverton's project most immediately were problems on the newly formed editorial board of the magazine and the publication's deepening financial difficulties. Ultimately the major difficulties Calverton confronted in attempting to fashion a political praxis based on the concept of an Americanized Marxism had less to do with the political climate in the larger voting populace than with the American Left itself and its unstable, shifting factions and alliances.

THE RELUCTANCE with which Wilson and Eastman joined, as well as their already diffused energies and interests, presaged ill for the future of a jointly edited *Modern Monthly*. But it was Calverton, long used to being his own master, who was the immediate source of conflict even before Eastman and Wilson formally joined the editorial board in February of 1934. Calverton called a staff meeting in October 1933 so that the prospective editors could meet with the existing editorial board (in addition to Calverton, there were Sterling Spero, a teacher and free-lance writer, Nina Melville, S. L. Solon, the student editor, and Calverton's close friend and literary critic, Ernest Sutherland Bates), so that they might work out future directions of the magazine. The group decided to prepare for publication a statement delineating the magazine's policy. Both Wilson and Eastman were in general agreement with the lines Calverton had already developed in the magazine, but it was unanimously felt that a clearly delineated statement of policy was appropriate, in view of the new additions to the staff. Calverton was to write the statement, stressing the magazine's commitment to a continuing tradition of independence and to the specifics of the American situation.

Calverton submitted a statement to the board that echoed the editorials he had been writing for the *Monthly* in the past few months. It reiterated that the *Modern Monthly* would continue its policy of intensively analyzing the "American scene" in "American terms and in the American language." Neither Eastman nor Wilson disagreed with this. But the statement went on to call for a new revolutionary organization that would unite workers, farmers, and middle-class intellectuals. This native revolutionary party should refuse the directive of the Communist International: only under terms of international equality should it participate in an international organization. Such a party had yet to be formed, read the statement, but should it be, the *Modern Monthly* would support it. In the meantime, the magazine would maintain its independent course.[7]

Obviously the talk of a new revolutionary party in Calverton's statement was a veiled reference to the gestating AWP. Apparently, Calverton believed that he would have no difficulty getting Eastman and Wilson to accept the statement. Indeed, Eastman initially approved it, but he began to have reservations when he received a highly critical letter from Wilson questioning its wisdom. While Wilson agreed with the ideal of making Marxism appeal to the American mind, he offered the following objections:

> I don't know whether it is a good thing for a magazine like the *Modern Monthly* to declare itself against the existing radical parties in favor of a hypothetical party which does not exist, and which the editors of the magazine itself have no intention of organizing. It is not that I don't agree with most of what the statement says, but that I question the advisability of having the magazine take so definitely hostile a stand toward the socialists and official communists. It seems to me that this kind of criticism might be better brought by the editors and contributors as individual writers—because, after all, our aim should be, shouldn't it? to persuade Socialists and Communists—as well as other people and even have them contribute to the paper.[8]

Ironically, Wilson upheld the magazine's long-established stance as an "open forum" for radicals of all factional persuasions. Calverton, who had espoused the policy of independence for years, now seemed ready to compromise it for a not so hypothetical party whose Provisional Organizing Committee had already been formed in the fall of 1933, and on which Calverton was busily working with Muste.

Wilson no doubt would have been concerned about the magazine's continued independence had he been aware of Calverton's involvement in the formation of the AWP. Had he read the letter from Calverton to Muste, promising not only to further the cause of the party in the pages of the magazine, but to persuade others on the editorial board to support the party, he would have had particular cause for worry:

> In January we are adding several people to the staff of the Modern Monthly among whom will be Edmund Wilson and Mauritz Hallgren, both of whom are radicals and who write in the American instead of the European lingo and both of them will be, I can as-

sure you after I talk to them about it, most enthusiastic about such a party as we discussed today.[9]

If Calverton had, as his letter implies, intended to talk to his coeditors about these proposed ties between the magazine and the nascent AWP, he did not. Rather he kept his coeditors in the dark about the party and the degree to which he had committed the magazine to it. Perhaps Calverton felt that providing space for AWP opinion would not endanger the magazine's overall objectivity and independence; perhaps he felt that Eastman and Wilson, who already thought along the lines the new party was articulating, would have no objection once the policy was known. Yet Calverton's approach at the very least seems imperious, since he did not consult his colleagues on the matter and attempted to install the policy unilaterally. At any rate Wilson wanted to delete completely the section of the statement in which the magazine declared itself in favor of a "hypothetical party" while denouncing the Socialist and Communist Parties. This was unacceptable to Calverton, who wrote to Eastman that "I think we should either run the statement more or less the way it is now, or not run it at all."[10] Because of the disagreement between Wilson and Calverton, the Statement of Policy was never published.

But in the February 1933 *Monthly*—the very issue in which a full-page advertisement appeared announcing that Eastman and Wilson had joined the editorial board—Calverton ran an editorial calling readers' attention to the organization of the American Workers Party as "the most hopeful sign that has appeared on the American horizon for years."[11] And by March 1934 Calverton's affiliation with the AWP became public knowledge. An "Open Letter to American Intellectuals" appeared in the March issue of the *Modern Monthly* sharply condemning the "Madison Square Garden Incident" in which Communist Party members broke up a crowd of 20,000 that the Socialist Party and members of various trade unions had managed to assemble. Such "hooliganism" simply aped fascist tactics and could not be acceptable to any self-respecting intellectual, read the statement. The "Open Letter" called on all intellectuals to repudiate the Communist Party, to leave the Party if they were members, and to offer relentless opposition to the "desperate and criminal adventures of the communists." The organizational and intellectual bankruptcy of the official Communist Party made the building of a new revolutionary party even more imperative. The "Open Letter" announced that just such a party, the American Workers Party, was hastily being built. The "Open Letter," an outright call for intellectuals to rally behind the AWP, was signed, along with other members of the AWP (such as A. J. Muste, Sidney Hook, James Rorty, J.B.S. Hardman), by Calverton.[12]

Calverton's political allegiances, now a matter of public record, brought into question the independence of the *Monthly*. Soon after the "Open Letter to American Intellectuals," Muste reported to Calverton that there was a growing impression that the magazine was an AWP organ. Mike Gold, for one, had concluded just that. Muste felt it essential to prepare a statement disclaiming any official connection between the AWP and the *Modern Monthly*. A statement was soon drawn up and adopted by the AWP's Provisional Organizing Committee to the effect that the *Monthly* was not an AWP organ, but remained an independent radical journal and as such could print articles either for or against the party. As an AWP member, however, Calverton himself could not write articles that were hostile to the party. If other members of the editorial board wished to do so, that was their prerogative.[13]

Yet in spite of this disclaimer it was obvious that Muste and the AWP still looked upon the *Modern Monthly* as an ally. Muste viewed Calverton's influence on the *Monthly*'s editorial board as a strategic advantage. He saw the magazine as a forum in which party opinion would always be welcome. Thus he urged officials and members of the AWP to read and promote the sale of the *Monthly*. Consequently this matter emerged as a topic of heated discussion at an editorial board meeting prior to the publication of the June 1934 issue. The board members agreed that, although the magazine continued to print the views of various parties and factions, the impression persisted that it was becoming the semiofficial organ of the American Workers Party. They therefore decided that an editorial must be printed at once, denying any connection with the American Workers Party and reaffirming the *Monthly*'s status as "an independent radical magazine affiliated with no party." The writing of this editorial was left to Calverton, who was preparing the June issue for publication.[14]

The June issue, however, appeared without the editorial statement. When his coeditors objected, Calverton told them that it was left out for lack of space. But this explanation seemed odd, particularly in view of the fact that Calverton had found space at the end of an article by Louis Berg and Eliot E. Cohen in the June number to answer the author's charge that the AWP had "flunked [the] first test of its declared purpose to build unity in the American Working Class," because AWP members had not marched in the May Day demonstration with other radical parties.[15] This was not all that seemed strange: the rebuttal tacked on at the end of the article bore no signature and was not even designated as an editorial note. Moreover, it read like an official statement of the American Workers Party. Calverton had not only managed to find space for the rebuttal, but had allowed AWP officials to inspect the article before publication and had extended them the privilege of printing their response at the end of the article.

Sterling Spero was incensed by the incident. He fired off a letter to Calverton complaining about the omission of the editorial statement and charging that the unsigned comment at the end of the Berg and Cohen article raised some fundamental questions about the magazine's editorial policy:

> 1) Why should a magazine which is not an AWP organ and whose editors had just voted to disclaim all party connections give the AWP the privilege of inspecting an attack on it prior to publication when other groups have never been given this privilege? 2) Why should a statement of the AWP be made to appear like an editorial without any editorial designation? These questions raise the unpleasant issue: has the MODERN MONTHLY been pursuing a policy of having its cake and eating it? Has it been a party organ without having the courage to say so? [16]

If the magazine was to preserve its status as a nonpartisan radical forum, argued Spero, it would have to "stop the attempts of various groups to profit by the strategic position of their friends on the editorial board." If it wished to change its policy and become an organ of the AWP, that was another matter. But it should adopt such a policy openly and honestly, realizing that such a move would entail dramatic changes in the editorial staff and changed relations with its readers.[17]

Calverton, "sore as hell" at Spero's letter, defended himself, recounting that only a short time earlier, the American Workers Party had offered to pick up the tab on the *Monthly*'s deficits and support it financially; Calverton had refused the offer even though the magazine was in "desperate financial straits." He declined the aid, he told Spero, precisely because he wanted to keep the magazine independent.[18] Calverton added that the editorial statement regarding the magazine's independence would appear in the next issue. But, no sooner had Calverton managed to calm Spero down, than Eastman added his own protest over the comment at the end of the Berg and Cohen article and the nonappearance of the statement of independence. Eastman informed Calverton that he was in complete agreement with Spero. However, Eastman went a step further, charging that Calverton's rejection of an essay by Paul Mattick, which was critical of the AWP, "must have been politically motivated. . . . I should like," Eastman admonished Calverton, "to see both the statement of our independence and Mattick's article to prove it in the next number—or some other article which would definitely correct the erroneous impression that seems to have gotten abroad." [19]

The statement of independence outlined jointly by the board members did in fact appear in the following issue, and Mattick's article appeared later in the year. "To avoid any misunderstanding of the purpose and policy of the *Modern Monthly*," the July 1934 editorial read, "the editors wish to make it clear that the magazine is an independent, radical journal, affiliated with no party." The *Monthly* was to continue its policy of being an independent forum of radical opinion "uncensored by party and undoctored by dogma." While the individual editors might differ in their political sympathies, they stood as one in their belief that the magazine best served the radical movement in the United States "by opening its pages to any individual or group that has anything of importance to contribute to the American revolutionary scene." This was to include all factions ranging from the Socialist Party to the official Communist Party. Articles submitted to the *Monthly* would be judged "solely on their literary and social merit and not on the ground of their particular party bias or conviction." [20]

It was only because this statement of independence finally appeared in the July issue that the Lovestonites decided not to ban the *Monthly* from the New Workers' School. Bertram Wolfe reported to Calverton that although the Lovestonites had previously considered the magazine mandatory reading, its obvious connection with the AWP had resulted in the organization of a boycott that was halted at the last moment only because of the appearance of the statement of independence. Still, Wolfe felt the magazine's closeness to the AWP was cause for concern and criticized Calverton for his bias toward the AWP as well as his inability to distinguish "between personal views and editorial policy." [21]

But distinguishing between personal views and editorial policy was always difficult for Calverton, who had always considered the magazine his own journal. Thus, no doubt, Eastman's and Spero's feelings that the AWP had an undue amount of leverage in the magazine's editorial practices because of Calverton's strategic position were correct; and indeed their belief that the *Monthly* was coming to be regarded as an AWP organ was corroborated by Wolfe. Once Calverton had published the editorial statement declaring the magazine's independence, however, the conflict among the editors abated—at least on this issue.

But other difficulties soon emerged. For one, the addition of such prominent and independent figures to an editorial board, which had for so many years been dominated by a headstrong and independent editor, created a situation that was ripe for conflict. This was exacerbated by the fact that both Eastman and Wilson were too busy with their own projects to participate actively in the duties of daily editorial work, while Calverton was notoriously inattentive to editorial details due to his own hectic schedule.

Predictably, problems cropped up. Wilson, for example, returned to

New York from one of his frequent trips to find the May 1934 *Monthly* carrying a John Sloan cartoon that portrayed Michael Gold in an uncomplimentary way. "I was shocked," Wilson wrote Calverton immediately after perusing the issue that came out in his absence, "to see my old friend Mike Gold depicted in a chamber pot and I don't think you ought to have done it." Wilson conceded that he had no right to complain too vociferously, since he had been away when the May number was put together. Nevertheless, he wanted to disassociate himself from the magazine because of the matter: "I really ought to take my name off the editorial staff so that I won't be made editorially responsible for anything else of the kind that occurs."[22]

Calverton pleaded with Wilson to stay with the magazine, arguing that a breakup in the editorial board at this point would give the Stalinists ammunition to direct against the *Monthly*. Indeed, the Stalinists had already attacked Wilson and the magazine when the *Monthly* was launched, announcing in the *New Masses* of February 20, 1934, that "Edmund Wilson has formed an unholy alliance with the 'shady' Max Eastman and the still 'shadier' Calverton and Hook."[23] Wilson therefore took Calverton's point and agreed to remain.

But even as Calverton was persuading Wilson to stay on the editorial board, Eastman came forth with "a considerable grouch" against Calverton's editing. After ten years of presiding over the *Masses* and *Liberator*, Eastman, admittedly, was not prepared to take a back seat in the job of editing,[24] and he was occasionally given to fits of egotism and petulance. Eastman began his list of "grouches" by complaining about an assertion Calverton made in the *Monthly* to the effect that Ramon Fernandez's *Messages* was the most important critical work since Eliot's *Sacred Wood*. "You forget that both Wilson and I have published books of literary criticism," wrote Eastman. "I think mine is about five thousand times as important as either of these, and so no doubt does Wilson think of his." Eastman went on to complain that Calverton had the habit of "plugging" his own works in the *Modern Monthly* while failing to give any notice to books written either by Eastman or Wilson in editorials and book reviews. On one occasion Calverton had advertised the fact that one of his own articles had been chosen for an essay collection, a "piece of self-aggrandizement pure and simple," Eastman charged, and a practice that was "damned irritating." Furthermore, all the circulars and ads for the magazine referred to it as "V. F. Calverton's *Modern Monthly*," in spite of the fact that editorial responsibility was now supposed to be shared equally. This, coupled with the fact that Calverton did not list the editors alphabetically on the banner of the magazine but rather put his own name at the top of the list, conveyed the impression that Calverton was *the* editor and that the magazine was his. Probably the most irksome thing to Eastman was that this in fact was true notwithstanding his and Wilson's putative status as coeditors:

> Well you are [the editor]. This is the fact of it. It is also a fact that the magazine belongs to you. It *is* V. F. Calverton's *Modern Monthly*. Our monthly meetings do not profoundly alter these facts. That, I suppose, is why it is so distressing to see them announced. It means that I will be held responsible for views I do not hold, without even getting the credit of being an editor.[25]

Eastman felt the whole situation was "quite a mess" and complained that being responsible for views he did not hold "doesn't help me raise money for the magazine." Finally, Eastman concluded that "I feel almost like Edmund Wilson at our last editorial meeting that editorial responsibility without continual active co-operation is impossible to me."[26]

Calverton assured Eastman that the reference to V. F. Calverton's *Modern Monthly* was a carry-over from the days before the new editors came aboard, something he intended to change as soon as possible.[27] But Calverton continued to regard the magazine as his own, a major stumbling block to working effectively with Eastman and Wilson. Moreover, at the bottom of these editorial conflicts was the lack of "continual active co-operation" to which Eastman referred. The needed cooperation was simply not forthcoming on either side. Thus, ironically, while Eastman and Wilson complained that they lacked control in editorial matters, Calverton continually admonished the two men to "come in and really edit the magazine"; while Calverton asked for more participation, both men protested that they did not have enough time.[28]

The history of Wilson's and Eastman's association with the magazine was comprised in great part of this double-bind, deadlock situation. It was also replete with their continual objections to Calverton's self-aggrandizement, lapses in taste, and slap-dash format, on the one hand, and Calverton's apologies as well as blandishments to keep them from resigning, on the other. At one point Wilson objected to the fact that when he wrote an introduction to André Malraux's novel, *The Conquerors* (a translation of the novel was published in the *Monthly* in installments), his own name was printed in larger type than Malraux's. This, he felt, was in very bad taste.[29] On another occasion, when Wilson went to the Roger E. Smith Grill on 41st Street to attend the *Modern Monthly* tenth-anniversary celebration and found Carl Van Doren making a speech on the magazine's behalf, he "felt a little like the way the communists said they felt when they saw Matthew Wohl on the platform" (Wohl was vice president of the American Federation of Labor and had made a report to its Executive Council urging withdrawal of support from Brookwood Labor College because of "communist influence").[30] On still another occasion, Eastman wrote Calverton an angry letter protesting a derogatory remark directed at him by Sidney Hook that appeared in the *Monthly*. The exchanges between Eastman and Hook had been full of disparagement for years, but now that he was on the editorial board, Eastman maintained, things were different and the remark should never have appeared.[31]

For Calverton it was a continual battle to keep his two prominent editors from resigning every time one of these mishaps occurred. He bent over backward apologizing to Eastman for the Hook remark. He reiterated his argument that a breakup in the editorial board would damage the *Monthly*'s position as the focal point for a united front against the Stalinists. He recounted to Eastman the details of the disastrous dinner engagement at Blankfort's and the confrontation with the Stalinists:

> I cite all this because I want you to see what kind of venomous rats they are in the drawing room and what we're up against. They're determined to wipe out you and me and any others that get in their way. . . a division in our ranks at the present moment . . . would be just what they would love to see—just as they loved to see the Trotskyite split in Russia.

Calverton argued that the Stalinists had a "strangle hold" on the publishing houses. Hence "guys like [Bennett] Cerf would rather Kunitz edit a volume than Max Eastman." The *Modern Monthly* was the only real threat to the Stalinists "because the *Monthly* reaches an audience they fear, and influences people of influence in the newspaper and book world as well as functions as a buffer against their controls among the students and working class."[32]

Eastman was swayed by Calverton's very persuasive argument and agreed to remain on the editorial board. But both Eastman's and Wilson's skittishness continued. Finally in February 1935, Wilson sent Calverton a letter of resignation that had a tone of finality. "I really have to resign from the Monthly editorial staff, as I expect to go abroad for five or six months, if I can make it, and I shan't be able to give the magazine any attention," Wilson wrote. In spite of his differences with Calverton over certain editorial matters, Wilson asserted that he left the magazine with a positive sense of his association with it: "I believe the magazine's been keeping up well as far as interest in the contents is concerned—though I disagree with some of your editorial handling."[33]

Little more than a week later Calverton received Eastman's resignation. Eastman was away on a trip at the time. He chose the time purposely to write the letter of resignation, he said, because "I want to get it in your hands before I get home and under my affection for you and Nina." Eastman again cited his desire to devote himself exclusively to writing books as his reason for giving up journalism, at least for the time being. He was determined to throw all his energies into writing books and would have no time for the *Monthly*, he wrote. This time he had no intention of relenting.[34]

Calverton was saddened by the resignations of the two men he was obviously proud to have associated with the *Monthly*. And he was hurt by Eastman's resignation: "You are a close friend and your resignation creates more of an ache, a poignant piercing ache than a disappointment," he wrote Eastman.[35] But neither Eastman nor Wilson was to be dissuaded. The April 1935 issue was the last in which Eastman and Wilson appeared as editors. Their association with the magazine in an editorial capacity had lasted slightly over a year.

Calverton had now lost two valuable partners in the battle against the Stalinists and in the venture of Americanizing Marx. But Calverton's handling of the *Monthly* had a distinct shortcoming—he recruited major figures to the editorial board and yet continued to view the magazine as exclusively his; he asked for cooperation and yet made unilateral decisions. His harried schedule meant that failures of communication were bound to occur, while his occasional efforts at self-promotion were sure to offend. And if Calverton was headstrong and independent, so were his co-editors. The anti-Stalinist radical group Calverton had formed therefore could not be at all cohesive. This same difficulty was perhaps the essential conundrum of the independent Left: the very independence it espoused and defended made it difficult to form an effective united front against Stalinism.

Yet during the period Eastman and Wilson sat on the editorial board, the *Modern Monthly* excelled itself, continuing its specific political and economic critiques of the American scene while extending the effort to Americanize Marx with symposia on the topic and articles by writers like Herberg and Budenz on the problem of winning America to the Marxist cause. Eastman's series of articles entitled "Bunk about Bohemia" was a reevaluation of American radicalism, specifically the Village radicalism of the 1910s. Eastman asserted the political seriousness of this phase of American radicalism in the face of the Stalinists' charges that Eastman himself was a "bohemian esthete" and that the Greenwich Villageism from which Eastman's radicalism sprang was unscientific and romantic in character. Eastman protested the Stalinists' rewriting of American radical history, defended the activities of the young rebels of the Village as bearing a relation to the scientific enterprise of utopian socialists such as Charles Fourier and Robert Owen, and reasserted the continuity of American radicalism, the degree to which present-day radicalism was the legacy of the Village Left.[36]

Wilson's presence on the editorial board injected new literary life into the publication. The magazine had long embodied an ethnic and racial cosmopolitanism, yet in literary matters such a cosmopolitan spirit had been lacking. Wilson opened the magazine to a literary cosmopolitanism; he introduced André Malraux to the *Monthly*'s readers, and in his prefatory comments to Malraux's *The Conquerors*, he called attention to the fact that Malraux's works were not in the tradition of realism, but rather attempted "the expression of emotional and psychological truth." Nevertheless Malraux's works, including his later novel *La Condition Humaine*, were politically radical and written from a Marxist viewpoint.[37] Later in the decade Malraux's works would receive attention in the pages of *Partisan Review* from Philip Rahv and William Phillips. But Wilson's remarks in the *Modern Monthly* early in 1934 inaugurated a new interest in radical European literature. In addition they provided alternatives to the usual criticism in the magazine during this period— for example, Calverton's rather predictable "Sinclair Lewis: The Last of the Literary Liberals" (one of Calverton's less discerning examples of radical criticism) and Thomas Hart Benton's aesthetic of nationalist realism in "Art and Nationalism."[38] Wilson published some of his own creative writing in the *Monthly* during this period, including his play *Beppo and Beth*, adding to the literary tone of the publication. And although the *Monthly*'s primary emphasis was on political and social issues, such commentary as defenses of the artistry of Diego Rivera and outraged reports on the destruction of his New York murals by order of the Rockefellers gave the publication a vigorous political–cultural thrust. As well, creative writing by Thomas Wolfe and Claude McKay, translations by Lionel Abel, and drawings by the *Monthly*'s art staff—Diego Rivera, Art Young, and George Grosz—made the magazine during Eastman's and Wilson's tenure a vital and dynamic artistic forum, more so in fact than at any time in its history.

BESIDES these contributions to the *Modern Monthly* by Eastman and Wilson, there were other reasons for regretting their resignations. Eastman, particularly, had been a great help financially, donating fifty dollars to the magazine each month and seventy-five during the summer months.[39] On more than one occasion Eastman had provided money to pay contributors when they refused to write for nothing. Eastman was also good at soliciting donations from others. During his association with the magazine he had managed to obtain money from several sources, including Corliss Lamont, a "friend of the Soviet Union," whose father, Thomas Lamont, was a banker in the house of Morgan. When Eastman resigned, Calverton flatly told him that the magazine could not continue to exist without his financial help.[40] Eastman agreed to continue assisting the magazine financially even though he was no longer an editor.

Extreme financial difficulties were nothing new to Calverton, but at the beginning of the *Monthly* venture, he had entertained hopes that the magazine would become, unlike the *Quarterly*, economically self-sufficient. At the outset, Calverton had written editor–scholar Angel Flores to express his belief that the *Monthly*, handled by the American News Service, would reach 5,000 in newsstand sales alone. Such a response to the magazine would enable him to pay contributors at least a cent a word and cover operating expenses.[41] But Calverton's expectations did not materialize. The financial history of the *Monthly*, like the *Quarterly*, quickly became a study in financial brinkmanship with Calverton facing one crisis after another.

A new wave of interest in the magazine and markedly increased subscriptions during the early thirties had made Calverton optimistic that the *Modern Monthly* would thrive. But circulation alone does not reflect the health of a magazine. The *Monthly*, in fact, was born out of financial difficulties: part of the reason for forming a new magazine was to avoid paying the unpaid taxes that had accrued on the *Modern Quarterly*. In December of 1932, Huntington Cairns, a long-time friend of Calverton's from his Baltimore days who frequently advised him on financial and legal matters, reported on the status of the *Modern Quarterly*'s charter. "It was decided, as you recall," he wrote Calverton, "to allow the charter of the MQ Inc. to be forfeited for nonpayment of taxes." "The charter has not actually been forfeited," Cairns continued, "but in view of the taxes which have accrued on it I think the cheapest thing to do is organize a company under a new name."[42] Two months later, the Modern Quarterly Inc. was dissolved, and the magazine appeared as the *Modern Monthly*.

After the withdrawal of support for the *Modern Quarterly* by Alex Hillman and William Godwin, Inc. in 1932, Calverton had been faced with personal responsibility for the magazine's debts—as well as having to placate irate contributors pressing for payment and raging printers suing for past due bills. Consequently, he was more than agreeable to Cairns's suggestion that the magazine be incorporated to protect him from any personal responsibility. But Calverton insisted that he remain the controlling partner of the corporation and wrote Cairns that:

> As to the names to be used in connection with incorporation, use mine, my brother's, Wiscott's [for a time the *Monthly*'s art director], yours. If you simply have to have another name put my god damn sister on. She'll never know anything about it. If three are not enough you might use mine and Wiscott's and yours, or my brother's or what you will. I don't give a god damn. The main thing is to make me some kind of president of the organization, so that I retain 51% of the stock, so as to prevent outsiders from seizing control.[43]

There is a certain irony that, in all this talk of forming a corporation and retaining a controlling interest in the shares, the subject under discussion should be a socialist magazine. But in his determination to keep the direction of the magazine under his control, Calverton could hardly be particular about the way he managed to do it. And certainly from a capitalistic point of view, owning stocks in a corporation whose profits were nonexistent and whose financial future looked abysmal could scarcely be considered a sound financial venture. By the end of 1933, Calverton's hopes that the *Monthly* would become self-supporting seemed more unrealistic each day. In November of that year he wrote Eastman that "we are in one hell of a jam. . . . I am putting every cent I can of whatever monies I can spare to keep the magazine alive," Calverton gloomily reported, "but it is hellishly hard sledding."[44]

To make matters worse, Sidney Hook, who had been contributing seventy-five dollars an issue, suddenly decided to stop his assistance to the magazine, upset because his arch enemy in the long drawn-out series of debates on Marxism, Max Eastman, had joined the editorial board. Although Hook relented when Calverton pleaded with him to continue assistance, financial matters had deteriorated so badly that Calverton wrote to Eastman in the summer of 1934 that "I have been living on about $14.00 a week subsistence level and have had to borrow additional money of late to keep up."[45]

The Long and Smith bankruptcy and the debacle with William Godwin meant the termination of any steady income for Calverton. Nina Melville, too, had worked for Long and Smith, and after the firm's collapse she also was without a job. Now even with Eastman's and Hook's help, Calverton was continually operating in the red. After Eastman's donations, Calverton still had to raise money to cover the remaining expenses, which ran anywhere from fifty to one hundred dollars a month. During these years this was an enormous amount of money, and Calverton was often simply unable to raise it. In a letter that was sent to *Monthly* subscribers in 1934, Calverton reported that not a cent had been paid to any of the editors, managers, or office staff, and that contributors seldom received a penny for their articles, yet the magazine was still running at a deficit of $1,500 a year. "We need approximately $1,200 to continue publication; with $1,200 we can continue another year, without it we must close with the next issue," read the letter. Calverton requested pledges of any amount from fifty cents to a hundred dollars from subscribers.[46]

The pledges, however, did not yield enough money to cover expenses. Eastman began to feel the strain of bearing his own share of the financial burden. Apologizing for a late check, Eastman wrote Calverton that "I have dipped so deeply into my own bank account that I am dead broke and if we don't get some money out of our friends, I am afraid we are lost."[47] Eastman and Calverton then began writing to anyone who might contribute money and set about working out a scheme to form a *"Modern Monthly* Club" with honorary membership at ten to twenty dollars apiece. They were able to raise enough money to keep the magazine going for several more months, but by March of 1935 Calverton wrote Eastman that the *Monthly*'s treasury was again exhausted.

During this bleak period Calverton resorted to every conceivable device for keeping the *Modern Monthly* alive—debates, fund-raising dinners, out-and-out pleas for money. Because of his many contacts in the literary world, he was usually able to get a big name to speak at the fund-raising dinners and attract a large number of participants. Indeed, Calverton displayed a great deal of chutzpah when it came to recruiting artists and intellectuals to speak at these gatherings. But occasionally he overextended himself with disastrous results.

The appearance of the April 1936 number of the *Modern Monthly* hinged entirely upon whether Calverton could raise enough money at a promotional dinner to fund the issue. Calverton contacted Thomas Wolfe, who had been contributing stories to the magazine from time to time. He asked Wolfe to attend the dinner and perhaps say a few words in order to make the affair a success and help the *Monthly* in its struggle for survival. Wolfe agreed to attend, but since he loathed public speaking he intended to say very little; Calverton, on the other hand, meant to exploit his appearance as much as possible. Accordingly, Calverton sent out letters announcing to subscribers that Wolfe would be the guest speaker at the fund-raising dinner. To make sure the event was well publicized, he ran the same announcement in both the *Modern Monthly* and the *New York Times*.

This time Calverton's opportunism had taken him too far. When Wolfe saw the advertisement in the *New York Times* he shot off a letter to Calverton announcing he had changed his mind and wouldn't attend the dinner after all. But by now a large number of people had bought tickets for the affair with the expectation of hearing Thomas Wolfe speak. Calverton was reduced to pleading in order to avoid catastrophe. "Your letter fell like a bombshell today, knocking me both flat and cold. . . . Jesus, I feel like I've aged a year since I got your letter." He implored Wolfe to come to the dinner and "say any god-damned thing you want for a minute or two," or simply "extend your felicitations to the Modern Monthly."[48]

Wolfe finally agreed to attend the function, which was to take place at the Roger E. Smith Grill on East 41st Street. But on the evening of the event he arrived looking nervous. Moreover, he proved to be uncommunicative and consumed one drink after another. After dinner George S. Counts gave a speech in which he complained wryly of Calverton's tendency to corral speakers for his fund-raising exercises; several people present tonight, he said, were "trapped here by our host." The audience laughed and warmed to his introduction of Thomas Wolfe, who, by now drunk, slowly and deliberately stood up to his six-foot-six-inch height, weaving a little, and said, "Our host asked me to come to dinner just to be present, and then he said 'maybe you could take a bow,' and then I read in yesterday morning's paper that I would make a major address. Of course when you read in the *New York Times* that you are going to make a major address, you have to make a major address." But Wolfe was simply too inebriated to continue his "major address." Apologizing, and attempting to sit down, Wolfe fell on the floor, where he stayed for the remainder of a rather abbreviated after-dinner discussion.[49]

It was episodes like this—often a mixture of the humorous and the painful—that characterized Calverton's struggle to keep the magazine alive through the worst years of the depression. The Baltimore dowager Elsie Sise made occasional contributions, but it was primarily Corliss Lamont's contributions during these bad times that kept the magazine from dying. Calverton suffered from increasing bouts of ill health and depression (some of which were enough to prevent an issue of the magazine from appearing). He was deeply despondent about the *Liberation of American Literature*'s failure to bring in money; not only had it been a financial flop but it had not received the critical attention he felt it deserved. The paltry book sales made his financial situation even more dire. He was often exhausted from writing, lecturing, and editing. As he wrote Nina Melville, "I'm wearing out at thirty-four, my gums, my stomach, my libido— all seem to be undergoing a change that frightens me and makes me want to drink more than ever." He was thrown into panic about his declining libido and complained that his anxieties were affecting his sexual performance: "I'm afraid to have sexual intercourse with you at night . . . for fear I can't maintain an erection. . . . This sex thing is becoming the bête noire of my life. . . . I'm afraid of it, of myself."[50] Indeed as fatigue and anxiety grew his drinking increased markedly; he often drank excessively at lunch or dinner dates and he began to drink himself to sleep at night.

Yet the larger period of the *Monthly*'s duration between 1933 and 1935 marked a high point in the history of the magazine. In spite of Calverton's allegiance to the AWP during part of this period, the *Modern Monthly* continued to include a variety of factional opinion. It remained a focal point for high-velocity intellectual output with provocative articles by writers such as Louis Hacker (analyzing the plight of the American farmer in the depths of the depression), David Saposs (examining the conservative influence of Irish Catholicism on the American Labor movement), Bertram D. Wolfe (writing on the problem of "American exceptionalism"), Carleton

Beals (an expert on Latin America, writing on the intervention of the Roosevelt administration in Cuban affairs), George Schuyler (a black journalist, writing on racial intermarriage and its consequences in the United States), Edmund Wilson (writing on the Indian Bureau in Washington and the plight of American Indians), S. L. Solon (writing on student radicalism in America), and Nina Melville (writing perceptive theater reviews in a regular column).

During this period the *Monthly* also featured articles on American labor from the differing political viewpoints of Jay Lovestone, A. J. Muste, and Mauritz Hallgren, critiques of Trotskyism by Allen Stiller and defenses of the Trotskyist position by Max Schachtman. It featured a transcription of a discussion between H. G. Wells and Stalin, a conversation and debate between Wells (who visited Russia in July 1934) and Stalin on revolutionary socialism. It included Max Eastman's translation of Leon Trotsky's *Farewell to Prinkipo (Pages from My Diary)* and the leading German Marxist theoretician, Karl Korsch, in one of its symposia on Marxism. Sidney Hook's articles on Marxist theory ran in continuing installments (including a whole series on Marx and the "Young Hegelians"), while many articles during this period were devoted to the analysis of fascism. Calverton himself wrote a number of pieces on fascism examining Father Coughlin and Huey Long, while George Britt wrote on "Jew Baiting in America," Eliot Janeway discussed "Fascism in England," and Jean Burton examined the phenomenon of "The Silver Shirts." On the cultural front, several controversial articles appeared examining Upton Sinclair's role, as head of the financial backers of Eisenstein's *Que Viva Mexico*, in the editing of the film that destroyed its original conception. Stories appeared by Thomas Wolfe and Jack Conroy. Lewis Feuer recalls the intellectual electricity the *Monthly* generated at the time: it was circulated, he says, among intellectuals, young radicals, and students and avidly read "like the reports of the great theologians' disputes in the middle ages."[51]

The *Modern Monthly* was primarily an intellectuals' forum, and never had a wide influence in the labor movement, yet occasionally it fell into the hands of an appreciative worker. Jerry Allard, the head of the Illinois Progressive Mine Workers Union, member of the organizing committee of the AWP, and writer for *The Fighting Miner* (a journal that came out of Springfield, Illinois, and was put together by a group of left-wing miners), wrote to Calverton in 1934 that he had not discovered the magazine soon enough:

> After reading the magazine from cover to cover I came to the conclusion that I had lost some of the most valuable material along revolutionary lines published in America today. So impressed were

the editors of *The Fighting Miner* with your magazine that they gave it a strong recommendation in the current number of *The Fighting Miner.*[52]

As a member of "a genuine group of workers who get their dope from the rock bottom of our putrid industrial arrangement," Allard gave his whole-hearted endorsement to the *Monthly*. And as "an actual coal digger," he disagreed with the notion that the *New Masses* was the only magazine that would interest real proletarians. "Personally," wrote Allard, "I get a pain in my ass when I read magazines like the *New Masses*."[53]

If the middle of the decade saw the twelve-year-old magazine thriving in spite of editorial and financial difficulties, it marked the end of Calverton's short-lived political activism. With the merger of the AWP and the Trotskyists in late 1934, Calverton resigned from the AWP. Calverton, J.B.S. Hardman, Louis Budenz, and Ludwig Lore were the dissenters on the AWP Provisional Organizing Committee who opposed the merger of the party with the Left opposition. Nevertheless, with the blessing of A. J. Muste, and the support of Sidney Hook and James Burnham, this became a fait accompli in December of 1934. Initially lukewarm in his opposition to the merger, Calverton quickly became dissatisfied with the new party when it became obvious that the unique American emphasis of the AWP had been lost.

The middle of the decade also saw the worst years of the depression passing. The emergency relief measures of the Roosevelt administration and the Works Progress Administration (WPA) programs were helping many to survive, while the Wagner Act seemed to open new areas of opportunity for the labor movement. Meanwhile, both liberals and Communists viewed the moment as ripe for the formation of a broadly based political coalition dedicated to socialist goals. But for Calverton, the midpoint of the decade marked another low in the manic-depressive swing of events that he felt himself living through. His vision of uniting left-wing groups into a truly revolutionary united front to combat decaying capitalism and incipient fascism now seemed unrealistic. The political party that he had expected to provide the vehicle for realizing this broadly based and uniquely American political coalition had disappeared in the rapidly shifting and changing factional alliances that characterized American radicalism.

After the Seventh World Conference of the Communist International held in 1935, which ratified the need for a broadly based coalition to fight fascism, the Communists began to adopt the same concepts that Calverton had been espousing for some years: the idea of making communism twentieth-century Americanism and stressing the revolutionary implications in the writings of great Americans like Jefferson and Paine; the notion of preserving the American democratic tradition as a bulwark against fascism; the assumption that in order to be a revolutionary force the workers needed allies among the white-collar workers and the middle class. Yet when the Popular Front was initiated in 1935, Calverton did not endorse it. He was opposed to the conservative manifestations of the Popular Front—the blurring of distinctions between Marxism and progressivism (distinctions Calverton took great pains to make), and the reformist nature of the Popular Front program in which, as Calverton saw it, the Communists surrendered radicalism to expediency in their eagerness to enter into an alliance with any middle-class group or government that would join the Soviet Union in an antifascist entente. Holding fast to his ideal of the independent radical intellectual, he felt that the Popular Front's ideal of solidarity with other Progressives for a cause even as important as antifascism threatened debate and critical discourse. And later in the Popular Front period, Calverton became increasingly critical of the Party interpretation of the Spanish Civil War, as well as the Stalinists' role in the events of the war. Calverton's critical response to the Popular Front placed him close to the positions of Eastman and Wilson, but put him in opposition to an extraordinarily lengthy list of American intellectuals and artists ranging from the *New Masses* group (Hicks, Freeman, Gold, et al.) to liberals like Lewis Mumford (who had opened the first American Artists' Congress in 1936 urging the need to rally around the cause of antifascism in order to avert world catastrophe).[54]

At the conclusion of 1935, with the demise of the AWP, and the leave-taking of Eastman and Wilson from the magazine, Calverton's goal of Americanizing Marxism seemed farther away than ever. Instead of tangible progress, he had experienced contradiction after contradiction: he had written about the inconsistencies of an objectively revolutionary situation and a working class that was ideologically unprepared to take revolutionary action. He had felt the contradictions involved in forming a party at once radical in a Marxist sense yet truly American in its orientation. He had lived with the ironies of running a socialist magazine in a capitalist context. He had experienced the tensions inherent in a steadfast political commitment to a radical ideal in the context of the unstable and protean character of the American radical parties. These were the ineluctable ironic tensions that ran through the very essence of the American radical experience. Yet this did not make it any easier to accept that the prospects of Americanizing Marxism looked increasingly problematic, that the promise of an American-style socialism would have to be deferred to a future that seemed to recede indefinitely.

CHAPTER ELEVEN

The craze for myth is the fear of history.
—Philip Rahv, *The Myth and the Powerhouse*, 1965

Marxism and Death: Calverton and the Old Left's Crisis of Reason

For the American Old Left the appeal of Marxism lay in great part in its emphasis on reason and scientific utility. Lincoln Steffens's famous remark on returning from Russia shortly after the revolution, "I have been over into the future and it works," set the tone for a whole generation's response to Marxist ideas. Steeped in a pragmatic and instrumentalist philosophy, American left-wing intellectuals were impressed by Marxism's claim to scientific validity and by the idea that Marxism provided the conceptual tools to discover historical laws and "engineer" social change. For the American Old Left the Soviet Union came to represent a "gigantic laboratory" (as it was often called), a scientific experiment in socialism that reaffirmed the rational and humane values of the Enlightenment.[1]

Yet by the mid thirties radical intellectuals were becoming increasingly plagued by a sense that Marxist science was powerless to explain history's "whirl of events" or to shed light on the dark chaotic forces it was unleashing. For many the growth of totalitarianism in both its fascist and Stalinist forms symbolized unreason in human affairs; for others the successful use of myth, propaganda, and the manipulation of mass media on the part of both Fascists and Stalinists attested to the growing power of the irrational. Some American radicals speculated that Marxism's major flaw stemmed precisely from the fact that it had absorbed the illusions of the Enlightenment—the notion of reason and science as agents of human progress and human freedom.

Max Eastman's early critique of Marxism in the late twenties questioned its teleology and scientific status. Although the original thrust of his critique was to hold up Leninism as an antidote to the "animistic" taint of Marxism's Hegelian heritage, Eastman would eventually arrive at a kind of antinomian position that saw history as a riddle for which abstract ideological systems offered no solution.[2] Eastman became convinced in the light of Stalinism that the rationalistic and optimistic assumptions that permeated Marxist philosophy needed to be reexamined. Similarly, Will Herberg would come to believe that Marxism's failure stemmed from the fact that it had absorbed the heritage of Enlightenment reason with its dangerous tendencies to worship science and technology.[3] This crisis of belief in Marxist reason ultimately led Eastman from radicalism to conservative libertarianism and Herberg from Marxism to Christian existentialism.

Calverton himself was not unaffected by this "crisis of reason." In 1933, ten years after its inception, Calverton rededicated his magazine to "radical re-education" and continued to view Marxism as a conceptual tool rather than a source of dogma or authority. In December 1934 he publicly debated Reinhold Niebuhr on the topic "Marxism and Religion," and this debate was extended in the February 1935 issue of the *Modern Monthly*; opposing Niebuhr's argument that "Marxism is a religion," Calverton vigorously argued that Marxist methodology, by virtue of its scientific approach, has "provided an interpretation of history which is more valid than any that has preceded."[4] Yet in spite of his stress on reason, education, and social theory, a new strand in his thinking was beginning to emerge. Calverton was discovering, like many of his contemporaries (as Bruce Bliven put it), "how profound is the role of emotions and subconscious impulse in men's actions, how little intellectual processes really matter."[5] "Fascism is theater," as Jean Genet declared; in Germany, torchlight parades and Hitler's skilled use of the media bore this out. Closer to home, the "radio priest," Father Charles Coughlin, "the demagogue of the airways," suggested the persuasive power of rhetoric and the awesome capacity of the mass media for shaping the minds of the people.[6]

Moreover, darkness and irrationality seemed close at hand. Calverton's journalist friend Walter Liggett, muckraking editor of the *Mid-West American* in Minneapolis, had been writing on corruption in the administration of Floyd Olson, governor of Minnesota, and the "strangle hold" of the Olson gang on the Farmer–Labor Movement. Olson retaliated by framing Liggett on a sodomy charge. Calverton was to attend Liggett's trial; as a character witness and expert in psychology, he was to testify that Liggett could not have commited such an act. But in early November of 1935, before the trial, Liggett was gunned down on the street by mobsters who, the evidence suggested, were Olson's henchmen.[7] Calverton and Melville were crushed and heartbroken when they received the news from Liggett's wife and agreed with her assessment that "Walter gave his life to free the radical movement from the Olson gang."[8]

Calverton was, then, becoming aware of the brute forces that hindered radical advance. But he was also conscious of the more subtle yet no less effective means of social suggestion that drew people away from reason and toward the forces of reaction. Troubled by the inadequacies of Marxist theory to shed light on the power of propaganda and suggestion in its various manifestations, he began to formulate some theories of his own, and what resulted was one of the more unusual hybrids of American intellectual history.

During the late twenties Calverton had been interested in Freud and the new psychologists, and his fiction reflected a persistent concern with a deep core of irrationality at the center of human behavior. Examining the problem of the subrational mind's susceptibility to suggestion and political exploitation, however, he drew upon the unlikely combination of Marx and Søren Kierkegaard, finding at the core of man's alienation the fear of death. Given his own obsessions, it is hardly surprising that he assumed a gloomy Kierkegaardian position that the final terror of self-consciousness is the knowledge of death. But more than this, Calverton felt that understanding and controlling the human subterranean fear of death provided the key for the success or failure of the communist society of the future.

During the mid thirties, Calverton began for the first time to write extensively about and to speculate on the fear of death. His preoccupation at this point took on a new resonance, a concern with the forces that the "sweet reason" of Marxist ideology could not explain. Thus, besides revealing the rare spectacle of an Old Leftist wrestling with such an unorthodox subject as death, Calverton's writings during the mid thirties provide a case study of the "crisis of reason," which afflicted radicals during the latter part of the decade. His writings from this period also reveal a darker side to the intellectual directions that followed from this crisis of reason: the temptation of manipulative solutions, the lure of social control, the fascination with propaganda, mythology, and symbolism that enticed some intellectuals, like him, after mid decade.

THE PASSING OF THE GODS (1934) was Calverton's first excursion into myth and unconscious motivation. Ostensibly a study of the religious impulse, the book's primary concern is the issue of death. Calverton began his work confident that Marxism provided the key to the history of religion as well as the perplexing question of mortality, although the more he probed, the more the answers eluded him. His argument in fact reflects a retreat from reason and social theory. For he initiates his study in the spirit of Marxist science only to fall back, by the end, on the utopian content of Marxist philosophy.

Calverton claimed that religion developed because it promised power over the environment. However the emergence of science under capitalism, which brought about greater environmental control, began to erode religion's control over minds and initiated a lengthy historical process that would ultimately conclude in the "passing of the Gods." Religion's domination would disappear only in a socialist society where the fruits of science benefited the majority of men. Yet the scientific control of the material world was not sufficient to undermine religious belief; a more difficult problem lay in the psychological realm. Here Calverton's argument, thus far reading like that of an unswerving rationalist committed to a vision of historical progression from capitalism to socialism and from superstition to science, takes an unexpected turn. Religion would be abandoned completely only when humanity was free of the primary conditions that gave religion its raison d'être—the fear of death.

Capitalism's role in the decline of religion, Calverton suggested, was paradoxical. While it provided scientific control of the environment, it brought about a greater sense of individualism. And "the individual's fear of death or personal extinction developed in direct relation, it is reasonable to assume, with the emergence of the individual ego."[9] The rise of capitalism did more than any other factor to develop the individual ego, to promote a sense of the separate and isolated self cut off from any organic connection with the social whole. "It is only with the emergence of the ego, and the differentiation of its interests from those of the group that the fear of death was to develop into an individual obsession."[10] The fear of death, according to Calverton, was the curse of a capitalistic individualistic civilization.

Much of human behavior was devoted to attempts to restore the feeling of primary ties between the self and group and thus assuage the death anxiety. In the past, religion was the chief means of gaining a sense of "identificatory fusion" between individuals and the group, but in the modern world where religion's influence was waning, mass movements such as communism and fascism provided this function. Yet for Calverton a basic difference existed between the two movements' ability to unite self and society in the long term. Although fascism could relieve the anguish of the isolated self, its aim—to perpetuate an individualistic economic structure with a private-property base—contradicted and undermined a developing, long-term, and organic reconciliation of the individual with the group. Thus fascism coerced people into a false community. Only a socialized society constructed around a collective economic system could provide genuine communion and bring freedom from social and spiritual isolation. Calverton concluded that a communistic society "is the only satisfactory and lasting solution to the ego problem of our age."[11] Death would diminish in significance as humans felt themselves to be part of a larger entity that endured after their personal extinction. After the fear of death had been conquered under socialism, the "passing of the Gods" would finally become an accomplished fact.

Probably the most significant and unusual aspect of *The Passing of the Gods* was Calverton's variation on the theme of alienation. Rather than focusing on man's relationship to the means of production, as in the classical Marxist model, he looked primarily at the breakdown of community and saw alienation manifesting itself in the fear of death—bourgeois man's constant companion, the real specter that haunts bourgeois society. Another unusual aspect of the book is that Calverton, a Marxist, views death as the most intractable cause of alienation and resurrects the latent Christian paradigm in the socialist myth. His study of the demise of religion sketches a version of man's "fall"—the fall into selfhood in which man experiences his own separateness as an involuted fixation of his own ego and its mortality.

His work draws heavily on the Christian idea of redemption in the socialist ideal, for socialism ultimately overcomes the problem of death. The vision that emerges from Calverton's book is chiliastic and reconciliatory; it implies a millenarian conception of redemption beyond history. Perhaps this suggests that Calverton's early religious interests and his training for the ministry were now manifesting themselves in his analysis of socialism. Yet this religious dimension to Calverton's thinking reveals a disenchantment with the telos of rationality that underlies the Marxist view of history. Desperately, reason gives way to the theological terms of utopian socialism. Calverton in fact concluded his work with the observation that, with the disappearance of traditional religious faith in the contemporary world, "man is everywhere seeking a new faith—a faith that will give him a sense of alliance with the group."[12] It was only in socialism that such a faith could be sustained; it was only in socialism that the profound "religious" yearnings of the individual to merge with the group in true community could be satisfied. The conclusion seemed to be that what the Left had to offer was not theory but faith.

Warren Susman's observation that the Communist Party's Popular Front, with its enthusiastic efforts to link communism and Americanism, indicated one expression of the quest to belong, the need to identify with collective mainstream America, seems relevant here.[13] Although Calverton was basically opposed to Popular Front policies, his book, with its ideal of a quasi-religious "identificatory fusion" between the individual and a socialist community, suggests this urge toward a collective identity. Moreover, the *Passing of the Gods* raised questions that were to haunt Calverton for the next few years, and which the American Left would ultimately have to confront. If the attraction to mass movements and the impulse to political action sprang from dark and unconscious fears and desires, could such impulses be used for the radical cause? To what extent could radicals manipulate such fundamental impulses, the fear of death and drive to merge self and group, to change the course of history? If humans were essentially irrational creatures, shouldn't the Left master the necessary techniques to appeal to their irrational nature? Calverton moved into an examination of these sticky and problematic questions in his next work, *The Man Inside*.

LATE in 1936 Calverton sent a copy of his new novel, *The Man Inside: Being the Record of the Strange Adventures of Allen Steele Among the Xulus*, to George Santayana with the following note: "My argument is that the human mind, with but rare exceptions is far more susceptible to suggestion than to logic. Hence the fact that whoever gets hold of the suggestive mechanisms of society can change the minds of the people, viz. the change even over the German people before and after Hitler's seizure of power." [14]

Even more than the *Passing of the Gods*, the novel reflects a pessimistic view of reason in human affairs; far more than in the earlier work, irrationality and death become absorbing, obsessional issues. If Calverton had once subscribed to an optimistic brand of American Freudianism with an emphasis on the positive value of instinctual liberation, he was now influenced by Freud's later works with their psychological categories of destructiveness and emphasis on the death instinct. In *Beyond the Pleasure Principle* (1920) Freud outlined the complexities of the death instinct: the fundamental aim of all instincts is to revert to an earlier stage, thus it represents a regression, ultimately of living forms to the original condition of inanimate matter. But a portion of the death instinct was directed toward the external world in the form of aggressiveness and destructiveness thus saving the organism from the innate self-destructive impetus of the death instinct: the desire to kill replaces the desire to die. [15] And in *Civilization and Its Discontents*, Freud suggested that the evolution of civilization itself was a product of a dynamic conflict, a struggle between Eros and Thanatos. The "fateful question" Freud asked in this work— whether the human species would ultimately master its inherent instinct of aggression and self-destructiveness, or whether indeed humans would exterminate one another "to the last man"—left the struggle between Eros and Death unresolved, but it did suggest the potential of the death instinct to gain dominance over an entire culture. [16]

Calverton was influenced by this suggestion. He saw Freud's pervasive death drive as well as aggression, child of this drive, operating in a society mobilizing for a major war; indeed one of the novel's concerns is the inexorable movement toward war in Europe. Yet his is an odd intellectual bricolage that combines Freud's ideas on death with a smattering of Kierkegaardian existentialism. Calverton elaborated on his earlier argument in the *Passing of the Gods*: if society is in the grip of an irrational drive toward death in the Freudian sense, it is because bourgeois man lives in a condition distorted by the flight from death, a neurosis and despair engendered by the "denial of death" in the Kierkegaardian sense. As against Freud, Calverton thus concluded that aggressive and self-destructive propensities arise not because of a death drive, but rather because of a death flight.[17] The fear of death that haunts the isolated, monadic consciousness under capitalism and the anxiety that results from the burden of separation, individuality, and mortality that emerges in the absence of community results paradoxically in a morbid wish to "die" as individual, to escape the specter of individual extinction by regressing to the deindividualized social atoms that form fascist collectives. In a sense, then, Calverton retained the Freudian notion that regression was fundamental to the death instinct while modifying it with Kierkegaardian insight. Yet unlike the Freudian death drive, Calverton's death-fear/death-drive dynamic was not characteristic of civilization, but rather, specific to capitalism. The problem for the radical therefore became the creation of a society in which the fear of death—and man's related destructive propensities—were minimized, a society in which true community vanquishes Thanatos and reason is once again restored in human affairs. Calverton's novel addresses the issue of how such a society might be created or, conversely how the human personality might be altered to make the engineering of such a society possible.

As a work of fiction the *Man Inside* is tedious and relentlessly didactic. In the manner of an Edward Bellamy or B. F. Skinner, wooden characters mouth a series of essays on social ideas. The novel's narrator is a disillusioned scientist, Allen Steele, who deserts the wasteland of Western society, characterized by a vast technology of destruction and the dark impulses of fascism, for the African jungle. Steele there meets an American doctor, banished from the American medical establishment for his experiments with hypnosis. Joli Coeur, the doctor, expounds his notion of revolution and initiates Steele into the secrets of the subrational and the subtleties of social control. The doctor, who has established himself as a leader of a Xulu tribe through his powers of "social hypnosis," articulates the central theme of the book when he tells Steele: "Those who control the means of suggestion control the community."[18]

The key to social suggestion and social control, claims the doctor, is the fear of death. Mouthing Calverton's theory that man aggressively bands together and submerges himself in militaristic mass movements to flee death, the doctor proposes that the use of psychological tactics must be used to eradicate the fear of death: "We can never change the world until we get rid of that fear."[19] He insists that only in true community of socialism can fear of death as radical separation be ultimately overcome. Yet the transition to community involves more than a revolutionary restructuring of society; the deep layers of the self, the "man inside," must be altered to prevent reaction and ensure lasting change. Above all, radicals must give up their cherished Marxian notion that reason is the foremost instrument of revolution. "The mind is not logical. . . . Radicals who believe that they can persuade people to follow their own interests because of the truth involved in them simply do not understand the nature of human behavior. People are not convinced by truth, but by suggestion."[20] Hitler and Mussolini skillfully waged a battle for the unconscious minds of the people— the doctor argues, "If we could but get hold of the radios, the newspapers, the schools, the churches, and all the agencies of social hypnosis, we could do the same thing to the world in a miraculously swift manner."[21] By exploiting psychological devices and ideological apparati, the myth of individuality would succumb to the concept of the group and the psychological impediments to true social community would be removed. Man would be "convinced" (as the doctor puts it) through the various means of suggestion that the group is "fundamental" while individuals are "accidental." A revolution would be accomplished not by class analysis, not by guns, but by hypnosis. And once a true communist community had been established, the burden of individuality—and consequent fear of death— would be removed. The doctor concludes on a millenarian note: "Socialism, the negation of individualism, will give birth to a new man, a man freed from the illusion of individuality, who, unhampered, can explore the life force of the man inside."[22]

There is something remarkably tautological in Calverton's argument in the *Man Inside*. Individuals join groups to flee the fear of death; therefore, they should be hypnotized away from individualism into group life where they will lose their fear of death. For Calverton there was a difference in these "alternatives": in the first instance, a regression born of fear, one gets fascism, in the second, an engineered restructuring of the human self, one gets communism. Nevertheless his novel is marred by fuzzy thinking, and it has some disturbing implications. For although it holds up the ideal of a vital connection and organic tie between the individual and social self, its emphasis lies rather on the deindividualization of man, a kind of cryptomystical dissolution of the self in the group. Equally disturbing is the uncritical way in which Calverton advances the idea that the Left should appropriate the new techniques of social suggestion, or, for that matter, the uncritical depiction of the doctor as an imperialist "great white father" figure (ruling the Xulu Tribe by hypnosis!) vaguely reminiscent of Joseph Conrad's Kurtz. Indeed the irony of the name "Joli Coeur" is apparently unintended. Calverton's novel conveys no sense of the darkness at the heart of the doctor's ideas.

Calverton was by no means the only thinker of the period who saw the promise of socialism not simply as an economic transformation but as the creation of a totally new state of mind. John Dewey, who visited the Soviet Union in the late twenties, saw in positive terms what he interpreted as an attempt there to substitute a collectivist mentality for an individualistic psychology. Yet if, as Richard Pells observes, Dewey's Russia "resembled a model progressive school, committed to experimentation and cultural conditioning, devoted to communal and collectivist values, interested in socializing every person in the land," Calverton's socialist society took this progressive bias a step farther, employing psychological and managerial experts to achieve total socialization by eradicating individualistic psychology, by uprooting the offending self.[23] As Joli Coeur, the doctor in Calverton's work puts it: "Annihilation—there is the dread idea. Complete disappearance. If there were no selves there could be no annihilation."[24]

Shortly after the *Man Inside* was published, Calverton wrote to George Santayana explaining that one of the ideas he had attempted to convey in the novel was that socialism would usher in "a fusion of the oriental and occidental outlook on life. . . . The orient has been too concerned with the man inside and too little concerned with the man outside, the Occident has been the reverse. We have to achieve a dynamic mean between the two."[25] Yet Santayana, a philosopher who advocated a life guided by reason (he had written a five-volume study entitled *Life of Reason*), was not favorably disposed to Calverton's notions of social hypnosis, whether practised by the Left or Right. "Who shall unhypnotize the hypnotizer?" Santayana asked Calverton. "Who shall hit upon the blessed prescription that might liberate instead of constraining this 'man inside'?"[26] Calverton insisted that hypnotic techniques, which had always existed in some form whether religion, myth, or propaganda, had been considerably augmented by advanced technology. "The spell binders in the old days were as nothing compared to the spell binders of today," he contended.[27] While acknowledging that Santayana's questions were "crucial," he could only suggest that devices capable of arousing submissive responses from the masses be controlled by the "progressive" elements of society rather than the "reactionary" ones.[28] In an article he wrote for *Scribner*'s magazine early in 1937, Calverton went so far as to advocate social engineering on the part of "disinterested scientific experts" who would use social hypnosis for progressive ends:

> Hypnosis is even more powerful as a social device than an individual therapeutic, and . . . all those who recognize its powers can turn them to advantage only by directing them towards healthy and progressive ends. In the hands of individual quacks and fakirs, it can give as great a menace as, in the hands of scientists and political progressives, it can prove an inestimable boon to the human race.[29]

Along with Santayana, F. Scott Fitzgerald harshly criticized Calverton's novel. As his *Tender Is the Night* suggests, Fitzgerald was interested in the psychology of the unconscious, yet he was "alternately attracted and repelled" by Calverton's novel. He objected not only to its discursive nature, but to its muddled conception. Calverton, he charged, failed to pursue clearly and logically the consequences of his line of thought. "I feel that the more nebulous your thought has been, the more inclined you are to throw a cloud around it," Fitzgerald wrote.[30]

Yet Calverton's work was praised by Max Eastman, Herbert Read, Havelock Ellis, and Harold Laski, suggesting a prevailing fascination with the "positive" uses of symbol and myth.[31] Indeed, as early as 1932 Reinhold Niebuhr's *Moral Man and Immoral Society* had asserted that man's social impulses are "more deeply rooted than his rational life."[32] The strength of Marxism, Niebuhr contended, lay not in its scientific character but precisely the reverse—its messianic and apocalyptic view of history, which offered faith that a new society would bring about social salvation. Such salvation consisted in the substitution of "new illusions for the abandoned ones"; thus intellectuals became the mythmakers who provided the illusions and "emotionally potent oversimplifications" that people needed in order to be inspired to change society.[33]

By 1935, this interest in the mythic and the manipulative had grown. Kenneth Burke read a paper to the Congress of American Writers that year in which he argued that familiar symbols should be used by the Left in such a way as to unify and rally the masses. Burke analyzed the significance of Hitler's rhetoric and suggested the importance of the development of a revolutionary symbolism in the United States.[34] Economist Stuart Chase published his *Government in Business* the same year, which argued for technocratic planning on the national level accompanied by the use of "thoroughly modern psychological methods" for behavioral control, techniques "for arousing popular interest, for dealing with recalcitrant minorities, and for helping citizens in their personal adjustments."[35] In 1936 and 1937 Harold Lasswell and Thurman Arnold carried this a step further, maintaining that men in groups were seldom rational, and that the heads of state needed to perform much like "psychiatrists," manipulating the psychological realm as much as the social and demonstrating a deep understanding of how the subrational of public ritual and ceremony could be used to mobilize the people.[36] In *Faith for Living* (1940), Lewis Mumford, influenced by Reinhold Niebuhr, speculated that evil and irrationality were constants in human life. He criticized intellectuals for underestimating the "dark forces of the unconscious" in human behavior and argued the need for fostering national myths as well as for a "religious faith" based on community, land, and family to counteract the religious faith of the Nazis.[37] Upton Sinclair, himself strong on propaganda and pageantry in his campaign for the governorship of California, undoubtedly represented an extreme case of the retreat from reason on the Left when, in a letter to Calverton, he praised the *Man Inside* for its movement away from materialism and its concern for "mental powers."[38]

If the Old Left generation had rejected, in the late twenties, the new psychology of Freud because it had little to do with history and social revolution, some now began to feel that the key to revolution lay precisely in the depths of the human psyche. Any future revolution would be psychological rather than social, yet this fact did not necessarily signal a renewed interest in Freud and the new psychology. Freud's therapeutic goal had been based on a thoroughgoing Enlightenment hope of understanding and controlling the irrational; in the intellectual climate of the late thirties the tools of psychology were relevant only insofar as a managerial understanding (reason defined in its narrowest sense) was required to rationalize the irrational, to manipulate the "man inside."

Calverton's doctor in the *Man Inside* exemplifies a prevailing mood as he sums up the case against reason and advances an argument for managerial control, declaring that Western civilization is "being taken over by the forces of darkness, by Fascism, because those forces understand more of the truth of human psychology than the radicals and revolutionaries do, who are still ensnared by the rational arguments of the eighteenth century."[39] But in attempting to escape the "snare" of supposedly outmoded rational arguments, Calverton underwent a lapse of radical vision. Ironically, his response to the threat of fascism became a fascination with those ideas most closely associated with the fascist mentality. Much as he spoke out against the philosophy and politics of the Communist Party's Popular Front, he seemed, nevertheless, to be expressing the same glorification of power and expediency at the expense of social theory, the same techniques of suggestion to mobilize the masses, and the same tendency to see ideas not as tools but as weapons or myths in the battle between the Left and the Right for social control. Like other radicals who became enraptured with the "beneficial" effects of social hypnosis, Calverton's speculations, as the *Man Inside* suggests, were taking him dangerously close to totalitarian ideology.

O NE OF the ideals of the thirties Left was collectivism, that is, the socialization of the means of production and the fair distribution of economic resources. Yet American radicals in the latter part of the decade, Calverton included, were grappling with a crucial and perplexing question: does the collectivization of a country's economic institutions bring one closer to a truly socialist society? Obviously, the state capitalism of the Fascists was one form of collectivization. At the other end of the spectrum, economic collectivization in Russia had scarcely resulted in introducing the ideal of a socialist community. On the contrary, Calverton increasingly felt that the USSR was following the pattern of capitalistic development in the West; its collectivist institutions were in no sense politically democratic, nor were they economically classless. As he wrote a friend in 1937:

> Most of the editors of the *Modern Monthly* are convinced that what is developing in Soviet Russia is a form of state capitalism in which the resources of the nation are owned by the state. . . . Soviet Russia represents a new form of capitalism in which the bureaucracy becomes the exploiter using different slogans, instead of the private capitalists. We further believe that the tendency of fascism is in the same direction. Only by people smoking out the bureaucracies and establishing general individual democracies can state capitalism be converted into a socialist society.[40]

The distinction between community and collectivity was emerging as an important issue. According to Calverton it was only within the context of a socialist community that humans could hope to transcend alienation, only in community that the individual could, as Calverton put it, be "reborn into the group." At one point in the *Man Inside* the doctor holds up the Soviet Union as the best hope for the human transformation, the one place where "social hypnosis" is being carried out to accomplish such a "rebirth." Yet Calverton was painfully aware that the Soviet Union was a collectivity, not a community and that the Soviet Union furthermore provided a stark example of the ease with which collectivism could become authoritarian. And now the horrifying Moscow Purge Trials, in fact living examples of "social hypnosis," underscored malevolent possibilities of a "rebirth" of the individual mind into group deception. As he wrote Max Eastman, even while writing the *Man Inside*, "Christ, what has Stalinism brought the personality to? Where is that old belief, so cherished by all of us, that communism will make a higher order of character?"[41]

Calverton's ambivalence, his divided mind on this issue, is obvious. In his call for community and "individual democracies" as opposed to mere collectivism, he held on to the libertarian bias of American radicalism. Yet ironically, he had prescribed social hypnosis—replete with totalitarian possibilities—as a necessary measure to attain this ideal. While envisaging the freedom of the "new man," reborn in community, released from the bondage of individualism and the fear of death, he had written a work that seemed actually to describe an escape from freedom into collective deception. Trapped in theoretical contradiction, caught between a fascination with the positive uses of mass suggestion on the one hand and the obvious repressive implications of social hypnosis on the other, Calverton pursued the lure of "social hypnosis" no further than his imaginative speculations in the *Man Inside* and his prescription for social hypnosis in *Scribner's* magazine.[42] Abandoning the idea, he turned instead to the exploration of the American past and its communal experiments in his pursuit of the socialist dream of uniting the "man inside" and the "man outside" within the framework of true community.[43]

Nevertheless, Calverton's works are reminders of a growing interest among social and political thinkers of the thirties in the role of symbol, myth, rhetoric, and the power of the mass media to manipulate consciousness. This interest developed alongside the new and sophisticated uses to which the photograph, radio, and motion pictures were being put during the thirties as they became a pervasive aspect of the American political climate. In this highly charged exchange of rhetoric and image, it certainly seemed true, as Calverton's novel posited, that the crucial battle was not over ideas but over suggestion.

Calverton's works are also reminders that fear, anxiety, and preoccupation with death were salient characteristics of the thirties. Warren Susman writes that the era was characterized by "shame and fear"—a profound sense of humiliation as a response to social collapse and consequent personal failure and a pervasive fear of an uncertain future and a culture in crisis. One might add that this fear included an anxiety about personal extinction arising out of what seemed the collapse of the natural, moral, and metaphysical order of things. Henry Miller, writing to Calverton about the *Man Inside*, objected to the novel's "banal form," but seized perceptively on the fact that the novel captured precisely the ambience of the period in its "death theme. . . . As a matter of fact," Miller wrote about the novel's preoccupation with death, "it is a world-wide obsession today."[44] Susman further observes that the psychological background of shame and fear then led "to a search for metaphysical certainty, a search for a sense of transcendent being, a collective identity deeply responding to deeply felt needs and aspirations."[45] Certainly Calverton's exploration of the relationship between Marxism and death reflects the effort to find an answer to the angst of the period in the ideal of a socialist collective identity.

Yet if Calverton's quest for some sort of collective and transcendent being reveals a general psychological background of anxiety characteristic of the decade, it also reflects his own profound and obsessive concern with loneliness and death, as well as his pursuit of the relationship and the group as a means of surrendering the self and its burden of fears. Now his periods of exhaustion and depression curbed his affairs with other women and drew him closer to Nina Melville. From the lecture circuit he wrote her, "This isolation is becoming too much. . . . I need you now, love, in a myriad of ways—to give me strength and to fortify me against the loneliness that is eating me like a cancer, and to give me sexual closeness which these weeks of absence have made more imperative than at any other period of my life since I was an adolescent."[46] And while working on the *Man Inside* he wrote her that "only our love, our oneness, our fusion of selves stands out against . . . the living death which pervades all things animate."[47] Thus, he looked to his relationship not only to assuage chronic loneliness but somehow to vanquish death's presence, to conquer the inherent propensity of the animate to seek the inanimate, to defeat the death instinct itself. The surrender of the self in the love relationship could relieve that sense of life's inexorable slide toward and treacherous complicity with death. And if the intimacy of a relationship could not obliterate death's presence, then perhaps the group could. If not love, then community; if not the group, then a socialist millennium that would transform the *vetus homo* into the *novus homo*, eradicate the fear of death by the creation of a radically new "man inside."

Yet in spite of such hopes his anxieties hounded him; his heavy drinking was now habitual. He had recurring nightmares in which he and old friends and acquaintances appeared as corpses. "Last night," he told Melville, "I jerked about in my sleep dreaming that Waldo Frank was dead and Sherwood Anderson was looking at corpses including mine."[48] Chronically fatigued, he was often ill. Melville assumed that many of his symptoms were psychosomatic, yet his health was visibly deteriorating and she implored him to seek medical help. But even here the fear of death intervened: he refused, terrified of being diagnosed with something serious. In spite of the vision of relief from anxiety and death expressed in his *Passing of the Gods* and *Man Inside*, the gathering sense of a "living death" that permeated his life drove him more deeply into despair.

But in Calverton's works of this period the personal and historical intersect: ultimately his study of religion and his novel, with their moody concern about the realm of inwardness and death, their retreat from social theory, as well as their new interest in unconscious manipulation, suggest a sense of disorientation and despair on the Left. In part, the preoccupation with social hypnosis represented a hope, albeit desperate, that the chaos of history could be countered, if not by Marxism and its outmoded rationalistic epistemology of the eighteenth century, or by a socialist revolution, then by means of managerial social control. If the socialist millennium could not be achieved by reason and revolution, then it might be achieved by manipulative techniques directed at the man inside.

In a sense, Calverton's response to the crisis of reason was to fall back on a strain of American thought—the psychology of adjustment, which, as Christopher Lasch has pointed out, is part of the tradition of American progressivism.[49] His novel in particular drew on a fundamental conviction of an earlier generation of radicals—that the recovery of the inner secret self through the new psychology was not only a way of liberating the spirit, but of bringing about positive social change as well, that the discovery of the man inside provided a primary means of achieving social control. Perhaps Calverton's work also suggests the way in which the pragmatic frame of mind with its concern for adjustment and social control, a legacy of the turn-of-the-century new radicals, lent itself to manipulative solutions. Calverton was no systematic student of Dewey like Sidney Hook, and perhaps for this reason his reading of and response to pragmatism was not entirely consistent. To some degree, the inconsistencies in his thinking were part of the contradictions of the pragmatic tradition of discussion, which stressed voluntarism on the one hand and instrumental control on the other. Thus, if Marxism's claim to scientific validity appealed to a pragmatic strain in American thought, so did the idea of the scientific management of society through the psychology of influence. If American thinkers were attracted to the Marxist notion of radical as a voluntarist "engineer of the revolution," they had little distance to travel to entertain the managerial notion of "engineer" as disinterested expert who wielded not abstract reason and social theory but the apparently more effective tool of social suggestion.

To a degree, then, Calverton's novel draws on the earlier writings of the Progressives with their implicit manipulative note. For example, Walter Lippmann's ground-breaking work on propaganda, *Public Opinion*, had concluded as early as 1920 that the Enlightenment concept of democracy was inadequate in a mass society and recommended that competent opinion be left to the "specially trained."[50] Calverton's novel also anticipates writings of the forties when the manipulative note becomes explicit and dominant, and reason now comes to be regarded with utter cynicism. It looks ahead, for example, to works that announce the emergence of a "managerial" society, such as James Burnham's *The Managerial Revolution* (1941) and *The Machiavellians* (1943).[51] Like Calverton's novel, these works advance the premise that contemporary society will be increasingly ruled by a group of elites who legitimize and maintain their leadership by using the suggestive potential of myth, symbol, and the techniques of the "science of power" to govern a public that can never be made to think logically or intelligently.

Calverton's works of the mid thirties capture a pervasive intellectual temper and tone emerging from the period. At the midpoint of the decade Calverton debated with Reinhold Niebuhr, arguing for Marxism's scientific validity against Niebuhr's contention that Marxism proffered a religious and apocalyptic vision. Yet as his works with their crisis of reason demonstrate, he had more in common with Niebuhr than he would have cared to admit. Moreover, Calverton's mid-thirties works, with their "fear and trembling" hint at existential directions taken by some intellectuals during the postwar era. His works convey a mood that looks ahead, for example, to works like Lionel Trilling's *Middle of the Journey*, a novel in which the protagonist John Laskell loses belief in the reason of Marxist ideology and experiences a queasy "vertigo of fear," a sense of existential anxiety and a preoccupation with death.[52] Calverton's concern with alienation, anxiety, and the fear of death look ahead not only to postwar writers of an existentialist bent like Trilling, but also to writers like Daniel Bell who continued to look to forms of socialism to address such issues and solve the problems they posed.

Thus if Calverton provides the spectacle of a leftist lured by the tempting and sinister ideas of social hypnosis, if his works provide case studies of the American Left's "crisis of reason," they also suggest something incubating within the thirties as a legacy for post-Marxist thought. In their retreat from radical theory they suggest the future direction of American postwar thought. Although Calverton would now turn his attention back to radical thought and socialist ideals, his mid-thirties works suggest a deradicalizing impetus. In an uncanny way they portend the beginning of the end of ideology.

CHAPTER TWELVE

After each death, he is like a Georgian tribesman,
putting a raspberry in his mouth.
—Robert Lowell, "Stalin 1934"

The "Bankruptcy of Bolshevism"

T he demise of the American Workers Party and the deterioration of revolutionary aims on the Left, particularly after
the Popular Front policies were initiated in 1935, pushed
Calverton closer to the Socialist Party. During the Detroit convention of
the Socialists in 1934, the left wing of the Party (the "Militants") wrested
power from the right wing (the "Old Guard"). The militants asserted
that the victories of reaction in Europe challenged the traditional socialist
notion of a legal and peaceful transition to socialism.[1] Consequently, the
Socialist Party adopted the militant faction's "Declaration of Principles,"
which dedicated the Party to active, and if necessary extralegal, resistance
to war, and to the task of creating a genuine workers' democracy. Hail-
ing the victory over the Old Guard as a triumph of a revolutionary over
a reformist outlook within the Party, Calverton praised such militants as
Maynard Krieger, Andrew Biemitter, Murray Baron, Paul Porter, as well
as his old friend Haim Kantorovitch. By January 1936, Calverton had
added David P. Berenberg, Herbert Zam, and Bruno Fischer—all militants—to the editorial board of the *Modern Monthly*, placing his magazine
solidly against the policies of the Popular Front and staking out a position
he felt to be genuinely revolutionary and thoroughly anti-Stalinist.

Calverton had returned full circle to a close association with the Party
from which he had become estranged nearly ten years before, following
the rupture of his relationship with James Oneal and the socialist *New
Leader*. Oneal, however, as a member of the Old Guard, was now out of
the picture. Calverton unequivocally supported the Socialists in the 1936
presidential campaign, publishing a "Declaration for Thomas and Nelson"

in the *Modern Monthly*. Calling the New Deal Franklin Roosevelt's "political insurance against radical social change," the manifesto asserted that the Socialist Party was "the sole alternative to continued reaction and fascism."[2] Besides Calverton, the declaration was signed by Max Eastman, Lewis Gannett, Louis Hacker, Sidney Hook, Reinhold Niebuhr, James Rorty, and Art Young. After the middle of the decade—and particularly after the Trotskyists merged with the Socialists in June of 1936—a reversal of sorts occurred in which the Socialists assumed revolutionary rigor, accusing the Communists of capitulating in the struggle for revolution. If the *New Masses* swore its allegiance to democracy and the New Deal in accordance with Popular Front policy, the *Modern Monthly*, supporting the Socialist Party, reiterated its commitment to the class struggle and to the realization of radical change.

Yet in spite of his support for the Socialist Party, Calverton was wary of the Trotskyist connection. The rendezvous between the Socialists and Trotskyists had been supported by Sidney Hook,[3] but Calverton, who had been unhappy to see the Trotskyists take over the AWP and sabotage its aims, saw no reason to believe they would not do the same to the Socialist Party. For this reason, and because he was a maverick whose radicalism had always been highly personal, Calverton never joined the Socialist Party. Rather, throughout the remaining years of the decade he stayed politically unattached. Moreover, over the course of the next few years his intellectual direction veered toward social democracy. In part, his practical experience of the difficulties of realizing an American socialism caused this change of direction. These difficulties had included not only directing the magazine toward the goal of Americanizing Marx, but finding a lasting political party capable of embodying this goal and acting upon it. In part, his individualistic habit of mind and his commitment to intellectual independence accounted for this change in the final years of the decade, because social-democratic politics allowed him to speak his own mind without regard to dogma or ideological rigidity. Finally, his move toward social democracy was a result of his efforts to find an indigenous American basis for Marxism; looking to the democratic tradition in America as a basis on which to build a socialist future led logically toward a social-democratic outlook.

During the late thirties amid continuing financial and editorial difficulties, Calverton continued his freewheeling and independent commentaries in the *Modern Monthly*. One of the most trenchant and insightful critics of the Left during the final years of the decade, he paid dearly for his critical independence through isolation and ostracism. His final battle against Stalinism—during its most influential phase of Popular Front hegemony—was his most lonely and difficult one.

DURING 1935 and 1936, *Modern Monthly* editorials aimed their most penetrating criticisms at two targets: the Roosevelt administration and the Communist Party. Calverton insisted that both groups were guilty of "reactionary" agrarian politics. Roosevelt's appeal to farmers, his "trek back to populism," was calculated to capitalize on a deep-rooted populism in American liberalism. Even worse was the Communists' call for a farmer-labor coalition, a "complete lapse of judgment." Farmers had a vested interest in private property; only the landless tenant farmers and sharecroppers had any desire for fundamental social change, and even they would have to be led by labor. Furthermore, the Popular Front Communists had swung far and foolishly right and now reductively conceived of the elections of 1936 as a debate between fascism and democracy (ludicrously embodied in Alfred M. Landon and Roosevelt respectively) rather than between capitalism and socialism.[4]

Calverton's arguments notwithstanding, in 1936 many American intellectuals, both liberal and radical, endorsed the Popular Front. The Party's policy of de-emphasizing revolution and calling for radical and progressive elements to form a united front against the threat of fascism seemed to many not merely sensible and salutary, but a tactic that might well avert world catastrophe. But, in 1936, two momentous events occurred that profoundly called into question the integrity of the Communist Party and the Stalinist regime: the Spanish Civil War and the Moscow Purge Trials. The first, at least initially, gave new vitality and purpose to the Popular Front as a clear antifascist cause on which liberals and radicals could unite. The second, the Moscow trials, was a veritable explosion that convulsed the Left, the crucial disillusioning event for many American radicals. Yet if the Moscow trials provoked a number of important writers to break with the Popular Front and condemn the Soviet government, many others continued to support the Soviet regime, or suppressed their doubts about it.

From its inception, Calverton had been critical of the Popular Front's call for broad-based unity on the Left. As he wrote to a friend, "we all believe in revolutionary unity, but not when that unity is destructive to revolutionary progress."[5] But the Moscow trials made it apparent that the last vestiges of the October Revolution itself were being destroyed in the Soviet Union. Like many other intellectuals, Calverton was shocked by the news of the trials. For him they were not so much a disillusioning as a confirming event: it now seemed patently evident that Stalin was presiding over the destruction of socialism itself.

The verdict of the first trial was announced in September. Calverton's response was immediate. In October, when a majority of American radical intellectuals were still reeling from the news and struggling to formulate

an opinion, he ran an editorial in the *Monthly* denouncing the Purge Trials
with their "weird Raskolnikovian admissions and confessions, less convinc-
ing than a Hollywood court scene." The confessions, Calverton concluded,
were no doubt "forced either by third-degree technique or solicited by
false promise and sentence." In any event, the execution of Kamenev,
Zinoviev, and the fourteen other Bolsheviks, was not some bizarre anomaly
but the logical outcome, the "climax" of a policy initiated by Stalin a decade earlier, that is, the exile of Trotsky to Siberia and the imprisonment
of thirty thousand Trotskyists.[6]

Calverton ran editorial after editorial condemning the Moscow trials
and questioning the Popular Front notion of the Soviet Union as a "bulwark" against fascism. More than that, he linked Stalinism and fascism
as reactionary forces. "What sort of 'socialism' is Stalin building in Russia
which leads to the shooting of old Bolsheviks and creates a bureaucracy
which spreads terror over the land?" he asked. "Where does Stalin's socialism begin and where does his terroristic reign which has so much in common with the methods of fascist countries end?"[7] In another editorial he
designated the trials "the most important issue of our time" and called for
an impartial committee to investigate all aspects of the events in Moscow.[8]
He dedicated the *Monthly* to an almost single-handed attack on the Moscow trials during late 1936 and early 1937: the *Partisan Review* would not
crystalize into an anti-Stalinist publication until its revival in mid 1937;
and even then Rahv and Phillips, troubled by the trials, resisted any direct
condemnation.[9] Believing that the trials should be a subject of constant
commentary and critical scrutiny, Calverton ran a symposium in March
1937. The participants—including Theodore Dreiser, John Chamberlain,
Leo Huberman, Ludwig Lore, Henry Hazlitt, Clifton Fadiman, and John
Hayes Holmes—expressed bewilderment and confusion about the trials,
but they also clearly expressed a loss of confidence in the Soviet Union.[10]
Calverton and Eastman saw eye to eye on the trials, and the following
month Calverton ran a letter from Eastman to the *Nation*—a letter the
Nation refused to print. Eastman castigated the *Nation* and the *New Republic* for "voluntary blindness," singling out the former for its advocacy
of a "suspended judgment" (the belief that no one in New York was in a
position to pass a meaningful judgment on the trials) and the latter for
upholding this official "know-nothing" attitude.[11]

The battle lines were now being clearly drawn between the anti-
Stalinists (consisting of Independents, Trotskyists, and Socialists) and
those who would "defend the Soviet Union" either because they believed
in the validity of the Moscow trials or because, subscribing to the Popular
Front perspective, they saw the Soviet Union as a critical buffer against
fascism. Malcolm Cowley, appealing to the first of these reasons, defended

the trials and executions in the *New Republic* on the basis that those found guilty had "formed a loose alliance with the Trotskyists and begun a series of schemes for political assassinations and palace insurrections." [12] Granville Hicks, appealing to the second, asserted that "most of the men were guilty," but even if they were not, the Soviet Union had to be defended because "she is on our side in the struggle against fascism." [13] In the world of leftist publications in the spring of 1937, the unadulterated Stalinist viewpoint was expressed by the *New Masses*; for Mike Gold, Trotsky was "the most horrible Judas of all history." [14] Meanwhile, the *Nation* and *New Republic* upheld the Popular Front generally, the former arguing that damage to Russian prestige in foreign relations would disrupt the unity necessary among democratic nations to fight fascism, the latter arguing that disputes among radicals on the issue could cause the domestic Popular Front to collapse. Even the liberal journal *Common Sense* hesitated to take a position; then in March 1937 it published an article supporting the trials' authenticity.[15] In the spring of 1937, the *Modern Monthly* was the lone voice opposing the trials; if it was putting up a good battle against Popular Front hegemony, it was clearly outnumbered.

The Moscow trials kept Calverton in an almost-continuous state of outrage and dismay, but another momentous event nearly as disruptive to his equilibrium was the Spanish Civil War. Here was another front on which Stalinism must be fought, he believed. Accordingly, he devoted large portions of the *Monthly* to attacks on the Stalinist interpretation and guidance of events in Spain. He became one of only a handful of isolated anti-Stalinists to publicize Stalinist repression in Spain. The *Modern Monthly* was the primary focal point of dissident opinion on what amounted to a hallowed cause for most literary intellectuals.

If the Communists viewed the Spanish Civil War as the supreme test of the Popular Front, Calverton saw the events in Spain as further tragic evidence of the Popular Front's failure. Here he was in agreement with radicals such as Will Herberg and Max Eastman. Like them, Calverton was incensed that the Spanish Communists, on orders from the Comintern, suppressed revolutionary action. He saw this as another example of the Stalinist repudiation of the October Revolution. The real forces of radicalism in Spain were the Trotskyists (POUM) and the anarchists who were establishing collective farms and workers' councils in an attempt to transform the civil war into a genuine revolution. Instead of building on this popular movement, the Spanish Communists in Barcelona were putting down popular uprisings and liquidating anarchist leaders. The Communists justified these outrageous counterrevolutionary procedures by the Popular Front notion that the battle should be waged not between socialism and capitalism, but between democracy and fascism. In so doing the Communists were throwing away the revolutionary potential of the moment. "It is an ironic fact," Calverton wrote in a May 1937 editorial,

> that the Spanish Communists and Socialists today should be fighting the two organizations, the Anarchists and POUM, which want to create a communist or socialist Spain. The Anarchists and POUMites believe that it is not only important to beat Franco, but also to create a socialist state. They further believe, especially in Catalonia, that the best way to beat Franco is by socializing production, and establishing a workers and peasants government.[16]

Calverton argued that contemporary Spain formed an "ironic parallel" to Russia of 1917: the Communists with their Popular Front strategy were now the Mensheviks while the anarchists and POUMites were the modern Bolsheviks of the Spanish Civil War. Extending this parallel, he concluded that only one way existed to defeat Francisco Franco and conquer fascism: the establishment of a workers' state in Spain:

> The Spanish populace, familiar as it is with revolutionary doctrine, particularly of an Anarchist variety, will never be stirred or inspired by Stalinist doctrine with its bourgeois-democratic promises and pro-capitalist slogans. . . . With all the nations of Europe against them, the Loyalists cannot possibly win unless they can do what the Russians did in 1917, namely, arouse the populace to fight for them. . . . The Spanish workers and peasants have to be promised the factories and the land just as Lenin promised them to the Russian workers and peasants in 1917. Once promised that, the Civil War will take on a new cast.[17]

Unless such a revolutionary policy was adopted, he predicted, Franco would soon defeat the Loyalists and Spain would become a fascist nation.

Calverton's insistence that the war in Spain be transformed into a proletarian struggle once again placed him outside the mainstream of American radical opinion. In September 1937, he devoted an entire number of the *Modern Monthly* to Spain, filled with articles condemning the "counter-revolutionary" role of Stalin's regime in the Spanish conflict. Documents by the National Committee of the CNT (anarchists) and POUM (Trotskyists) appeared describing the imprisonment and executions conducted by the "Spanish Cheka" against the Spanish revolutionaries. An "Elegy for the Spanish Dead" by James Rorty in the same issue, accompanied by an "In Memoriam," suggested more powerfully than any of the articles just how the *Monthly* viewed the Stalinist influence in Spain: a list of the "Martyrs to the Spanish Revolution," those killed by the Fascists, was placed side by side with an inventory of those killed at the hands of the Communists. Calverton's editorial summed up the tone of the entire issue and gave pro-Loyalists the following challenge:

> Stalin's Russia is not concerned with the creation of a socialist Spain; it is concerned with the destruction of a socialist Spain and the resurrection, or rather a continuation, of a so-called "democratic" Spain which means a Spain dominated as before, by capitalist forces, but capitalist forces favorably disposed to the Soviet Union instead of to German and Italian interests.[18]

The Spanish Civil War and the plight of the People's Front held an enormous appeal for American intellectuals, most of whom viewed the conflict from a liberal and antifascist point of view. Calverton's statements therefore put him far afield of both the dominant radical and liberal positions. At the American Writers' Conference of 1937, attended by prominent radical and liberal intellectuals and artists gathered under the ideological umbrella of the Popular Front (including Ernest Hemingway, who was the star of the conference), Calverton was named as one of the "renegade" defenders of Trotsky (along with James T. Farrell, Edmund Wilson, John Chamberlain, Dwight Macdonald, Mary McCarthy, Joseph Wood Krutch, Charles Yale Harrison, and others).[19] The Conference, in Dwight Macdonald's words, "assumed an a priori agreement on Stalinist Policies"; Calverton, and the other "defenders" of Trotsky, all of whom were affiliated with the American Committee for the Defence of Leon Trotsky, were to be excluded.[20] Calverton's name, listed along with Farrell, Macdonald, and McCarthy, aligned him with an embryonic group of anti-Stalinists, a group that would soon play an important role in the formation of *Partisan Review*.

The American Writers' Conference verdict reflected the pervasive hostility among Popular Front supporters toward the American Committee for the Defense of Leon Trotsky, a commission of inquiry headed by John Dewey, which conducted hearings in Coyoacan, Mexico, in mid April 1937. Indeed, when the commission defended Trotsky and published its findings in *Not Guilty*, a storm of controversy erupted. One hundred and fifty "American Progressives" signed a statement supporting the Moscow trials. Believing that the "countertrial" outside the Soviet Union would conceivably uncover new and important facts about the Moscow trials, Calverton added his name to the list of members of the American committee. Although he played no direct role in the committee's activities, he opened the pages of his magazine for articles written in defense of Trotsky and for the findings of the commission that met in Mexico. By providing an outlet for discussion about the investigation, however, Calverton involved the magazine in further editorial conflicts.

IN EARLY 1937 Carleton Beals, an expert on Latin America, had only recently joined the editorial board of the *Modern Monthly*. Calverton had met Beals in 1931, in one of the discussion groups to generate a symposium or book on American culture from a Marxist perspective. Beals was appointed to the Dewey commission and went to Mexico for the interrogation of Trotsky. During the hearings Beals claimed to have special information that Trotsky had sent an emissary to foment revolution in Mexico seventeen years earlier. Dewey and other commissioners felt this had no bearing on the charges raised during the Moscow trials and that such claims jeopardized Trotsky's status as an exile in Mexico.[21] Beals resigned from the commission in the middle of the hearings and published an article in *El Universal* of Mexico City denouncing it as biased in favor of Trotsky. In May of 1937 *Soviet Russia Today* printed an article by Beals calling the investigations "utterly ridiculous" and a "schoolboy's joke."[22] Ernest Sutherland Bates, another associate editor of the *Monthly*, then wrote an "Open Letter" to Beals, charging that Beals's conduct reflected adversely on the personal integrity of the commission's head, John Dewey. In the same issue of the *Monthly* in which Bates's "Open Letter" appeared, Beals retorted that he considered the proceedings of the commission "unworthy of the name of a serious investigation."[23]

The conflict threatened to rip the *Monthly* apart from the inside. Bates was furious that a member of the *Monthly*'s editorial board had attacked the Dewey commission. Diego Rivera, head of the magazine's art department and an avowed Trotskyist, was similarly outraged and threatened to resign. In the midst of this furor, Calverton was busily preparing for a lecture tour in England and was forced to leave with the altercation unsettled. He and Melville sailed for England. The lecture tour took them away from the conflict, gave them some time together, and allowed Calverton the opportunity to visit his daughter Joy who was attending Dora Russell's Beacon Hill School. After their stay with Herbert Read, Calverton's nerves were eased considerably.

By the time they returned to New York the situation had worsened. Corliss and Margaret Lamont had long been supporters of the Communists; Corliss Lamont was national chairman of the "Friends of the Soviet Union." Both were adamant in their support of the Soviet Union and increasingly uneasy with the *Monthly*'s policy of printing articles defending Trotsky. Corliss Lamont was now debating whether to continue his financial assistance to the magazine. In spite of Calverton's assertions that the Trotskyists were as much opposed to the *Modern Monthly* as were the

Stalinists, Margaret Lamont, who had joined the editorial board in June of 1936 and had functioned only nominally, resigned.[24]

In fact, even though the *Monthly* was publishing defenses of Trotsky, Calverton was correct in that the Trotskyists found the publication objectionable. Ironically, after Margaret Lamont's resignation, Calverton received a paranoic letter from Trotsky himself charging that the *Modern Monthly* had been "contaminated" by Stalinism and infiltrated by agents of the Russian secret police, the GPU. Trotsky challenged Carleton Beals's impartiality as an associate editor: "After his 'participation' in the trials," Trotsky wrote scathingly, "there cannot be the slightest doubt about the moral physiognomy of this gentleman. Beals' article on the Inquiry Commission hearings in Coyoacan was nothing but a series of lies and falsifications dictated by the interest of the GPU." Trotsky flatly refused to write anything for the *Monthly* so long as Beals remained on the staff:

> I can give an article to a bourgeois, even a conservative publication without any concern about the other contributors, as I may ride on a bus without the concern of the identity of the passengers. Totally different is the case with a magazine which appeals to Marxism and revolution. Every contributor in this case is bound by a reciprocal bond to all others. I consider it impossible to carry on any responsibility not only for Beals but also for a publication which tolerates him in its ranks. . . . Stalinism is the syphilis of the worker's movement. Anyone who chances to be a direct or indirect cause of such contamination should be submitted to pitiless quarantine.[25]

Calverton may have shared Trotsky's feeling that Stalinism was pathological, but he remained unconvinced that Beals had contracted the Stalinist malady. But Trotsky's letter notwithstanding, he now felt a great deal of pressure from inside the magazine to drop Beals from the editorial board. Not only was Rivera protesting, but Eastman advised Calverton to drop Beals. "His whole conduct, aside from its political implications, has been in conflict with the spirit of the *Modern Monthly*, and damaging to its reputation," Eastman wrote Calverton. "I think the only suitable reply to Trotsky's letter is to remove his name from the editorial board."[26]

Although Eastman was no longer on the staff of the magazine, Calverton held his opinion in high regard. He finally relented and formally dropped Beals, who in any case had never been an active member of the magazine's staff, from the editorial board. But he emphasized in his reply to Trotsky that Beals's removal "is in no way to be interpreted as indicating agreement that he acted as a G.P.U. agent." After "a thorough examination of the available evidence," Calverton and the *Monthly* staff had concluded that "Carleton Beals is not, and at no time, was an agent of the G.P.U." He insisted that he had made the decision to drop Beals "to avoid any possible misunderstanding of the magazine's position vis-à-vis the Moscow trials and the Stalinist regime."[27]

Unfortunately, the dismissal of Beals now made it appear that Calverton was buckling under to Trotsky's demand. It seemed to confirm the suspicions of those, like Corliss and Margaret Lamont, who believed that he was siding with Trotsky. But at this point Calverton was bound to be condemned no matter which way he turned. Given the extreme factional tension in the political atmosphere—a tension now as great as it ever had been during the height of the Third Period—he found it next to impossible to walk the razor's edge of independent radicalism. Having removed Beals from the editorial board to avoid even the slightest taint of Stalinism, he brought upon himself the charge of selling out to the Trotskyists. While being denounced as a Trotskyist by orthodox Communists, he found himself under fire from Trotsky himself. No sooner had Calverton removed the supposed Stalinist Beals from the editorial board than the Trotskyist Diego Rivera resigned in a huff: Rivera was not satisfied with the mere removal of Beals's name from the editorial board; he wanted to see Beals's ejection accompanied by some sort of public censure and condemnation by the *Monthly*.[28]

Calverton continued to insist that, in spite of Beals's dismissal and the magazine's hard line against Stalinist Russia, the *Monthly* was no Trotskyist publication. As for his own feelings regarding the differences between the Trotskyists and the Stalinists, he revealed them to Beals after the fracas had died down. While he felt the Trotskyists were, for the moment, fulfilling a progressive role in Spain, he believed they bore an uncomfortable resemblance to the Stalinists:

> I don't think we think very differently about either the Stalinists or the Trotskyites. Both are pathological, the Stalinists being worse in one but most tremendous respect, namely that they have fatherland as state property in which they can murder off all their opponents. Fortunately, the Trotskyites have no such equipment.[29]

Beals, disgruntled by the whole affair, yet "a bit amused for apparently I am kicked off for believing the same things as you do" (as he wrote Calverton), had only one comment to make about the Stalinists and the Trotskyists:

> It is all cockeyed to me, all these strange revolutionary egos running around loose. In neither Stalinists nor Trotskyites have I found decency and honor. Stalin to me is a menace to the world. Poor Trotsky reveals all the symptoms of a disordered temperament. I repeat: a plague on both their houses.[30]

In spite of the criticisms of the Dewey committee—Beals's included—Calverton saw the committee as an important step in critical thinking on the Left. He hoped that the committee signaled a growing independent and anti-Stalinist Left in America. For a brief time these hopes buoyed him up. Yet in general his spirits were flagging not only because of contention on the editorial board, but because of the financial difficulties that continually dogged him.

A TTEMPTING to maintain a critical and independent position in a highly factional atmosphere not only invited attacks from all directions, but made the matter of getting funds from supporters delicate. A critical stance was guaranteed to alienate someone. After Calverton wrote an article on the Left's failure to anticipate the dangers of the demagogue Huey Long, C. Hartley Grattan sent him an indignant letter, charging that his article was less an attack on Long than on the radical movement. Grattan concluded that "I can best underline my disappointment at your present phase by ceasing my small contributions to the Monthly."[31]

Financial problems were exacerbated by the fact that Calverton's books were bringing in little money. *The Man Inside* had sold only 2,200 copies by January 1937. And the magazine was in need of continuous financial transfusions. Corliss Lamont was the magazine's main benefactor during this period. In early 1936 he donated a thousand dollars to the publication, but by the end of the year Calverton was begging him for additional funds. A careworn letter to Lamont outlined the grim situation: "Three times a week the printer calls for money which I strive to raise until I am half mad with desperation in my inability to do so in any sufficient form."[32] Lamont agreed to make further contributions of $250 a year to the publication. But even with Lamont's assistance the financial situation was desperate. By early 1937, Calverton confided to a friend that he was "in a terrifying state of indebtedness."[33]

The struggle to keep the magazine alive in the face of internal dissension among editors and financial adversity was beginning to take its toll. In early 1937 Calverton confided to Eastman that he was suffering from exhaustion and was seriously considering relinquishing the magazine or handing it over to someone else.[34] But he could never bring himself to take this step. He continued to work furiously, laboring over his many projects and at the same time trying to make ends meet. Besides editing the *Monthly*, working on a projected three-volume history of the American people, and writing a regular column in *Current History* called "The Cultural Barometer," Calverton lectured anywhere he could get billing in order to raise extra cash. He lectured in every state of the Union, as well as in Canada and Mexico. He would cram into his hectic tours as many engagements as possible, even if they lay across the country from one another. During one trek, he was to lecture in Ithaca, New York, Chicago, Houston, and San Antonio, Texas. "I lecture in Chicago on the night of the 28th and I don't think I could get from Chicago to Houston in 20 hrs, or could I?" Calverton asked his agent.[35] This sort of high-pressure schedule increased his gross for a given lecture tour, but it did little good for his already precarious health. After one of these ordeals, a harried Calverton wrote a friend that "I have been lecturing every god-damned place, in Niagara Falls, Buffalo, Detroit, Chicago, St. Louis, Toledo, etc."[36]

These lecture tours were draining, yet occasionally they had their high points. One was a tour early in 1938 through Texas and Louisiana, lured on by a $350 fee at Wiley College in Marshall, Texas, a predominantly black institution where the poet M. B. Tolson was a faculty member. In spite of political differences—Tolson favored the Popular Front and sympathized with the Stalinists—Calverton and Tolson had become close friends. Tolson had become aware of Calverton through his *Anthology of American Negro Literature* and initiated a correspondence with him. Calverton introduced Tolson's work to Maxwell Perkins of Scribners; he also published Tolson's poetry in the *Modern Monthly*. Calverton was to deliver several lectures at Wiley College, but he became so engrossed in working with the students that he extended his stay, giving informal seminars and critiquing the efforts of the school's drama club.[37]

Calverton's warmth, personal magnetism, and socialist convictions inspired the students. One of the students, James Farmer (later a civil rights advocate and founder of CORE) was profoundly impressed by him, the first man from the literary world of the East he had ever met. Farmer later cited Calverton as an important influence on his decision to take up civil rights work. He remembered Calverton for his egalitarian ideals and, more important, for his actions. Calverton, according to Farmer, was the first white man to visit Wiley College who did not patronize the students. He lacked any trace of condescension or paternalism, communicating only "the feeling of comradeship and equality on his part." But Farmer also noted that he was exhausted and drank heavily. On one occasion Calverton was so thoroughly and obviously drunk that college administrators were outraged.[38]

Calverton wrote Nina Melville from Texas that he was weary to the bone, had been drinking too much, and had been vomiting frequently. He wanted above all else to come home.[39] But on returning to New York, frayed and run down, he found a letter from Huntington Cairns waiting for him.

The Baltimore Daily Record today carried a notice signed by His Excellency Governor Nice, that the charter of the Modern Monthly Inc. has been repealed, annulled and forfeited, and the power conferred by law upon the corporation shall be, and become inoperative, null and void upon the expiration of 60 days from February 7, 1938 unless all taxes due by the corporation, together with interest and penalties due thereon, are paid before the expiration of said 60 days. Immediately upon the expiration of said 60 days the charter of incorporation of the Modern Monthly Inc., if it has not then paid all taxes, interest and penalties due as aforesaid, shall be *ipso facto* repealed, annulled and forfeited, and the powers granted to the Modern Monthly Inc. shall be inoperative, null and void without the necessity of proceedings of any kind either at law or in equity.[40]

An exhausted Calverton contemplated more lecture tours, more fundraisers, more appeals to Lamont for financial help. Lamont's interest in giving money to the magazine had dissipated, particularly after the *Monthly* came out with an article by Sidney Hook entitled "Corliss Lamont: 'Friend of the GPU,'" casting Lamont in the role of apologist for Stalin's atrocities.[41] The soundness of Calverton's decision to publish an article attacking a principal financial backer of the magazine is questionable, but he no doubt felt there was little chance Lamont would continue contributing funds after the magazine's support of the Trotsky Defense Committee. Thus he decided to run Hook's article as part of the anti-Stalinist campaign. In any case, the *Monthly* now had to survive without assistance from Lamont.

If the Trotsky campaign brought together a core of independent anti-Stalinist intellectuals such as those that had now formed around the *Partisan Review*, the effects of this new group of independent radicals were only just beginning to be felt on the American Left in early 1938.[42] During this year the situation at the *Modern Monthly* grew increasingly worse, both in terms of morale and finances. Although the publication continued its battle against Stalinism and the Moscow trials, the *Monthly* issues grew thinner and thinner. Sometimes they ran only fifteen pages, with gaps between issues of two and even three months. Floundering due to lack of funds, almost totally alienated from the dominant strains and factions of the Left, the magazine appeared once again as a quarterly publication in the fall of 1938. Calverton's editorials cited the co-option of radical values by the New Deal, the splintering of radical groups, and the accompanying lack of support for an independent radical journal as reasons for cutting the *Monthly* back once again to a quarterly:

The editors feel that the time is opportune for a thorough re-examination of radical doctrine and that this work can be accomplished only by combatting the dual tendencies of opportunism and sectarianism. With only limited resources available the Editors have therefore concluded that a Quarterly journal which is large enough to publish extended discussions is preferable to a small monthly which must of necessity limit itself to brief articles.[43]

The fall 1938 issue was also the last issue on which Socialist Party militants Berenberg, Zam, and Fischer served on the editorial board. As part of this contracting process, the board reverted to Ernest Sutherland Bates, Nina Melville, S. L. Solon (student editor), and Lillian Symes. The reversion to the *Modern Quarterly* was in the main the outcome of both economic difficulties and Calverton's flagging energies. What remained was the will to continue even if on a less ambitious basis, to continue independently, and to persevere in an ongoing evaluation of radical theory.

THE "thorough re-examination of radical doctrine," which the editors vowed to carry out, reflected their desire to explore in varying ways their own continuing relation to radical ideas. As many other intellectuals on the Left were beginning to do, they wished to reassess concepts like individualism and collectivism, democracy and totalitarianism. Calverton held that the vicious and opportunistic policies Stalin had initiated almost ten years before had almost single-handedly destroyed socialism in Soviet Russia. But as the initial numbness induced by the horrifying trials wore off, as the USSR seemed increasingly indistinguishable from other totalitarian countries, some painful questions emerged. Was there something fundamentally wrong with the development of socialism in Russia, something more basic than Stalinism? By 1938 Calverton had reached just this conclusion. In an editorial he argued against Trotsky's thesis that the revolutionary state in Russia had reached the phase of Thermidor, like the French Republic in 1794, and degenerated into a servile bureaucracy ruled by the new Bonaparte, Stalin. Denying that a workers' state existed in any form whatsoever in Russia and refuting the idea that the state capitalism that existed in the Soviet Union represented a higher economic form than private capitalism (as some had asserted), Calverton then made the following startling comment:

In another quarter, Trotsky and his adherents will continue to rail against the "Stalinist bureaucracy" while professing a faith that the substantial triumphs of the October revolution still remain. They will continue to call for the "defense of the Soviet Union" because Russia is still in essence a "workers' state." Trotsky, for political reason, cannot admit *that the bankruptcy of Bolshevism dates not from 1926 but must be traced back to the early years when objective conditions of industrial backwardness and Bolshevik one-party philosophy forced the regimentation of the insurgent working class.* (emphasis added)[44]

Calverton's gloomy conclusion was that Stalinism, far from being an aberration, was a logical outcome of the mechanisms of repression that the Bolsheviks had erected in the first place. He contended that instead of creating a classless society out of old feudal Russia, the Bolsheviks had created an entrenched privileged class. This view was later expressed succinctly in Edmund Wilson's *To the Finland Station*: the Bolsheviks had "encouraged the rise and the domination of a new controlling and privileged class, who were exploiting the workers almost as callously as the Tsarist industrialists had done."[45]

Ironically, Calverton here very nearly embraced a position articulated by Haim Kantorovitch in one of the early issues of the *Quarterly*, a position he categorically rejected at the time. In his "Rise and Decline of Neo-Communism," Kantorovitch had come to an even gloomier conclusion: that the mechanisms of repression the Bolsheviks erected indicated that socialism could not be brought to an unindustrialized country, that Marx was right and Lenin wrong.[46] If Calverton did not subscribe completely to such a position, he did run, in the next issue, a symposium entitled "Was the Bolshevik Revolution a Failure?" in which the participants considered the terms of the question Kantorovitch had asked in the same publication some thirteen years earlier.[47] In his preface to the symposium, Calverton asked the overriding question: "If, as Trotsky and other dissidents contend, the Russia of Stalin is a distorted workers' state, enveloped in a 'Thermidorian reaction' then the question arises: what elements contributed to the degeneration, what were the weaknesses in the Bolshevik principle and tactic?"[48] The participants included radicals and liberals such as Max Eastman, Paul Mattick, Herbert Zam, Norman Thomas, Max Nomad, and Lewis Gannet. To the question, "Did the Bolshevik Revolution achieve its proletarian objectives?" most participants answered in the negative. To the question, "Does Lenin's thesis that in the imperialist epoch the proletariat alone can lead a revolution to complete the 'Bourgeois tasks' retain validity?" a number responded that Lenin's thesis had now been thrown fundamentally into question. The symposium evoked a variety of responses about the reasons for the "degeneration" of the Bolshevik revolution. In any case there was no doubt in Calverton's mind about the failure of the revolution. He insisted that the old ideas dating back to the Bolshevik revolution had "lost their significance as guiding principles to action." Lenin's question, "What is to be done?" had to be asked all over again.[49]

During 1938, discussion in the Quarterly centered on the pivotal questions: was Soviet communism a natural and logical outcome of Leninism? Did the socialist vision necessarily point toward a totalitarian state? Late that year the luminary Karl Korsch entered the dialogue with his own criticism of the Soviet state. Calverton had long admired Korsch's work and had even managed to get Korsch to participate in a symposium on Marxism in 1935.[50] But it took Sidney Hook, who corresponded regularly with Korsch, to persuade him to participate in the American discussion on Stalinism. The appearance of an article on such a momentous topic by Korsch in the winter 1938–39 issue was something of a coup.[51]

In an article entitled "State and Counter-Revolution," Korsch agreed that "the Russian state has abandoned more and more its original and proletarian features." But as against Calverton and those arguing for the "direct line" between Bolshevism and Stalinism, Korsch indicated that the counterrevolutionary situation in Russia could not be traced back to the phenomenon of "revolutionary dictatorship" or the system of a single party. Rather the revolution's failure stemmed from the frustration of all revolutionary movements outside of Russia that reduced the workers' state to "a mere driving belt, transmitting the curbing and destructive effects of a capitalist world economy to the exceedingly small beginnings of a true socialist economy."[52]

But by early 1939 the anti-Stalinism of some articles that appeared in the Modern Quarterly began to shade into a disillusionment with Marxist premises. In one issue James Marshall wrote on the "political fiction" of the withering state.[53] Max Eastman and Sidney Hook, who had once filled the pages of the Quarterly with raging arguments regarding the dialectic and its relation to radical theory, now joined in repudiating dialectical materialism, but from differing positions. Hook harshly characterized as "the new obscurantism" the "orthodox dialectical materialism" that the Stalinist regime used to validate everything from Party policy to Soviet science.[54] But if Hook's was essentially a criticism of the Stalinist use of the dialectic, Eastman, whose radical philosophy had always been infused by a libertarian bias and a latent individualism, spoke openly of the need to "abandon the religion of the collective will." Stressing the totalitarian potential of Marxism, Eastman asserted that Russian communism meant "a general surrender to some authoritative concept of the collective good." True socialism, on the other hand, would mean "individualism generalized and made accessible to all." Foreshadowing his later conservative utterances, Eastman stressed the need to "preserve the liberties that came with capitalism and foster their extension into the future."[55]

Nevertheless, most of the writers—Calverton included—who rallied to the *Modern Quarterly* were still committed to the idea of socialism. Increasingly, however, they defined it in terms of democratic values. Here, Dewey was seen as important, since his thought stressed a radical democracy that was felt to be congruent with socialist ideals. Hook contributed an article in 1939 on "The Importance of John Dewey in Modern Thought," which asserted that Dewey's most valuable legacy was "his faith in democracy as a way of life." The central concepts of Dewey's social philosophy, "cultural freedom, creative experience, and organized intelligence" led logically to a socialized economy "*democratically* controlled by producers and consumers, into whose fabric is built an educational system both critical and progressive."[56] This rediscovery of the virtues of the democratic process was also reflected in Calverton's symposium in the summer of 1939, "Can Democracy Survive?" The participants, veterans of the anti-Stalinist crusade including John Chamberlain, Upton Sinclair, David Berenberg, McAlister Coleman, Scott Nearing, and James Rorty, agreed that democracy was incompatible with monopoly capitalism. But most also agreed that the very essence of socialism was democracy—not only political but industrial—in which political rule existed by virtue of the majority of voters, and industrial rule existed by virtue of the majority of the workers.[57]

The rediscovery of a democratic tradition in the American past, a vital heritage of indigenous egalitarianism upon which a socialist vision might be based, was a central concern of Calverton's *The Awakening of America*. This first (and only) volume, in Calverton's projected three-volume study of American history from a radical point of view, appeared in 1939. He described his new work as "the first extended Marxian history of America," a history "of the underdogs instead of the top dogs."[58] Yet Calverton explained that he had attempted to avoid dogmatism or narrowly economic interpretations in his study. "Although its primary object is to interpret the lives of the American people in terms of their diverse and dissident economic interests," he wrote of the book, "it aims to trace the evolution of these interests in political and social form."[59]

The scope of the book encompassed the early colonial revolts, "those incipient class struggles that embodied the early outcroppings of the rebellious spirit and prepared the way for the Revolutionary War and the establishment of what today is known as the American democratic tradition."[60] Calverton raised a question that has troubled many contemporary historians: Whence did American democracy spring? In part he fell back on Frederick Jackson Turner's thesis and the environmental explanation of the open frontier; in part he attributed democratic beginnings to the dissenting religious denominations—particularly the Baptists and Methodists—that came from Europe. The Dissenters, he believed, played the largest role in establishing the democratic tradition in America. Unlike the Puritans, who were upper-middle-class entrepreneurs owning vessels and involved in a network of commerce, the Dissenters were the *little entrepreneurs,* simple people who were democratic not merely from philosophical conviction or political creed, but from experience and necessity. The Dissenters transplanted to the new country a battle they had carried on in the old country for some time—the battle for religious freedom, individualism, and democracy. "The independence of the Dissenters . . . was of ancient tradition, tempered by a new environment, out of which emerged a new concept of life and a new civilization."[61]

Beyond this individualistic ideology and democratic impulse provided by the dissenting groups, Calverton wished to search out the communitarian basis of American democracy. Repelled by the totalitarian collectivity of the present he looked to the past for models of community. Thus he examined the anti-authoritarian and egalitarian philosophy of the Quakers, Anabaptists, Hutterites, and the community-oriented Moravians. If the communism of these early groups like the Moravians was of feudal derivation, and its monastic discipline caused their demise, such sects "made *Gemeinschaft* and *Gemeingeist* sacred words."[62]

Like Dos Passos, who was later to write about them in *The Ground We Stand On,* Calverton now saw the heroes of Parrington—figures like Roger Williams and Thomas Hooker—as early American radicals, apostles of democracy at a time when it was "nothing more than a nebulous aspiration." Calverton perceived in Hooker's stress on decentralized authority the historic roots of Jeffersonian philosophy. Roger Williams was "the man of the masses" whose belief in the rights of the individual and his libertarian ideals "made him a revolutionary of his day, a fugleman of a new philosophy." The individualism and democratic principles of the early revolutionaries were their most important contribution to the modern world. Extending an argument he had used in *The Liberation of American Literature* and *For Revolution,* Calverton asserted that although the early revolutionaries were thoroughgoing individualists, their philosophy was progressive in its day:

It was not until the coming of the machine and modern capitalism, with the creation of an industrial proletariat and the institution of wage slavery, that a different type of social prophet was born, who believed in a collective instead of an individualistic form of society. It was not the task of Zenger, Paine, and Freneau to work for a collective society. It was their task to free the rising capitalist order of the vestiges of feudal tyranny and to encourage an individualistic attitude in economics and a democratic one in politics.[63]

Calverton was no doubt guilty, as Dos Passos later was, of a somewhat slanted rewriting of history when he made the conservative Williams into an apostle of democracy and a torchbearer of the idea of toleration.[64] But Calverton's search for a usable past was conducted, as was Dos Passos's, with the pressing sense that the ideal of collectivism in the modern world had gone awry, that democracy itself was threatened by the forces of totalitarianism.

The *Awakening of America*, then, represented not only a revaluation of the American past but a reappraisal of the convictions of a decade. The study emerged out of a desire to revaluate the distinctions between community and collectivity (something Calverton had begun after his *Man Inside*) and to redefine and extend the concept of democracy. Perhaps there is no better way to define this process of reappraisal than to compare *The Awakening of America* with *The Liberation of American Literature*, written earlier in the decade. In the first, Calverton claimed that the Dissenters had forged the ideology of individualism. Additionally, the American frontier had given rise to and sustained a "petty bourgeois ideology," which made Americans resistant to the collective ideals of communism. In the later book, the Dissenters are heroes of democracy, and the individualism that the frontier nurtured is not "petty bourgeois," but democracy pure and simple. Thus Calverton writes that "in the cabin settlements of the frontier democratic America was born." If he concluded *The Liberation of American Literature* by prescribing collectivism as the means for the "liberation" of American life and culture, he poses democracy as "the way out" in the *Awakening of America*.[65]

The fact that Calverton could now embrace an overriding concept of democracy attests to the distance he had traveled in his thinking since 1934 when the *Liberation of American Literature* was published. He had opposed the Popular Front because (apart from its Stalinist ideology) it blurred the distinctions between radicalism and reformism, Marxism and progressivism. Yet he was obviously moving closer to the Progressives in his desire to find sustenance in the American democratic tradition. Certainly Parrington had influenced his earlier work, but the "liberation" Calverton there envisaged was the overturning of the bourgeois order by proletarian values. Yet Calverton's emphasis on a lineage of historical heroes like Williams and Hooker, as well as his stress on democratic values to the exclusion of revolutionary ideals, make the progressivist historiographical emphasis much more dominant in this later work. Calverton was also familiar with the works of Charles A. Beard and Arthur Schlesinger's early work on the American revolution, both of which had a strong influence upon him. In his historical vision, at least, Calverton was moving toward a position closer to his progressive beginnings.

Indeed, the notion of an embracing democratic socialism went back to his own intellectual origins and to the idea of a "complete socialism," a concept fashioned largely from the legacy of the prewar intellectuals of the Village and from writers such as Van Wyck Brooks. In *America's Coming-of-Age*, a book that had a profound effect on the young Calverton, Brooks had proposed as a counter to the "base privateness" of capitalist America a robust democratic American spirit. "Socialism flows from this as light from the sun," Brooks had asserted.[66] This notion of a natural and inevitable linkage between socialism and democracy, which had always influenced Calverton's thinking to some degree, was a guiding principle in his work of the late thirties.

Yet some of the impulse to revise the progressive strain in a Marxist direction remained if only in his call for "a radical reevaluation and readaption of the concept of democracy." The democracy achieved in colonial days was the outgrowth of an agrarian nation and could only be sustained in an agrarian context. But America had since been transformed from an agrarian into an industrial society. In an industrial nation *industrial* democracy was necessary if the democratic tradition was to be perpetuated. Calverton defined "industrial democracy" as follows:

> Industrial democracy means endowing every individual with the right to hold his job, in bad times as well as good, and with the right to vote in terms of his job and not in terms of his residence. It means emancipating the individual from economic bondage—bondage to an employer before whom he is defenseless. It means protecting him against economic disaster and defeat—protecting him not against kings, proprietors, and governors, as in the colonial days, but against industrial barons, financial magnates, and political demagogues.[67]

Calverton thus continued to hold out socialist ideals, albeit ideals of a democratic socialism. The "awakening" of America to which the title of the book referred was the awakening of the democratic spirit in colonial America. This awakening, he believed, constituted one of the most important contributions to the development of freedom in the modern world. But it was the task of Americans now, he submitted, to maintain the democratic heritage, keeping democracy dynamic and progressive rather than static and retrogressive by extending it to include not only politics but industry.

Instead of looking to the communist millennium as he had done in the *Liberation of American Literature*, Calverton called for a social democracy to be created on the basis of an already existing American democratic tradition. Although he did not specify how this was to be accomplished politically, such a call obviously meant continuing to fight Stalinism and keeping the socialist ideal alive. In a sense his call for social and industrial democracy grew logically out of his long-time desire to Americanize Marxism, to reassert or reinstate within the vision of social transformation the ideals of egalitarianism and community. More to the point, however, his effort to reassess and extend democratic ideals came—as it did for many other anti-Stalinists in 1938 and 1939—as a response to the growth of totalitarian institutions that threatened the individual conscience. And for Calverton, now in his sixteenth exhausting year of editing a journal of independent radical opinion, individual conscience and individual opinion seemed more important than ever.

The book emerged in a hospitable intellectual climate; a number of intellectuals were impressed with its antitotalitarian impulse. As George S. Counts, the advocate of progressive education, wrote Calverton, "this is precisely the kind of history that must be written if American democracy is to check the spread of totalitarian pestilence."[68] But the reception of the book came generally from a different place on the ideological spectrum than Calverton's earlier books. Liberal and progressive historians such as Harold U. Faulkner and Arthur Schlesinger praised the book highly. Allan Nevins invited Calverton to Columbia University to introduce him to Henry Steele Commager. And the venerable Progressive Van Wyck Brooks added his congratulations, explicitly comparing Calverton's book to the works of Parrington: "It is a revelation, as Parrington was for me; and I marvelled as I read it, that you should have been the first to see our own tradition, so far as I am aware, with your range of feeling, with reference to the 'masses instead of classes.' "[69]

Calverton was elated by such praise from Brooks, whom he considered one of his chief early intellectual influences. "I can think of no one in this country whose praise I would value more than yours, and damn few I would value as much," Calverton responded to Brooks. He conceded that his point of view had changed considerably over the past decade. As for the *Liberation of American Literature*, written in the optimistic early thirties, he would "never write it in that vein today." Yet he still considered himself a Marxist in the broadest sense, if only because "I feel that originally I owe such a debt to Marx and that a certain number of his theses hold true today."[70] In this connection, he prefaced *The Awakening of America* by stating that "the author is Marxian only to the extent that he believes Marx did more to illuminate the historical processes than any other thinker of the modern age, and that no one who aims to write history intelligently today can escape the influence of his work."[71] Marxism thus remained a valuable analytic tool, while its socialist ideals of democracy and its vision of *Gemeinshaft* were still worth striving for.

The late thirties also saw Calverton reevaluating his notions of literature and striking out at Stalinist notions of proletarian literature. Reviewing John Howard Lawson's *Marching Song*, he charged that the play was marred by the "polyannistic fallacy," a vulgar proletarian precept that assumed that "all proletarian literature must be optimistic in conclusion" in order to support revolution. Such an aesthetic assumed that "literature is nothing more than the hand-maiden of politics, and has no rights and privileges of its own, no intrinsic laws which politics must respect and revere." Calverton castigated what he considered to be a related attitude, namely, that "tragedy is an expression of the decadent classes," and has no place in proletarian art. He insisted that "we can never, under any regime, escape the tragic sense of life." Tragedy would continue to be a dominant literary genre "under proletarian auspices or otherwise."[72] Accordingly, he rejected the complete aesthetic and historical relativism of his early years. He told a friend that he had abandoned his theory of the "impermanency of aesthetic values," which he had advanced in his first book, *The Newer Spirit.*[73]

Calverton spoke out for the relative autonomy of art, defending it against the blatant political incursions and the destruction of aesthetic integrity that the Stalinists were carrying out in such a roughshod fashion. He embraced the position Eastman earlier articulated in *Artists in Uniform.* Stalinism, Calverton maintained, exercised as pernicious an influence in the cultural as in the political realm; it had "retarded the growth of an autonomous and authentic culture in the Soviet Union" and threatened seriously to debilitate American literature as well.[74] Once a lonely spokesman for sociological criticism during the art-for-art's-sake twenties, Calverton now ironically found himself defending aesthetic values to one-time art-for-art's-sakers who had more recently adopted a Stalinist point of view. In a letter to Harold Salemson, who, nearly a decade earlier had signed the *transition* "Revolution of the Word" proclamation, Calverton wrote:

> I can still recall with warm affection the picture of you, Sam Schmalhausen, and me walking up 5th Avenue, Sam and I trying to convince you that literature should have social meaning and significance. You were all for the supremacy of the aesthetic. And now you tell me your political development is "definite and definitive." . . . I presume you mean you have gone over to the Stalinists, despite Stalin's murder of every son of the revolution he could lay his hands on. If that is the case, where is the sensitivity which once made you such a passionate defender of art? How can you stomach such atrocities and the complete destruction of art values which have occurred in the USSR?[75]

Calverton and the *Modern Monthly* confronted the implications of the Moscow trials and the Popular Front—including its policies in Spain—at a time when most writers on the Left did not. He spoke out against the Moscow trials some two years earlier than did the *Partisan Review* group, often considered the first independent anti-Stalinist radicals of the late thirties.[76] He openly defended Trotsky's right to a countertrial in spite of his own critical view regarding the Trotskyists and in spite of the risk of losing financial backing for his magazine. He opened the pages of his magazine to searching questions about the meaning of the Russian revolution and the possibility of preserving a socialist vision in the face of totalitarianism by drawing upon an indigenous democratic tradition in America. He devoted his magazine, in spite of flagging energy and dwindling financial resources, and in spite of increasing alienation from the broad spectrum of the liberal and radical Left, to a single-minded attack on Stalinism in politics and art.

But the Moscow trials weighed heavily on all radical thought and posed important questions that haunted Calverton in the last years of the decade. He had sided ideologically with the Socialist Party militants in 1936. He had even brought several Socialist Party militants to the editorial board of the magazine. At the time he saw hope in their undogmatic yet unqualifiedly revolutionary program, feeling that theirs might be the best party for the purposes of Americanizing Marxism. During the later years of the decade his independence of mind and his effort to find an American basis for Marxist thought had moved him toward a social-democratic position. But, by 1939, the specter of the "bankruptcy of Bolshevism" seemed, in spite of his best hopes for a socialist society, to threaten even the vision of socialism itself. Now, like other radicals of the late thirties, Calverton found himself facing some painful questions about the feasibility of a socialist society. An interchange between Calverton and Scott Nearing reveals the depth of the distress and anguish that accompanied this searching inquiry. Sixteen years earlier the two men had articulated their hopeful vision of socialism in the fledgling *Modern Quarterly*; now as battle-scarred veterans they asked themselves fundamental and agonizing questions about long and dearly held beliefs. Nearing wrote Calverton telling "how very helpless I feel re: the Moscow Trials." He then revealed his innermost doubts to his old friend:

> This is another thought—maybe this is socialism—the servile state. Ideally, the content of socialism is quite different but actually what will it be? Perhaps the U.S.S.R. is the best answer.
>
> Ever since national socialism got power in February, I have been asking myself: what is socialism after all? Does it necessarily involve a bureaucratic system; conspiracy and plotting; a drastic regimentation within a bureaucratic military set-up.
>
> And if we win socialism and lose our freedom—are we paying

an excess price? . . . It needs a lot of rethinking. The history of the past twenty years has made mincemeat of more than outstanding theories of K. Marx.[77]

Indeed it seemed that the past—along with its assumptions and ideals—was being ground to pieces as raw materials for a future that was unthinkable. Calverton responded:

Your observation that maybe this is socialism, the servile state, made me gasp a little. If that were the case, and I am willing to confess that it might be, although I hate to admit it, it would certainly render meaningless years and years of effort, which many of us extended in hopes that socialism meant something different, something superior. . . . Your question—"if to win socialism and lose all our freedom"—is a crucial one. After much reflection I am convinced that if socialism can only be won in that way the price is too great a one to pay. I don't think any of us can be sure that will be the case until socialism is attempted in a more industrialized country than Russia.[78]

For the moment, then, Calverton fastened onto the hope that, indeed, Lenin was wrong and Marx right, or rather that the only way of testing their respective positions would be to witness the emergence of socialism in an industrialized country. He continued to hold to the ideal of a democratic socialism. But the questions remained, despairing questions that arose out of the crisis of the late thirties: Calverton's and Nearing's doubts were the doubts of the decade. For both men, only time and history could prove or disprove socialism's viability. For the present, it appeared that Soviet socialism had emerged from a gruesome theodicy grimly similar to that which had produced fascism in Germany; both Hitler and Stalin presided over the "servile state."

CHAPTER THIRTEEN

War determines its own end—victory, and government
crushes out automatically all forces that deflect, or
threaten to deflect, energy from the path of organization
to that end.

—Randolph Bourne, "A War Diary," 1917

Where Angels Dared to Tread

By the early summer of 1939 two groups emerged that indicated a growing anti-Stalinist intellectual mainstream on
the American Left. The first was the Committee for Cultural Freedom, organized largely through the efforts of Sidney Hook and
chaired by John Dewey. The committee printed a manifesto protesting
the growth of totalitarianism and the suppression of civil liberties as well
as artistic and intellectual freedom:

> Under varying labels and colors, but with an unvarying hatred for
> the free mind, the totalitarian idea is already enthroned in Germany,
> Italy, Russia, Japan and Spain. There, intellectual and creative in-
> dependence is suppressed and punished as a form of treason. Art,
> science and education—all have been forcibly turned into lackeys for
> a supreme state, a deified leader and an official pseudo-philosophy.[1]

The statement went on to say that the totalitarian idea, triumphant in a
large part of the world, also threatened democracy and cultural liberty
in the United States. Besides this direct reference to the Popular Front
apologies for Stalinism in the United States, the statement drew an explicit connection between the Soviet Union and fascist Germany, both
manifestations of the totalitarian spirit.

The second group, the League for Cultural Freedom and Socialism,
was organized and directed by Dwight Macdonald and other writers asso-

ciated with *Partisan Review*. The league made a public statement that denounced both Stalinism and fascism and deplored the debasement of art under both systems. Unlike the Committee's statement, which directed its attention solely to totalitarianism in the dual form of fascism and communism, the league pledged itself to a liberation of culture through liberation of the working class. Because Calverton felt ideologically closer to Hook and Dewey (and because the league, with its *Partisan Review* constituency had a Trotskyist bent), he signed the statement of the Committee for Cultural Freedom.

The *Nation* printed the Statement of the Committee for Cultural Freedom, yet ran an article in the same issue that castigated its linking of the Soviet Union and fascism; the *New Republic*, on the other hand, declined to print the statement. And a response came swiftly from defenders of the Popular Front in the form of a manifesto issued from a "Committee of 400." They attacked the Committee for Cultural Freedom and "other committees" that promoted "the fantastic falsehood that the U.S.S.R. and the other totalitarian states are basically alike." The Soviet Union represented a "bulwark against war and aggression," read the statement of the "Committee of 400," which was printed in the *Nation*.[2]

One of the first within the Left to link fascism and Stalinism as reactionary forces, Calverton had been drawing comparisons between Stalinist Russia and Hitler's regime since 1936. Lecturing in 1938 Calverton had made the extraordinarily prescient statement that "undoubtedly Stalin . . . is going to bend all efforts to renew an alliance with Germany . . . . Hitler and Stalin will become allies."[3] On August 24, 1939, the Nazi–Soviet nonaggression pact was signed, which sent a convulsive moral shock through the entire intellectual community. The mass exodus from the Communist Party and the vocal resignations from the ranks of its intellectual entourage is by now a familiar episode in the history of the American Left. For many orthodox radicals and Party members like Granville Hicks it came as a terrible blow ("this knocks the bottom out from everything," he said when he resigned from the Party).[4] For fellow travelers like Cowley the pact confirmed his worst and most private suspicions. For Calverton it reaffirmed what he had been saying all along—that Stalin was as ideologically opportunistic as any leader in the capitalist or fascist countries.

After the Nazi–Soviet pact was signed, the Communists discarded their Popular Front alliance with liberals and took, for a time, a strong antiwar position, now insisting that war was a manifestation of the imperialistic interests of the Western democracies. Calverton agreed that war was, in a larger sense, part of an imperialistic impulse, but did not exempt the Soviet Union from such imperialistic intent. Calverton had always opposed war in principle. As early as June 1935, feeling the drift toward war, Calverton put together a symposium entitled "What Will I Do When America Goes to War?"[5] The response of the participants had been almost unanimously opposed to U.S. participation. Moreover, in 1936 Sidney Hook had written an article in the *Monthly* asserting that war would weaken the proletarian struggle: "From the point of view of the working class," Hook argued, "any measure which strengthens the military arm of the state power weakens the workers in their struggle for socialism."[6]

Hook would later change his mind on this issue, but Calverton agreed strongly with his earlier analysis. By 1938 he also found himself in agreement with the editors of *Partisan Review* who attacked the Popular Front intellectuals for their promotion of patriotism and war. Like the editors of *Partisan Review*, Calverton saw U.S. involvement in the war as potentially devastating for democracy. "Nothing will hasten the growth of fascism in this country as our entrance into war," he wrote, adding that entering the European conflict "will unleash, as it did in the last war, those frontier primitivisms from which we have never disencumbered ourselves, and convert us from a democratic into a totalitarian people. It will multiply difference, aggravate antagonism, intensify hates."[7]

Remembering his own childhood days and the patriotic hysteria, xenophobia, as well as hatred directed at the German community in which he lived, it is only natural that he turned to Randolph Bourne as a model of inspiration. Calverton cited Bourne as one who "had the courage to see through the lies, the propaganda, the exaggerations" of the war effort some two decades earlier, and that his "unflagging efforts in the cause of sanity hastened his death."[8] Like the editors of *Partisan Review*, Calverton echoed Bourne, insisting that war was an expression of imperialism and a diversion from the problem of building socialism. There could be no end to war until a social system was created that democratized industry, wealth, and power.[9] He criticized radicals whose analysis of the war had shifted from that of a fundamentally interimperialist conflict to a fundamentally antifascist struggle. And he lamented that many of the same intellectuals who had earlier opposed war in the *Monthly* symposium of 1935 now favored it. As Bourne had done earlier, he castigated intellectuals for their prowar stances. "Fine minds like Lewis Mumford and Waldo Frank are typical of what war does to disequilibriate the mental faculties," he wrote. "They have become so hysterical in their fear of Hitler that unwittingly they are encouraging tendencies in the United States that will produce an American Hitler."[10] Throughout 1939 and 1940, an antiwar editorial or article appeared in every issue of the *Modern Quarterly*. In the summer of 1940, Calverton again endorsed Socialist Party candidate Norman Thomas and his running mate, Maynard Krieger, in the presidential elections. "They will not be elected in November," he lamented, "but every vote cast for them will represent a challenge to the dark forces that are leading the country to militarism and worse."[11]

Yet history now seemed controlled by these "dark forces" that Calverton had earlier explored in *The Man Inside*. As it had for Henry Adams, history now appeared to be a dynamo of change, a process of deterioration leading to the inescapable destruction of the ideals of the past, if not the destruction of humankind. The realization that Soviet communism had little to do with classic socialist ideals was, in itself, a slow and agonizing process, but the discovery that it crushed human liberty with an arbitrary violence (as the Moscow trials proved) was shattering. The historical process, Marxism notwithstanding, seemed marked by tragedy, extremity, and irrationality rather than by logical patterns. The events of the late thirties from the Moscow trials, to the defeat of the Loyalists in Spain, and now the retreat from socialist ideals by American intellectuals backing the war effort, all contributed to the feelings of dismay that pervaded the last years of George Calverton's life.

In his unpublished autobiographical novel "This Thing of Darkness," completed in 1938, Calverton depicts himself as an adolescent, wrenched out of his personal and private world into an awareness of events around him by World War I. Yet if that war caused him, as a teenager, to be "reborn" as he put it, the impending second World War, at age forty, did quite the opposite: it "worried and broke him," as a friend remarked.[12] At the very least, it contributed to a growing sense of despondency and powerlessness that plagued him.

His antiwar stand reinforced his friendship with some of his like-minded old friends—the pacifist Scott Nearing, Michael Blankfort (who had now abandoned Stalinism and joined the Left opposition), and Bertram D. Wolfe, who declared, "This war is no different from any other imperialist war," and broke a lifelong friendship with Jay Lovestone over the war issue.[13] But his stand served primarily to alienate him further from the general intellectual community. Lonely and depressed, he turned to a project he had begun in the *Awakening of America*—the study of utopian communal experiments of early America. Faced with the demise of socialist norms and values in the contemporary world, Calverton sought to extend his project in the *Awakening of America*—to find a tradition in the American past that embodied classic socialist ideals.

The premise upon which Calverton built his study grew out of a reinterpretation of the American dream itself. The depression experience now made that dream appear as deceptive and hollow as the Maltese Falcon in Dashiell Hammett's novel. Yet in his search for an alternative to the crisis of the late thirties, Calverton discovered cooperation and community at the heart of the American dream. In the broadest sense, he argued, the American dream was that of a decent society, a "better life." Those who pursued such a life had been primarily members of the persecuted and hungry classes. Little had been said about those groups in the American past who were spiritually idealistic yet economically "materialistic"—the utopian groups who practiced communism on a simple but comprehensive scale. Their communal ideals were an important part of the American dream, Calverton insisted:

> These groups dreamed of an America in which men might be able to carve out the contours of a new society—a society which should be cooperative and not competitive, communal and not individualistic. They were not all of America, but they were an important part of it and their philosophy represents as much of the American dream as the competitive philosophy of the rest of the country.[14]

As though he felt time running out, Calverton worked furiously on the new book he called "Where Angels Dared to Tread." The work sought to examine religious and economic experiments in which communal practices existed to varying degrees—the Owenites, Mormons, Labdists, the Fourieristic groups like Brook Farm and Hopedale—and groups in which sexual as well as economic communism was practiced (such as the Oneida Colony), as well as anarchist groups like "Modern Times." Calverton portrays their efforts to establish various cooperative commonwealths in an individualistic land as close to heroic. He concludes hopefully that their vision of communal life persists deep in the American psyche, that their ideal of cooperation and community will live on: "for it may very well be that ultimately, before this century is ended, it will be their philosophy, and not the individualistic one, which shall triumph."[15]

Calverton was acutely aware that the yearning for community had been distorted over the course of the decade into a gross denial of individual liberty by the repressive apparatus of the totalitarian state. But he turned to the past in his moment of despair, at a time when socialist values of true community and human fellowship seemed farther away than they ever had been. His attempt to recapture the communal impulse in early America was in one sense a way of asking his contemporaries to appreciate a world that was lost. On another level, it represented a hope that communalist philosophy was so deeply embedded in the American tradition that, given continuing economic and social injustice, it would ultimately surface and carry with it aspirations for a decent society, for a thoroughgoing egalitarianism, and for freedom from oppression. For Calverton the communitarian philosophy of the early utopian groups provided the ground upon which to build a native variety of socialism, a ground that might be enriched by the notion of a culture of radical democracy gleaned from the progressive tradition outlined in his previous book, *The Awakening of America.*

Yet in spite of this positive reaffirmation of his belief in the enduring nature of socialist ideals, daily life for Calverton was growing increasingly grim. He had always considered sleep a waste of time, but now he was plagued by chronic insomnia. If he went to bed at night, he lay awake worrying, his muscles twitching nervously.[16] Calverton's yearly income from books and lecturing had dwindled to less than a thousand dollars a year, and he and Nina Melville quarreled about money and worried themselves sick over debts.[17] In Baltimore he appealed for money to Elsie Sise, who had contributed money sporadically since the early twenties, but the effort required was more than it was worth: "The old lady here is driving me mad. . . . She wants me to invite people to dinner like Bates and Wittels who will impress her friends."[18] He did a lecture tour in the Midwest in the spring of 1940 and came back with enough money to make little more than a dent in his debts. The magazine had reverted to its status as a quarterly; now he was losing the struggle to support and maintain it. His stand against the Popular Front and against war made it increasingly difficult to find financial assistance. He lay awake nights in a cold sweat feeling that his seventeen-year effort to preserve a tradition of independent leftist thought was disintegrating and that socialist ideals were being destroyed by a tide of irrational forces.

In order to combat his fatigue and continue the frenetic pace on his book, Calverton began using benzedrine.[19] And he was drinking more heavily than ever. When he went out to dine with friends he would simply order a drink and watch the others eat. Still making his weekend trips from New York to Baltimore, he appeared at a "2110" gathering haggard and yellow-skinned. When a friend expressed concern about his appearance, he shrugged off a liver inflammation exacerbated by alcohol as a slight case of jaundice. The degenerative state of his life is suggested with a certain pathos by the *New York Telegram*, which had once quoted Calverton as a radical freethinker; now it quoted him as an expert on hangovers: "Cheese is the best thing I have found for mitigating the effects of alcohol."[20]

Calverton was stunned and further depressed by the death of Thomas Wolfe, one of the few men, he told Max Eastman, who really understood the *Man Inside* with its thesis that "the fear of death is the key to man's life."[21] Shortly after Wolfe's death, Calverton's closest friend, Ernest Sutherland Bates, also died. Calverton had known "Brachy" Bates since the early thirties; he and Bates had worked together on the *Modern Quarterly* during most of the decade. If Wolfe's death deeply disturbed Calverton, Bates's death devastated him.[22] Meanwhile a friend was succumbing

to madness. Calverton had patched up his friendship with Sam Schmalhausen after their rift in 1933, but now Schmalhausen was confined to a
mental institution in Michigan. For Calverton the end of the decade had
left in its wake a sense of entropic disorder and decay. Only a few days
after the New Year of 1940 he wrote Nina Melville that "death is closer
than we ever realized and here with Sam [Schmalhausen] in Battle Creek,
madness too."[23]

Now his lifelong preoccupation with death utterly possessed him and
he talked about death incessantly. Profoundly disturbed by his behavior,
Melville attempted to persuade him to see a doctor. He flew into a rage:
"I'd rather die not knowing I had a disease . . . fuck all doctors."[24] When
a couple who were close friends died as a result of a suicide pact, Calverton proposed to Melville that they do the same. She, now worn down and
utterly depressed herself, agreed that it would be "easy" with "an extra
dose of nembutal," but Calverton relented: "I won't let you do it with
me."[25] Later, he picked out and financed a cemetery plot in King David
Memorial Park, signing one of his letters to the mortuary, "your old friend
and death wisher."[26] He told Melville, "I am not going to live long. . . . Why
don't you go live with your family while I die."[27] She was near distraction,
but refused to leave.

Scott Nearing wrote several times from Jamaica, Vermont, inviting
Calverton and Melville up for a visit and rest in the country. But Calver-
ton continued to work, even initiating a new project with Ludwig Lore
for the formation of an American Labor Party that would supplant the
"effete" Socialist Party and be truly responsive to the American situation.
Nevertheless Calverton was clearly slipping more deeply into depression.
His long-time desire to be a successful creative writer began to obsess him.
After Maxwell Perkins rejected his autobiographical novel, he sent it to
Simon and Schuster, where it was again rejected. Thereafter he brooded
deeply about his failure as a fiction writer. Melville implored him to stop
drinking, but he refused, telling her that his drinking was an act of suicide: "Don't think my drinking is casual. I'm not a casual person," adding
"I'm half mad besides." He warned her that he was verging on a mental
breakdown: "I'm lost, my darling, utterly, and can't find my way back to
myself."[28]

Noticing that his physical and mental health was deteriorating, Calverton's family doctor advised him to make an immediate appointment.
But Calverton refused. Drinking continually, eating almost nothing, and
vomiting several times a day, he worked on, fatigued, bleary-eyed, and
yellow-skinned. It was as if Calverton, always sensitively attuned to the
historical forces of his time, was now being wrenched and sundered, men-
tally and physically, by the crisis of the late thirties, by the Stalinization

of radical values, by the exhaustion of socialist ideals. Overwhelmed by a sense of desperation, he was driving himself to death.

Yet even though contemporary events were taking an enormous toll on Calverton's psyche, he had not utterly given up. He worked incessantly on "Angels" and continued talks with Ludwig Lore on the proposed American Labor Party. He remained convinced of the need to oppose the war-preparation effort, and on November 18, 1940, he called Bertram Wolfe to question him about the efforts and possible success of the Keep America Out of War Conference.[29]

On November 20, he finished the manuscript of "Angels" and urgently dashed off a preface describing the heroes of his book: communitarians who at once embodied socialist values and whose example underscored the extent of radical failure at the end of the present decade, those who "sought to create a new life, a new world." When he finished, drained yet enormously relieved, he struggled up from his chair and dropped on the couch for a nap. Later Melville noticed that he was sleeping peacefully for the first time in months. But when she tried to wake him, she felt his hand was cold and he failed to respond. In a panic she called the doctor and two friends. George Britt and Charlie Abrams arrived first, and when the doctor finally arrived, George Calverton was pronounced dead.[30]

Calverton's friends and associates were shocked at the news of his death. Many learned of his death suddenly, unexpectedly, over the telephone or from a mutual friend. Because he had been so energetic and active, few understood the degree of his exhaustion before death, nor the degree to which his physical and mental health had deteriorated. Nor did the cause of death in the doctor's report—"pernicious anemia"—suggest the mental and physical torment he had gone through before he died, the physical deterioration and the developing cirrhosis of the liver.

After his death Melville, feeling herself on the brink of a nervous breakdown and wishing a reprieve from the scene of so much agony, sailed for Cuba. On board ship, she set down the details of George's last days in her notebook, observing that they were "sheer torture. . . . He talked about death so much . . . that I would reach the point of screaming. . . . When he had dwelt on death and its funereal aspects for the millionth time I suddenly burst out 'darling you must stop this, why are you torturing me this way?'"[31] She returned from Cuba grieving and still exhausted and checked into Roosevelt Hospital. She wrote a friend, "The collapse which has been threatening since George's death is now occurring."[32] She cited the sleeplessness, "which started when I stayed up with George night on end," as the cause of her condition, as well as "just the living with a too intimate consciousness of death, a consciousness which I have been trying to push away for months—keeping a face when I really wanted to scream."[33] Added to this, in spite of his torment about death, Calverton left no formal will, and now there were the conflicting claims of Una Corbett, Bessie Peretz, the Goetzes, and other Baltimoreans to contend with.[34] Ultimately the emotional dependence on women George Calverton had always exhibited meant that the women in his life would have to deal with these final matters.

The magazine, in its editorial policy and direction, was always virtually a one-person operation, and it was clear it would now die too. But the people who had known Calverton for years gathered to put out one more issue. George Britt, Max Eastman, Nina Melville, and Lillian Symes were among those who formed the editorial committee of the last issue of the *Modern Quarterly*—the "V. F. Calverton Memorial Issue." Among the "Tributes, Appreciations, Memories" were pieces by an impressive list of liberals and radicals, ranging from Lewis Corey, Norman Thomas, Michael Blankfort, and James Farmer, to literary figures like Sherwood Anderson and James Rorty. Lewis Corey (Fraina), who was active in the early communism of twentieth-century America, and whose analysis of the professional classes was so influential on the policy of the magazine during the mid thirties, spoke of "the quiet, unappeasing but unbreakable intellectual and moral independence of George Calverton."[35] Henry Hazlitt wrote that Calverton "brought writers together . . . and their ideas fructified each other."[36] Benjamin Stolberg wrote that "his passing seemed to me . . . like the passing of a generation, the closing of an era in my own life." Norman Thomas wrote that Calverton "worked with the high standard of integrity that Randolph Bourne had set himself in the First World War, and like Bourne he died when we needed him most."[37]

As Calverton would have wanted it, there was an article in this final issue of the *Modern Quarterly* on the imminent danger of war, and it was written by Scott Nearing, who had contributed to the magazine's first issue. Continuing the fight against fascism, there was an article by Gunter Reimann on the threat posed by the fascist ideology on a global level. There was an article by Max Eastman, who had shared with him the difficulties of keeping the magazine alive throughout most of the 1930s. And appropriately there was an account by Una Corbett, Calverton's early lover, mother of his daughter Joy, and lifelong friend, of the old days and the parties at 2110 East Pratt Street in Baltimore, and a poem by Eli Siegel, who had initiated Calverton into the world of socialism nearly two decades earlier. So the *Modern Quarterly* came to an end, seventeen years after its birth.

HENRY James once said that being an American is a complex fate. Irving Howe has added that being a Socialist in America makes such a fate even more complex.[38] Calverton's career embodies the com-

plexities as well as the contours of American radicalism in the early twentieth century, particularly the tension between individualism and collectivism. Calverton's "American cast of mind" with its individualistic premises,
as well as the radical personalism he had absorbed in his early years, a
legacy of the distinctively American Village Left, clashed resoundingly
with the adamant ideological and collective cast of the later twenties and
thirties Left. Throughout his career, Calverton found himself oscillat-
ing between the two poles of individualism and collectivism, striving to
overcome his own inner loneliness by organizing and joining in group
activity and simultaneously struggling to avert the group's demands for
ideological conformity. Moreover his sense of self—his singularity—often
ran counter to his plans to act collectively. This was the case in his capacity
as editor with the difficulties that emerged from attempts to share editorial responsibility with others such as Eastman and Wilson. And certainly
also this collision between individualism and collectivism was evident in
the radical groups of the early thirties he himself helped organize and
which then excluded him because he ultimately could not conform to their
narrow ideological agenda.

Calverton longed for the group, the collective, yet could never fit com-
fortably into it. He was a social animal but a solitary creature too, subject
to private neurotic anxieties. His yearning for an organic community, for
the group, was not only a desire to overcome loneliness, but a wish to transcend the chief fear of the lonely bourgeois monad—the fear of death.
Yet even here, searching for solace from his most profound and disturbing fears, Calverton could not in the last instance embrace an idea of the
collective that obliterated the individual conscience and merged the self
totally with the group.

In this sense Calverton shared with Randolph Bourne more than just
an opposition to war. Both men shared the American propensity to be
single, separate persons yet to long for the condition of being "en masse";
both shared the American tragedy of being unable to reconcile the separate impulses toward individuality and collectivity. The tragedy of V. F.
Calverton is precisely that he could never overcome his chronic sense of
personal loneliness nor his sense of alienation within American culture in
the context of a revolutionary community. Perhaps his situation suggests
something about the American political psyche itself, about the limits and
conditions of revolutionary activity within American political culture. Yet
he also shared with Bourne the fate that this "tragic" characteristic—his
burden of singularity—sustained his independence and enabled him to
be one of the severest critics of the very movements he advocated and
to which he wished to belong.[39] Certainly Calverton was one of the Old
Left generation's most outspoken critics of collective oppression and au-

thoritarianism in its manifold forms: of the increasingly inflexible and ironhanded stance of the Party in the late twenties, of full-blown Stalinist ideological rigidity and oppression of dissenting opinion at the height of the Third Period, of the hegemony of the Popular Front, and of the threat of fascism itself both from within and from without America.

Calverton's intellectual movement toward social democracy, as has already been suggested, was doubtless in part a consequence of his efforts to discover an indigenous basis for Marxist analysis within an American tradition that stresses democratic norms as the overriding criteria of political action and historical evaluation. But it was also very likely the result of a search to balance the two stresses of the communal and individual, the shared and the alone. As Irving Howe has suggested, socialism of the democratic variety represents a kind of middle position between the solitary individual and the intensities and propensities for mass psychology of the overheated community.[40] What Calverton found in the early communitarianism of the American past were the classic socialist values of cooperation, mutuality, communal provision, and public life—things starkly absent from the America in which he lived. Yet he did not take from his study of the American communal experiments a Rousseauian communitarianism, but an outlook that stressed the democratization of the economic processes as well as political institutions, the extension of democracy as a political mode into every area of social and economic life. A socialist society was crucial for overcoming alienation of the isolated self, yet enlarging democratic freedom was also crucial if a new kind of social exploitation that crushed individual liberty was not to emerge. While he strongly believed that the ideal of community and collective vision should be preserved, Calverton was not willing to abandon the concept of democracy in the name of a chimerical community without alienation that sacrificed the individual to larger and ever more repressive collectivities.

To be sure, Calverton was a nonacademic, public intellectual who sometimes caught ideas on the fly or failed to develop them sufficiently. His theory was not always consistent; indeed his Marxism swayed between a libertarian impulse and an excessive veneration of group psychology. The influence of pragmatism led him to stress voluntarism and historically specific radical praxis on the one hand, and dubious notions of social control on the other. Although he harshly criticized positivistic and scientistic versions of Marxism (as he did in his theory of cultural compulsives), he at times exhibited (particularly in his earlier literary criticism) a wooden determinism. There was an obvious contradiction between the flexible, interdisciplinary radical cultural analysis Calverton somewhat sketchily assembled by wedding Freud and Marx and the undialectical and deterministic analysis of ideas and culture he constructed from his readings of Plekhanov. Nevertheless the trajectory of his intellectual career suggests an increasing appreciation for a culture of radical democracy uniting the individual and the communal. Moreover, enormously influenced by the progressive and pragmatic spirit of the prewar Village intellectuals, Calverton consistently held up the notion of an oppositional cultural criticism. And his magazine exhibited a variety of pragmatic or "Deweyan" Marxism with its critical spirit and oppositional sentiments, its criticisms of doctrine and rigid ideology, and its ideal of radical community based on dialogue between various intellectual groups and factional persuasions.

Calverton was not a "vulgar Marxist," who quickly reduced ideas to ideology. On the contrary, his major efforts were in the direction of breaking through the iron cage of ideology so that political ideas could be the subject of speculation and debate. Certainly also, it was in this speculative spirit that he investigated new and often unpopular topics associated with cultural radicalism—psychology, sexuality, and marriage, and the possibility of uniting Marx and Freud. He was an American voice speaking in terms consistent with early- and mid-twentieth-century Western Marxism. His advocacy of a marriage between Marx and Freud paralleled efforts to bring about this union by the Frankfurt School. His notion of the pedagogical and educative role of politics, his opposition to a Leninist concept of the Party as an elitist vanguard, and his sense that political theory and praxis must be grounded in the precise cultural reality of American workers are strikingly similar to Gramsci's concerns and priorities.

Finally, it was Calverton's unswerving individualism combined with his commitment to the ideal of the group, specifically his commitment to this Gramsci-like notion of the educational role of politics in the process of social and cultural transformation, that ultimately made him such an important and creative editor. Retaining his own individualistic perspective, opposing the collective mentality of the Party, Calverton dedicated his publication with its debates and dialogue to the larger community of American leftists, to "radical education and reeducation." His sense that the intellectual should be linked to public life, that intellectual work should have public consequences, places him in the tradition of radical social critics. It is also the key to his importance as an editor.

If Russell Jacoby is right in his contention that the public intellectual is disappearing from American life,[41] then Calverton might be seen as another of this vanishing breed. Indeed, in the late twentieth century it is difficult to imagine an editor of a journal devoted to social, cultural, and political analysis having a profound influence on the direction of American intellectual and cultural history. And from our vantage point it is also easy to overlook the significance of the editor in shaping the course of the American Left in the early and mid twentieth century. For it is as editor, shaping and defining the key questions of his age—rather than author or political activist—that Calverton was most influential.

Calverton never succeeded in providing a detailed theoretical program for a possible Americanized Marxism. Nor did he found a political party that wedded Marxist ideas to American conditions. The *Modern Quarterly* nevertheless approached left-wing ideas in the best pragmatic spirit. It embodied the practice of a free and unfettered play of political ideas while holding to the ideal that community and communication—the exchange of ideas—are inextricably linked, that (in John Dewey's words) "democracy is a name for a life of free and enriching communion."[42] Calverton's steadfast dedication to the *Modern Quarterly*, and to these ideals, was, in retrospect, a unique contribution to an American approach to radical theory and speculation.

Epilogue

I n the summer of 1983, 2110 East Pratt Street in Baltimore stood empty, and the silence of its rooms seemed to echo with the conversations and learned and heated arguments that characterized the soirees there from the early 1920s to 1940. Its rooms saw the passing of an older generation, devoted to small business and a complacent middle-class routine, which had come to maturity in the late nineteenth century. They saw the emergence of a new generation pitted against Victorian gentility and devoted to socialist ideals, a group of young people, inspired by the prewar intellectual Left, conspiring to launch their own magazine devoted to radical thought. Countless editorial meetings took place here, with writing, copy-work, and typing until the early hours. Its rooms also witnessed the drama of unconventional and experimental relations and love affairs, the disruption of severed relationships, and the continuity of perduring relationships. Even when the magazine moved to New York, its rooms provided the base for weekend radical gatherings and remained the first and proper home of the magazine and its editor. Now 2110 East Pratt Street was empty and up for sale, the character of the neighborhood transformed, and the events that took place there forgotten by the surrounding community. The fate of "2110," offered for sale to me, a passing traveler, by its immigrant owner who was oblivious to its history, suggests the profound difficulty of realizing a vision to which radicals like Calverton were devoted—the difficulty of realizing community in a constantly changing, fluid, American reality.

Indeed when Calverton lived at "2110" he felt the fluid sense of social instability, the sense of being part of an immigrant family without strong roots, subject to the changing realities of American political and social conditions. Calverton embraced radicalism for deeply personal reasons: community promised a sense of stability, a context in which the self might transcend its own fears and preoccupations and turn its creative efforts to social renewal; social and self-renewal would thus be coextensive. In a sense then, the changing American reality, hostile to the stability implied in a notion of community, was precisely the reason Calverton sought community.

Yet Calverton also faced the dilemma that not only was the Left unstable, its strategy and policies subject to profound historical upheaval and change, but the terrain of radicalism itself was one of mutating factional alliances and sectarian dispute that undermined the possibility of community. The radical group projects to which Calverton dedicated himself in the early thirties were torn asunder by the Party's shifting policies and the increasing factionalism on the Left. The hope of a genuinely American party collapsed when the AWP was swallowed by the voracious and Machiavellian Trotskyists. Ironically, during the Popular Front period, when a sense of solidarity and fraternal community ran high, Calverton could not accept the uncritical spirit of the Popular Front's radical and liberal coalition. And during the mid to late thirties Calverton's opposition to Stalinism made him a pariah in both liberal and radical camps. Calverton embraced the Left in search of community, and his failure to find it there was profoundly dispiriting and a major factor in the intense depression and declining outlook of his last years.

Calverton's dilemma is suggestive of the phenomenon of intellectual deradicalization in the post–World War II years. Alan Wald argues that intellectuals turned away from radicalism in the postwar years because of cold-war pressures and economic self-interest.[1] But although Calverton did not live to experience a postwar world, and although he held to a socialist ideal until his death, his example supports Terry Cooney's contention that the chief reason intellectuals turned away from radicalism was that radical thought seemed to have reached a cul-de-sac, that it "seemed increasingly tired, unable to generate a significant body of work in either literature or social thought."[2] By the mid thirties Calverton's writings expressed the sense that Marxian reason could not explain the ruses of history; by the late thirties they expressed the inescapable fact that the Left could not answer the dilemmas of the isolated self, could not provide in theory or practice a way of reconciling self and group. And if sectarianism undermined the hope of community, the Roosevelt administration's NRA and the Popular Front's alliance between Communists and New Dealers co-opted radical analysis and resolve. Like other radicals, Calverton experienced, in Howard Brick's words, "an oppressive sense of how ongoing social development frustrated or blocked their aims."[3] Finally, like the *Partisan Review* circle that Cooney examines, Calverton assumed that true socialism promised an invigoration of intellectual life and the free circulation of ideas. But Stalinism was antithetical to this assumption. Calverton groped with crucial questions that would later be addressed by the *Partisan Review* circle: was Soviet communism the logical outcome of Marxist–Leninism? Did the socialist vision point inevitably to the totalitarian "servile state"? Calverton's response to these disorienting questions was, on the one hand, growing depression and desperation, and, on the other hand, an attempt to salvage basic socialist ideals by embracing his progressive and pragmatic roots and turning to communitarian models in the American past.

In spite of the changing factional and ideological terrain of the American political landscape on the Left, and in spite of Calverton's personal disappointments, the notion of community was central to his life and project. It shaped his encounters with various radical traditions from the progressivism of the prewar Left to Stalinism to the amalgam of Marxist and American liberal ideals that constituted his final social-democratic vision. From the prewar intellectual Left Calverton inherited a sense of the realization of self in dialogue with community. From the prewar intellectual Left, with its Deweyan cast, Calverton fashioned an idea of an intersection of personal and social life based on a common culture of critical exchange. He absorbed from Deweyan progressivism the ideal of the necessary connection between community and communication; indeed his magazine was devoted precisely to the ideal of "keeping up the conversation" among radical groups. If he was briefly attracted to the social control and the technocratic strain of the pragmatic tradition, he ultimately drew upon progressive and pragmatic strains to form a vision of communal participation that would preserve the diversity and plurality of a democratic way of life. Diversity of point of view (whether political, ethnic, or cultural) and intellectual community were the guiding principles of his editorial vision.

The history of the magazine not only embodies the ideal of intellectual community as critical dialogue and debate, but expresses a particular conception of intellectual responsibility, also gleaned from the pragmatic and progressive tradition—the ideal of the organic intellectual who revels in ideas and relates them to action by creating constituencies for moral and political purposes.[4] For Calverton, the way in which this conception could be realized was by initiating the discussion, setting the agenda for dialogue, and preserving the possibility of the exchange of diverse ideas. Indeed the *Modern Quarterly* established itself on precisely those terms, setting the agenda for discourse on the Left between 1923 and 1940, sometimes taking up issues that reflected dominant concerns among radicals, more often taking up prescient and forward-looking issues spurned or ignored by orthodox radicals, frequently offering critical perspectives that fundamentally challenged the Left's central ideas and policies. A center of discussion of cultural radicalism in the twenties, the magazine became, during the thirties, the primary forum where radical thought could be independent and freely speculative, where intellectuals could enter into debate on contentious issues, could voice heretical positions, and could deliberate on the relationship between Marxist ideas and American conditions.[5] The chief voice of the anti-Stalinist independent Left after 1933, from 1936 to 1938 (when the second *Partisan Review* was formed) it was virtually the sole radical voice to protest the Moscow trials and the primary opponent on the Left of the Communists' Popular Front program.

Wanting to keep political speculation in his publication open-ended, Calverton eschewed an alliance with either Lovestonites or Trotskyists. Late in the decade when it became clear to Calverton that Stalinism, far from being an aberration, was a logical outcome of Leninism, and of the Bolshevik antidemocratic regime of which Trotsky was so integral a part, Trotskyism could scarcely be seen as the purveyor of a "true" revolutionary Marxism. In spite of the fact that Trotsky was the most significant symbol of opposition to Stalin, the publication's stance continued to be nonpartisan. Throughout its life, with the exception of the brief and unofficial alliance with the AWP, it remained exactly what Calverton insisted it should be—independent and unallied.

This ideal of independence, intellectual autonomy, and pluralistic flexibility which the *Quarterly* preserved during the twenties and thirties, provides a line of continuity between the radicalism of the pre–World War I intellectuals and the anti-Stalinism that asserted itself on the Left in the late thirties. Not only did this strain provide an intellectual climate and context in which a critique of Stalinism could readily emerge, but it created an atmosphere in which speculation could flourish. The collective discussions on Americanizing Marx as well as individual efforts, such as Calverton's own theory of cultural compulsives—in itself an intriguing contribution to radical theory—would have been unthinkable without this speculative atmosphere. Similarly unthinkable would have been the attempted conjoining of Dewey and Marx that took place in the pages of the *Quarterly*, arguably one of the major contributions the journal made to the intellectual culture of the thirties, and one of the distinct points of continuity between the *Quarterly* and more recent intellectual directions.

In one sense, then, the *Quarterly* continued a project begun by the prewar intellectual Left, that of fashioning the ideal of the "organic" intellectual as an independent critic of politics and culture, of establishing a cultural commentary that was uniquely American, and that attempted to explain America to itself at a particular historical moment. This legacy was made vital by the magazine's uncompromising commitment to radical thought; it was cross-fertilized by the array of radical intellectuals (Gentiles, Jews, and blacks) who were attracted into the magazine's orbit. In preserving the independent radicalism inherited from the prewar Left for later generations, the *Quarterly*'s contribution is incalculably important to American intellectual culture. The magazine's fundamental Deweyan

note of critical intelligence and creative democracy, as well as its speculations on how a pragmatic strain might intersect with Marxist analysis,
were later taken up in the writings of C. Wright Mills, for example. Mills
criticized pragmatism for its neglect of social conflict and struggle, yet he
was nonetheless involved in a neo-Deweyan project of genuine individuality and democracy.[6] Like writers who contributed to the *Quarterly*, Mills
was intent on fashioning a social criticism that combined these ideals with
the discourses of the social sciences, including Marxism. Like a number
of *Quarterly* writers, Mills was interested in professionals and intellectuals
as agents of radical change. And, like the *Quarterly* writers, Mills worked
out of a tradition of critical discourse hinging on the idea of intellectual
autonomy, which attempted to interrogate and explain the larger field
of American political and intellectual culture. Indeed it would be hard
to imagine the work of Mills, or for that matter of other independent
Left intellectuals like Michael Harrington, without the preservation of the
ideals of autonomy and democratic values to which the *Quarterly* substan-
tially contributed.

Moreover, the dialogue that emerged from this spirit of independence,
particularly the speculations on the relationship of pragmatism and Marxism, looked ahead to recent intellectual developments such as the revival
of pragmatism among neo-Marxists like Richard Bernstein and neoliber-
als like Richard Rorty. Articles in the *Quarterly* during the thirties anticipated recent pragmatic and postmodern critiques of Marxism's penchant
for totalizing history, for its tendency to overlook heterogeneity. And the
Quarterly's place in the continuity of pragmatism is suggested symbolically
by the fact that Richard Rorty's father, James Rorty, was associated with
the magazine, and Richard Rorty's earliest recollections are of Sidney
Hook, "a man upon whose knees I was bounced as a baby and a philosopher who forgot more about Dewey than I shall ever learn."[7]

Certainly, without the preservation of this uniquely American strain
of radicalism, it is difficult to imagine what developments on the intellectual Left during the post–World War II years might have looked like.
It would be impossible to imagine the New Left of the 1960s without
something of the indigenous radicalism of the Village Left—with its individualistic and antinomian character—surviving the years of communist
hegemony. Calverton's politics, in which personal issues were so much at
stake, represent a harbinger of the New Left. And it might be added that
in his quest for fraternity on the Left—a logical development not merely
of his own psychological needs but of the ideal of a complete socialism—
Calverton was seeking what the New Left later sought, that is, the abolition
of alienation through the creation of community.

The project of Americanizing Marx, another significant contribution of the *Quarterly*, was not only challenging at the time, but presaged future developments. Calverton's writings during the mid thirties served to remind radicals that America would not fit many of the dogmatic notions that the Communist Party embraced. And while calling for an American approach to Marx, Calverton rejected the notion that the Popular Front either contributed to or constituted an expression of a distinctive American radical tradition.[8] If the *Partisan Review* group was never able to get past its negative assumptions about a native American radical tradition, the *Quarterly* often too uncritically invoked this tradition in its call for radical social change.[9] Yet the *Quarterly* at least provoked speculation about the problematic relationship between Marxist theory and American conditions. This was also forward looking: the birth of the free-speech movement, youth culture, and the women's movement in the sixties strongly suggests that American radicalism cannot be constructed from foreign examples.

The *Modern Quarterly*, reflecting the intellectual odyssey of its editor, began the thirties denouncing liberalism and calling for revolutionary values, but became increasingly preoccupied with democratic values as the decade wore on, and with how the American democratic tradition might not only be reconciled with Marxian ideas but might also revitalize them. It ended the decade pitting these values against the virulence of Stalinism. Calverton, persecuted son of the revolution, able to see the chilling dimensions of Stalinism more clearly and more quickly than others, concluded the decade fighting a lonely battle against the Communists. He wrestled with the strenuous decade, succumbing at the end of his lifetime to the intellectual exhaustion of nurturing radical ideas and strategy and the physical and emotional exhaustion incurred in that pursuit. Yet his life struggle was for an independent Left and for a "human" socialism, and he remained committed to these ideals to the end.

Calverton and the *Modern Quarterly* belong to a unique period of American history. In the contemporary period with the effacement of concepts such as commitment, authenticity, belief, and community, it is difficult to imagine the intellectual excitement of New York in the thirties when the *Modern Quarterly*, that "intellectual brokerage house for the revolution,"[10] was displayed in the New York University bookstore window, alluring and provoking students and faculty and causing administrators concern about faculty members whose names appeared in symposia with titles like "Why I Am a Communist."[11] From the vantage point of the present, it is difficult to imagine the strange admixture of radical politics and socializing, of collective outcry and group celebration that characterized the *Modern Quarterly* fund-raising dinners, which included such speakers as Max Eastman, Scott Nearing, Sidney Hook, Clarence Darrow, A. J. Muste, Claude McKay, James Rorty, and on occasion music by Duke Ellington. Remote and distant seems that unique phenomenon of American radicalism, the Calvertonian weekly soiree, with its strange combination of intellectual intensity and amiability, its political arguments and factional wrangles lasting long into the night, its illegal liquor and camaraderie. Today, walking by "2110," the rowhouse on East Pratt Street in Baltimore, the laughter and talk that once issued forth from its crowded rooms seems a chimera, a ghostly recollection. But without the focal point of nonpartisan radical activity that collected there between the wars, it is difficult to envision the continuity of a democratic Left, of autonomous radical speculation, of an independent American radicalism. And without them it would be difficult to envision an heir of this radicalism in the American grain that may yet again come to life in future decades.

Notes

Introduction

1. Daniel Aaron, *Writers on the Left* (New York: Avon Books, 1965), p. 337.
2. Alfred Kazin, *Starting Out in the Thirties* (Boston: Little, Brown, 1962), pp. 65–66.
3. See Aaron, *Writers on the Left*, pp. 335–46.
4. Christopher Lasch, *The New Radicalism in America (1889–1963): The Intellectual as a Social Type* (New York: Knopf, 1965), p. ix.
5. Quoted in Lewis Perry, *Intellectual Life in America, A History* (New York: Franklin Watts, 1984), p. 354.
6. Van Wyck Brooks, ed., *History of a Literary Radical and Other Essays*, by Randolph Bourne (1920; New York: Biblo and Tannen, 1969).
7. V. F. Calverton to Leon Trotsky: "The Crisis in Communism," *Modern Monthly* (hereafter *MM*) 7, no. 3 (April 1933): 140.
8. Moses Rischin, "When the Savants Go Marching In," *Reviews in American History* 17, no. 2 (June 1989): 297.
9. Alan Wald, *The New York Intellectuals: The Rise and Decline of the Anti-Stalinist Left from the 1930s to the 1980s* (Chapel Hill: University of North Carolina Press, 1987), p. 111.
10. Ibid., p. 6.
11. Ibid.
12. For an account, see John P. Diggins, *Up from Communism: Conservative Odysseys in American Intellectual History* (New York: Harper & Row, 1975), pp. 17–66.
13. Quoted in Sidney Hook, *Out of Step: An Unquiet Life in the 20th Century* (New York: Harper & Row, 1987), p. 244.
14. Terry Cooney, *The Rise of the New York Intellectuals: Partisan Review and Its Circle, 1934–1945* (Madison: University of Wisconsin Press, 1986), pp. 35–36.
15. Alexander Bloom, *Prodigal Sons: The New York Intellectuals and Their World* (New York: Oxford University Press, 1986), p. 103.
16. Irving Howe, quoted, in ibid.
17. Ibid., p. 104.
18. Daniel Bell, *Marxian Socialism in the United States* (Princeton: Princeton University Press, 1967), p. xii.

19. Russell Jacoby, *The Last Intellectuals: American Culture in the Age of Academe* (New York: Basic Books, 1987), pp. 3–26.

20. Ibid., p. 192.

Chapter One. George Goetz: Baltimore Beginnings

1. This account of the Goetz family and the young George Goetz that follows is taken from several sources. The first is his unpublished autobiographical novel "This Thing of Darkness," which is in the V. F. Calverton Collection, The New York Public Library, Manuscript Division (hereafter referred to as VFC). Other accounts that contributed to an understanding of the early years as well as his life generally are: Calverton's "Between Two Wars," a short fragment of what was intended to be an autobiography, in *Modern Quarterly* (hereafter *MQ*) 11, no. 7 (Autumn 1940): 5–6; a short autobiographical sketch written for S. J. Kunitz and H. Haycraft, in *Twentieth Century Authors: A Bibliographical Dictionary of Modern Literature* (Englewood Cliffs, N.J.: Prentice-Hall, 1942), p. 240; an article, which V. F. Calverton wrote for the *Socialist Call* (22 June 1940), entitled "What Socialism Means to Me," containing sketchy autobiographical material he intended to expand on in his planned autobiography; George Britt, "V. F. Calverton: Notes Toward His Autobiography," as well as Britt, "V. F. Calverton," *MQ* 11, no. 7 (Autumn 1940): 7–12; also a number of short sketches written by Calverton's friends and associates in *MQ* 11, no. 7 (Autumn 1940). Finally my interviews and correspondence with Calverton's associates helped in filling out the picture and in distinguishing between factual and fictional materials in Calverton's autobiographical novel.

2. Calverton, "This Thing of Darkness," p. 17.

3. Ibid., p. 255.

4. Calverton, "Between Two Wars," p. 5.

5. Baltimore *Morning Sun*, 12 April 1917: "PACIFIST MEETING ENDS IN RIOT: MOB BREAKS IN: POLICE USE CLUBS: PROMINENT ARE BADLY BEATEN: ONE MAN RENDERED UNCONSCIOUS." See also Henry F. May, *The End of American Innocence* (New York: Knopf, 1969), p. 340.

6. Joseph Freeman, *An American Testament* (New York: Farrar & Rinehart, 1936), p. 222.

7. Haim Gnizi, "V. F. Calverton: Independent Radical," doctoral dissertation, City University of New York, 1968, p. 21.

8. George Goetz to Ries, 25 August and 2 September, 1919, VFC.

9. Herman F. Miller to Goetz, 26 August 1919, VFC. The letter includes quotes from a letter from Goetz to Miller and thus supplies much of the information about this exchange.

10. Miller to Goetz, 8 May 1920, VFC. Goetz's quote is included in the letter.

11. Miller to Goetz, 18 December 1919, VFC.

12. Calverton, "What Socialism Means to Me," *Socialist Call*, 22 June 1940.

13. Eli Siegel to Goetz, 11 October 1920, VFC.

14. George Goetz, "Concerning Partnership in Poverty," VFC.

15. Author's interview with Helen Letzer-Solidar, Baltimore, 5 May 1983.

16. Gnizi, "V. F. Calverton," pp. 35–36.

17. Russell Jacoby, *The Last Intellectuals: American Culture in the Age of Academe* (New York: Basic Books, 1987). See especially his chapter, "The Decline of Bohemia," pp. 27–53.

18. Quoted in ibid., p. 21.

19. Malcolm Cowley, *Exile's Return: A Literary Odyssey of the 1920's* (New York: Viking, 1951), pp. 27ff.

20. Ibid., p. 28.

21. Miller to Goetz, 28 January 1922, VFC.

22. Calverton, "Between Two Wars," p. 5.

23. Christopher Lasch, *The New Radicalism in America: The Intellectual as a Social Type* (New York: Knopf, 1965), p. 90.

24. Randolph Bourne, "Trans-national America," in *The Radical Will: Randolph Bourne Selected Writings, 1911–1918*, ed. Olaf Hansen (New York: Urizen, 1977), p. 264.

25. See Chapter Eleven.

26. Van Wyck Brooks, Introduction to Randolph Bourne's *History of a Literary Radical* (New York: Biblo and Tannen, 1969), p. xvii.

27. Bourne, quoted, Thomas Bender, *New York Intellect: A History of Intellectual Life in New York City, from 1750 to the Beginnings of Our Own Time* (New York: Knopf, 1987), p. 234.

28. Calverton submitted "This Thing of Darkness" to Maxwell Perkins at Scribner's. Perkins conceded it was an intriguing account of "the representative experiences that shaped the minds of a generation," but he declined to publish it, explaining that its "complete candor of statement" made the novel more like pornography than art. Calverton had argued that the specific intent of the novel was to explore adolescent sexuality, but Perkins was not persuaded. Very likely, Perkins also saw little literary merit in the book. Calverton to Perkins, 6 February 1938; Perkins to Calverton, 28 February 1938, VFC.

29. "This Thing of Darkness," p. 152.

30. Calverton to Nina Melville, no day, May 1928, VFC.

Chapter Two. Birth of Calverton, Genesis of Modern Quarterly

1. James Gilbert, *Writers and Partisans: A History of Literary Radicalism in America* (New York: John Wiley, 1968), p. 55.

2. Kerr & Co. was not encouraging: "You will need to work up a circulation of 20,000 or more before you can expect to sell much advertising. . . . We pay $40.00 in the *Liberator*, which has probably ten times the circulation you will start with." Charles H. Kerr & Co. to George Goetz, 9 September 1922, VFC.

3. Harry W. Laidler to Goetz, 27 December 1922, VFC.

4. Mercer Green Johnston to Goetz, 27 December 1922, VFC.

5. Thomas Bender, *New York Intellect: A History of Intellectual Life in New York City, from 1750 to the Beginnings of Our Own Time* (New York: Knopf, 1987), pp. 231–33.

6. C. Hartley Grattan in letter to author together with Grattan Notebook of Reminiscences on V. F. Calverton, Canberra, Australia, June 1971.

7. Richard Pells, *Radical Visions and American Dreams* (New York: Harper & Row, 1973), p. 14.

8. Editorial Preface: "Modernism and the Modern Quarterly," in *MQ* 1, no. 1 (March 1923): 1–2.

9. Ibid.

10. Eli Siegel, "The Scientific Criticism: The Complete Criticism," *MQ* 1, no. 1 (March 1923): 7.

11. V. F. Calverton, "The Great Man Illusion: A Study in Causes with Reference to William James," *MQ* 1, no. 1 (March 1923): 13–27.

12. Richel North (A. D. Emmart), "The Limitations of American Magazines," *MQ* 1, no. 1 (March 1923): 2–12.

13. For a discussion of Lippmann's notion of science, see David A. Hollinger, "Science and Anarchy: Walter Lippmann's Drift and Mastery," *American Quarterly* 29, no. 5 (Winter 1977): 463–75.

14. Siegel, "The Complete Socialism," *MQ* 1, no. 1 (March 1923): 37. For a discussion of the conflict between Siegel and the SLP, see Haim Gnizi, "V. F. Calverton: Independent Radical," doctoral dissertation, City University of New York, 1968.

15. John Marcey to V. F. Calverton, 3 May 1923, VFC.

16. Joseph Freeman to Calverton, 28 March 1923, VFC.

17. Calverton to Freeman, 7 May 1923; the *New Age* to Calverton, 19 March 1923, VFC.

18. Siegel to Goetz, 3 March 1923, VFC.

19. Goetz to Siegel, 3 March and 7 June, 1923, VFC.

20. In the late 1960s and early 1970s, Eli Siegel headed a small but zealous group known as "Aesthetic Realists" that met in the Terrain Gallery in the Village. He claimed to explain metaphysical issues and cure psychological problems by the "unification of opposites."

21. Haim Kantorovitch lamented that "the most characteristic sign of our time is the lack of confidence in the prewar conception of how we are going to realize our ideals." Kantorovitch to Calverton, 10 June 1924, VFC.

22. Karl Marx, *Theses on Feuerbach*, in C. Wright Mills, *The Marxists* (New York: Dell, 1962), p. 71; Kantorovitch to Calverton, 5 June 1924, VFC.

23. Kantorovitch to Calverton, 6 May, 15 July and 3 April 1924, VFC.

24. Haim Kantorovitch, "The Rise and Decline of Neo-Communism," *MQ* 1, no. 4 (Spring 1924): 21–43, 21.

25. Ibid., p. 33.

26. See Calverton, "Is State Capitalism Progressive?" *MM* 10, no. 11 (March 1938): 2–3.

27. Kantorovitch to Calverton, 14 April 1924, VFC.

28. Daniel Aaron, *Writers on the Left* (1961; New York: Avon, 1965), p. 114.

29. Kantorovitch to Calverton, 14 April 1924, VFC.

30. Boni & Liveright to Goetz, 12 December 1924, VFC.

31. See Charles Glicksburg, *American Literary Criticism* (New York: Hendricks House, 1951), p. 30.

32. Calverton, "On Sherman, Mencken and Others," *MQ* 2, no. 3 (Spring 1925): 162–77.

33. Calverton, *The Newer Spirit* (New York: Boni & Liveright, 1925), p. 21.

34. Ibid., p. 50.

35. Ibid., p. 91.

36. Ibid., p. 145.

37. Calverton, "Trotsky on Literature," *New Leader*, 16 May 1925, p. 5.

38. Calverton, *Newer Spirit*, pp. 29–30.

39. John Dewey to Calverton, 13 May 1925, VFC.

40. Herbert Read to Calverton, 2 January 1926, VFC.

41. *American Mercury* 5 (June 1925): 252.

42. Waldo Frank, "No Spirit at All," *New Republic* 43 (24 June 1925): 131–32.

43. Kenneth Burke, "The Scientific Critic," *New York Herald*, 10 May 1925.

44. James Oneal, "A Remarkable Book," *New Leader*, 25 April 1925, p. 9.

45. H. M. Wicks, "Another Professor Discovers Marx," *Daily Worker*, 24 September 1925, p. 6.

46. Michael Gold to Calverton, 4 May 1925, VFC.

47. Ibid.

48. Walter Rideout identifies Marcus Hitch's *Goethe's Faust: A Fragment of Socialist Criticism* (1908) as "the first extended piece of Marxist literary criticism by an American to be published in this country." See Rideout, *The Radical Novel in the United States, 1900–1954; Some Interrelations of Literature and Society* (New York: Hill and Wang, 1956), p. 97.

49. Mike Gold, *Liberator*, February 1921, pp. 20–21.

50. Editors, the *Modern Quarterly*, to American Fund for Public Service, no date, 1925, VFC. The letter specified the deficit for the year 1924–1925 at $1,938, and the estimated deficit for 1925–1926 at $2,538. It indicated that all editors had in fact donated over $300 each per year to keep the magazine alive.

51. Algernon Lee (Educational Director of the Rand School of Social Sciences) to Calverton, 1 April 1925, VFC.

52. Gold to Calverton, no date, VFC.

53. William Z. Foster to Calverton, 10 August 1925; Foster to Calverton, 8 September 1925, VFC.

54. William F. Dunne to Calverton, 3 October 1925, VFC.

55. Foster to Calverton, 8 September 1925, VFC.

Chapter Three. Red Love and Lost Innocence

1. Author's interview with Helen Letzer-Solidar, Baltimore, 10 May 1983.

2. Leonard Davin, "I Remember Friday Nights at Cal's Black House," *Baltimore Sun*, 13 April 1975.

3. James Oneal, "The Work of V. F. Calverton," *New Leader*, 17 April 1926, p. 6.

4. Harvey Klehr, *The Heyday of American Communism: The Depression Decade* (New York: Basic Books, 1984), p. 20.

5. Irving Howe and Lewis Coser, *The American Communist Party: A Critical History, 1919–1957* (Boston: Beacon Press, 1957), p. 253.

6. V. F. Calverton, "Four Revolutionary Thinkers," *MQ* 3, no. 3 (May–July 1926): 245.

7. William Z. Foster to V. F. Calverton, 2 June 1926, VFC.

8. Calverton to Foster, 10 June 1926, VFC.

9. *Daily Worker*, 16 June 1926.

10. Calverton's rejoinder was published in the *Daily Worker*, 16 June 1926, under the title: "The Case for Mr. Calverton"; William F. Dunne to Calverton, 29 June 1926, VFC.

11. James Oneal to Calverton, 16 June 1926, VFC.

12. "Socialists 'Bankrupt' Hints V. F. Calverton in Lecture at C. P. Hall," *Daily Worker*, 10 March 1927, p. 3: "'In spite of the bankruptcy of the socialist party of the United States,' declared V. F. Calverton, editor of the 'Modern Quarterly,' speaking on 'The New Negro,' at the Workers' School, 108 E. 14th St., Sunday night, 'there is no doubt that the Communist Party would join with it to fight some fundamental major issues.'"

13. Calverton to Edward Levinson, 16 March 1927, VFC.

14. Oneal to Calverton, 12 March 1927, VFC.

15. Haim Kantorovitch to Calverton, 22 February 1927, VFC.

16. Haim Gnizi, "V. F. Calverton: Independent Radical," doctoral dissertation, City University of New York, 1968, p. 131.

17. Calverton to John Dewey, 18 April 1927, VFC.

18. Earl Browder's letter to Calverton was published in *MQ* 4, no. 1 (January–April 1927): 72–75.

19. Foster to Calverton, 10 May 1926, VFC.

20. Scott Nearing to Calverton, 8 March 1927, VFC.

21. Calverton to Horace Liveright, 7 March 1927, VFC.

22. Calverton to Lee Furman, 22 June 1927, VFC.

23. Calverton, *Sex Expression in Literature* (New York: Boni & Liveright, 1926), p. 309. Calverton's analysis of the relationship between literature and society in this work was influenced by Floyd Dell's *Intellectual Vagabondage* (1926), as Calverton himself acknowledged in a letter to Dell in which he apologized for failing to cite Dell's work in his bibliography. Calverton to Dell, no date (Sherwood Anderson Collection, Newberry Library, Chicago).

24. Quoted in John P. Diggins, *The American Left in the Twentieth Century* (New York: Harper & Row, 1973), p. 120.

25. Una Corbett in letter to author, 11 September 1973; author's interview with Helen Letzer-Solidar, Baltimore, 10 May 1983.

26. Author's interview with Una Corbett, Baltimore, 9 May 1983. Una Corbett had absolutely no bitterness about Calverton's many women, and only praise for his loyalty. Nor was there any bitterness about raising Joy as a single parent, since she and Calverton had talked the matter over thoroughly beforehand, since she understood what she was undertaking (although it proved to be a greater burden than she had ever imagined), and since Calverton abided by his promise to see the child when he could and provide support where he could. One of the most striking things in Una Corbett's residence was a large painting of Calverton that hung in the living room, forty-three years after his death.

27. Author's interview with Helen Letzer-Solidar, Baltimore, 10 May 1983.

28. Author's interview with Una Corbett, Baltimore, 9 May 1983.

29. Calverton, "Red Love in Soviet Russia," *MQ* 4, no. 3 (November–February 1927): 180–91, 189.

30. Ibid., p. 190.

31. Ibid., pp. 190–91.

32. Max Eastman, *Love and Revolution* (New York: Random House, 1964), p. 435.

33. Daniel Aaron, *Writers on the Left* (1961; New York: Avon Books, 1965), p. 153.

34. John Darmstadt to Calverton, 27 January 1927, VFC.

35. Roger Baldwin in letter to author, 31 March 1971.

36. Calverton to H. M. Wicks, 22 September 1927, VFC.

37. Editorial: "The Pulse of Modernity," *MQ* 4, no. 3 (November–February 1927–28): 176.

38. Ibid., p. 177.

39. *Daily Worker*, 4 February 1928, p. 7.

40. Eastman, *Love and Revolution*, p. 598.

41. Joseph Freeman, "Bulgarian Literature, or the Perfect Critical Method," *New Masses* 2 (August 1927): 9–10. The attack was a personal venture and, unlike later attacks in the magazine, did not represent the publication's outlook or policy.

42. Bertram D. Wolfe, "America Discusses the Opposition," *Communist* 7 (January 1928): 46–56.

43. Samuel D. Schmalhausen's dismissal is discussed in Upton Sinclair's *The Goslings: A Study of American Schools* (Pasadena, Calif.: Sinclair, 1924), pp. 73–77.

44. Schmalhausen to Calverton, 31 July 1927, VFC.

45. Schmalhausen, "These Tragic Comedians," *MQ* 4, no. 3 (November–February 1927–28): 195–229, 218.

46. Ibid., p. 218.

47. Wolfe, "America Discusses the Opposition," p. 55.

48. Editorial: "The Pulse of Modernity," *MQ* 4, no. 4 (May–August 1928): 315.

49. "Correspondence," *MQ* 4, no. 4 (May–August 1928): 395.

50. Ibid.

51. Editorial: "The Pulse of Modernity," *MQ* 4, no. 4 (May–August 1928): 319.

52. Schmalhausen was to have officially joined the editorial staff at this point, but he proposed to omit his name from the editorial board of the November–February 1927–28 issue because Calverton expressed disagreement with the article and refused to take editorial responsibility for it. Schmalhausen to Calverton, 26 September 1927, VFC.

53. Calverton to Wolfe, 28 January and 2 February, 1928, VFC.

54. Jack Wasserman to Calverton, 12 March 1928, VFC.

55. Joseph Freeman to Calverton, no date, 1928, VFC.

56. Serge Dinamov to Calverton, 4 August 1928; D. Riasanov to Calverton, 18 November 1927, VFC.

57. *Daily Worker*, 12 January 1929, p. 2; Calverton to Jay Lovestone, 16 February 1929.

58. Calverton to Michael Gold, 28 December 1928, VFC.

59. Editorial: "The Pulse of Modernity," *MQ* 4, no. 4 (May–August 1928): 316.

60. Editorial: "The Pulse of Modernity; The American Scene," *MQ* 5, no. 1 (November–February 1928–29): 1.

61. Editorial: "The Pulse of Modernity," *MQ* 4, no. 3 (November–February 1927–28): 177.

62. Editorial: "The Pulse of Modernity," *MQ* 4, no. 4 (May–August 1928): 315.

63. Calverton to Edmund O'Brien, 22 December 1928, VFC.

64. Editorial: "The Pulse of Modernity," *MQ* 4, no. 3 (November–February 1927–28): 176.

65. Ibid.

66. A. J. Muste, "Militant Progressivism?" *MQ* 4, no. 4 (May–August 1928): 332–41.

67. Eastman, "State Philosophy of Soviet Russia," *MQ* 4, no. 1 (January–April 1927): 19–24.

Chapter Four. Karl Marx of the Sexual Revolution

1. See Floyd Dell, "Psychoanalytic Confessions," *Liberator* 3 (April 1920): 15–19; and Max Eastman, "Lenin Was an Engineer," *New Masses* 3 (November 1927): 14.

2. Max Horkheimer and Theodor Adorno's interest in Freud extended back into the late twenties, but Horkheimer's first article on the merger of psychoanalysis and Marxism, "Geschichte und Psychologie," was published in 1932. Similarly, Erich Fromm's work on this topic dates from 1932. See Martin Jay, *The Dialectical Imagination: A History of the Frankfurt School and the Institute*

of Social Research 1923–1950 (London: Heinemann Educational Books, 1973), pp. 100, 317.

3. Floyd Dell, *Love in Greenwich Village* (New York: G.H. Doran, 1926). See also Dell, *Love in the Machine Age* (New York: Farrar & Rinehart, 1930), which draws on material Dell published in the *Liberator* during the twenties.

4. Nathan G. Hale, Jr., *Freud and the Americans: The Beginnings of Psychoanalysis in the United States, 1876–1917* (New York: Oxford University Press, 1971), 1:309–10.

5. For a discussion of Samuel Tannenbaum's "liberative" Freudianism, see I. H. Matthews, "The Americanization of Sigmund Freud: Adaptations of Psychoanalysis before 1917," *Journal of American Studies* 1, no. 1 (April 1967): 39–62.

6. V. F. Calverton to Havelock Ellis, 8 November 1926, VFC; V. F. Calverton, *Sex Expression in Literature* (New York: Boni & Liveright, 1926), p. 75.

7. Calverton to Horace Liveright, 22 July 1926, VFC.

8. Samuel Schmalhausen to Calverton, 6 February 1924, VFC.

9. Samuel Schmalhausen, "Psychoanalysis and Communism," *MQ* 6, no. 2 (Summer 1932): 63–69; Schmalhausen, "Psychological Portrait of Modern Civilization," *MQ* 6, no. 3 (Autumn 1932): 85–95.

10. *MQ* 4, no. 1 (January–April 1927): 40.

11. *MQ* 5, no. 1 (November–February 1928): 300–301.

12. Ibid., p. 287.

13. Schmalhausen to Calverton, 24 November 1924, VFC.

14. Calverton, "Radical Psychology," *New Masses* 2 (July 1927): 29.

15. Calverton, "Love and Revolution," *New Masses* 1 (October 1926): 28.

16. Floyd Dell, "A Literary Self-Analysis," *MQ* 4, no. 2 (June–September 1927): 148–52.

17. *New Masses* 3 (March 1927): 11.

18. Calverton, "Sex and Economics," *New Masses* 3 (March 1927): 11–12.

19. Calverton, *The Bankruptcy of Marriage* (New York: Macaulay, 1928), p. 11.

20. Ibid., pp. 13–14.

21. Ibid., p. 13.

22. Ibid., p. 46.

23. For a discussion of this issue in relation to Wilhelm Reich, see Richard King, *The Party of Eros: Radical Social Thought and the Realm of Freedom* (New York: Delta, 1972), p. 63.

24. Huntly Carter to Calverton, 3 August 1929; Robert Briffault to Calverton, 14 October 1928; H. G. Wells to Calverton, 21 April 1929; Havelock Ellis to Calverton, 6 December 1928; Ben Lindsey to Calverton, 22 June 1929, VFC.

25. Bennett Stevens, "Sex Under Capitalism," review of *The Bankruptcy of Marriage*, *New Masses* 3 (December 1928): 26–27.

26. Michael Gold to Calverton, 28 December 1928, VFC.

27. Upton Sinclair to Calverton, 24 September 1928, VFC.

28. Quoted in John Darmstadt's "The Sexual Revolution," *MQ* 4, no. 2 (June–September 1927): 142.

29. Ibid.

30. H. M. Wicks, "An Apology for Sex Anarchism Disguised as Marxism," *Daily Worker*, 9 June 1927, p. 4.

31. Ibid.

32. James P. Monroe to Calverton, 2 April 1928, VFC.

33. Leonard Wood to Calverton, 6 January 1929, VFC.

34. *New York Telegram*, 30 October 1929, p. 8.

35. *New York Times*, 9 June 1929, p. 7.

36. Calverton and Schmalhausen, *Sex in Civilization* (London: George Allen & Unwin, 1929), p. 248.

37. Calverton, "Sex and Social Struggle," in *Sex in Civilization*, pp. 249–84.

38. *Los Angeles Times*, 9 June 1929, p. 21.

39. See Calverton and Schmalhausen, "Preface," *The New Generation* (New York: Macaulay, 1930), p. 13.

40. Calverton and Schmalhausen, eds., *Women's Coming of Age: A Symposium* (New York: H. Liveright, 1931), p. xx.

41. Havelock Ellis, "Women's Sexual Nature," in ibid., pp. 230–40, 236.

42. Charlotte Perkins Gilman, "Parasitism and Civilized Vice," in ibid., pp. 110–27, 125.

43. For a discussion of these two strains, see William O'Neil, *Everyone Was Brave: The Rise and Fall of Feminism in America* (Chicago: Quadrangle, 1969), pp. 304ff.

44. Dora Russell, "The Poetry and Prose of Pregnancy," in *Women's Coming of Age*, pp. 343–54, 350.

45. Lorine Pruette, "Why Women Fail," in ibid., p. 258.

46. Calverton, "Are Women Monogamous," in ibid., pp. 475–88, 488.

47. George Britt, "Women in the New South," in ibid., pp. 409–23, 423.

48. Ben B. Lindsey, "The Promise and Peril of the New Freedom," in ibid., pp. 447–71, 470.

49. *New York Times*, 28 May 1929, p. 17 (Henry James Forman, reviewer).

50. *New Masses* 2 (January 1927): 5.

51. Daniel Aaron, *Writers on the Left* (1961; New York: Avon, 1965), p. 184.

52. Calverton, "Love and Revolution," *New Masses* 1 (26 October 1926): 28.

53. Calverton to Dell, 15 October 1926, VFC.

54. Michael Gold, "Floyd Dell Resigns," *New Masses* 4 (May 1929): 41.

55. *New Republic* 65 (November–February 1929–30): 227–28.

56. *New Republic* 66 (March 1930): 102.

57. Malcolm Cowley, *Exile's Return: A Literary Odyssey of the 1920's* (New York: Viking, 1951), p. 309.

58. Aaron, *Writers on the Left*, p. 234.

59. Sidney Hook, *Open Court* 42 (1928): 20. In 1928 Hook challenged Eastman's contention that Freudianism would advance Marxian analysis. Hook charged that Freud's theories represented the "grossest violation of the sci-

entific method." See Hook's "Marxism, Metaphysics, and Modern Science," *MQ* 4, no. 3 (May–August 1928): 388–94.

60. Long and Smith advertisement for *Bankruptcy of Marriage*, no date [mid 1930s].

61. Serge Dinamov to Calverton, no date, 1930, VFC. Dinamov later disappeared during the Stalinist purges.

62. John Chynoweth Burnham, "The New Psychology: From Narcissism to Social Control," in *Change and Continuity in Twentieth Century America: The 1920s*, ed. John Braeman, Robert H. Bremner, and David Brody (Columbus: Ohio State University Press, 1968), p. 374.

63. Calverton to Schmalhausen, 20 August 1930, VFC.

64. See Jay, *Dialectical Imagination*, p. 317. Jay notes that even after members of the Frankfurt School had become émigrés in New York, they consciously resisted "Americanization" by writing in German and refusing to integrate their work into the American social scientific mainstream. This effort to retain their "purity" explains in part why their work was so little known by the Old Left (p. 114).

65. In 1929 Calverton challenged Eugene Jolas, editor of *transition* (an expatriate little magazine published in English in Paris and dedicated to experimental writing) to a debate over "the revolution in the word." In the resulting symposium Calverton stolidly maintained the position that surrealism amounted to no revolution at all, but rather a "chaotic Greenwich Village literary riot." See Calverton's "The Revolution-in-the-Wordists," *MQ* 5, no. 3 (Fall 1929): 277; see Chapter Six for a discussion of this issue.

66. King, *Party of Eros*, p. 51.

Chapter Five. New York: Metropolitanism and Love

1. See Thomas Bender, *New York Intellect: A History of Intellectual Life in New York City, from 1750 to the Beginnings of Our Own Time* (New York: Knopf, 1987), p. 252.

2. Joshua Kunitz to V. F. Calverton, 18 December 1929, VFC.

3. For a discussion of this cosmopolitan ideal that emerged from Greenwich Village, see David A. Hollinger, "Ethnic Diversity, Cosmopolitanism and the Emergence of the American Liberal Intelligentsia," *American Quarterly* 27, no. 2 (May 1975): 131–51.

4. Robert I. Vexler, comp. and ed., *Baltimore: A Chronological and Documentary History, 1632–1970* (Dobbs Ferry, N.Y.: Oceana, 1975), p. 76.

5. Abraham L. Harris to Calverton, 6 April 1925, VFC.

6. Harris to Calverton, no date, VFC.

7. W.E.B. Du Bois, "The Social Origins of American Negro Art," *MQ* 3, no. 1 (October–December 1925): 54; Charles S. Johnson, "The New Negro," *MQ* 3, no. 2 (February–April 1926): 128–34; Alain Locke, "The American Literary Tradition and the Negro," *MQ* 3, no. 3 (May–July 1926): 215–

22; Clarence Cameron White, "Labor Motif in Negro Music," *MQ* 4, no. 1 (January–April 1927): 79–81; E. Franklin Frazier, "La Bourgeoisie Noire," *MQ* 5, no. 1 (November–February 1928): 78–84.

8. For a discussion, see Harold Cruse, *The Crisis of the Negro Intellectual: From Its Origins to the Present* (New York: William Morrow, 1967), pp. 154–58.

9. Carl E. Gehring, "The Western Dance of Death," *MQ* 5, no. 4 (Winter 1930–31): 497.

10. V. F. Calverton, ed., *Anthology of American Negro Literature* (New York: Modern Library, 1929), p. 4.

11. *New Masses* 5 (February 1930): 18.

12. Cruse, *Crisis*, p. 152.

13. Ibid.

14. Alain Locke, ed., *The New Negro* (New York: Albert and Charles Boni, 125), p. 15.

15. Calverton, *Three Strange Lovers* (New York: Boni & Liveright, 1929), p. 75.

16. Wilhelm Steckel to Calverton, 15 June 1930; Fritz Wittels to Calverton, 16 February 1930, VFC.

17. Details of Nina Melville's early life are from Margo Berdeshevsky in letter to author, 1 May 1990.

18. Calverton to Nina Melville, no day, January 1929, VFC (restricted). The Mann Act was an act of Congress (1910) prohibiting the interstate transportation of women for "immoral purposes."

19. Calverton to Melville, no day, April 1928. Private letters of Margo Berdeshevsky, hereafter Berdeshevsky Letters.

20. Joseph Wood Krutch, *The Modern Temper: A Study and a Confession* (New York: Harcourt, Brace, 1929), p. 72.

21. Calverton to Melville, 29 July 1929, Berdeshevsky Letters.

22. Una Corbett to Calverton, no date, Berdeshevsky Letters.

23. Author's interview with Una Corbett, Baltimore, 9 May 1983.

24. Calverton to Melville, no date, 1928, Berdeshevsky Letters.

25. Calverton, *Three Strange Lovers*, p. 81.

26. Haim Kantorovitch to Calverton, 15 June 1924, VFC.

27. For a discussion, see Daniel Aaron, *Writers on the Left* (New York: Avon, 1965), pp. 73ff.

28. Calverton to Melville, 3 November 1928, Berdeshevsky Letters.

29. Calverton to Melville, 29 July 1929, Berdeshevsky Letters.

30. Calverton to Melville, 2 February 1929, Berdeshevsky Letters.

31. Calverton to Melville, no day, April 1928, Berdeshevsky Letters.

32. Melville to Calverton, no date, Berdeshevsky Letters.

33. Alfred Kazin, *Starting Out in the Thirties* (Boston: Little, Brown, 1962), pp. 75–76.

34. Calverton to Melville, no date, 1934, VFC.

35. Author's interview with Una Corbett, 9 May 1983.

36. Melville to Calverton, no date, Berdeshevsky Letters.

Chapter Six. New Agenda: Radicalism and Revolution

1. Malcolm Cowley, *Exile's Return: A Literary Odyssey of the 1920's* (New York: Viking Press, 1951), p. 309.

2. Quoted in David Shi, *Matthew Josephson: Bourgeois Bohemian* (New Haven: Yale University Press, 1981), p. 141.

3. Matthew Josephson, *Infidel in the Temple: A Memoir of the Nineteen Thirties* (New York: Knopf, 1967), p. 145.

4. *Culture and Crisis: An Open Letter to the Writers, Artists, Teachers, Physicians, Engineers, Scientists, and Other Professional Workers of America* (n.p.: League of Professional Groups for Foster and Ford, 1932).

5. V. F. Calverton, "The Decade of Convictions," *Bookman* 71 (August 1930): 486–90.

6. Editorial: "Exit the Forgotten Man," *MQ* 6, no. 3 (Autumn 1932): 6–9, 9.

7. Symposium: "Marxism and Social Change," *MQ* 5, no. 4 (Winter 1930–31): 422–66.

8. Sidney Hook, "Marxism, Metaphysics, and Modern Science," *MQ* 4, no. 4 (May–August 1928): 388.

9. Max Eastman, *Marx and Lenin: The Science of Revolution* (London: G. Allen & Unwin, 1926), pp. 13–18. For further discussion of Eastman's position, see John P. Diggins, *Up from Communism: Conservative Odysseys in American Intellectual History* (New York: Harper & Row, 1975), pp. 39–51.

10. Hook, "As to Max Eastman's Mentality," *MQ* 5, no. 1 (November–February 1928–29): 88–90.

11. Calverton finally stepped in and put an end to the battle. *MQ* 7, no. 8 (September 1933): 511.

12. John Dewey, "Social Change and Its Human Direction," *MQ* 5, no. 4 (Winter 1930–31): 425.

13. Eastman, "The Doctrinal Crisis in Socialism," ibid., pp. 426–29.

14. Hook, "The Meaning of Marxism," ibid., pp. 430–35.

15. Arthur Calhoun, "The Doctrinal Crisis in Eastmanism," ibid., pp. 436–48; Louis Boudin, "Marx and His Revisers," ibid., pp. 439–47; Waldo Frank, "Socialism and Value," ibid., p. 448.

16. Lewis Mumford, "A Challenge to American Intellectuals: A Controversy: The Evolutionary Approach," *MQ* 5, no. 4 (Winter 1930–31): 407–10.

17. Calverton, "A Challenge to American Intellectuals: A Controversy: The Revolutionary Approach," ibid., pp. 411–21.

18. For a discussion of Mumford's conception of the relationship between self and society, see Casey Blake, "The Perils of Personality: Lewis Mumford and Politics after Liberalism," in *Lewis Mumford: Public Intellectual*, ed. Thomas P. Hughes and Agatha C. Hughes (New York: Oxford University Press, 1990), pp. 283–301.

19. Hook, "The Non-Sense of the Whole," *MQ* 5, no. 4 (Winter 1930–31): 504–13.

20. See Dougald McMillan, *transition: The History of a Literary Era 1927–1938* (London: Calder and Boyars, 1975), esp. pp. 179–203.

21. The proclamation is reproduced in ibid., p. 49.

22. Eugene Jolas, "Necessity for the New Word," *MQ* 5, no. 3 (Fall 1929): 273–75.

23. Calverton, "The Revolution-in-the-Wordists," ibid., pp. 276–83.

24. Ibid., p. 283.

25. Harold Salemson, "James Joyce and the New Word," *MQ* 5, no. 3 (Fall 1929): 309.

26. Stuart Gilbert, "Why a Revolution of the Word?" ibid., p. 284.

27. *transition* 19/20 (June 1930): 140. See also McMillan, *transition*, p. 97, for a reproduction of "The Little Agitator."

28. Editors of *MQ* to Editorial Staff, *New Republic*, 18 January 1927, VFC.

29. V. F. Calverton to Scott Nearing, 18 December 1928, VFC.

30. See Terry A. Cooney, *The Rise of the New York Intellectuals: Partisan Review and Its Circle, 1934–1945* (Madison: University of Wisconsin Press, 1986), p. 41. According to Lionel Abel, Rahv believed during the early thirties that Michael Gold was "a much greater writer than Paul Valéry." See his *The Intellectual Follies: A Memoir of the Literary Venture in New York and Paris* (New York: Norton, 1984), p. 50.

31. Questionnaire: "Whither *the* American Writer," *MQ* 6, no. 2 (Summer 1932): 12.

32. Calverton, Editorial: "The Pulse of Modernity," ibid., p. 6.

33. Calverton, *American Literature at the Crossroads* (Seattle: University of Washington Chapbook no. 48, 1931), pp. 9–13; see also Calverton, "Humanism: Literary Fascism," *New Masses* 5 (April 1930): 9–10.

34. *New Republic* 64 (22 October 1930): 14.

35. Edmund Wilson, "The Literary Class War," *New Republic* 70 (4 May 1932): 319.

36. Ibid.

37. Henry Hazlitt, "Communist Criticism," *Nation* 131 (26 September 1930): 583–84.

38. Calverton, *American Literature at the Crossroads*, p. 49.

39. Hazlitt, Editorial, *Nation* 132 (1 April 1931): 354–55.

40. Hazlitt, "Art and Social Change: The Eclectic Approach," *MQ* 6, no. 1 (Winter 1932): 12.

41. Calverton, "Art and Social Change: The Radical Approach," ibid., p. 17.

42. Ibid., p. 16.

43. Ibid., p. 17.

44. Ibid., p. 27.

45. Granville Hicks, "Literary Criticism and the Marxian Method," *MQ* 6, no. 2 (Summer 1932): 44–47, 47. Newton Arvin, "Literature and Social Change," ibid., pp. 20–25, 25.

46. Calverton, *The New Ground of Criticism* (Seattle: University of Washington Chapbook no. 34, 1930), pp. 13ff.

47. Calverton, Editorial: "The Pulse of Modernity," *MQ* 6, no. 2 (Summer 1932): 6.

48. Calverton, "Can We Have a Proletarian Literature?" *MQ* 6, no. 3 (Autumn 1932): 39–51, esp. pp. 46–47, of his article.

49. Calverton, Editorial: "The Pulse of Modernity," *MQ* 6, no. 2 (Summer 1932): 8.

50. Ibid., p. 10.

51. Calverton, *American Literature at the Crossroads*, p. 9.

52. Walter Rideout, *The Radical Novel in the United States 1900–1954; Some Interrelations of Literature and Society* (New York: Hill and Wang, 1956), p. 166.

53. Maxwell Perkins to Calverton, no date, 1932, VFC.

54. Calverton, "Leftward Ho!" *MQ* 6, no. 2 (Summer 1932): 147.

55. Besides Gold's "prolet-cult" manifestos such as "Toward a Proletarian Art" (1921), Floyd Dell's *Intellectual Vagabondage* (1926), which explained literary developments in terms of general social themes, and Calverton's earlier work *The Newer Spirit*, little Marxist criticism had been attempted in America.

56. Calverton, *The Liberation of American Literature* (New York: Scribner's, 1932), p. xi.

57. In a turnabout from his position in *The Newer Spirit*, Calverton contended that "Whitman was not a believer in social revolution and was not a fugleman of the proletariat. He was just as much a petty bourgeois individualist in social philosophy, just as much a believer in private property, as were most of his contemporaries." Ibid., p. 296.

58. Ibid., pp. 479–80.

59. John Chamberlain, "Marxism and Literature," *Nation* 135 (7 December 1932): 571.

60. John Dos Passos's works were neither guided by a principle of historical explanation nor inspired by a socialist vision of historical meaning. Gold's lyric celebration of New York tenement life in *Jews Without Money* (1930) scarcely embodied a rigorous Marxist perspective. And to include Charles Yale Harrison in the group of proletarians was, as Haim Kantorovitch pointed out to Calverton, scraping the bottom of the barrel. Kantorovitch suggested that Calverton should have omitted the last two chapters, "then you would not have had to demonstrate the poverty of American radical literature." Kantorovitch to Calverton, 16 June 1932, VFC.

61. Richard Ruland makes this point in *The Rediscovery of American Literature* (Cambridge: Harvard University Press, 1967), p. 193.

62. Vincent B. Leitch's appraisal on this point is similar; see his *American Literary Criticism from the 30s to the 80s* (New York: Columbia University Press, 1988), p. 10.

63. Charles Beard to Calverton, 29 April 1932; Newton Arvin to Calverton, 26 November 1931, VFC; Granville Hicks, "American Literature: A Marxian Interpretation," *New Republic* 7 (September 1932): 104–5.

64. Ruland, *Rediscovery of American Literature*, p. 193.

65. Calverton, "The Decade of Convictions," *Bookman* 71 (August 1930): 486–90.

66. Hicks, "Writers in the Thirties," in Ruth Simon, ed., *As We Saw the Thirties* (Urbana: University of Illinois Press, 1967), p. 86.

67. Warren Susman, ed., *Culture and Commitment, 1928–1945* (New York, George Braziller, 1973), p. 19.

68. Calverton, *Liberation of American Literature*, p. 479.

69. Richard Pells, *Radical Visions and American Dreams: Culture and Social Thought in the Depression Years* (New York: Harper & Row, 1973), p. 126.

70. For a discussion of this pragmatic tradition in American criticism, see Giles Gunn, *The Culture of Criticism and the Criticism of Culture* (New York: Oxford University Press, 1987), pp. 23–26.

71. "The future of our civilization," wrote Lewis Mumford, "depends upon our ability to select and control our heritage from the past." Mumford, *Sticks and Stones: A Study of American Architecture and Civilization* (New York: Boni & Liveright, 1924), p. 51.

Chapter Seven. The "Literary Rotary"

1. Richard Pells, *Radical Visions and American Dreams: Culture and Social Thought in the Depression Years* (New York: Harper & Row, 1973), pp. 111ff.

2. Newton Arvin, "Literature and Social Change," *MQ* 6, no. 2 (Summer 1932): 20–25, 20.

3. V. F. Calverton, "Leftward Ho!" *MQ* 6, no. 2 (Summer 1932): 26–32, 32.

4. Pells, *Radical Visions*, p. 119.

5. Christopher Lasch, *The Agony of the American Left* (New York: Knopf, 1969), p. 56.

6. For an account of the "Meeting Place," see Max Eastman, *Love and Revolution* (New York: Random House, 1964), p. 546.

7. Membership list for 1930, VFC.

8. Garmont to Nina Melville, 10 January 1941, VFC.

9. Louis Adamic, *My America, 1928–1938* (New York: Random House, 1964), p. 87.

10. Author's interview with George Britt, New York, 5 July 1971; Bertram D. Wolfe in letter to author, 2 November 1971.

11. Adamic, *My America*, pp. 89–91.

12. Bertram D. Wolfe in letter to author, 2 November 1972.

13. Author's interview with Hazlitt, Wilton, Connecticut, 10 July 1971.

14. Harry Hansen to Calverton, 6 October 1932, VFC.

15. George Britt, "V. F. Calverton," *MQ* 11, no. 7 (Autumn 1940): 9–12, 9.

16. According to Michael Blankfort, Calverton was extraordinarily encouraging to young writers; he recalls that "whenever Calverton had an opportunity, whenever he wrote essays on the young writers . . . he would almost always include my name and the names of his young friends. Well, for a young writer that is sensational: here is this critic of some reputation writing 'consider the plays of Eugene O'Neill, Sidney Howard, and some young writers

like Clifford Odets and Michael Blankfort.'" Author's interview with Michael Blankfort, Los Angeles, 9 May 1971.

17. See Alfred Kazin's account in *Starting Out in the Thirties* (New York: Little, Brown, 1962), pp. 61–89.

18. Author's interview with George Britt, New York City, 5 July 1971.

19. Adamic, *My America*, p. 98.

20. Henry Hazlitt recalls Thomas Wolfe's remark about Calverton: "I've never met a man who could look so much like a crook and not be one." Author's interview with Hazlitt, 10 July 1971.

21. V. F. Calverton to Michael Gold, 16 April 1930, VFC.

22. Ibid.

23. Calverton to Gold, 26 April 1930, VFC.

24. Calverton to John Dos Passos, 27 June 1930, VFC.

25. Calverton to Gold, 9 October 1930, VFC.

26. Calverton to Gold, 16 April 1930, VFC.

27. Calverton, "Democracy *vs.* Dictatorship," *MQ* 5, no. 4 (Winter 1930–31): 397–402.

28. William Z. Foster, "Calverton's Fascism," *Communist* 10 (February 1931): 107–11.

29. Gold to Calverton, no date, 1932, VFC.

30. Granville Hicks to Calverton, 10 February 1932, VFC.

31. Daniel Aaron, *Writers on the Left* (1961; New York: Avon Books, 1965), p. 262.

32. Calverton to Scott Nearing, 18 December 1929, VFC.

33. Author's interview with Suzanne La Follette, New York City, 19 July 1971.

34. Calverton to La Follette, 27 February 1930, VFC.

35. William Godwin, Inc. to Calverton, 12 July 1931, VFC.

36. Alex Hillman to Calverton, 11 December 1931; 23 January 1932, VFC.

37. R. P. Dutt to *MQ*, no date, VFC.

38. Calverton to Samuel Schmalhausen, no date, VFC.

39. Calverton to Henry George, 11 July 1929, VFC.

40. C. C. Robbe, President, Broadway Savings Bank, Baltimore, to Calverton, 14 May 1930, VFC.

41. Calverton to Albert H. Gross, no date, VFC.

42. Oakley Johnson to Calverton, 22 October 1931, VFC.

43. Schmalhausen to Calverton, 7 November 1932, VFC.

44. Calverton to Schmalhausen, 18 January 1933, VFC.

45. Schmalhausen to Calverton, 10 January 1933, VFC.

46. Haim Kantorovitch to Calverton, 11 November 1932, VFC.

47. Calverton to Melville, 27 June 1930, Berdeshevsky Letters.

48. Calverton to Melville, no date, Berdeshevsky Letters.

49. Calverton to Melville, 23 December 1928, VFC.

50. Calverton to Melville, no date, Berdeshevsky Letters.

51. Ibid.

52. Ibid.

53. Ibid.

54. Reminiscence written by Nina Melville, December 1940, Berdeshevsky Letters.

55. Adamic, *My America*, pp. 87–96.

56. Wolfe in letter to author, 2 November 1972; author's interview with Hazlitt, Wilton, Connecticut, 10 July 1971.

57. Author's interview with Michael Blankfort, Los Angeles, 8 May 1971.

58. Sidney Hook, *Out of Step: An Unquiet Life in the 20th Century* (New York: Harper & Row, 1987), p. 145.

59. Ibid.

60. Kazin, *Starting Out in the Thirties*, p. 74.

61. Ibid.

62. James B. Gilbert, *Writers and Partisans: A History of Literary Radicalism in America* (New York: John Wiley, 1968), p. 72.

63. Pells, *Radical Visions*, p. 115.

64. This "thin line" between social commitment and group mentality during the thirties is discussed by Pells, ibid., p. 118.

65. Quoted in ibid., p. 117.

Chapter Eight. Excommunication and Exorcism

1. Max Schachtman, "Radicalism: The Trotskyite View," in *As We Saw the Thirties: Essays on Social and Political Movements of a Decade*, ed. Ruth Simon (Urbana: University of Illinois Press, 1967), p. 11.

2. Quoted, Irving Howe and Lewis Coser, *The American Communist Party: A Critical History* (New York: Praeger, 1962), p. 183.

3. Howe and Coser, ibid.

4. Bertram D. Wolfe, "America Discusses the Opposition," *Communist* 7 (January–February 1928): 45–57, 111–17, 55. Also V. F. Calverton to Wolfe, 28 January and 2 February 1928, VFC.

5. Jack Wasserman to Calverton, 12 March 1928, VFC.

6. *Daily Worker*, 12 January 1929, p. 3.

7. Ibid.

8. Calverton to editor of *Daily Worker*, 17 January 1929.

9. Calverton to Jay Lovestone, 16 February 1929, VFC.

10. For Calverton's account, see his "An Open Letter *to the* New Masses," *MM* 7, no. 2 (March 1933): 111. See also Daniel Aaron, *Writers on the Left* (1961; New York: Avon Books, 1965), p. 340.

11. A. B. Magil, "The 'Marxism' of V. F. Calverton," *Communist* 8 (May 1929): 282–85.

12. Aaron, *Writers on the Left*, p. 238.

13. Calverton, "Democracy *vs.* Dictatorship," *MQ* 5, no. 4 (Winter 1930–31): 397–402.

14. William Z. Foster, "Calverton's Fascism," *Communist* 10 (February 1931): 107–11, 111.

15. Calverton to Foster, no date, VFC. Calverton refers to Foster's promise to publish his letter in "An Open Letter to William Z. Foster," *MQ* 6, no. 2 (Summer 1932): 91.

16. Julius Davidson to Calverton, 14 February 1931, VFC.

17. Earl Browder to Calverton, 4 August 1931, VFC.

18. *Daily Worker*, 8 October 1931.

19. Haim Kantorovitch to Calverton, no date, 1933, VFC.

20. *Communist* 10 (October 1931): 851–64; *Communist* 10 (November 1931): 941–59.

21. Calverton, "The Compulsive Basis of Social Thought as Illustrated by the Varying Doctrine as to the Origin of Marriage and the Family," *American Journal of Sociology* 6 (March 1931): 695–720.

22. Ibid., p. 719.

23. Will Herberg to Calverton, no date, VFC.

24. For a discussion of this point in Max Eastman's *Marx and Lenin: The Science of Revolution* (London: G. Allen & Unwin, 1926), see John P. Diggins, *Up from Communism: Conservative Odysseys in American Intellectual History* (New York: Harper & Row, 1975), p. 48.

25. For a discussion of Georg Lukacs and the question of true vs. false consciousness, see Martin Jay, *Permanent Exiles: Essays on the Intellectual Migration from Germany to America* (New York: Columbia University Press, 1985), p. 65.

26. Karl Mannheim makes this observation in his introduction to the 1929 edition of *Ideology and Utopia*; Diggins, *Up from Communism*, p. 48.

27. Karl Mannheim, *Ideology and Utopia: An Introduction to the Sociology of Knowledge*, trans. Louis Wirth and Edward Shils (New York: Harcourt, Brace & World, 1966), p. 265.

28. Jay, *Permanent Exiles*, pp. 65–66.

29. A. Landy, "Cultural Compulsives, or Calverton's Latest Caricature of Marxism," *Communist* 10 (November 1931): 959.

30. Ibid., p. 853.

31. Foster, *Toward Soviet America* (New York: Coward-McCann, 1932), p. 206.

32. Calverton, "An Open Letter to William Z. Foster," *MQ* 6, no. 2 (Summer 1932): 91–94, 120.

33. Jim Cork, "Third Period Communism in Action: Sectarian Sterility and Culture," *Workers Age*, 23 July 1932, pp. 3–4.

34. Will Herberg, "About the Theory of Cultural Compulsives: Marxism and the History of Science," *Revolutionary Age*, 14 (14 November 1931): 12–18.

35. *New Masses* 7 (April 1932): 10.

36. Calverton to Joshua Kunitz, 5 April 1932, VFC; Kunitz to Calverton, 11 April 1932, VFC.

37. Newton Arvin to Calverton, 5 April 1932, VFC.

38. Sidney Hook to Calverton, no date, 1932, VFC.

39. A. Elistratova, "The Masses," *International Literature* 1 (1932): 107. Another journal, the *Left* (a journal of radical and experimental art that came out of Davenport, Iowa) was censured by *International Literature* for accept-

ing articles from Calverton and was admonished to "break completely with those social fascists who managed to find a place among the magazine's contributors." When the magazine complied, *International Literature* held up its example as "healthy self-criticism." See "Left #2," *International Literature* 2–3 (1932): 146ff.

40. David Ramsey and Alan Calmer, "The Marxism of V. F. Calverton," *New Masses* 8 (January 1933): 9–27, 9.

41. Ibid., p. 10.

42. *MQ* 7 no. 2 (March 1933): 110–14, 127–28.

43. Ibid., p. 110.

44. Ibid., p. 111.

45. Ibid., p. 128.

46. Max Eastman to Nathan Adler, Edwin Rolfe, and S. Funaroff, 9 June 1933 (Eastman Mss., Lilly Library, Indiana University, Bloomington).

47. *Virginia Pilot* (clipping), no date, VFC.

48. M. B. Schnapper to Calverton, 29 January 1933, VFC.

49. See Terry Cooney, *The Rise of the New York Intellectuals: Partisan Review and Its Circle, 1934–1945* (Madison: University of Wisconsin Press, 1986), p. 116.

50. William Phillips, *A Partisan View: Five Decades of Literary Life* (New York: Stein and Day, 1983), p. 56.

51. Cooney, *Rise of the New York Intellectuals*, p. 117.

52. Calverton to Henry Gage, 23 October 1933, VFC.

53. *MM* 7, no. 3 (April 1933): 140–45, 140.

54. Eastman, "Artists in Uniform," *MM* 7, no. 7 (August 1933): 397–404. Sidney Hook, "The Fallacy of the Theory of Social Fascism," *MM* 8, no. 6 (July 1934): 342–53.

55. Calverton, "The Crisis in Communism," *MM* 7, no. 3 (April 1933): 140–45.

56. A. Stork, "V. F. Calverton and His Friends: Some Notes on Literary Trotskyism in America," *International Literature*, no. 3 (1934): 97–124.

57. Granville Hicks to Calverton, 8 January 1933, VFC.

58. Quoted in Aaron, *Writers on the Left*, p. 342.

59. Michael Blankfort to Calverton, no date, 1933, VFC.

60. Quoted in Aaron, *Writers on the Left*, p. 343.

61. Michael Gold, *Daily Worker*, 2 November 1933, p. 4.

62. Author's interview with George Britt, New York, 29 July 1971.

63. Hook, *Out of Step: An Unquiet Life in the 20th Century* (New York: Harper & Row, 1987), p. 146.

Chapter Nine. The Americanization of Marx

1. Other intellectuals who felt the same prior to 1935 included John Dewey, Lincoln Steffens, George Soule, Bruce Bliven, John Chamberlain, Edmund Wilson, Alfred Bingham, and Lewis Corey. See Richard Pells, *Radi-*

cal Visions and American Dreams: Culture and Social Thought in the Depression Years (New York: Harper & Row, 1973), p. 94.

2. Louis Budenz, *This Is My Story* (New York: McGraw-Hill, 1947), p. 97.

3. V. F. Calverton, *For Revolution* (New York: John Day Company, 1932). *For Revolution* has no pagination.

4. See Daniel Bell, "Socialism: The Dream and Reality," in *Socialism in American Life*, ed. Donald Drew Egbert and Stow Persons (Princeton: Princeton University Press, 1952), vol. 1, p. 21.

5. Calverton, *For Revolution* (no pagination). For a discussion of the Musteite stress on an American revolutionary tradition, see A. J. Muste, "My Experience in Labor and Radical Struggles," in Rita James Simon, ed., *As We Saw the Thirties* (Urbana: University of Illinois Press, 1969), p. 139.

6. See Chapter Eleven.

7. Later works on this topic include George Soule, *The Coming American Revolution* (New York: Macmillan, 1934), and Lewis Corey, *The Crisis of the Middle Class* (New York: Covici Friede, 1935).

8. Waldo Frank to V. F. Calverton, no date, VFC; Michael Gold to Calverton, no date, VFC; Benjamin Gitlow to Calverton, 15 June 1933, VFC.

9. Leon Trotsky, "An Open Letter to V. F. Calverton," *The Militant*, 31 December 1932, p. 8.

10. Ibid.

11. Calverton to Leon Trotsky: "The Crisis in Communism," *MM* 7, no. 3 (April 1933): 140.

12. Ibid., p. 145.

13. *MQ* 6, no. 3 (Fall 1932): 5.

14. *MM* 7, no. 1 (February 1933): 5.

15. Ibid., p. 6.

16. John Dewey, "Who Might Make a New Party," *New Republic* 66 (1 April 1931): 177–78.

17. Alfred M. Bingham, *Insurgent America: Revolt of the Middle-Classes* (New York: Harper & Brothers, 1935); Corey, *Crisis of the Middle Class*.

18. Thorstein Veblen, *The Engineers and the Price System* (New York: Harcourt, Brace, & World, 1963), pp. 83–91.

19. For a discussion of Chase's position, see Robert B. Westerbrook, "Tribune of the Technostructure: The Popular Economics of Stuart Chase," *American Quarterly* 32, no. 4 (Fall 1980): 387–408.

20. Soule, *Coming American Revolution*.

21. Bingham, *Insurgent America*, p. 47.

22. Corey, *Crisis of the Middle Class*, pp. 140, 164.

23. Ibid., pp. 361–65.

24. See, for example, Sidney Hook, "The Meaning of Marxism," *MQ* 5, no. 4 (Winter 1930–31): 430–36.

25. *MM* 7, no. 8 (September 1933): 511.

26. Dewey, "Why I Am Not a Communist," *MM* 8, no. 3 (April 1934): 135.

27. Ernest Sutherland Bates, "John Dewey: America's Philosophic Engineer," *MM* 7, no. 7 (August 1933): 396.

28. Louis Budenz, "Winning America," *MM* 9, no. 3 (May 1935): 143.

29. Theodore B. Brameld, "John Strachey Was Wrong," *MM* 9, no. 3 (May 1935): 139–41.

30. Jerome Rosenthal, "What is Dialectical Materialism: Science or Mental Healing?" *MM* 9, no. 3 (May 1935): 147–59.

31. Quoted in Calverton's review of Corey's *Decline of American Capitalism*, *MM* 8, no. 10 (December 1934): 582.

32. *MM* 7, no. 1 (February 1933): 5.

33. John P. Diggins, *Up from Communism: Conservative Odysseys in American Intellectual History* (New York: Harper & Row, 1975), pp. 142–44.

34. Ibid., p. 142.

35. Will Herberg, "The Viewpoint of the International Communist Opposition," *MM* 7, no. 5 (June 1933): 283–88, 285.

36. Calverton, "For a United Front," *MM* 7, no. 3 (April 1933): 133–34.

37. Calverton to Mauritz Hallgren, no date, VFC.

38. Calverton, "For a United Front," pp. 133–34. (See note 21.)

39. Calverton, "What is Fascism?" *MM* 7, no. 6 (July 1933): 325–32, 331.

40. For a discussion of the dominant Marxist interpretations of Nazism during this period, see Pierre Aycoberry, *The Nazi Question: An Essay on the Interpretations of National Socialism (1922–1975)* (New York: Pantheon, 1981), pp. 47–68. Calverton's emphasis on the lower middle class is similar to Harold Lasswell in "The Psychology of Hitlerism," *Political Quarterly* 4 (1933): 70–85. Lasswell's discussion forms the basis for Erich Fromm's discussion of the role of the lower middle classes in the formation of Nazism in *Escape from Freedom* (New York: Avon Books, 1965), pp. 231–64.

41. Calverton, "What is Fascism?", p. 332.

42. "The Pulse of Modernity," *MM* 7, no. 8 (September 1933): 452.

43. Ibid., p. 453.

44. Ibid.

45. Editorial: "In Defense of the Democratic Tradition," *MM* 7, no. 2 (March 1933): 69–70.

46. Calverton expressed these ideas in several articles: "The American Revolutionary Tradition," *Scribner's* 47 (May 1934): 352–75; "Phillip Freneau, Apostle of Liberty," *MM* 7, no. 9 (October 1933): 533–46. See also Calverton, "Thomas Paine, God-Intoxicated Revolutionary," *Scribner's* 45 (January 1934): 16–24. Calverton planned to do a series of studies of American rebels and revolutionaries, which was to include Roger Williams, Andrew Jackson, Wendell Phillips, Daniel De Leon, William Haywood, and William Z. Foster. As with many other projects, he was overcommitted and never completed it.

47. James P. Cannon, *History of American Trotskyism* (New York: Pathfinder Press, 1972), pp. 112–15.

48. Calverton to A. J. Muste, 28 October 1933, VFC.

49. Editorial: "The Pulse of Modernity," *MM* 7, no. 9 (October 1933): 518.

50. Such was the description of the Party as Muste outlined it in his article, "An American Revolutionary Party," *MM* 7, no. 12 (January 1934): 713–19.

51. Muste to Calverton, Western Union, 5 December 1934, VFC.

52. Muste to Calverton, 20 December 1933; 29 January 1934, VFC: "This is to inform you officially of your election to the Provisional Organizing Committee of the American Workers Party."

53. See, for example, Will Herberg, "Bourgeois and Socialist Political Theory," in Donald Drew Egbert and Stow Persons, eds., *Socialism and American Life* (Princeton: Princeton University Press, 1952), vol. 1, p. 495.

54. In his discussion of the Independent Textile Union of Woonsocket in *Working Class Americanism: The Politics of Labor in a Textile Factory, 1914– 1960* (Cambridge: Cambridge University Press, 1989), Gary Gerstle points out that the effort to build an Americanized radicalism was precisely this sort of double-edged endeavor. If it imparted some sense of ideological unity to a disparate working-class culture, it also promoted traditional values, "anticapitalist but anticommunist, patriotic but parochial, militant but devout" (p. 195).

55. Edmund Wilson, "An Appeal to Progressives," *New Republic* 65 (14 January 1931): 238.

56. See Kenneth Burke's "Revolutionary Symbolism in America," in *The Strenuous Decade: A Social and Intellectual Record of the Nineteen-Thirties*, ed. Daniel Aaron and Robert Bendiner (New York: Doubleday, 1970), pp. 311– 20. Here Burke advocates using the term "the people" rather than the "proletariat" because the former is a familiar American term with broad appeal and the latter is not.

57. This issue of "political" Marxism is still important in discussion on the Left. See Robert Brenner, "Agrarian Class Structure and Economic Development in Pre-Industrial Europe," *Past and Present*, no. 70 (February 1976): 30–75, and Ellen M. Wood, "The Separation of the Economic and the Political in Capitalism," *New Left Review*, no. 127 (May–June 1981): 66–95.

58. See Paul Piccone, "From Spaventa to Gramsci," *Telos*, no. 31 (Spring 1977): 35.

59. For a discussion of Gramsci as a "pragmatist," see Cornel West, *The American Evasion of Philosophy: A Genealogy of Pragmatism* (Madison: University of Wisconsin Press, 1989), pp. 230–32.

Chapter Ten. "Hellishly Hard Sledding"

1. The incident is described in V. F. Calverton to Max Eastman, 29 September 1934, VFC.

2. Calverton to A. J. Muste, 28 October 1933, VFC.

3. Mauritz Hallgren to Calverton, 24 September 1933; Calverton to Eastman, 19 November 1933, VFC.

4. Max Eastman, *Love and Revolution: My Journey Through an Epoch* (New York: Random House, 1964), p. 611.

5. Edmund Wilson to Eastman, 4 November 1933, VFC.

6. Sidney Hook, *Out of Step: An Unquiet Life in the 20th Century* (New York: Harper & Row, 1987), p. 197.

7. Statement of Policy of the *Modern Monthly*, no date, VFC.

8. Wilson to Eastman, 4 November 1933, VFC.

9. Calverton to Muste, 28 October 1933, VFC.

10. Calverton to Eastman, 18 November 1933, VFC.

11. "The Pulse of Modernity," *MM* 8, no. 1 (February 1934): 6.

12. "An Open Letter to American Intellectuals," *MM* 8, no. 2 (March 1934): 87–92.

13. Minutes of the Provisional Organizing Committee: "Statement of the Relation between the AWP and the Modern Monthly," 8 March 1934, VFC.

14. This is Sterling Spero's account in Spero to Calverton, 14 June 1934, VFC.

15. See Louis Berg and Eliot E. Cohen, "May Day—1934, Record and Prospect," *MM* 8, no. 5 (June 1934): 286–91. The rebuttal follows the article.

16. Spero to Calverton, 14 June 1934, VFC.

17. Ibid.

18. Calverton to Spero, 14 June 1934, VFC.

19. Eastman to Calverton, 26 June 1934, VFC.

20. Editorial: "Left Face," *MM* 8, no. 6 (July 1934): 325.

21. Bertram Wolfe to Calverton, 6 August 1934, VFC.

22. Wilson to Calverton, 2 June 1934, VFC. The Sloan cartoon accompanies Eastman's article "Bunk About Bohemia" and depicts the head of Mike Gold emerging from a chamber pot, which sits on several stacked stone monuments, the bottom engraved with the name Piet Vlag, founder of the *Masses*, the next with the name "Masses," and the third (and top) "New Masses." Bob Brown is depicted as a small bulldog, about to urinate on the bottom stone monument commemorating Vlag. Brown once contributed to the *Masses* and *Liberator* and later wrote in the *American Mercury* that Eastman's role in editing the *Masses* was one of "remote aestheticization." He further asserted that the *Masses* was merely an Eastman family organ. The Sloan cartoon suggests that Brown's attacks have about as much significance as a small dog pissing on a monument. But it also implies that Brown is befouling the foundation of American radicalism upon which the *New Masses* rests, and that Gold is the unwitting recipient of this befoulment. The implications of the cartoon are in accord with Eastman's defense of Greenwich Village radicalism in "Bunk About Bohemia," particularly his contention that the "Old" *Masses* and *Liberator* provided the foundations of American radicalism in the twentieth century. See *MM* 8, no. 4 (May 1934): 206, for the Sloan cartoon.

23. Quoted in C. Hartley Grattan, "The Leftwing Spectrum," in Daniel Aaron and Robert Bendiner, eds., *The Strenuous Decade: A Social and Intellectual Record of the Nineteen Thirties* (Garden City, N.Y.: Doubleday, 1970), p. 274.

24. See William L. O'Neill, *The Last Romantic: A Life of Max Eastman* (New York: Oxford University Press, 1978), p. 152.

25. Eastman to Calverton, 2 June 1934, VFC.

26. Ibid.

27. Calverton to Eastman, no date, 1934, VFC.

28. Calverton to Eastman, no date, 1934, VFC.

29. Wilson to Calverton, 12 March 1934, VFC.

30. Wilson to Calverton, 19 March 1934, VFC.

31. Eastman to Calverton, 25 September 1934, VFC.

32. Calverton to Eastman, no date, 1934, VFC.

33. Wilson to Calverton, 25 February 1935, VFC.

34. Eastman to Calverton, 4 March 1935, VFC.

35. Calverton to Eastman, 16 March 1935, VFC.

36. Eastman, "Bunk About Bohemia," *MM* 8, no. 4 (May 1934): 200–208.

37. Edmund Wilson, Introduction to *The Conquerors*, *MM* 8, no. 2 (March 1934): 69–70.

38. Calverton, "Sinclair Lewis: The Last of the Literary Liberals," *MM* 8, no. 2 (March 1934): 77–86; Thomas Hart Benton, "Art and Nationalism," *MM* 8, no. 4 (May 1934): 232–36. Benton's article, however, was so provincially nationalistic it elicited the disapproval of the editors, particularly Benton's contention that the destruction of Diego Rivera's art in the Rockefeller Center was of no importance because Rivera's art was not American.

39. Calverton to Eastman, 29 September 1934, VFC.

40. Ibid.

41. Calverton to Angel Flores, 7 January 1933, VFC.

42. Huntington Cairns to Calverton, 8 December 1932, VFC.

43. Calverton to Cairns, 19 December 1932, VFC.

44. Calverton to Eastman, 18 November 1933, VFC.

45. Calverton to Eastman, 2 June 1934, VFC.

46. Letter from *MM* to Subscribers, no date, VFC.

47. Eastman to Calverton, no date, 1934, VFC.

48. Calverton to Thomas Wolfe, 8 April 1936, VFC.

49. Author's interview with Henry Hazlitt, Wilton, Connecticut, 10 July 1971.

50. Calverton to Nina Melville, no date, 1934, VFC.

51. Quoted, John P. Diggins, *The American Left in the Twentieth Century* (New York: Harcourt, Brace, Jovanovitch, 1973), p. 148.

52. Jerry Allard to Calverton, 25 May 1934, VFC.

53. Ibid.

54. See Matthew Baigell and Julia Williams, eds., *Artists Against War and Fascism: Papers of the First American Artists' Congress* (New Brunswick, N.J.: Rutgers University Press, 1986), pp. 62–74.

Chapter Eleven. Marxism and Death

1. David Caute argues that the phenomenon of fellow traveling itself during the thirties signified "a return to the eighteenth-century vision of a rational, educated, and scientific society based on maximization of resources and the steady improvement (if not perfection) of human nature as visualized by objective, unprejudiced brains." See his *The Fellow Travellers: A Postscript to the Enlightenment* (London: Weidenfeld and Nicolson, 1973), p. 250.

2. Eastman's critique of Marxism appeared in his *Marx and Lenin: The Science of Revolution* (London: G. Allen & Unwin, 1926).

3. For Eastman's and Will Herberg's rightward movement, see John P.

Diggins, *Up from Communism: Conservative Odysseys in American Intellectual History* (New York: Harper & Row, 1975), pp. 17–73, 269–305.

4. Reinhold Niebuhr, "Marxism and Religion," *MM* 8, no. 12 (February 1935): 712; V. F. Calverton, "Marxism and Religion," ibid., pp. 717–18.

5. Bruce Bliven quoted in Richard Pells, *Radical Visions and American Dreams: Culture and Social Thought in the Depression Years* (New York: Harper & Row, 1973), p. 322.

6. The "demagogue of the airways" is Matthew Josephson's phrase in *Infidel in the Temple: A Memoir of the Nineteen Thirties* (New York: Knopf, 1967), p. 317.

7. Calverton, "Who Killed Walter Liggett?" *MM* 9, no. 7 (January 1936): 390–96. Liggett had, in fact, written an exposé of Olson in the *Modern Monthly*. See Walter M. Liggett, "Third Parties for Sale," *MM* 8, no. 12 (February 1935): 721–26. For an account of Liggett's death and Farmer-Laborism's possible connections to urban crime, see Millard L. Gieske, *Minnesota Farmer Laborism: The Third Party Alternative* (Minneapolis: University of Minnesota Press, 1979), pp. 212–13.

8. Edith Liggett to Calverton, no date; Edith Liggett to Calverton, 24 October 1935, VFC.

9. Calverton, *The Passing of the Gods* (New York: Scribner's, 1934), p. ix.

10. Ibid., p. 284.

11. Ibid., p. 319.

12. Ibid., p. 324.

13. Warren Susman, *Culture and Commitment 1929–1945* (New York: George Braziller, 1973), p. 18.

14. V. F. Calverton to George Santayana, 25 November 1936, VFC.

15. Sigmund Freud, *Beyond the Pleasure Principle*, in *The Standard Edition of the Complete Psychological Works of Sigmund Freud*, trans. J. Strachey (London: Hogarth Press, 1961), vol. 18, pp. 38, 54.

16. Sigmund Freud, *Civilization and Its Discontents*, in *The Standard Edition of the Complete Psychological Works of Sigmund Freud*, trans. J. Strachey (London: Hogarth Press, 1961), vol. 21, p. 145.

17. On this point, Calverton anticipates Norman O. Brown by more than twenty years. See Brown, *Life Against Death: The Psychoanalytic Meaning of History* (New York: Vintage, 1959), p. 101.

18. Calverton, *The Man Inside: Being the Record of the Strange Adventures of Allen Steele Among the Xulus* (New York: Scribner's, 1936), p. 112.

19. Ibid., p. 79.

20. Ibid., p. 112.

21. Ibid., p. 242.

22. Ibid., p. 182.

23. Pells, *Radical Visions*, p. 67.

24. Calverton, *Man Inside*, p. 80.

25. Calverton to Santayana, 25 November 1936, VFC.

26. Santayana to Calverton, 2 November 1936, VFC.

27. Calverton to John Chamberlain, 10 February 1936, VFC.

28. Calverton to Santayana, 25 November 1936, VFC.

29. Calverton, "Our Hypnotized World," *Scribner's* (20 April 1937): 38–42, 89.

30. F. Scott Fitzgerald to Calverton, 4 November 1936, VFC.

31. Max Eastman to Calverton, 18 March 1936; Herbert Read to Calverton, 20 February 1937; Havelock Ellis to Calverton, 20 February 1937; Harold Laski to Calverton, 1 May 1937, VFC.

32. Reinhold Niebuhr, *Moral Man and Immoral Society: A Study of Ethics and Politics* (New York: Scribner's, 1934), p. 26.

33. Ibid., p. 277.

34. Kenneth Burke, "Revolutionary Symbolism in America," in *American Writers' Congress*, ed. Henry Hart (New York: International Publishers, 1935), pp. 87–90.

35. Stuart Chase, *Government in Business* (New York: Macmillan, 1935), pp. 269–72. For a discussion of Chase's paternal technocratic progressivism, see Robert B. Westerbrook, "Tribune of the Technostructure: The Popular Economics of Stuart Chase," *American Quarterly* 32, no. 4 (Fall 1980): 387–408. For a discussion of Chase and of intellectuals and experts as agents of radical change—as well as the "technocratic," managerial dimensions of the discussion—see Jean-Christophe Agnew, "A Touch of Class," *Democracy* 3, no. 4 (Fall 1983): 59–72.

36. See Richard Pells's discussion of Lasswell's *Politics: Who, What, When, How* (1936), and Thurman Arnold's *The Folklore of Capitalism* (1937), in *Radical Visions*, pp. 323–25.

37. Lewis Mumford, *Faith for Living* (New York: Harcourt, Brace, 1940). For a discussion, see Donald Miller, *Lewis Mumford: A Life* (New York: Weidenfeld & Nicolson, 1989), pp. 395–98.

38. Upton Sinclair to Calverton, 23 October 1936, VFC.

39. Calverton, *Man Inside*, p. 296.

40. Calverton to Weprinski, 22 August 1937, VFC.

41. Calverton to Eastman, 26 April 1935, VFC.

42. A similar dilemma, particularly the identification of centralized economic planning with Stalinism and fascism, led Stuart Chase away from notions of social control toward a greater appreciation of democracy and a position that might best be described as "left Keynesianism." See Westerbrook, "Tribune of the Technostructure," p. 404.

43. See Calverton, *Where Angels Dared to Tread* (New York: Bobbs-Merrill, 1941).

44. Henry Miller to Calverton, no date, VFC.

45. Warren Susman, ed., *Culture and Commitment 1929–1945*, p. 19.

46. Calverton to Nina Melville, no date, 1938, VFC.

47. Calverton to Melville, no date, 1935, VFC.

48. Calverton to Melville, no date, 1938, VFC.

49. Christopher Lasch, *The New Radicalism in America: The Intellectual as a Social Type* (New York: Knopf, 1965), p. 146.

50. Walter Lippmann, *Public Opinion* (New York: Macmillan, 1922), p. 161.

51. James Burnham, *The Machiavellians: Defenders of Freedom* (London: Putnam, 1943); James Burnham, *The Managerial Revolution* (New York: John Day, 1941).

52. Lionel Trilling, *The Middle of the Journey* (New York: Penguin, 1964), p. 9. For Trilling, death and the Freudian death instinct would become important concerns in his post-thirties thought. Yet, for Trilling, Thanatos would provide a ground for the "opposing self" and its modernist adversary role in cultural resistance. As against Calverton, for whom the fear of death led to embracing the group, death for Trilling would become a way to affirm the self in its ultimate confrontation with reality. See, for example, Lionel Trilling, *Beyond Culture: Essays on Literature and Learning* (New York, Viking, 1965), esp. the chapter "Freud: Within and Beyond Culture," pp. 77–102. For a discussion of Trilling's idea of death in relation to *The Middle of the Journey*, see Mark Krupnick, *Lionel Trilling and the Fate of Cultural Criticism* (Chicago: Northwestern University Press, 1986), p. 91.

Chapter Twelve. "Bankruptcy of Bolshevism"

1. See Haim Kantorovitch's "Towards Reorientation," *American Socialist Quarterly* 2 (Autumn 1933): 13–19, and Reinhold Niebuhr, "The Revolutionary Moment," *American Socialist Quarterly* 4 (June 1935): 8–13.

2. "Declaration for Thomas and Nelson," *MM* 10, no. 1 (October 1936): 13–14.

3. See James P. Cannon, *The History of American Trotskyism* (New York: Pathfinder Press, 1972), p. 226; Sidney Hook, *Out of Step: An Unquiet Life in the 20th Century* (New York: Harper & Row, 1987), p. 226.

4. Editorial: "The Trek Back to Popularism," *MM* 9, no. 11 (July 1936): 3–4.

5. V. F. Calverton to Menefee, no date, VFC.

6. Editorial: "Stalin on Trial," *MM* 10, no. 1 (October 1936): 3–4.

7. Ibid., p. 4.

8. Editorial: "The Moscow Trials," *MM* 10, no. 4 (March 1937): 3.

9. See Terry Cooney, *The Rise of the New York Intellectuals: Partisan Review and Its Circle, 1934–1945* (Madison: University of Wisconsin Press, 1986), p. 99.

10. Symposium: "Is Leon Trotsky Guilty?" *MM* 10, no. 4 (March 1937): 4–6.

11. Max Eastman, "A Letter the NATION Did Not Print," *MM* 10, no. 5 (April 1937): 4–7.

12. Malcolm Cowley, "Moscow Trials II," *New Republic* 95 (25 May 1938): 4.

13. Granville Hicks, "Communism and the American Intellectuals," in Irving Talmadge, ed., *Whose Revolution* (New York: Howell, Soskin, 1941), p. 97.

14. Michael Gold, quoted in Harvey Klehr, *The Heyday of American Communism: The Depression Decade* (New York: Basic Books, 1984), p. 359.

15. For a discussion of the positions of the *New Republic, Nation,* and *Common Sense,* see Frank Warren III, *Liberals and Communism: The "Red Decade" Revisited* (Bloomington: Indiana University Press, 1966), pp. 171ff.

16. Editorial: "Bolshevism in Spain," *MM* 10, no. 6 (May 1937): 2.

17. V. F. Calverton, "Will England Give Spain to Franco," *MM* 10, no. 7 (August 1937): 7–8.

18. Editorial: "Beyond Franco and Stalin," *MM* 10, no. 8 (September 1937): 2.

19. Daniel Aaron, *Writers on the Left* (New York: Harcourt, Brace and World, 1962), p. 462.

20. Dwight Macdonald, quoted in Aaron, *Writers on the Left,* p. 376.

21. See Alan Wald, *The New York Intellectuals: The Rise and Decline of the Anti-Stalinist Left* (Chapel Hill: University of North Carolina Press, 1987), p. 136.

22. Warren, *Liberals and Communism,* p. 168.

23. Ernest Sutherland Bates, "An Open Letter to Carleton Beals," as well as Beals's reply, *MM* 10, no. 6, (May 1937): 9–10.

24. Margaret Lamont to Calverton, 4 September 1937, VFC.

25. Leon Trotsky to Calverton, 15 October 1937, VFC.

26. Max Eastman to Calverton, 23 October 1937, VFC.

27. Calverton to Trotsky (Mexico City), 26 November 1937, VFC.

28. Diego Rivera to Editors of the *Modern Monthly,* 18 January 1938, VFC.

29. Calverton to Carleton Beals, 24 April 1938, VFC.

30. Beals to Calverton, 11 April 1938, VFC.

31. C. Hartley Grattan to Calverton, 21 February, no date, VFC.

32. Calverton to Corliss Lamont, 31 December 1936, VFC.

33. Calverton to Grant C. Knight, 30 January 1937, VFC.

34. Calverton to Eastman, no date, 1937, VFC.

35. Calverton to Miss Smith, 6 November 1937, VFC.

36. Calverton to Knight, 30 January 1937, VFC.

37. Author's interview with James Farmer, New York, 9 July 1971.

38. Ibid.

39. Calverton to Nina Melville, no date, Berdeshevsky Letters.

40. Huntington Cairns to Calverton, 21 February 1938, VFC.

41. *MM* 10, no. 11 (March 1938): 5–8.

42. See Cooney, *Rise of the New York Intellectuals,* pp. 136–39. Cooney points out that Rahv was not ready to make explicit connections between Stalinism and fascism until well into 1938. Even in early 1938, Rahv was not yet prepared to indict Stalinism with a stronger label than "reformism." Later in the year he did link fascism and Stalinism with the result that the League of American Writers filed suit against him, demanding the return of a hundred dollars that had been lent to the old *Partisan Review* before its break with the Party.

43. Editorial: "The Modern Quarterly," *MQ* 11, no. 1 (Fall 1938): 2–3, 3.

44. Editorial: "Is State Capitalism Progressive," *MM* 10, no. 11 (March 1938): 2–3, 3.

45. Edmund Wilson, *To the Finland Station* (New York: Doubleday, 1940), p. 445.

46. Haim Kantorovitch, "The Rise and Decline of Neo-Communism," *MQ*, 1, no. 4 (Spring 1924): 21–43. See Chapter One.

47. Symposium: "Was the Bolshevik Revolution a Failure?" *MQ* 11, no. 1 (Fall 1938): 7–28.

48. Ibid., p. 7.

49. Editorial: "Was the Bolshevik Revolution a Failure?" ibid., p. 5.

50. Karl Korsch, "Why I Am a Marxist," *MM* 9, no. 2 (April 1935): 88–95.

51. John P. Diggins, *The American Left in the Twentieth Century* (New York: Harcourt Brace, Jovanovich, 1973), p. 446.

52. Korsch, "State and Counter-Revolution," *MQ* 11, no. 2 (Winter 1939): 60–67, 67.

53. James Marshall, "The 'Withering' State," *MQ* 11, no. 3 (Summer 1939): 68–80.

54. Sidney Hook, "Science and the New Obscurantism," *MQ* 11, no. 1 (Fall 1938): 66–86.

55. Eastman, "Motive Patterns of Socialism," *MM* 11, no. 4 (Fall 1939): 45–55, 54.

56. Hook, "The Importance of John Dewey in Modern Thought," *MQ* 11, no. 4 (Fall 1939): 30–35, 35.

57. Symposium: "Can Democracy Survive?" *MQ* 11, no. 3 (Summer 1939): 68–80.

58. Calverton to Charles A. Beard, no date, 1939, VFC.

59. Calverton, *The Awakening of America* (New York: John Day, 1939), pp. vii–viii.

60. Ibid.

61. Ibid., p. 66.

62. Ibid., p. 184.

63. Ibid., p. 340.

64. For a discussion of John Dos Passos's treatment of Roger Williams and the Founding Fathers in this light, see John P. Diggins, "Dos Passos as Historian," *American Literature* 46, no. 3 (November 1975): 329–47; esp. 339.

65. Calverton, *Awakening of America*, p. 436.

66. Van Wyck Brooks, *America's Coming-of-Age* (New York: B. W. Huebsch, 1915), p. 180.

67. Calverton, *Awakening of America*, p. 437.

68. George S. Counts to Calverton, 30 April 1940, VFC.

69. Allan Nevins to Calverton, 10 October 1939; Harold U. Faulkner to Calverton, 10 December 1939; Arthur M. Schlesinger to Calverton, 11 December 1939; Van Wyck Brooks to Calverton, 26 December 1939, VFC.

70. Calverton to Brooks, 27 December 1939, VFC.

71. Calverton, *Awakening of America*, p. vii.

72. Calverton, "A Plea for Proletarian Tragedy," *MM* 10, no. 4 (March 1937): 14.

73. Calverton to Grant C. Knight, 25 July 1935. Knight Collection, University of Kentucky Library, Lexington, Kentucky.

74. Calverton, "The Cultural Barometer," *Current History* 46 (April 1932): 89.

75. Calverton to Harold Salemson, 10 July 1939, VFC.

76. See, for example, Irving Howe, "The Thirties in Retrospect," in Ralph F. Bogardus and Fred Hobson, eds., *Literature at the Barricades: The American Writer in the 1930s* (University: University of Alabama Press, 1982), p. 25.

77. Scott Nearing to Calverton, 13 March 1938, VFC.

78. Calverton to Nearing, 21 March 1938, VFC.

Chapter Thirteen. Where Angels Dared to Tread

1. James Gilbert, *Writers and Partisans: A History of Literary Radicalism in America* (New York: John Wiley, 1968), p. 201.

2. *Nation* 159 (26 August 1939): 226.

3. V. F. Calverton, "After Munich What? Or, a Treaty Between Germany and Soviet Russia Which is Now in the Air" (lecture), VFC.

4. Granville Hicks, *Where We Came Out* (New York: Viking, 1954), p. 185.

5. Symposium: "What Will I Do When America Goes to War," *MM* 9, no. 4 (June 1935): 199–204.

6. Sidney Hook, "Against Sanctions," *MM* 10, no. 1 (April 1936): 15.

7. Editorial: "The Second World War," *MQ* 11, no. 3 (Summer 1939): 2–7, 3.

8. Editorial: "The Road Back," *MQ* 11, no. 6 (Summer 1940): 2–6, 2.

9. Editorial: "The Second World War," p. 7.

10. Editorial: "The Road Back," p. 2.

11. Ibid., p. 6.

12. George Britt, "V. F. Calverton," *MQ* 11, no. 7 (Autumn 1940): 12.

13. See Alan Wald, *The New York Intellectuals: The Rise and Decline of the Anti-Stalinist Left from the 1930s to the 1980s* (Chapel Hill: University of North Carolina Press, 1987), p. 286.

14. Calverton, *Where Angels Dared to Tread* (New York: Bobbs-Merrill, 1941), p. 17.

15. Ibid., p. 17.

16. V. F. Calverton to Nina Melville, no day, December 1939, VFC.

17. Calverton to Melville, 15 March 1940, VFC.

18. Calverton to Melville, 23 December 1939, VFC.

19. Calverton to Melville, no date, 1939, VFC.

20. *New York Telegram*, 2 November 1939, p. 10.

21. Calverton to Max Eastman, 4 August 1938, VFC.

22. "On top of the general misery of our civilization, my dearest and closest friend Ernest Sutherland Bates just died, and that has made me feel worse than ever. For several weeks I didn't know whether I was coming or going." Calverton to Grant C. Knight, 11 January 1940, Grant C. Knight Collection, University of Kentucky, Lexington.

23. Calverton to Melville, 5 January 1940, VFC.

24. Calverton to Melville, 7 January 1940, VFC.

25. Memoir of Nina Melville, December 1940, Berdeshevsky letters.

26. Calverton to Herbert, 7 June 1940, Berdeshevsky Letters.

27. Memoir of Nina Melville, December 1940, Berdeshevsky Letters.

28. Calverton to Melville, no date, VFC.

29. Bertram Wolfe in letter to author, 2 November 1972.

30. Nina Melville, reminiscence, no day, December 1940, Berdeshevsky Letters.

31. Ibid.

32. Melville to Charlie Abrams, 23 July 1941, Berdeshevsky Letters.

33. Ibid.

34. Ibid.

35. "Tributes, Appreciations, Memories," *MQ* 11, no. 7 (Autumn 1940): 45.

36. Ibid., p. 48.

37. Ibid., p. 54.

38. Irving Howe, *Socialism and America* (New York: Harcourt, Brace, Jovanovitch, 1985), p. 144.

39. For a discussion of Randolph Bourne in these terms, see Thomas Bender, *New York Intellect: A History of Intellectual Life in New York, from 1750 to the Beginnings of Our Own Time* (New York: Knopf, 1987), p. 234.

40. Howe, *Socialism and America*, pp. 163–64.

41. Russell Jacoby, *The Last Intellectuals: American Culture in the Age of Academe* (New York: Basic Books, 1982), esp. the first chapter, "Missing Intellectuals," pp. 3–26.

42. John Dewey, *The Public and Its Problems* (Athens, Ohio: Swallow Press, 1954), p. 184.

Epilogue

1. Alan Wald, *The New York Intellectuals: The Rise and Decline of the Anti-Stalinist Left from the 1930s to the 1980s* (Chapel Hill: University of North Carolina Press, 1987), pp. 345–65.

2. Terry Cooney, *The Rise of the New York Intellectuals: Partisan Review and Its Circle, 1934–1945* (Madison: University of Wisconsin Press, 1986), p. 257.

3. Howard Brick, *Daniel Bell and the Decline of Intellectual Radicalism: Social Theory and Political Reconciliation in the 1940s* (Madison: University of Wisconsin Press, 1986), p. 13.

4. Cornel West, *The American Evasion of Philosophy: A Genealogy of Pragmatism* (Madison: University of Wisconsin Press, 1989), p. 6.

5. The other independent radical journal during the mid thirties was the *Marxist Quarterly*, the editorial board of which included such notables as Louis Hacker, Lewis Corey, James Burnham, George Novak, Felix Morrow, Bertram Wolfe, and Sterling Spero. But the publication ran for only three issues. Toward the end of 1932 *Common Sense* appeared, a magazine edited

by Alfred Bingham and Selden Rodman. Although it published many of the same writers as did the *Modern Quarterly*—Mumford, Dewey, Eastman, Nearing, A. J. Muste, and James Rorty—the journal reflected the philosophy of Alfred Bingham, which stressed a virtually technocratic "central planning" approach to social change in America. See Richard Pells, *Radical Visions and American Dreams: Culture and Social Thought in the Depression Years* (New York: Harper & Row, 1973), p. 74.

6. See Cornel West, *American Evasion of Philosophy*, p. 127.

7. Richard Rorty, *Philosophical Papers*, vol. 1: *Objectivity, Relativism, and Truth* (Cambridge: Cambridge University Press, 1991), p. 17, n. 30.

8. For a critical discussion of recent Left historians who argue that the Popular Front represented an expression of indigenous American radicalism, see Theodore Draper, "The Popular Front Revisited," *New York Review of Books*, 30 May 1985, pp. 44–50.

9. For a discussion of the *Partisan Review* group's cosmopolitanism and its dismissive view of an indigenous American radical tradition, see Terry Cooney, *Rise of the New York Intellectuals*, p. 276.

10. Daniel Aaron's term in *Writers on the Left* (New York: Avon Books, 1961), p. 335.

11. See Sidney Hook, *Out of Step: An Unquiet Life in the 20th Century* (New York: Harper & Row, 1987), pp. 205–6.

Index